. . . But I Promised God

. . . But I Promised God

Malamateniah Koutsada

Library of Congress Control Number: 2018914332
ISBN: Hardcover   978-1-9845-0456-2
                Softcover   978-1-9845-0454-8
                eBook   978-1-9845-0455-5

Print information available on the last page.

Rev. date: 09/05/2019

To order additional copies of this book, contact:
Xlibris
1-800-455-039
www.Xlibris.com.au
Orders@Xlibris.com.au
768008

Contents

PART 2

PART 3

PART 4

I dedicate this book to my daughter, my sons, my grandchildren, and the rest of my family, so that they may know me better.

I would like to thank the people who made this book possible: My daughter, M. Rose, who introduced me to a motivational speaker in Melbourne, and who inspired and encouraged me to keep on going when I wanted to give up. My friend Yvette, who did the initial editing and correcting of the manuscript. An author friend who made many valuable suggestions regarding the manuscript. My grandchildren, whose curiosity spurred me on when my enthusiasm waned. And God, who walked beside me through dark and stony paths, holding me up and leading me on.

The purpose of this book is to inspire others to follow their dreams. There is nothing people can't achieve as long as they have focus, set their minds to it, and work hard towards achieving it. The universe is waiting for us to ask so that it can give. "Ask, and it shall be given you," said Jesus (Matthew 7:7).

A portion of profits from the sale of this book go to support The Fred Hollows Foundation and MSF (Medicins Sans Frontieres).

Introduction

This is the story of an impoverished Greek girl told with courage and brutal honesty. She experienced domestic violence, civil war, she lived as a refugee in a church compound where she witnessed cruelty, injustice, and childhood adversity first-hand.

Motivated by childhood desire and need, she immigrated to Australia, alone at twenty-one, with very little money and even less English. She worked hard and studied diligently. At thirty-two, married and with two children, she obtained her year twelve school certificate.

Working as a clerk in an aeronautics facility while living in Papua New Guinea made her determined to fulfil her ambition to become a nurse. Upon returning to Australia with her Australian-born husband and children, she became a general nurse, a midwife, and later a psychiatric nurse, where she worked most of her working life.

Her changing vicissitudes forced her to re-enter the work force aged sixty-four when others her age were retiring. She worked hard and faced many obstacles, the most daunting of which were uncertainly and self-doubt. But with faith in God and determination, she went forward, becoming successful in real estate.

She considers herself blessed. Her dream now is to be a blessing to as many people as possible.

Part 1

Chapter 1

My Childhood

This is my life story. I will try to be honest and open with events and my feelings. My earliest memories begin when I was two and a half years old.

I was born in north Greece in a small village of twenty families. My mother's name was Georgia. She was the youngest of thirteen children and the odd one out. She was blonde, blue-eyed, and pretty. The others were dark and tall. Her father's name was George, and her mother's name was Ellie. The names of her siblings were Soula (twenty years older than my mother), Saphy, Dan, and Magdalena.

My father's name was Alexis. He had a brother, Minoas, and an older sister, Sonia. His father's name was Grigoris, and his mother's was Anthea. My grandparents and parents were born in Turkey. My father's family lived in Istanbul and were Orthodox. My paternal grandfather was a seaman. He travelled over the seas, bringing home the delicacies of the world. They owned a nice house and were comfortable.

My mother's family lived inland, not far from Istanbul. They were farmers and Protestants. In the 1920s, during the exchange of population between Greece and Turkey, all the Greeks in Turkey returned to Greece, and all the Turks in Greece returned to Turkey. Both sets of my grandparents ended up in Macedonia, north Greece, but in different parts. My maternal aunt Soula, who was married with a son, Kostas, ended up in Peria, close to Rodia, where my father's family was. At the time of resettlement, my father was twenty and my mother was seven. Peria was a bigger village. It had a school, church, and a cafenio (coffee shop). All the socialising and festivities took place in Peria, where people from the nearby villages met to socialise, barter, and party. They all knew each other.

My maternal grandmother died when my mother, Georgia, was seven years old. She lived with her father and was thrown from pillar to post. She didn't know what it was to be loved, to be hugged. She was not important to anybody. Georgia was a nuisance as far as some family members were concerned, and she was aware of it. She was emotionally neglected and abused. She told the story of when she was eight years old, the family gathered around the fireplace, talking. Georgia was playing with the first pair of socks she had knitted for herself. She was proud of them, throwing them up and catching them. After a few tosses, her brother, Dan, an adult at the time, caught them and threw them in the fire. She was devastated.

When Mother was eleven years old, she went to Thessaloniki with her father to visit his brother who lived there. He met an old friend, and while chatting, the friend said they had a baby son, and his wife was looking for some household help. He asked her father if he knew of anybody. Her father looked at my mother and unemotionally and without hesitation said, "Here she is. Take her," as if she were an unwanted, scungy dog. He took her. No wages were negotiated; no promises to take care of her were given or asked for. Mother's father took it for granted his child would be looked after. When her new boss presented her to his wife as the helper, she said, "Why did you bring her here? She is so young!" He coldly told his wife my mother would grow up.

Mother was treated humanely by her boss's wife, but he was hard on her and heartless. She told the story of how one day, she took the nine-month-old son out for a walk. While she was walking, baby in her arms, a bicycle went past, knocked her and the baby down, and sped off. The commotion and the crying baby brought out the family. The mother picked her baby up and comforted him. He picked my mother up and belted her for dropping the baby. They didn't ask what happened or whether she was hurt.

Mother spent her young life working as a housekeeper in Thessaloniki. The only people she knew were her father's brother and his family. My mother's family was Protestant. My grandfather and his brother were the first converts from the Greek Orthodox church to the Seventh-day Adventist church in Turkey. The story of their conversion is an interesting one. My grandfather and his brother were religious men, and they wanted to become hajes. About the time they were planning to go to Jerusalem to be baptised in the Jordan River and receive the desired title, a man in the area was preaching a new religion that prohibited the making and worshipping of images. He proved it using the Bible, the Word of God. They heard him but dismissed him. They were Orthodox and would remain so.

In Jerusalem, a great icon of the Holy Mary was set up on a gentle hill by the Orthodox Church, and it was said that Mary was weeping for the sins of the world. Many people went to see the miracle, including my grandfather and his brother. They were intrigued by this unnatural phenomenon and decided to investigate it. At night, they went up to the hill. Real tears ran down the icon's face. How could this be? They looked around and behind the icon. What they found astounded them. Two branches of a grapevine growing behind the icon were trimmed and attached at the back of the icon's eyes, in which two small holes were made at the point of the pupils. Because it was spring the sap ran down, imitating tears. They were disgusted. (No disrespect or slander meant to the Orthodox faith.) They were baptised all right, but by the preacher of the new religion, the Seventh-Day Adventist Church. They were so enthusiastic about their new-found faith that they converted not only their own families but the whole village as well.

As my mother grew older, she occasionally visited her oldest sister, Soula. The rest of her family ended up in north-east Macedonia, too far away to visit. They grew tobacco.

My mother was twenty years old when she visited Soula. After getting off the bus, she went past the cafenio, heading to her sister's.

My father was sitting in the cafenio playing backgammon with another man. "Who is that girl?" he asked when he saw her.

"She is my wife's sister. She will stay with us for a few days," the man replied.

"I will marry that girl."

He was eligible, well respected, had money, and could well afford to be confident. In the same week, he asked for her hand from Aunt Soula and Uncle Panos. Mother refused. She didn't like living in the country. Aunt Soula was devastated. "How could you refuse such an offer? How stupid can you be?" My mother stood her ground and planned to leave the village the following week. The shock was too much for Aunt Soula. She took to her bed ill, not eating and fainting. When she came to, she did not fail to point out that if Mother married him, they would be close, and she wouldn't have to work as a housekeeper. She would be "a lady in her own house."

Mother could see the advantages in marrying him. She relented and stayed in the village. They were soon engaged and were married a year later, in 1937. My father was thirty-five and my mother twenty-two. They lived with my paternal grandparents as the custom was. The Turkish house was plenty big enough for them all.

Mother's pain started the moment they were on their own. My father held her hand and ruefully said, "I feel as if I'm holding her hand," referring to another girl. My mother was shocked! She felt like leaving him there and then. But she believed she could make him respect and love her and eventually forget the other girl.

My father was madly in love with a girl in the village named' Desmy, but she had jilted him because she was in love with another man. I found out later my father married my mother to spite Desmy. He died still loving Desmy, who never married.

Things turned against my mother when, after three months, she was not pregnant. For this she was treated with contempt. She was branded "the mule" by her sister-in-law's mother, who rejoiced and added fuel to the fire by pointing out to my father that if she hadn't conceived by then, she never would, and he would be left childless.

My father was anxious to have children. He was expecting a girl first because everybody else in his family had had a daughter first, but it was not happening. My grandmother was concerned and often murmured that her son would be left childless. Mother was looked down on by the villagers and the family. She was treated as unworthy by all. I'm not sure she wanted to have children and stay in that backwards little village. My mother often voiced regret for staying there as long as she did.

Then someone suggested a "treatment" for infertility that was guaranteed to work. It had worked for countless other couples, and it would surely work for them. It sounded horrible, but she was prepared to try anything. They needed some blankets, a bucket, a shovel full of fresh chicken manure, a large quantity of hot chilli, and a bottle of vinegar. They put all the ingredients in the bucket and poured boiling water in it. The patient, my mother, sat on the bucket while wrapped up in blankets, making sure the steam didn't escape till the water was nearly cold. This was done from day one of the cycle till day fifteen, for as long as it took. My poor mother must have been sitting on the shit bucket, sweating in the middle of summer, in a country where summers got over forty degrees and there was no air conditioning. It worked!

When my mother was four months pregnant, they let out the secret. My father had the privilege of telling his brother and his wife's family. His brother's mother-in-law, Thana, refused to believe the good news and said to my father, "If my leg produces another leg, then she will produce a baby." My father believed her and was upset. He wanted reassurance from my mother. The only thing she could show was her constant vomiting. She suffered from morning sickness till the day I was born. She had a very rotund figure, and her pregnancies didn't show till near the end. All the while, Thana maintained that when her leg reproduced, Georgia would too.

The time came. My mother had a very long, hard labour. The experienced village midwife ordered my father to fetch the doctor from town or else she'd lose both mother and baby. The doctor came on his horse. I was born in March 1939. They named me Malamateniah, Mallie, after my deceased aunt. I gave everybody hell on my way to this world and carried on like it most of my life. I couldn't help myself, having started on chook shit! One thing though, all that fresh manure helped me live and thrive when nobody, including my mother and grandmother didn't think I would survive. I was tiny.

With the birthing business over, the midwife gave Thana the good news on her way home.

"Georgia had a little girl. When is your leg due?"

Thana crossed herself, and repentantly said "I have sinned; may God forgive me."

While my mother was bathing me, one of the neighbours called in. She looked at me pitifully and in all seriousness said, "Georgia, let the poor little thing die in peace."

My mother replied "I will do the best I can, and if God wants to take her then let His will be done."

I wasn't about to kick the bucket I started on. I pulled through. I was the pride and joy of my father. He was on cloud nine, for months. He bought me a pair of aquamarine earrings when I was three months old and insisted I wear them immediately. They made him wait till I was older. I must have been a sight to behold—a square, bumpy head, and earrings!

After my birth, life for my mother was easier for a while. The Second World War was in full swing by the time I was few months old, but it didn't affect us in the way it affected people in cities, where they died from starvation by the thousands and where the Jewish people were hunted and killed like wild animals, and their property confiscated by greedy, unscrupulous people. Life in the village was quiet. The only things they missed were sugar, coffee, and other imported things. Oil was in short supply, but lard and suet were plentiful.

My mother fell pregnant again, she was no longer looked down upon. My father was delighted. It'd be a son, he was sure. Everybody in his family had a son next, and so should he. The time came, and in January 1941 the baby was born quick and easy even though it was big and had lots of dark hair. My father was devastated. How could this happen? A girl, when it should have been a boy? He concluded the child was not his. My mother was distraught. Grandmother tried to tell him he was being unreasonable and stupid, but he wouldn't have it. He wouldn't talk to my mother and completely rejected the baby, who was the image of him, deep dimples and all.

After six months, he started talking to my mother, but he didn't acknowledge the baby. He must have been doing so secretly, because the baby was very fond of him. She'd stand by the window upstairs, waiting for him to come home. When she spotted him in the distance, she'd get very excited, saying, "Daddy, Daddy." But he ignored her. It broke Mother's heart. My sister was twelve months old before he picked her up and openly cuddled her.

I don't remember the following incident, but I heard it so many times that it has been imprinted in my memory as if it were my own. When my sister was six weeks old, my mother took her to church for the blessing of the baby and the cleansing of the mother, just as Mary and Joseph had taken baby Jesus to the temple. After the ceremony, she went to see her sister. She left me and the baby on the couch, in the room on our own, and went looking for her sister, leaving the door open. I wasn't two yet, but I picked the baby up and headed for the door. I dropped her on the ledge at front of the door. The screams of the baby brought my mother running upstairs. The baby had a fractured right collarbone and a bump on her spine.

Mother took the baby and ran all the way to the midwife's house, banging on the door madly. The midwife, Haj Nene, said she was having a bath and couldn't come out now. My mother kept yelling, "My baby, my baby! Come out, come now!" Haj Nene wrapped a towel around her and went out to see what the problem was. She took the baby, put her on her knees, and gently pushed the bump on her spine down. The baby was OK. The collarbone healed but had a ridge on it.

When the issue of naming the baby arose, my father said, "Karis is going to be the godfather and wishes to name the baby after his sweetheart."

My mother was upset. "And what might the name be, then?"

"Eva," he said flatly, and despite her protestations, Eva it was. Mother was hoping she would be named Ellie after her mother, but the privilege was denied her again. She wanted to call me after her mother, but instead I was called Malamateniah after my deceased aunt.

From then on, their marriage went downhill. They argued more often than not, mostly verbal abuse. When Eva was about eight months old, they split up. My mother took Eva and me and went to her sister Soula's place till she sorted out accommodations. She found a room with one of the villagers. I clearly remember living in another house, in a room with just a table and chairs in it. I can see my mother sitting at the table with the baby on her lap, feeding her bean soup with pieces of bread in it. I remember that horrid soup; the smell still lingers in my nostrils. I hated it, it nauseated me, and I couldn't stomach it for years. I waited for my mother to turn her head away from me to feed the baby, and I'd quickly take some bread and liquid from the bowl without the beans.

My father forcefully took me to Rodia, where I lived with him and my grandparents. I wondered where my mother was and missed her. The next time I saw her, it was on the road outside our house just before our gate. My mother was lying on her back, on the dirt road, screaming, trying to disentangle herself from my father's grip. He was sitting on her chest, legs astride, holding onto her long, blonde, dishevelled hair while bashing her head on the hard ground. I was expecting my mother to die or for blood pour out of her head any moment. I saw the whole thing happening, including myself, from high up on my left and in great detail, including what I was wearing and doing. I was wearing a finely knitted burgundy dress; the collar had a white trim around it, and it had buttons down the front. I was chewing the neckline and was very distressed. It was a very weird experience.

My parents remained separated for six months or so. My mother had no support at all. Her only relatives, her sister, Soula, and Soula's son, Kostas, urge her to shut her mouth and obey her husband. Kostas, two years her junior, told her she was a disgrace to the family and should go back to her husband. She had no option but to go back. In those days, divorced women were thought off as prostitutes. My parents were together again, mother fell pregnant two years later.

It was during my parents' separation that I formed my memories of my paternal grandfather. They were sad but thankfully few. My grandmother sat on the floor at front of the open fire, in the position that was so typically hers: one leg folded under her bottom and the other bent at the knee with foot flat on the floor, he arms crossed over the bent knee, and talking with my grandfather. Suddenly he picked up the forty-centimetre-long fire poker and started beating her on the back. She made no effort to get up or defend herself. Simply cried saying, "Why, Grigoris? Why are you hitting me?" he stopped when he was satisfied.

After another bashing when I was nearly four, she asked me to rub her back. "It's sore," she said. I can still see the bruises. From the nape of her neck to her waist, there were black lines where the fire poker had fallen. I felt sorry for my granny. To me, then and for many years later, hitting, belting, and bashing was a normal part of life. If it weren't children or women being beaten, it was animals.

In North Greece, the winters were cold. I hated the freezing winds coming straight from the North Pole. They were so cold and sharp that they'd shave the hairs of your legs if you didn't have on your trousers and your long johns. I hated the snow even more. I couldn't understand how kids enjoyed playing in it. I preferred to sit upstairs on the window ledge and watch them. I tried playing "snow war" once, but when my hands got cold and painful, my toes curled up, and I couldn't feel my nose, nothing would induce me to play in the snow again, no matter what the bribe.

One day, my mother was cooking on the heater—that hated bean soup (a Greek national dish). she left the onions unpeeled in a bowl and went downstairs to get wood. I looked at the onions, picked one up, tried it for size, and decided it was too big to fit in my mouth. Eva was watching me. I said to her, "I'm sure you can't put it in your mouth. It's too big."

"Yes, I can," she said. She took the onion from my hand, opened her mouth wide, manoeuvred the onion around, and managed to put it in her mouth, anchoring it securely between her jaws. Now she couldn't shut her mouth or open it wider for me to it pull out. The onion juice dripped in her mouth, burning her and dribbling down her chin. When she realised I couldn't pull it out, she started screaming. Her screams frightened me even more than the prospect of her having an onion permanently planted in her mouth.

It wasn't long before my mother came up running out of breath; she was about seven months pregnant. With admirable dexterity, she pulled out the onion. I didn't get a belting. She told me to not tell Eva to do stupid things again, and she admonished Eva to not do everything I told her to do.

I was five years old when my second sister was born in May 1944. My mother got her wish, and the baby was called Ellie. When Ellie was six weeks old, my mother put her in a clothes basket and took her just outside our gate in the town square. She put the basket under the big shady trees, told me to look after her, and very firmly said, "Don't pick her up." I dare say she was scared of me dropping Ellie too. The baby wore a pink silk dress with smocking. It had been made for me, and all three of us wore it. I was so proud of that baby and would have loved to have held her, but I was not allowed. I sat there admiring her.

Then, horror of horrors, I saw a herd of buffaloes approaching in the distance. The herdsman was leading them, but that didn't reassure me. I was terrified of the big black animals with their huge blue eyes, thickly curved horns, and rhythmically swinging big heads sitting on their powerful necks. I was sure they were going to trample us to death. I panicked. Mum had said, "Don't pick up the baby." I thought of tipping the baby out of the basket and running away, at least saving it, but the frightful animals were getting too close. I didn't know what to do. I left baby and basket there and took off. I hid behind some blackberry bushes and watched, horrified. Any minute now, they would squash the baby! The animals went by, not even looking at the baby. The herdsman, Theophanis, kept looking at me, not at the baby. He knew I was terrified of the animals; they lived opposite us.

I scrambled out of the blackberry bushes, scratched and bleeding, but that was better than being killed. When I explained to my mother about the scratches and buffaloes, all she said was, "What a stupid kid. You know they won't hurt you!" For a child born and bred on a farm with animals around me, I was terrified of them. I didn't mind sheep, goats, donkeys, or pigs, but I dreaded horses and cattle. As far as I was concerned, I didn't go near them. They had fire in them! I concluded so by watching them.

My father trained and broke in horses during winter. He spent the summers up in the mountains making charcoal, which was his other trade. He sometimes worked with huge Hungarian horses. I would not go outside or stay downstairs when he was breaking them in, but curiosity always got the better of me. I'd go upstairs and watch, terrified. The horrid creatures would stand on their giant hind legs and let out a loud, blood-curdling neigh, their nostrils flaring and smoke pouring out them. I was sure they had fire in them—how else could they blow out so much "smoke"? It sent a chill down my spine. I admired my father for his courage. He was a small man, and he looked even smaller next to those huge creatures, which he controlled so well. They ended up being calm and humble like lambs.

My father tried to teach me to ride the horses he'd broken. I trembled with fear on the saddle, hanging on, but that didn't deter him. He was determined to teach me to ride because he loved his horses. He broke in a beautiful, proud, silver grey horse, which he called Fish. I couldn't believe it was the same horse when he finished with it. One day the horse was tethered to a tree in the backyard, eating his feed from a bag hanging around his neck and swinging his tail contentedly. My baby sister, Ellie, crawled behind it. The horse stopped dead like a statue. Ellie got hold of the horse's hind leg and pulled herself up, cooing and dancing on her little legs. That animal didn't move a muscle, and it didn't start eating again till my mother took away the baby. I was amazed! Mother growled at me for not taking the baby away, but I was paralysed with fear.

My father would force me to walk under Fish's belly to desensitise me. It didn't work. He would make me take the horses to the town trough to water them, and he would tell me they wouldn't hurt me, but I didn't believe him. My heart would pound with fear as they walked behind me, a rope in each of my hands. I knew they couldn't hurt me, but only because "they couldn't catch up to me." I walked fast as was told not to run. I'd look behind me, but the horrid creatures were always at my heels, breathing down my neck. I wished they stayed a bit farther away than that.

My and my siblings' favourite pastime was going for walks and collecting flowers for our parents. Eva, I, and two other girls, Noppy and her cousin Lella, went to get some flowers. It was Sunday, and we were wearing our best; Eva had new shoes. Shoes were an item of luxury for most people. Parents used to make shoes out of pigskin and were worn with at least two pairs of thick, knitted socks—and in winter only. In summer, we went barefoot or wore homemade wooden clogs. If we were lucky enough to own a pair of proper shoes, we didn't wear them every day. Our parents bought them a size or two bigger so we would grow into them.

We followed the older girls. We walked a long way to a place which was full of yellow bog irises. It was a beautiful sight. The ground felt a bit wet and mushy underfoot, but it was nice and soft. We kept walking till we were almost up to our knees in mud. Four-year-old Eva got bogged, started crying, and kept falling over in the mud. She was covered in it. We could see the whites of her eyes, and that was about all. We were pulling her while she was crying. We told her to shut up. "What the hell are you crying for? We are all in mud!"

"I lost my shoes!" she wailed. "My new shoes!"

Oh, no! I thought. I'm going to get belted for it!

She cried, and the rest of us were in mud up to our elbows looking in vain for the lost shoes. As it turned out, she only lost one. I was so pleased about it. We looked for the lost shoe for what seemed like hours, to no avail. We were tired, dirty, worried, and by now hungry. We went back without the shoe to face our fate. Going back was difficult. The ground seemed to be softer and mushier, and we kept falling at nearly every step. Eva was still crying, and I felt like crying too. Had it not been for the lost shoe, we would have kept going deeper in the marsh, and it would have been impossible to get back. We eventually managed to reach solid ground. We forgot about the flowers while looking for the shoe, but nothing in the world would induce us to go back for them.

We started for home as four bedraggled, mud-dripping kids. We were all very quiet. I was too busy thinking of the impending belting.

My mother, having been belted often as a child, was liberal dishing it to us. She knew no better. We got home late in the afternoon. Our parents sat in the front yard looking worried. They seemed greatly relieved to see us. I was surprised. I expected my mother to be waiting, stick by her side to save time, but she wasn't angry. They ask us in unison, "Where have you been all day?" We said we went to get some lilies. They knew where we had gone to. We told them we got bogged, and now it was my chance to telling of Eva's lost shoe. I thought I wouldn't get belted hard in front of all these people. All my mother said was, "And they were brand-new!"

"Never mind the shoes," said my grandmother. "They are alive. They could have perished in that marsh, and they wouldn't be the first ones either. Think of that." I didn't get belted, but we were told in no uncertain terms not to go anywhere near that place again, or they would kill us. They didn't need to worry about it; we wouldn't have even if they had made us.

One day, Lella came to our house with a pair of new scissors. She showed them to me and asked if I could cut fingernails. "Of course I can cut fingernails," I said.

"Good. You can cut mine now." She handed me the big scissors, putting her hand forward with her middle finger sticking up, all the others curled into a fist. I took hold of that finger, and the scissors went *crunch!* I had the nail taken off, all right—but a bit of the finger as well. Blood gushed out, she yelled and hopped around like a slaughtered chicken. All the yelling and hopping around brought her mother running to us. Just as well. I was terrified. I was sure she too was going to die like the chickens. Her mother quickly grabbed her finger and squeezed. After a while, it stopped bleeding. I was still holding the scissors. Lella kept yelling and hopping around her mother, who held her hand tightly. "Where did you get the scissors from?" she asked me angrily.

I was so scared that I couldn't talk. I simply pointed to Lella. She let go of Lella and took the scissors from me, and was giving me a good shake when my mother appeared. She let go of me. I thought my mother was going to take over where Lella's had left off, but she didn't. She figured the fright and the shaking would be enough for now.

The next disaster was on a summer's day. There were some tall "stinking plants" growing at the edge of the village square, close to our house. I decided to walk in there. There was lots of open, clear, grassy space to walk, but those plants looked perfect for hiding in. The stink was terrible, and the blueberries were falling on me as the plants shook, but I still walked in there. Then I walked on a broken bottle and got a deep cut in my right foot. I hobbled home, blood pouring out of my foot.

My mother and grandmother got into a flap. They sat me on a tree trunk which my father had cut, debarked, planed, and used as a seat. They put tobacco and plantain leaves on the wound and bandaged it well. Before it had stopped bleeding, I was told what a stupid kid I was for going in there, and if I went there again, I'd get belted as well. From then on, I went around the plants, keeping my distance just in case.

My grandfather was sitting on a chair, smoking his pipe, and completely unmoved and unconcerned by it all. It was then that I got the impression that he didn't love me. I was surprised and disappointed. He showed no interest in my plight, not even to say I was stupid. He simply looked at me with one hand on his knee and the other on his pipe. It was then that I noticed his missing middle finger and how unnatural it looked. I knew that he didn't love us. He referred to us "the little donkeys" and to my father "the jackass." He never showed us affection, and if we ran past him, he'd try to trip us with the handle of his walking stick. Later, I realised that father and son didn't get on. They argued a lot, and Granddad took every opportunity to humiliate my father. Granddad was jealous of my father and my grandmother's good relationship, and my father disapproved of Granddad treating Grandmother so poorly. As a child, I thought God looked like my grandfather.

Another favourite pastime was going to the forest to collect hazelnuts. The other kids would collect pockets full every time, but I never managed to collect any more than six nuts. I was too busy watching for caterpillars on the leaves. I could climb like a cat but didn't, fearing the caterpillars. I'd wake up with nightmares, throwing the blankets off and screaming, "Caterpillars in bed!" Still, I enjoyed what I picked and what the other girls generously gave me.

Another pleasant pastime was going to the dry riverbed in nearby Stakos and collecting smooth white stones, with which we played the game "volia," from the French word *voler*, to fly. We needed five stones for the game, but we'd bring home pockets full of them. The game would keep us busy for hours. We would sit on the ground, legs spread out, one hand on the ground at front of us, fingers well spread, and four stones placed haphazardly at front of the hand. We'd throw the fifth stone up in the air, high enough to give us time to put a stone in between our fingers and catch the falling stone before it hit the ground. If you missed the stone, you'd lose, and it would be the other players turn. There were several variations to the game. It is amazing what we could do with five little pebbles. It was a good exercise in eye-hand coordination. I have seen on TV African children play the same game.

We occupied ourselves for hours by making animal toys from zucchini, cucumbers, and eggplants (aubergine). We collected sticks and put four sticks under them for legs and one across the front on which to anchor the "reins." We dragged them along, pretending they were donkeys. We even put saddles on them by putting little sticks on a circle on their back. We made our own dolls out of rags, and we made them dresses either with leaves or cloth when we had some.

I loved our backyard, which was large and covered by a grapevine. My father would get grapes and have them with homemade bread and cottage cheese for breakfast. Against the mud brick wall which marked the boundaries between properties was a huge, red, climbing rose.

The best part of the day was the summer evenings, when all the work was done. After the evening meal, everybody would come out and sit under the trees on the wooden benches made by the villagers for a chat. In summer, the sun didn't set till late. There was a long twilight period, and when it was full moon, one could see to knit and even embroider. The women brought their knitting and the men brought their pipes. There was a man in the village named Elias, and I can still see his face clearly. He always smiled. He was bald. His wife couldn't all the knitting for his three daughters. He wasn't teased; trying to ruffle his feathers because he didn't care. My had great respect for him. He was killed in the civil war. I was very sad. When he was killed, his wife did the knitting, and she knitted well.

When the corn was ripe and gathered in, it was de-husked by hand. The outer leaves were used as fodder for the animals. Some leaves were left on and tied together in a loop to hang the corn to dry. The villagers would take turns helping each other. In winter, the dry corn would be stripped from the cob. This again was a combined effort. There was chestnut roasting, stories for us kids who helped, and news and gossiping for the adults.

In the village, there were people from different parts of the world. My grandmother used to say, "In this lice-ridden country, there are nuts from forty different nut trees." There were people from Pontus, Yugoslavian Macedonia, Turkey, and all around. They all had a different cuisine, and after a while they borrowed from each other, and the Greek cuisine developed. Neither my mother nor my grandmother could cook tsorva, and I had to go to Lella's or Noppy's place to eat it. It was a Pontiac dish made out of crushed corn, yoghurt, butter, onions, and cream. It was delicious. My mother tried to cook it, but it never tasted as good as Noppy's or Lela's mothers'. The people from Pontus thought drinking milk was repulsive. They maintained it was made for calves, not for people, but their kids drank it at our place. I ate snails and mushrooms at their houses. My grandmother thought cooking capsicums was silly, but she got to like them. She baked, stuffed, fried, and pickled them, and she even ate them raw. But she never ate snails or mushrooms—they were repulsive to her.

During the exchange of population in the 1920s (Greece to Turkey and vice versa), my grandparents were given that property in exchange for what they'd left in Turkey. "Unfair deal," my grandmother kept saying for as long as I can remember her. She hated Greece and everything associated with it, and I don't ever remember her referring to Greece by name—she always referred to it as "this lice-ridden country."

For her, there was nothing good in Greece. In Turkey, the cheese was tastier, the halvas were creamier, the watermelons were bigger and sweeter, the summers were not so hot and stinky, and the winters were not so cold. In her later years, when she injured her hand and couldn't wear a thimble, even the needles were no good. Their eye was "too sharp" and pricked her finger while sewing! It was the family joke.

As far as the house was concerned, she used to say, "It is the pits!" Upstairs, it had two large rooms and one small room. She thought the toilet was a disgrace. It had a hole in the floor, and the pipes were removed. I don't remember it ever being used. There was an outside toilet which had a pit. When the pit was full, they'd dig another one, and so on. At night, the potty was used. The murmuring and dissatisfaction went on and on. We grew up thinking poorly of Greece, particularly me. I felt as if I didn't belong there. I had no sense of patriotism or pride in Greece and her "glorious history." I knew I couldn't go back to Turkey. Even a child could work that out. If my grandparents were kicked out by the Turks, I would be too. Turkey held a mystique for me because Grandma always sang its praises. I was six years old when the seed to migrate was planted in me.

All the Turkish houses were two storeys. The ground floor was used to store fodder and to house the animals in winter. Ours had a very steep staircase. When I looked up at it, it seemed almost upright. The steps had no backing, just a plank to walk on and a flimsy balustrade. One day I was sitting on the top landing, taking in the view, and focusing at the climbing red rose. Suddenly I heard a commotion downstairs. The chickens were going berserk. I bent over to see what was wrong. I overbalanced, tumbling all the way down. When I regained consciousness, the whole neighbourhood was around me. My mother was white as a ghost and looked terrified. I couldn't understand what it was all about. I don't know how long it was before I regained consciousness. I had no injuries other than bruises, but for many years afterwards I'd dream that I was flying or falling from great heights, and I'd wake up terrified.

One day, my paternal cousin Yana visited, and together we went to her maternal grandmother's house. She gave us the usual snack:

home-baked bread with olive oil, salt, and mixed herbs—my favourite. What impressed me was that Yana's slice of bread was much thicker than mine and had more herbs on it. I immediately perceived the discrimination. I was glad that my bread wasn't as thick as hers. I hated thickly cut bread, but I would have liked some more herbs. I was about six years old. It was then that I made up my mind to be fair. Kids have a keen sense of justice and fairness and a very long memory. I learned later that Thana and her only daughter, Sassa, my uncle's wife, were nasty with a murderous streak in them. Ria, Yana's sister, was nearly as bad.

Another time at Yana's place they were watching me eat freshly sprayed, unripe grapes. They didn't stop me from eating them even though they knew I'd get sick at best or die at worst. They did the same thing with mulberries. My mother and grandmother couldn't understand their cruelty. Yana was kind, a different person altogether. We'd walk together for miles. Occasionally I'd walk with her to Peria, go to her house for a short time, and then head to Aunt Soula's for a sleepover. My cousin Ria would look at me with contempt and say, "Why did you bring this arsehole here?" It saddened me, but a child doesn't get rejection easily, and because she never spoke to me directly, I kept going back.

I loved birds and always wanted to be one. Yana knew it. One day she said, "Do you want some birdies?"

My ears pricked. "Yes, where are they?" I asked.

"Oh, at my place." And off we went. A tall ladder was leaning against the mud brick wall. She pointed to the ladder and said, "Up there on the wall, in the nest under the eaves."

I climbed up and put my hand in the nest. There were birds there all right, but I got a rude shock! It felt as if a pitchfork landed on my hand! Five little hawks stuck their sharp beaks on my hand. They weren't ready to fly, but they were more than ready to defend themselves. I yanked my hand out of the nest, licked off the blood, and put it in the nest again. I could just see their heads. I had one in my hand but had to let it go because it tore my fingers. The others joined in at pecking my hand. I let go of the bird, licking the blood again. We were told to do that; it was supposed to be good for us. I thought it was the blood that was good, or it was the saliva on the wound that was the good bit?

After the third time, I told Yana that I couldn't get them. "No, I know. I tried too," she said, showing me her hand, which was pecked at too. I got down, disappointed at getting so close to the birds and coming down empty-handed. The disappointment overshadowed the painful, bleeding hand. I was annoyed Yana hadn't warned me, but I thought she might have had a lot of confidence in me. I held no animosity towards her. I was fond of her and told her so when I saw her many years later.

Back home, my mother sent me to get some eggs from the henhouse. To my delight, I found a tiny egg, such as the ones hens lay at the end of their laying season. It was pigeon size. I wanted to keep it, but Mother wouldn't let me. She said, "Eggs this size must not to be eaten. You must put them in the middle of a crossroads for good luck for the household, and for the hens that laid it." What sort of good luck, especially for the hens, I didn't know. I figured they wouldn't end up in soup. She sent me to the crossroads about half a kilometre from our place with the egg and a broken roof tile in hand. I estimated the middle of the crossroads, carefully put down the tile, and placed the egg on it. Having done it as accurately as I could, I returned home fully reassured that good luck would follow us and the hen forever.

After that incident, my mother took the opportunity to give me a lesson in stealing. I don't know what prompted her because stealing was not a problem I had. We lacked nothing, and there was nothing to steal. Nobody had any bought toys; we made our own. Occasionally we'd hear of someone stealing tobacco or coffee, but that was rare. The village was small and very closely knit. People would borrow from each other "till next market day." Mother said that people who stole wouldn't go to heaven.

"Why?" I asked.

"Because the thing they steal will block their way."

"How?" I asked.

"Well, suppose you stole an egg. That egg will block your way, stopping you from going to heaven." "I will trample on it," I said.

"More and more eggs will come to take its place," she said.

I asked no more questions. I imagined millions and millions of eggs forming a huge wall all the way up to heaven, stopping me from entering the pearly gates. It was a lonely prospect when everybody else got in and I was left outside, where there was "gnashing and clashing of teeth"—which she never failed to mention either. I believed it till I was quite old.

Life in Rodia rolled on pleasantly, and I wasn't even aware that a big war had been going on since before I was born, or that thousands of people were dying of starvation in the cities only fifty miles from where I lived peacefully with my family. I lacked nothing and felt safe.

Chapter 2

End of the Second World War

Autumn arrived, and the first rains started falling. The road at front of our house was very muddy. There was great excitement in the whole village. "The Germans are going! The Germans are going!" people shouted. I didn't know what that meant. What were they? Animals or people? Where were they going?

In a few days, there were large convoys of trucks going past our place, full of soldiers singing and laughing. So that was what Germans were—truckloads of happy, singing soldiers! Their truck tyres left funny patterns on the muddy road. Between convoys, Yana and I would check out the patterns. We would stomp on every second one, saying, "You live, you die." It kept us busy for hours, going up and down the muddy road through the village.

One day a convoy stopped at front of our house, and a dozen or so soldiers jumped out and came in our yard. My grandmother looked terrified. They were talking to her, but she couldn't understand a word. She went inside and came out with a dishful of raw eggs. The soldiers proceeded to crack them and swallow them like the Greeks did. There was great commotion and much laughter. Some of them swallowed them, and others spat them out. I watched with great interest, but I wasn't scared. Suddenly a soldier picked me up, lifted me up above his head, spun around while shouting something with great joy. He stopped with me still in his arms above his head. He looked up and talked to me. I looked at him. I will never forget that youthful, childlike face. All my life, I wondered what he had said, and I wished I'd meet him again. His skin was fair, and his blond hair fell over his forehead. What struck me more than anything else were his eyes: they were laughing eyes just like my mother's. He put me down and gave me a hug. They jumped in their truck and continued on their way to Germany, followed by many more convoys.

Soon after the Germans left, some strange things took place in the village. There were celebrations whose meaning I didn't understand; they baffled me and eluded me. It was solemn and strange.

Late in the evening, the whole village was awake, including the children. Everybody was looking at the moon or waiting for it to rise, though I didn't know why. At a certain time, when the moon was in a particular spot in the sky, there was shouting and great joy. Men and women jumped up and down, clapped, hugged, and kissed each other, repeating a girl's name: "Eleftheria, Eleftheria!" We children were sent to bed while the adults celebrated.

The next day, something even stranger took place. They hoisted the effigy of a fat woman dressed in a bright red dress. Her hair was done in the style of the 1940s. They paraded her up and down the village, singing songs and shouting Eleftheria. I was confused. The effigy didn't look like the girl Eleftheria. To start with, Eleftheria was not fat; her hair was straight, sparse, and looked as if it needed a good wash. The hair on this effigy was blonde, wavy, and beautifully combed. It took me years to understand. I was twelve years old, and during a history lesson it occurred to me that they weren't honouring Eleftheria for anything she had done. They were celebrating the end of the war and freedom, which Eleftheria means. Why were they looking at the moon? Because the new day begins at midnight, and because they had no clocks or watches, they could tell the time by the position of the moon and stars in the night sky, or by the position of the sun during the day. My grandfather was a seaman and could tell the time accurately both day and night, as could others.

The effigy symbolised freedom. The red dress symbolised the blood shed to gain that freedom. After the war, life was peaceful for a little while.

Diagonally across from our house lived a family of four boys and a girl. The girl was youngest and about three years older than me. We used to spend a fair bit of time together when Yana wasn't there. Her name was Euthymia, abbreviated to Theme. She was a good-natured and happy girl, but she always took me to places where there were no adults or other children. One day she said, "Come. You and I are going to have an enema, because constipation is bad for you." I knew that; everybody said so. I knew what enema equipment looked like because we had one at home. I also knew one needed warm, soapy water; olive oil; and a pole to hang up the enema can. We had none of that.

She took me to a quiet spot. I waited for the enema equipment to appear miraculously, but it didn't. "Where is the enema can?" I asked.

"We don't need one" she said confidently. She proceeded to collect little sticks about the thickness of a pencil, which she cut about three to five centimetres long. She lowered her pants and ordered me to do the same. I obeyed. We squatted. She gave me half the sticks and told me to watch her and do the same.

She put the sticks in her rectum. Wonder of wonders! Before long, the sticks came out with lots of pooh stuck to them. It worked! Why the hell didn't the adults use this quick, easy method? Why all the rigmarole, wasting time and oil? Theme's way was much quicker and just as effective. I tried it under her supervision, and it worked for me too. I was going to recommend it to my mother, but she told me not to do so. "This is our secret. You must not tell anybody," she said. I agreed and never told anybody. She seemed to be preoccupied with bodily functions because every time we were together, we would be either peeing or giving ourselves enemas.

One day as we were urinating together, I noticed her urine was thick like pea soup; I swear I saw some solid pieces come out, whereas mine was clear. I wondered why the difference and thought something was wrong with my pee. I daren't ask anybody because those meetings of ours were clandestine. It was many years later that I realised that she most likely had an ano-urethral fistula, probably as a result of those enemas.

I liked walking on my own. My favourite spot was about 1.5 kilometres from home on the way to Peria, where the creek formed a deep, clear pool. I'd sit on the bridge, hang my legs down, and put my feet in the water. I would stay still. After a few minutes, there would be dozens of little fish swimming around, tickling and biting my feet. I loved the sensation and would amuse myself for hours. On the way home, I'd pick blue daisies which grew wild by the roadside in summer. The flowers didn't last long. In late winter and spring, women would pick the plant and cook it for salads. The water they were cooked in was used as medicine for high blood pressure.

In hot weather, I'd walk in the creek, my dress tucked up in my pants, carrying my shoes. One day while going to Peria, I saw a huge water snake swimming in front of me. Before I knew it, it slithered between my legs. I froze with fear! When I came to my senses, I looked behind me. It was swimming in caterpillar fashion, and it was gigantic. From then on, no matter how hot it was, I refused to walk in the creek. When I walked with Yana, she couldn't understand why I refused to walk in the creek. I didn't tell her because I would not say I was scared. Secretly, I hoped the snake would come along when she was in the creek not only to make up for her not telling me about the birds biting but also to humble her; she always said she wasn't scared of anything.

****

I'd walk for miles carrying my lunch in a tea towel. I'd ask my mother for bread, cottage cheese, olives, and a couple of spring onions. No need for water; there were lots of crystal-clear streams coming straight from the mountains. I'd sit down, crumble the bread and cheese, mix it up, squash it together, and eat it with relish. No cooked meal tasted so good. A favourite spot was the river, where I'd go fishing after lunch. I'd tie the tea towel ends together, forming a cradle and using it as a fishing net. I never caught any fish. I wonder if my mother would have let me go had she known where and how far I walked. When she'd ask where I'd gone, I'd simply say I walked.

When I tired of fishing, I'd go looking for turtles, and more often than not I'd find one. I'd turn it upside down so that it couldn't run away, and then I'd go looking for her eggs. It never occurred to me that it might have been a male.

I loved walking by the creek in the early spring when the grass was wet and slippery on the slopes. I'd pull myself up on the exposed tree roots or low-lying branches, to get where Holy Mary's tears grew. They were white- and pink-tinged, conical flowers an inch high and divinely perfumed. I'd kneel down to smell them. It was said they grew wherever Mary's tears fell when she followed Jesus carrying the cross. Nobody told me that Mary had never set foot in Greece, that Jesus was a Jew, and that he was crucified in Jerusalem.

In early summer when the privet was blooming, I'd go looking for green and golden beetles. The privet perfume was heavenly. I'd collect the beetles from the flowers, filling my hands and putting them in my pockets, and then I'd run home to put them in a jar. Every time they'd escape through my fingers, and I'd end up with just one in each hand. They tickled my hands, but I wouldn't squeeze too hard, fearing I'd squash them. It was a great disappointment to end up with just two beetles after all that effort.

Another highlight was visiting Aunt Soula and my cousin Andrea. They fussed after me and always had something nice to eat there. Aunt was a good cook, and my cousin showered me with attention, combing or cutting my hair. She got all her haircutting practice on my head. The job never took long; there wasn't much hair to cut.

Yana and I would walk from Rodia to Peria, talking about the Americans and "Uncle Truman," who was so good, sending us food and other goodies. That was the American aid to Greece during and after the war. I liked the taste of some of the tinned meats. Because Uncle Truman was so good to us, we decided we should be speaking American, not Greek. Yana told me that Uncle Truman spoke English. I told her not to be stupid; he was American and spoke American, whereas the English people spoke English. She didn't argue. We gibbered away, stopping regularly to interpret to each other. I loved speaking in "American" and wished I could really speak it—and go to America as well.

In winter and early spring, wolves were a real danger. Many times we'd get up in the mornings to find lambs missing and animals mauled if they weren't bolted inside at night or outside, untethered in the spring. A wolf, being intelligent, would not attack a tethered animal for fear of being tangled in the rope. All the stories we heard about wolves as children—especially the story of Red Riding Hood and grandma who they ate up—as well as hearing their howls and seeing the carnage they caused, terrified me. I didn't need a second reminder to go inside. All they had to say was, "The wolves are coming," and I'd run in. I saw them as supernatural, all-powerful, and wise. They were to be dreaded and respected.

One winter afternoon, my mother and I were walking to Peria. The sun was setting as we approached the village, we had a short way to go. My mother kept looking around and over her shoulder rather anxiously, but I felt safe in her capable hands. She was holding my hand a little harder than usual. Suddenly I knew why she was anxious. I heard that unmistakable, eerie, scary howl. He sounded very close. My mother held my hand, vice-like, and took off! She ran like fury, dragging me behind her. I can still feel my heels hitting my bottom. I hadn't seen my mother run before, let alone move so fast. She was built for comfort, not for speed. She was short, just under 150 centimetres, and was bottom heavy. However, the speed she worked up that day was record breaking. What's more, we didn't stop running till we reached the first houses of the village. We both panted like overheated dogs.

Chapter 3

Move to Peria

Time went by, and I was happy and carefree. I don't remember any arguments between my parents for a while, and Grandfather was out of the picture even though he lived with us. I was familiar with Peria, but Rodia was my home.

One day my parents said that we were going to live in Peria soon. I didn't like the idea and told them so. They said I would be starting school, and it would be better for me. I wouldn't have to walk such a long way in the middle of winter, in the snow and the cold winds. I promptly pointed out that the other kids did, and I would walk with them. They were just as quick to point out that the other kids weren't scared of wolves, but I was. I was having frequent nightmares of wolves chasing me where I couldn't run fast enough to get away from them. I had no answer to that.

The sad day came. We moved to Peria and lived in a rented house. My grandfather didn't come with us; I was told he stayed in Rodia to look after the house.

My father and grandfather argued. Granddad was hell-bent in humiliating my father and did it in the worst possible way a proud man could imagine or endure. The nasty, cunning old fox took a sugar bag, put a strap on it, threw it over his shoulder, and walked the nearby villages, begging and saying that his son Alexis didn't feed him, adding,

"Could you give me food and money, please?" He had two sons, but he never mentioned Minoas, whom he got on well with. My father was mortified. No matter what he did, how much money he offered, and how much food he gave Granddad, insisted on embarrassing him. In the end, my father gave up. We moved out of Rodia on false pretences.

The move wasn't a protracted one. There were no wardrobes; the clothes were hung from a rope or wire in the bedrooms according to the season, and the rest were kept in trunks till they were needed. The brass bed my parents had, and which was the talk of the village, was sold when they split up the first time. The bed had a circular mirror of shiny metal about six inches in diameter at the foot end. I can remember squatting in front of it and looking at my reflection. I remember exactly what I looked like. I had freckles on my nose and cheekbones, and I remember trying to count them. I could never count them all, but it kept me from getting bored and getting into mischief. I thought to myself, *My forehead is bigger than Lella's or Noppy's.* It didn't bother me; I simply accepted it as being me.

We all slept on mattresses which were rolled up during the day and covered with a fancy sheet. This was Turkish-style and was common practice in the village. We settled in quickly, and I had no trouble adjusting to our new house, which was exactly the same design as the one in Rodia except for the downstairs, where there was a huge room with a clay floor. It was used as kitchen/dining room, and lounge in the summer. In the middle of this room was a large round table about thirty centimetres high where everybody sat cross-legged for meals.

At one end was a sink with a four-gallon, semi-circular drum hanging on the wall above it. It had a tap and a pretty drawing on it. My mother or grandmother filled it up regularly with water carried in from the village tap. At the opposite end was a smaller room, which was used as a sitting room in winter, as well as to hatch the silkworm eggs and nurse them there till they were big enough to be put in "their own beds." It had a timber floor and an oval heater, which was used to heat the room and to cook on. The heaters were made of tin and lasted two to three winters; they were stored away in summer. Under the window was a divan, and above it was a shelf with Grandma's icons and a fancy oil lamp hanging from a yellow metal chain. The front of the house had been a shop in times gone by, but my parents used it to store fertilisers and poisonous sprays; it was always bolted. The three bedrooms were upstairs.

On the right side was the driveway for the cart. On the same side was the toilet, a chicken shed, and the huge oven under a tin roof. At right angles was the barn. The backyard was covered by a grapevine, and between it and the chicken shed was a pomegranate tree, under which I'd lie and daydream. A deep well marked the boundary between the two properties and was shared by both. Wells were used in the summer as refrigerators, to keep fruit and food cool, in which the villagers lowered in hessian bags.

In the front yard were two huge mulberry trees. The one on the left was opposite the upstairs window and had thick branches growing horizontally. One of them was hollow in the middle and cradle-like. I used to climb up and sit on it, keeping an eye on what was going on in the room upstairs and all around the village. I didn't see anything interesting or unusual. A little creek meandered past the house. The chooks drank from it, the ducks and the kids had fun in it, and my three-year-old sister Ellie did "her washing" in it.

I used to wait eagerly for the hens to hatch the ducks' eggs and take the ducklings to the creek for a drink. Ducks weren't very good mothers, so the villagers used hens to hatch and bring up the ducklings, which would take to the water as soon as they saw it. The mother hen would cackle frantically, flapping her wings and thinking they would drown. It was hilarious, and I laughed every time I saw them. The other kids were used to this scene and didn't take notice. Soon the hen realised her chicks were safe. She'd wait for them to come out of the water in their own good time. By the time she was clucky again, she'd forget, and the drama would start all over again

Soon after we moved to Peria, while playing with Yana I said to her, "Come in and see our new house."

"It's not your house. It's my godmother's house," she retorted.

"No, it's our house," I said defiantly, and the argument went back and forth. I told her to go away.

"No, I don't have to. It's my godmother's house." She stayed put, singing, "It's my godmother's house, tra-la-la."

I was furious. I went inside and slammed the heavy front door shut. My grandmother witnessed it all but didn't interfere. I went upstairs and told Yana to go away again. No matter how I asked, yelled, or spat at her, she would not go. She stayed there tormenting me. I was blind with rage. I looked around and saw a broken chair awaiting repairs. I picked up a leg and threw it at her. Fortunately, it missed her head, but it hit her on the shoulder. The yelling was deafening, and her screams brought Grandmother running. She checked and comforted Yana and then sent her to her mother, who came later, complaining and asking my mother to discipline me. I didn't get punished for trying to kill Yana. It was then that I knew what anger felt like.

Grandma told me what I'd done was terrible. I could have killed Yana. I must ask forgiveness from Holy Mary. I didn't want to. I didn't think it was as bad as what Yana had done to upset me, but I did it to please her. I knelt on the couch under her icons and prayed for forgiveness. I didn't think my cousin would ever come again, but before long there she was, smiling, happy and asking if I wanted to play. Never again, during the two years we lived in that house, did she mention that the house belonged to her godmother. She'd say, "Let's go to your house," emphasising the *your*.

The last summer before starting school was eventful. I got sick for the first time in my life with measles. I was miserable and thought I would never get better All three of us got measles, but Ellie was the sickest. She was about ten months old and had just started walking. After the measles, she got bronchitis and nearly died.

My grandmother stayed home to look after Ellie while my mother went to the field to cut mulberry branches, load them on the cart, and bring them home for the silkworms. This was another reason Grandma stayed home. It was silkworm season, and the worms had to be looked after like premature babies. One could say they needed intensive care, except they had voracious appetites. They took preference over everything and everybody, even sick babies. The room temperature had to be constant. If it dropped, they had to feed the heater. If it went over, they had to reduce the heat. With no central heating, it must have been a nightmare for them. The ventilation had to be perfect—not draughty and not too still. There were huge thermometers hanging on the four walls. My poor mother would come from the field, her face red and her eyes full of worry. The first question she'd ask was, "Mother, is the baby still alive?" Her face was anxious as to what the answer might be. I will never forget the look of relief when Grandma said, "Yes, it is." They both thanked God for another day and said, "Let His will be done."

I hated the silkworms. It was four months of continuous, unrelenting labour. Everybody worked hard, from the hatching of the eggs to the collecting of the silk. I remember them putting the silkworm eggs (tiny, round, grey beads) in a warm spot, looking at them several times a day, and regularly checking the temperature of the area. They rejoiced when the tiny, wriggly worms appeared. Their disappointment was palpable when the eggs didn't hatch. They always blamed it on the eggs being "no good," never on the environment, which was as critical in their hatching as was their fertility. One day, Grandmother came having fed the silkworms. A worm was stuck on her black head scarf. I froze while looking at it. She put her hand right on the worm and pulled it off, saying, "It won't hurt you, silly. It has no teeth." She went back and put it on its bed. I was terrified of them. I wouldn't go in the house for anything other than to sleep. I hated my toes and everybody else's because they moved and wriggled like silkworms. As the worms grew, they became white and thick as an adult woman's finger.

My poor grandmother must have been going out of her mind trying to look after a very sick baby and two rooms full of silkworms on triple-decker beds. We all slept downstairs or upstairs under the veranda. One day while Aunt Soula came to our place, the baby deteriorated, and they thought she was going to die. They "air baptised" her, which was to lift her towards heaven while saying, "We baptise you in the name of the Father, the Son, and the Holy Spirit." They called her Ellie, the name given to her officially then. A couple of months later, they baptised her properly, and Aunt Soula was the godmother.

Chapter 4

Starting School

The school year started soon after we moved to Peria. I was sure to start school with my cousin Yana and two friends, but I was told I was too young and would start next year. I was upset and angry, and I asked, "Then why didn't we move here next year?" No explanation was given, and I was told to shut up. The greatest disappointment was when the kids came home after their first day at school (September 22, 1945) with their new bags and new thick, colourful readers. They showed them to me and excitedly flicked the pages. I could have cried; I didn't have a book. No child had a book unless there were older children in the family. My mother took the reader from one of the kids, put it on her lap, and with me beside her started reading and pointing to the pictures. The first page had a picture of a mother rocking a baby with the letter "O" on top of the page, both capital and lower case. She said, "See? She is singing to the baby, o, o, o," which is the sound people make when rocking a baby. That day I learned five letters: one consonant, N, and four vowels, O, A, I, and E. My mother said, "Look: if you put N and A together, it sounds NA." She pronounced it *nah*, and she did the same with the other vowels.

I got the idea immediately, and within two weeks I knew all the letters of the alphabet and could work out all the words in the first half of the book, which I read when the kids came home from school. Then

joy of joys, I had a book of my own. The local te̶
father's close friend and Eva's godfather, saw ho̶
and gave me a book. I loved that bald-headed, ro̶
dimples and a lovely smile.

I came across words I couldn't work out. I wen̶
help. "Ah," she said. "These two letters together mak̶   ̶ only."
She taught me all seven of the diphthongs. Before long I was reading
well, which in Greek was easy once one knew the alphabet; they sound
as one sees them. I finished the first year's reader within a few weeks
and read it till I was bored.

The girl next door, Anastasia, was in grade six. She lent me her old
readers from grades two to five, one at the time. I was happy reading
and rereading them, but I soon realised I was at a disadvantage. The
other kids were learning to write, and I wasn't. I asked my mother to
teach me how to write. That was a big mistake. She was self-taught and
a terrible writer. I turned out to be as bad as her. Still, my preschool
year wasn't all bad.

The school year finished on June 22. August 15 was a big religious
holyday, Saint Mary's Day. My cousin Ria made me a new light coat in
navy blue out of a dress which didn't fit my mother anymore. It had long
sleeves and two pockets. I wore it on St. Mary's Day. It was traditional to
wear something new on that important day. She also made me a school
bag out of sailcloth. It was a pillow-like structure with handles, and I
was thrilled with it. The joy I got from that bag was indescribable. It
was by my side day and night. I looked after it lovingly, and it was the
most precious thing I had.

The day for the festival celebrations arrived. That fair in 1945 was
the most enjoyable, and the last one before the civil war affected us.
There were lots of people there from the nearby villages. There was
a band of all sorts of instruments: drums big and small, trumpets,
clarinets, and all sorts of jingles. I loved the music, the singing, and
the dancing. Above all, I loved the drums, and I will till the day I die!
I focused on the big one in front of me. I could see the man's head and
arms behind it, banging with all his might, skill, and enthusiasm. I
stood so close to it that I could feel the sound vibrations going through

nny little body. It was an indescribable thrill. Life in the village
as carefree. We could go anywhere we wanted to as long as we told
our parents.

During school holidays, we played and explored places, or I went
on long walks on my own, daydreaming and trying to find answers to
childish questions, of which I had many. As a group of four little girls,
our favourite place was the mill, which was in the next village, Lower
Loutraki. We'd ask the miller, Uncle George, to weigh us, which he did
with much fanfare. Every week we'd go, and every week he'd receive
us with enthusiasm and a big smile on his face as if we were long-lost
friends. He was a tall, thin, grey-headed man and was Anastasia's father.
We loved him. We were never too much trouble for him, and no matter
how busy he was, he'd always find time to weigh us, even if we had to
wait for a while.

The weighing never took long. The poor miller must have been
able to tell our individual weights in his sleep, but he always put us on
the scales, jiggled the bits and pieces, and feigned great surprise when
he called our weight out loud. I was the youngest, smallest, and the
lightest, and I didn't like it; it bothered me. No matter how much I ate,
it made no difference—every week I was the same weight.

One day while going to the mill, I dropped behind a little, filled
my pockets with stones, and caught up with them. We got on the
scales, and as usual I was the last one to get weighed. The miller must
have noticed my bulging, rock-filled pockets, but he said nothing as he
jiggled the weights. He was overjoyed in the increase in my weight. He
put his arms up and waved them in true Greek style. He had a big smile
on his face, and at the top of his voice he announced my weight for
everyone to hear. "Ooh, woo, you have grown so quickly! Nice and fat
too!" I thought I'd be happy, but I wasn't because I knew in my heart it
wasn't true. I was ashamed and didn't to do it again. That miller cared
for kids. Every time we went to be weighed, he always gave me the
higher weight. Regularly he'd tell us we were "all getting nice and fat
just like piglets," which we thought was a great compliment. Being thin
in Greece wasn't fashionable then; it indicated lack of nourishment, a
deep-seated jealousy (which was thought to destroy health), a worry of

some sort, or being struck by the arrows of the winged son of Aphrodite (being in love).

The mill was a very dangerous place to be, and I don't know if either the miller or our parents knew where we went after being weighed. The mill was water operated, and we'd go around the back, high up where the water rushed down and formed a dam from where it tumbled down through the huge pipes turning the millstones. We played around the dam. We weren't tempted to get in because we couldn't swim, but we could have fallen in; there was no fence around it. It was a miracle none of us got minced in those turbines. Our guardian angels worked overtime.

Summer nights were a delight as we chased fireflies. As they flew, they looked like a heavenly show of shooting stars. They never stopped to amaze and delight us. We were excited when we caught one. During the day, we tried to find their hiding place in the ground. Finding one was thrilling. Our other popular pastime was "decorating the earth." We'd scratch a shallow hole in the ground; get some flowers, colourful beads, string, paper, and whatever else we could find; arrange them as artistically as we could; cover it with a piece of glass; put a bit of soil around its edges; and look at each other's artwork, voting for the best one. We'd do them and redo them. I seldom won. Regularly we'd cut ourselves, but our immune systems coped well with dirt and cow and horse manure. The standard self-treatment was to suck the blood. If it started looking red, the next step would be a good scrub, a generous application of tobacco, and a bandage made of old sheets. Not too many of us died from septicaemia.

That summer I realised I was in deep love with Demosthenes, or Demos, two years older than me. He had two sisters. Marika was older than him and Toula was younger. Toula was Eva's best friend. He was a naughty kid, was always in trouble, couldn't pass by a challenge, and was always on the go. I looked forward to going to school with him. We'd be in the same classroom because grades one through three were in one classroom and grades four through six were in the other.

Summer nights were socialising time for the adults. Women would get together in the town square for a chat, ranging from innocuous gossip (often not so innocuous) to matchmaking. Men would go to the cafenio. My father was seldom home in the summer. He was up in the mountains making charcoal. In the winter, he helped with farm work, broke in horses, used his trade as a farrier, and at night went to the cafenio for a game of backgammon, a chat, and ouzo.

Soon before I started my first school year, a lady came to stay with us. I hadn't met her before. Her name was Sephora, and she was the kindergarten teacher in the village. The only thing I remember about her were her comments about my terrible handwriting, but I don't remember her offering to teach me how to write. She kept to herself.

The end of the school year came for my cousin and friends. I had read all five readers, and Anastasia lent me her sixth when she finished with it. I read it several times during the summer holidays. That was all very well, but when I started school, I became bored, and the teacher suggested to my parents that they put me up to grade two. For some reason, they disagreed. The only challenge I had was learning to write properly, which I never managed, and arithmetic, which I followed and understood. I'd finish my work early, and because I didn't have to do any reading, I'd listen to the arithmetic lessons of the higher grades. I couldn't follow them, and I thought the teacher had a speech impediment and was unable to pronounce a R sound. I didn't know the difference between the word decada, a unit of ten, and decara, a ten-cent piece. I enjoyed every day of school, even carrying the wood, which we had to bring for the heater in winter.

The school year finished, and the celebrations were held at night. People from the villages were there. We sang as a group or individually, or we recited a poem. Because I couldn't sing, I recited a poem. I was so nervous that I forgot it halfway. The teacher rescued me, and I still got a clap.

The prizes were given out together with the certificates, starting with first grade. I got a shock when my name was the first to be called. I got a straight ten for everything, including arithmetic. I had no clue what it all meant, but the look on my mother's face said it all. Her face beamed, and her blue eyes laughed and sparkled. I realised it was a great honour. Yana, Dinah, and Vicky got six, seven, and eight, respectively.

I won't forget the malevolent look on my paternal aunt Sassa's face. She looked at me with contempt and said, "My Yana will get ten next year."

"Yes, of course," said my mother, who only saw the good in others. Only one other pupil in the whole school got a ten, a girl in grade six.

Chapter 5

Religious Awakening

Easter was approaching. Women were busy cleaning their houses, dying eggs, and cooking the traditional chicken offal soup and sweets. Everybody went to church, men included, and everybody took communion. We got up early and put on clean clothes—undies, socks, and all. They had to be immaculate. They must not have not been farted on let alone pissed on; this was how important cleanliness was on this day.

I was dressed, my hair combed, waiting to go to church. Mother and Grandmother raced around doing the necessary chores and getting Eva and Ellie ready. I helped myself to breakfast thinking they had forgotten about it. I had bread, oil, and herbs.

We went to church, worshipped, prayed, took communion, and went home. I felt pious, happy, and very important. Ellie looked angelic in her new white dress with frills around the armholes. It was handmade by my mother from her silk wedding petticoat. I loved Ellie and was proud of her. I loved Eva too, but I didn't feel maternal towards her.

We returned home, and the table was set for breakfast. "I'm not hungry, I have already eaten," I said.

Grandma's blue eyes, dimmed by age and a hard life, opened wide. "When?" she asked.

"Before we went to church," I said casually.

I thought she was going to die. She raised her arms to her head in dismay. "Oh, no! My God, what have you done?"

I had no idea. I looked at my mother to assess the situation and work out how severe the punishment was going to be. She was unconcerned, trying to hide a smile. I was confused.

"Don't you know it's a terrible sin to eat before you take Holy Communion? You must ask Mary for forgiveness."

I figured out it must have been a bigger sin than farting on your knickers. I went to the little room, kneeled under her icons in fear, and sincerely asked Holy Mary to forgive me.

Religion and theological themes became very significant in my life from then on. I took them seriously. I wasn't sure whether I was forgiven or not, and because my mother had reacted differently, I went to her for reassurance. "Yes, of course God has forgiven you. He always forgives," she said. I realised then that they had different ideas and perceptions on religion. One said, "Ask Mary for forgiveness." The other said, "God forgives." I had heard a lot about Holy Mary's graciousness and greatness; she was dominant in the Greek Orthodox faith. God was in the background. I knew Jesus was Mary's baby; she carried Him in every icon.

I started asking questions about God. I asked everybody except the priest—he was too awesome. They always answered me honestly and to the best of their knowledge: where did God live, how far was heaven, how did he remember everybody's names, how big were his books, and did he have one book for good deeds and one for bad. I didn't have to ask what He wore because all the icons showed the saints wearing loose robes with wide sleeves, and they were all old men. I thought a person had to be old before becoming a saint. (There's some truth in that.) I imagined God to be an old man with a handlebar moustache and blue, stern eyes just like my grandfather's. He always carried pencil and paper to write down my sins, and he would gladly punish me when the time came.

After a while, it occurred to me to ask about God's origins. "Who made God?" But no one could give me a satisfactory answer. The most confusing one came from my father, who said, "God is not like us. He is a power, a bit like a strong wind." I knew all about strong winds. When the northerlies blew, they'd push me along whichever way they blew. They uprooted huge trees, ripped off roofs, and more. So God was an awful power to be reckoned with. I pestered my grandmother, who would always patiently say, "Child, I don't know. Nobody knows." She'd breathe with relief when I'd leave her alone.

One day my mother was baking bread. It was a hot day. She stood at front of the huge oven rushing to put the dough in with a long, flat-handled shovel kept for that purpose alone. The hot day combined with the hot oven made her face red hot, and her eyes looked bluer in contrast. I asked her again who made God. She rested her wooded shovel on the lip of the huge oven, looked at me, and in no uncertain terms told me that if I ever asked her this question again, she'd belt the daylights out of me. I knew she meant it and was glad she didn't say she'd throw me in the oven too. I fully believed she'd keep her threat; she never forgot things.

In great disappointment, I lay down under the pomegranate tree opposite the chook shed to continue pondering this awesome, fearful, all-knowing, ever-present God. The ideas eluded me. I gave up trying. I looked up in the sky and watched the clouds as they moved and formed different shapes. I saw all sorts of images. I saw birds, people, trees, huge rocks, a rabbit, and a wolf cross the sky. I knew it! I was thrilled and delighted. I knew then who made God, and I was sure of it. The wolves made God! They took the rocks I saw in the sky, put them together, built a great staircase, climbed up to heaven, made God, and came down again to terrify me and countless other villagers—except for Yana, who wasn't scared of anything. That belief of the origins of God satisfied me till I was about eleven years old.

I have pleasant memories visiting our neighbours Zizi and Michael, who had their first child, Vivika. I was besotted by her and was made welcome by the baby's whole family. I thought she was beautiful. Vivika smiled a lot and had dimples on her cheeks just like her mother, as well as a short curl of hair behind each ear and nothing on top. I remember comparing the colour of my skin with hers. She was darker.

Zizi was very pretty with fair skin, dark hair, big brown eyes, and sensual lips just like Eva's. Michael was a big man with a square jaw, broad face, thick and curly black hair, heavy eyebrows, and a big moustache. He seldom smiled, but I saw him as indifferent, not stern. I was never scared of him. I loved Vivika as I did all babies. She responded to me and got excited upon seeing me. By the time I started school, she was walking. I adored her.

There are many advantages to living in a small community. People know each other, and everybody seems to care for each other's children. I knew Zizi's mother as Mouzena (the wife of Mouzi). When a woman got married, she lost her identity. She even lost her first name. She was called by her husband's given name, and to make it feminine, they added the "-ena" suffix. For example, the wife of Gorge would be Georgena. I never knew what her own name was. Zizi had two sisters, one of whom I got to know well and love. Her name was Kiki. She was a lovely girl in her late teens. She was friendly and always welcomed me whenever I visited, which was often. They had a bitch, a terrier cross, that had a litter of four pups. When I wasn't at Zizi's. I was at her mother's place playing with the pups. I would have loved one, but my mother said I couldn't have it. I knew there was no use in asking again; her word was law.

The pups were growing up and scrambling around. They started eating solids. I'd play with them for hours. One in particular took my fancy, and I'd always keep it on my lap. It was a female that was black with white under its belly and neck, as well as a brown spot over each eye. One day Kiki said, "You'd like this puppy, wouldn't you?"

I said "Yes, but Mother won't let me have it."

"Well, I'll tell you what we'll do. You can take it home, and if your mother says you can't keep it, bring it back."

I thought it was a fair deal. I took the puppy home, but I didn't take it inside. I snuck in the barn unnoticed, made a bed for it in the straw, and was sure nobody would see it. I didn't say a word to anybody, not even to my grandmother. I was afraid they'd make me take it back.

The next day I went in the barn, gave it milk, and played with it. For a couple of days, the pup and I were happy playing secretly. My frequent comings and goings in the barn raised suspicions. Mum or Grandma must have gone and found the pup, which they left there. They got hold of me and started asking some awkward questions. "What do you have in the barn? Why are you there all day?" I hated lying. I soon realised telling the truth was better than lying. I told them I had a puppy, and Kiki said I could take back if I wasn't allowed to keep.

My mother asked, "How long have you had it?"

"A long time," I said. Three days seemed a long time to a six-year-old. I brought it out of the barn.

My mother was pleased with it. She picked it up, smiled, and said, "It is beautiful." To my surprise and delight, they allowed me to keep it! Then she asked, "What shall we call it?" I hadn't thought of that; to me, it was Puppy. She put the pup on the landing of the stairs. The pup waddled around, wagged its tail, and sniffed around, happy to be out in the daylight.

My mother looked at it again and decidedly said, "Irma, that's her name." She picked it up, put her mouth close to its ear, and gently called her name three times in each ear. Then she put down the pup, went a few steps away and called, "Irma, come!" To my amazement, the pup went to her. I liked the name.

We had great times playing together. Irma learned to jump, chase me, run after a stick, and bring it back. I loved that pup. Training dogs at our house wasn't much different to training kids, at least according to my mother. She believed in the biblical statement "spare the rod and spoil the child." She used the rod liberally, when necessary. She always had a stick nearby to make sure we weren't spoilt, and to save time.

One day we were playing outside. Ellie, two years old, had something in her hand and was eating it. The pup jumped up, took the food from her, and ate it. My mother saw it. she thought it to be bad manners for the pup. She picked up the pup by the scruff of the neck, went inside, put it on the stair landing, and rubbed the pup's muzzle on the timber floor, occasionally bashing it on the floor. She said, "No, no! Don't do it again," and kept on doing it. I felt like crying and telling her to stop. I watched in horror as the pup yelped helplessly. It seemed like ages. Then I saw some blood come out of its muzzle. She let go of the pup.

I picked up my puppy and tried to comfort her, trying very hard not to cry myself.

Time went by. Irma grew up, was a well-behaved dog, and became part of the family. She was even allowed to come inside during the day—rare treatment for a village dog, whose place was outside both day and night.

Chapter 6

To the Field for Watermelons

It was the summer of 1946. We had a visitor from the city: a girl, Ria, three years older than me. She was my father's god-daughter. My father was home from the mountains. He said he was going to the field to get watermelons to take to the market, and we could go with him if we wanted. Ellie was too young and stayed home. The cart was ready, and we all hopped on to head to the field. We helped as much as we could. The cart was filled to capacity. We couldn't all sit in the cart. He made room for Ria in the middle of the cart by moving a few watermelons; it was a special treat as a visitor. Ria sat there safely, if not comfortably, and we started on our way home. Eva and I walked.

On the way home, Father met a friend, and they stopped for a chat and a cigarette. Eva snuck behind my father, climbed up the bar of the cart, and tried to pull herself up on the cart by holding onto a watermelon, which rolled and fell to the ground, together with Eva. This scared the animals, which took off, and the front wheel of the cart ran over Eva.

I have never seen anybody move as fast as my father did that time. Simultaneously, his friend moved like lightning in front of the animals, stopping them. My father pulled Eva away before the second wheel ran over her. He held her in his arms, looked up towards heaven, and in the most pleading, frantic, painful voice I have ever heard yelled, "My child, my child! God, please!" Eva looked shocked and wet herself. My father was terrified and crying. Only a few years earlier, his brother's only son was killed in the same accident. The only difference was that the ground he was run over was hard, whereas Eva fell in a small dip on soft ground. He carried her home.

My mother was waiting for us. With an anxious voice, she asked if everything was OK. My father told her what had happened. She said, "I knew something bad was going to happen. I had a terrible premonition even before you left home. I pray to God she will be all right." My father's nephew had died within two hours of being run over. The next few hours were a most anxious time for the whole family. Eva survived by a miracle.

Autumn was my favourite season. I loved walking in the forest when the trees were bare. I'd stomp on the leaves, enjoying the rustling sound. I loved the sun streaming through the bare branches, the coolness, and the mellowness of the day. I collected dead leaves, especially the big leaves of the plane trees. I enjoyed going out with my family and the neighbours, sweeping leaves and putting them in piles, then in sacks. We used the leaves for the animals to sleep on in winter. That was the only other job I didn't mind doing. I hated every other farming job except collecting the eggs from the nests. I had made up my mind at an early age that I was not going to spend my life digging around onions, cleaning manure, ploughing, and milking cows.

Children of my age started learning about farming and were put to work. There were children's tools: hoes, picks, and even shovels. Kids had to help. I used to go with my mother to the field to weed and dig around the onion patch. The first time, I went gladly. I didn't realise we were going to be there all day. I wanted to go wandering around but wasn't allowed. We were there all day, and it seemed as if it would never end. The next day, we were back on the same job! I couldn't see the point in digging around onions. "It is killing them," I said to my mother, pointing at them flagging.

"Yes," she said. "But look at the ones we dug around yesterday." They looked very healthy, standing upright and much cleaner. I couldn't argue and had no choice but to stay and do as much as I could till the sun started going down—a mighty long time. For three days, we dug and weeded onions. When the job was done, I didn't go to the field again.

School started on September 22. I was thrilled to be going to school again. The church bell rang twice. The first was to wake the village children, and the second was for the classes to start. I'd be up and ready before the second bell rang. The school was close to home. I was glad I didn't have to get up at the crack of dawn and walk for miles in the snow, carrying wood for the heater.

Chapter 7

My First Holiday

One day I got home from school, and the shoemaker from town was at our place. Without an explanation, he told me to take off my shoes, and he measured my foot. My mother gave him her cream-coloured wedding shoes, and he left without saying anything. I didn't ask for an explanation. A week later, the shoemaker came back with a pair of child's shoes in black with a strap and a shiny black button. My mother took them from him and told me to try them. I couldn't believe they were for me. I put them on, and they fitted perfectly.

My mother paid him, and he left. I asked if I could wear them. "No," she said. "They are for best. You can wear them when you go to Eidesah." What a bombshell! What a privilege! I had never been away from the village before. For me, that was a bit like going around the world and back. I was delighted.

"When am I going? I asked.

"Next week," she said with a sparkle in her eyes.

"Are you coming?" I asked.

"No, you are going with Sapho for Christmas."

I couldn't wait to go to Eidesah. Every day I'd get the shoes out, look at them, literally spit on them, and polish them. I had seen kids put snot on their new shoes to shine them, but I wasn't going to do that to my new shoes.

School closed for Christmas holidays. The next day, we left for Eidesah, about forty kilometres away, but because of the bad roads and the snow, it took up to two hours to get there.

My mother packed a few clothes for me: some dresses; warm, knitted, long cardigans; knitted woollen socks; and a pair of bought ones to go with the new shoes. I didn't have a good winter coat, and so she put in the silky navy one to cover everything rather than to keep me warm. I wore the coat and the new shoes that day. We said our farewells and were on our way. The weather was icy.

We got to Sappho's house, which was a grand one. Beautiful dark timber doors, and decorated, open fireplaces which made the lounge room warm and cosy. The house had lots of rooms and a very big kitchen with a wood stove for cooking and heating. We were greeted by her mother, a very kindly old lady whose name I don't know; she was Aunty to me. Sappho had two sisters. The eldest one, Margarita, was in her late twenties, and the youngest, Aria, was about twenty. Sappho was the middle child. None of the girls was married. They were beautiful and had a lighter complexion than the average Greek because they were European Macedonians.

They all fussed over me and seemed happy to have me around. Their mother was busy making preparations for Christmas, and her cooking smelled delicious. She made the New Year's traditional Greek pie, vasilopita. She put the coin in the dough and kneaded it well so that nobody knew where it would end up. There was great excitement when it came to cutting the pie on New Year's Eve because the one in whose piece the coin was found was supposed to have good luck for the rest of the year. Anyway, the old lady mixed the dough, wrapped it up in blankets, and put it on a big sitting cushion close to the heater to rise. I didn't see her put it there, and when I went to the kitchen looking for somewhere to sit, I thought the dough was a cushion. I sat on it, and it was soft and warm.

I had been sitting there some time when Aunty came in, gave a loud shriek, and picked me up as fast as she could. The girls came running in to see what the shrieking was all about. When she told them in

Macedonian what happened, they burst out laughing, which didn't amuse her. The vasilopita turned out nicely despite my sitting on it.

The girls took me to places, but I don't remember much other than a big river, the famous cataracts of Eidesah, and an evening out to the cinema, my first time. I didn't know what to expect. I wore my light coat and my new shoes, and we were off. The movie was a musical one, with singing and dancing and lots of beautiful costumes. It was not a children's movie. One scene stayed with me: the dancer and singer's dress! It was odd. It was very short at the front, sitting just below her groin, and very long at the back, dragging on the floor. It had frills all the way around it, the neckline was too low, and half her bosom hung out. I didn't I like it. But I thought it was better this way than having it short at the back, showing her bottom (which would be rude) and tripping her when going forward.

Christmas and New Year's were celebrated by just us. Aria got the piece of vasilopita with the coin in it. Everybody wished her good luck, hoping the bloke would be a nice one. I overheard my mother and the other women in the village say, "Old maids," which was a derogative term. Aria was still young enough to marry according to them. Single women over twenty-five were considered too old to marry; the best they could hope for was to marry a widower. There were not too many divorcees then. Eva's godmother, a very pretty girl of eighteen, was referred to as the old maid till my father's friend came to the village as a teacher, saw her, fell in love with her, and married her. That friend was my much-loved teacher, John Karidis.

The two weeks flew by, and it was time to go back home. I had mixed feelings about going back because I enjoyed the attention I got at Eidesah. Aria came with us, and we were to travel back to the village by truck. The driver put all the luggage on the truck. The girls sat in the cabin. When the driver lifted me up, I thought he'd put me in the cabin too. Instead, he put me on the back of the truck and told me to sit in the middle just behind the cabin. He ordered me not to stand up on penalty of death, and they took off.

I didn't like sitting at the back of the truck. After all the attention I'd received in Eidesah, to be thrown at the back of the truck as if I was baggage was humiliating and upsetting. The weather was cold, and it had snowed heavily. I had on only my light coat, my jumper under it, and my short socks. I curled in a small ball, pulled my dress over my bare legs, and stayed huddled up at the back of the truck. I felt like crying. The truck jumped over potholes and roared and blew smoke from somewhere. We travelled like that for what seemed hours before the truck stopped.

The driver came out, took me off the truck, and put me in the cabin without a word. "Come, darling, come," the girls said. I sat on one of the girls' lap for the rest of the trip, which wasn't long after that. She remarked how warm I was.

By rights I should have frozen. It was the middle of winter, I wasn't warmly dressed, and I was sitting on the tray of an open truck I was a skinny kid and didn't even have on warm socks. Looking back now, I was in danger of falling from the truck with its low sides. But all along, I felt as if someone was hovering just above me, protecting me. I didn't feel the cold, and I didn't notice the wind rushing past. I had the same feeling of protection several times later in my life.

At home, my mother was glad to see me. Her blue eyes sparkled. She asked me how I enjoyed my holiday and a million other questions. I told her everything. The theatre, sitting on the vasilopita, the song Aria had taught me (or rather, that I learned because it was all she sang all day long). The song was all of two sentences and went something like, "Scondy's underpants are red and long and full of knots." My mother laughed. I couldn't work out the importance of the knotty underpants, let alone their colour. Everybody else wore white or grey underwear.

This was the same winter I witnessed my parents fighting angrily. Mother yelled at Father, which infuriated him. He demanded total submission and obedience, but she would not submit. They were screaming at each other, with my father calling her all sorts of undeserved, filthy epithets. He shook his fist close to her face, threatening to kill her. I was terrified that he meant it. Suddenly he rushed towards her, arm raised and a knife in his hand. I screamed. He turned and looked at me, letting her go. He wasn't aware that I was witnessing the fight. His face was red and his eyes were bulging. He swung around and furiously knifed the heater instead.

Hot coals poured on the floor, and smoke filled the room. My grandmother came running, and both women shovelled up the hot coals, preventing a fire. When the heater cooled down, my father patched it up with tin and wire. Many years later, my mother said they had been fighting because my father had gambled every cent they'd had for building a house in the coming spring. New Year's Eve was a big gambling night in Greece, and my father was a bit of a gambler.

Chapter 8

Spring 1947

Spring 1947 was rolling nicely, and I was blissfully unaware that a civil war was raging on. My father was away for a long time. When I asked after him, I was told that "he was in the war." My mother and grandmother looked after everything—the animals, the farm, the silkworms, and the kids—but this time it was a bit harder. My mother was six months pregnant with her fourth child. She had to go to the field to get mulberry leaves for the silkworms, and I had to go with her to help. She had to rest the long ladder against the tree, climb up, and cut the branches. I'd put them together neatly in bundles. When she cut down enough branches to fill the cart, I'd pass them to her on the cart, and we'd go home to feed the worms. We were both exhausted.

My grandmother was in the field all night, watering the sweet corn. Only so much water was allocated to each farmer and at a certain date, and so farmers had to water their crops at the appointed time or else they'd lose their turn. Watering was a man's job, and it involved digging tranches to direct the water to the field, blocking one waterway, and opening another till all the field was watered. It was hard, back-breaking work, but Grandma had to do it. She was a tiny woman, barely 147 centimetres tall, and she never weighed more than 45 kilograms. She was aged in her sixty's but she had to do it.

One day, Eva had to take breakfast and lunch to Grandma, a walk of about four kilometres. Eva was six years old and was scared to go on her own. She asked if Toula could go with her. My mother sent us to ask Toula to go with Eva.

I helped Eva carry the food, and together we walked to Toula's place, just across the road. Toula had nothing to do but decided she didn't want to walk all the way to the field. I didn't know what to do. Eva was scared to go on her own. I did a bit of quick thinking and asked her, "Would you go if I came with you as far as the vineyards?" That was about a kilometre.

"Yes," she said. "I will go."

We walked to the vineyards. They kept on walking, and I turned back to go home, where Mother was waiting for me to go to the field for mulberry leaves. It was Thursday, market day. People were going to Ardea for shopping as I was returning home. I thought I could hear my mother's voice calling my name: "Mallie!"

Vayia, an older lady, ran towards me and in great urgency said, "Run home! Your mother wants you. She will kill you."

I ran as fast as my skinny legs would take me for nearly one kilometre without stopping. I got home at the point of collapse. My heart thumped, and I was breathless and unable to speak.

Mother was lying on a mat on the ground, her face red hot and her eyes bulging with anger. She got off the ground with a grunt. Without a word, she picked up the stick next to her and started beating me mercilessly. After a few blows, I started crying, and all I could say was, "Mommy, Mommy!" I don't know how long she beat me. Suddenly, I felt all my strength ebb away. I couldn't cry anymore.

I became vaguely aware of the woman next door running towards us screaming, "You are killing the child. You are killing her!" I don't remember her rescuing me. I went blank. I don't know who carried me inside, how long I was conscious, or how long I slept.

When I woke up, I was on the landing of the staircase, not in bed. I was dazed and drowsy. The woman, Maria, was still at our house. My mother watched me with a worried look, but she didn't ask how I was. She never put her arms around me or showed any emotion or affection.

She looked stunned and let me be, but she didn't leave my side. When I was fully awake and remembered the whole episode, I realised she was angry because she needed to go to the field for mulberry leaves. The silkworms had to be fed. But she hadn't told me to come back quickly; if she had, it didn't register. And how did I know that Toula would be difficult to convince to go with Eva? If I hadn't gone the distance with them, my grandmother would have been hungry, and I didn't want that to happen.

Needless to say, I was in no state to do any work that day. I don't know how my mother managed to feed those accursed silkworms. She must have gotten leaves from the trees around the house and neighbourhood. Later that week, I heard her saying to the neighbours that she was so upset that she felt the baby thresh about in her. It was then that I knew we were going to have a baby, and I was thrilled. Anyway, I lived to tell the story—and to get a few more beatings like it. Grandma always comforted us after beatings, but this time she wasn't there to sooth my pain.

What Mother did to me then, might sound harsh and severe, but when I look into her own childhood and how her fanatically religious father had disciplined them, what I got was a reprimand, perhaps a bit more severe than necessary. My mother told the story of how her cousin had gone to her father saying, "Uncle George, Magdalena stole onions from the garden." He hung the twelve-year-old child on a tree by the ankles and beat her senseless.

The words *stealing* and *lying* were anathema for three generations in my family. My parents couldn't tolerate three things in us kids: lying, stealing, and disobedience. I was always willing to do their bidding, especially when they explained the reason to me. Mother didn't always have the time to do this, but my grandmother did, and I loved her for it.

Many times I thought of that beating that I'd gotten undeservedly. I thought I might tell her sometime, but I didn't. I didn't want to upset her. She never asked why I took so long to return. I knew she was very sorry for nearly killing me. She died without knowing the reason.

Chapter 9

The Civil War

The civil war was already raging, but it hadn't affected us yet. I was about to start my second school year. I was blissfully unaware and happy with the other children during the long vacation. We also had jobs to do, such as picking beans for home use or for marketing, harvesting corn, and my much-hated sedentary job, getting the silk off the cocoons. My bottom would get sore, and I'd spend more time wriggling than getting silk. Then after a while, my shoulder would ache from continuously turning the wheel of the silk-extracting machine, a simple square box about thirty centimetres deep and seventy centimetres square with a roll in the middle and a handle on the side to turn the rod. The cocoons would rotate, and the silk fibre would wind around the rod. When it was full of silk, they'd take the silk off it, throw the cocoons out, and refill the machine, and the torturing would start again. There seemed no end to it. It was times like this that I wanted to live in the city for ever. I would do anything but sit down all day and wind the handle of that hated machine. That was the time Mother growled at me most and told me not to be so lazy. I was glad when the stuff was packed up and the silk was taken to the market.

Another task was to collect our animals when the hired herdsman brought them back from grazing a long way from the village. He accompanied them just before the vineyard, a couple kilometres from the village, where we collected them. On a hot, dry summer's day late in the afternoon, Yana and I went to collect our animals. We got to the designated spot before the cattle arrived, we sat on the grass by the vineyard, and talked. Yana was a year older and stated with great authority that she knew more than me on every subject, including weather forecasting. She looked up towards the setting sun and said with great confidence, "See that?" She pointed towards a cloud that was half covering the sun. "It will rain."

"No, it doesn't rain in summer," I said.

"Yes, it will rain, and heavily too, before we get home" She was sure, but I was dubious. We waited to see the forecast fulfilled.

Just as we heard the bells of the animals coming, and while the sun was still shining, a few drops of rain started falling. Before long, the whole sky was black. Thunder and lightning tore the skies. We got drenched. We collected our animals and ran all the way home. We didn't know that milking cows shouldn't run, but we'd have ignored that even if we had known because we were so scared.

Just before we got to the village puffed and out of breath, Yana looked at me and gasped, "I told you so, didn't I?" I held her in awe ever after, and never again did I doubt her weather forecasting abilities.

My peaceful little world was about to be shattered, never to be the same again, but we had a few weeks to enjoy. My father was in the war, but I didn't miss him; he was away for long periods of time, and when he wasn't around, there were no fights or profane language.

One day I went with my cousin Ria and her mother, Aunt Sassa, to collect the animals from the herd. We sat on the grass as usual, and I got the distinct feeling I was an outcast in that small group. Aunt Sassa spoke in Turkish. I couldn't understand a single word, but occasionally they'd glance at me. Ria answered curtly in Greek, saying, "Why didn't you tell her the sewing machine is broken?"

I knew exactly what they were discussing. At home, I relayed the story to my mother exactly as it had happened. Both my mother and grandmother became upset. When they calmed down, my mother sent me to Aunt Sassa's, telling me to ask for the return of the four little camisoles she had asked Ria to machine stitch. I didn't understand the implications of it, and with the innocence of an eight-year-old, I asked her to give me back the clothes I'd brought this morning. "Please. My mother said."

She looked at me horrified. Her eyes flashed, and I thought she'd hit me. She threw the small bundle of baby clothes in my arms, and I went home.

Soon after I got home, Aunt Sassa arrived, flustered and dithering. My mother, always polite and civilised, asked her in. Before she sat down, Sassa said to my mother, "But we weren't talking about you! We were talking about someone else!"

"Well," said my mother coldly, "if the sewing machine is broken for someone else, it must be broken for me too. Never mind; it's only four little vests. I'll do them by hand as I did all the others." Aunt Sassa left empty-handed.

Chapter 10

Ellie Belted

The stress of the civil war, the heavy responsibility my mother and my grandmother had, Mother's pregnancy, and her fiery nature made her capable of nearly killing all the three of us in as many months. I have forgiven her because I had much time to reflect and understand her. Sometimes I still feel sad for her, wanting to cry.

Ellie was very advanced in her speech and reasoning, but she was late getting bladder control. She'd wet or dirty herself, take her pants off, and dip them in the creek running at the front of the house. Then she would bring them in dangling between fingers and thumb and say, "Mommy, don't smack me. I washed them." I wish I could forget those words. My mother and the neighbours didn't understand that bladder control was not a matter of learning or intelligence. Putting it simply, it is communication between bladder and brain.

It was a hot summer's day, and we were dressed in our Sunday best. I had the responsibility of taking my sisters to church. Ellie looked like a doll. My mother stayed home to carry on with the many jobs she had to do. I liked going to church. I loved the smell of the burning wax, the incense, the priest singing psalms, the flickering candles, and the light filtering though the stained-glass windows. I loved the icons beautifully painted and decorated, mostly with silver but some with gold, and the general atmosphere of the church. To me, it was like a festival. Most of all, I liked the priest making a fuss of us at the end of the service. I was delighted when the priest commented on Ellie's new dress and how beautiful she was. We were the children of a convert to the Orthodox religion. He baptised my mother and officiated at her marriage, and he was fond of her.

When church was over, I took them by the hand, and we walked home. At the front of the house, I let go of them and played with the other kids. Ellie wet herself, and as usual she took off her pants—as well as everything else—dipped her clothes and herself in the creek, and walked home stark naked, her "washing" over her arm. She saw Mother coming. "Mummy, don't smack me. I washed them." This would frustrate my mother and amuse the neighbours, but not today. No sooner than Ellie had finished speaking than Mother grabbed Ellie. She had the tethering steel rod in her hand, which was about fifty centimetres long. She attacked the child and bashed her naked little body indiscriminately and without control or mercy. Ellie screamed, but Mother didn't stop. I thought she was going to kill the baby, as we referred to Ellie. I withdrew into myself; I couldn't even cry. I felt helpless and angry, and I didn't dare go near her to intervene. I had seen and heard her tell my grandmother, "Go, or I'll hit you too."

When the child went limp in her hands, she let go. One of the neighbours came out, took the child, and cared for her and for my mother, who was shaking with fury and upset with what she had done. My grandmother didn't come home till late in the day. By then, the red marks on Ellie had turned blue. That little body was covered in black stripes where the iron rod had struck her, from her little shoulders to her ribs and down to her little legs. I will never forget the look on my grandmother's face when she saw the child's bruises and how subdued the usually active child was: it was a look of fear, anger, frustration, and pity mixed together. She murmured, "She will kill these kids one day. She will. But Grandmother never confronted her.

My mother was remorseful and very upset—and by punishing the child as severely as this, she'd punished herself even more. Many times, I saw her pick Ellie up and rub her hands up and down that bruised little body. I knew then that she was sorry for what she'd done. It was not till I had my own children and grandchildren that I knew how they each felt. I felt sorry for both because it wasn't easy for them.

I feel sick in the stomach as I am writing this, even seventy-one years later. The sound of the sentence, "Don't smack me. I've washed them," torments me, and I wish I could wipe it from my memory. Mother was under tremendous stress. She was heavily pregnant, had three children to look after, was doing the work of four people between them, and was living during a civil war. It must have been horrendous for her, and here was a three-year-old creating more unnecessary work for her. She disciplined us the only way she knew how, the way she and her siblings had been disciplined. She'd been beaten mercilessly by an overzealous and fanatic father because he, like my mother, believed literally in the "Spare the rod and spoil the child." I could not hold them responsible or guilty for their actions. They didn't know any better.

There was so much to do: cutting the corn, harvesting the wheat, and organising the silk to be taken to the market. There was no time to breathe, let alone rest. All the hard work caught up with my poor grandmother. She was doubled over with back and shoulder pain, and she couldn't stand up straight. I was convinced that she would be left crippled forever. I felt very sorry for her, but I never showed my feelings. I simply coped as best as I could. Nobody said to me that she would be OK when she rested in winter; it would have put my mind at rest. She walked bent over, moaning with every step, but there was no way she could or would have taken a rest. She did the "light jobs" such as cooking and feeding the chooks. My mother did the heavy ones: milking, feeding the animals, and cleaning the house not only because it had accumulated dust and dirt from the silkworms and neglect, but also because the baby was due, and they had to clean the house. My poor mother was on her knees, scrubbing and cleaning floors and putting colour (ochre) on them to make them look good. The whole house, upstairs and downstairs, smelled clean and looked impeccable. The floors looked like florins. I stood back to admire the staircase and the landing. I loved the fresh smell of the ochre and the clean look.

Chapter 11

Eva

One day, Eva was on her own and hungry. She decided to make a tomato salad for herself, Greek style. She went to the garden and got some tomatoes, a cucumber, and some spring onions. She chopped them up as best as she could, got the bottle of oil, put some in her salad, and put a whole lot more on the freshly cleaned landing. Then she got some bread, ate her self-prepared meal, and left everything on the landing where she ate, including the sharp knife. She came out to play with of us.

My mother came in before my grandmother and found the mess on the freshly cleaned landing. Overworked, heavy with child, tired, worried, and quick-tempered as she was, she went blind with rage. She picked up the knife from the landing and came out in the front yard, looking furious. Seeing the knife in her hand and the look on her face, I was sure she was going to kill someone. I don't know how she knew it was Eva who had messed up the place. Eva was in the village square just across the road from our house when my mother screamed at her and told her to come immediately. Eva had the sense to run away as fast as her chubby little legs could take her. I would have gone running to Mother because I knew if I didn't, I'd get double the belting, one for the offence and one for not coming quickly enough. Mother had lost all reason. She ran after Eva, brandishing the knife and calling her all sorts of names such as little ogre, little devil, bastard, and anything else she could think of. However, she couldn't catch up to Eva, not at nearly nine months pregnant, and Eva was a good runner.

Eva got to Aunt Soula's place out of breath and said, "Mum is going to kill me."

Aunt Soula didn't waste any time. She grabbed her and threw her in an empty flour barrel, told her to keep quiet, put the lid on, and sat down as if nothing had happened.

Not long after that, my mother arrived out of breath, shouting and brandishing the knife. "Where is the little devil? I will kill her! Bring her out here! She couldn't have gone anywhere else—she's got to be here."

"Who? what are you talking about? What happened?" my aunt asked calmly. In between breaths, my mother told her she was after Eva and what the girl had done. "I don't know where she is. I haven't seen her. she could have gone to Sassa's," Soula suggested. If anybody could look you in the eye and lie, it was my aunt. "But sit down for a minute, have a coffee, and then we will go look for her."

My mother, being out of breath and in a psychological upheaval and not thinking straight, did as was told. Eva was in the barrel all the time, not too far from where the two sisters were having coffee and talking; she could hear every word. She was scared my mother might hear her heart thumping, she said years later. Aunt Soula did a good job in pacifying my mother. She had a tongue that could charm a snake out of its hole, and that same tongue could be as venomous as a viper. Aunt Soula pointed out the facts. "The kid is six years old. She was hungry, with no one around to give her something to eat. She spilled a bit of oil on the landing. Is it worth belting the child for it?"

My mother cried saying, she was too tired, too busy, and too worried. She'd reacted more violently than she should. After Mother had a good cry and calmed down, my aunt got Eva out of the barrel, dusted her down, pretended to be smacking her bottom, and told her off for making a mess. She warned her she'd get a bigger smack if she did it again.

Chapter 12

The Draft Horse

My father loved animals. He couldn't resist buying any neglected or sick horse. He'd treat it, feed it well, train it, ride it for a while, and eventually sell it. Just before he was taken forcefully by the guerrillas to care for their horses and mules, he bought such a horse. It was a draft horse, a Hungarian, he said. The horse was strong and healthy, but "Some stupid idiot put the wrong size saddle on it and injured the horse's shoulders," causing two huge wounds below his neck on either side where the ill-fitting saddle rubbed. From upstairs, I could see the raw flesh when he was cleaning it and putting medicine on it. I could hear him swear at the idiot from whom he'd bought the horse. I can still see him gently pulling the skin up by the mane to clean under it. To my amazement, the horse didn't bolt or neigh. I can't explain how I felt. A mixture of nausea, wonderment, fear, and hope that it didn't hurt the horse and that he would get better.

The treatment was simple, inexpensive, and effective. Father cleaned the wound with fresh urine three times a day. We all had to contribute. They'd round us up, give us the potty, and order us to do it. Then we could go play. If there was no fresh urine, they had no option but to use the "modern medicine" salt, but that was expensive. I didn't enjoy watching my father treat the horse, but curiosity always won. To my amazement, the wound got smaller and smaller. When he was taken by the opposition, treating that animal became my mother's duty—one more amongst many. My grandmother and mother resented my father buying that horse in the middle of a war, but they were stuck with it, and they cared for it faithfully. Their saying was, "Animals don't know God. We are their God, and we must care for them well." They practiced their saying.

The day after my father was taken, we were rounded up and given the potty again. I went upstairs to watch my mother clean the wound, which by now was the size of a ten-cent piece on either side of the horse's neck. She too tethered the horse on the side of the bullock cart as my father did, and she climbed up with much grunting and difficulty considering she was small, chubby, and pregnant. Potty and cotton wool in hand, she started cleaning the wound and busily dabbing it.

What happened next amazed me. She got hold of the short mane and tried to lift it as my father used to do in the early stages of the treatment. She shouldn't have done it because the skin was now healing and attaching to the muscle. It must have hurt the horse, and he tried to move away, pulling the cart with him, which leaned sideways on the two wheels. My mother rolled with it, hanging onto the sides of the cart. I thought she was going to be run over and be killed. My grandmother was watching, terrified; she had her hands on her head and was unable to make a sound. In an instant, the horse took a step backwards and sideways, and with his huge body steadied the cart and then gently pushed it upright on all four wheels. We were all amazed and dumbfounded at the intelligence and understanding of that horse. From then on, there was no complaining about the extra work the horse created. They treated him till the wounds healed, and we all loved him.

Now they had a problem: "What will we do with the horse?" I don't know what happened to that beautiful, intelligent, and proud animal. He was gone before the baby was born. He was probably given to someone as a gift, because I know the cattle were sold for next to nothing, and we were lucky to get a butcher to take them off our hands. There was a glut, and everybody was selling, but butchers had no freezers those days. From then on, I have never ever thought of animals as dumb. Some might be less intelligent than others, but stupid they are not. I am also convinced that they can reason. I am thinking of Monty, my daughter's little Maltese dog, who had to share a kennel with Cleo, a Japanese Chin." Cleo wouldn't let Monty in no matter how much he barked in that peculiar, pleading way. We were amazed at how he worked out getting in. After a few pleading barks, he'd take off running towards the back fence, barking like mad and pretending to chase rabbits, which were plentiful in the area. Cleo would take off after him, chasing the imaginary rabbit. He'd let her run past him, make a U-turn, and sprint into the kennel. Once in, she had no choice but to share the accommodation. Try telling me that Monty and the horse couldn't reason.

Chapter 13

The Arrival of the Baby

One afternoon, my mother sent me to Rodia to tell the midwife, Haj Nene, to come see my mother. That night, all three of us children were bundled up and were sent to sleep at Aunt Soula's place. I was eight years old, but nobody told me that we would soon be getting our baby; I was left to guess. First thing the next morning, I went home to hear my mother screaming. I got worried and started to cry. Anastasia's mother took me aside and comforted me, telling me not to worry; my mother was going to have the baby very soon.

I was comforted but not reassured. Other women had babies, but I had never heard them scream like that! There was a lot of commotion, with lots of women coming and going, and there were two midwives in attendance whereas everybody else had one. I was worried. What seemed to be many hours later, Aunt Sassa came out with a big smile on her face, her gold dentures sparkling in the morning sun. She was very excited, her arms waving in the air. "It's a little boy! A beautiful little boy!" I was relieved, but I didn't care that it was a boy. To me, the thrill was we had had a baby. He was born on August 8, 1947. I wanted to run inside to see my mother and the baby, but we weren't allowed in yet. It seemed ages before my grandmother came out and said we could go in and see the new baby.

I ran in and looked at my mother. She looked ill! She looked pale, tired, and old. She was wearing a white nightie, couldn't keep her eyes open, and looked to me as if she was going to die. She looked at us without interest, and I didn't think she cared much for the baby either. No wonder! It was a long, hard labour and a big baby. I looked at the baby lying next to her, surprised to see it wrapped up like an Egyptian mummy with a white scarf around his head. I thought maybe the baby was sick too. It was a pretty baby with a chubby face. I wanted to stay there forever, but we were hustled out. "Mum is tired and needs to sleep. Go play." I went out, but didn't play, I sat outside the door, waiting for my mother to wake up so that I could go inside and play with the baby.

The next time I saw him, he didn't have that great thing on his head. He had a nice blue lacy bonnet my mother had made for him by hand. He looked bigger and better. There was no more gossiping about my mother being unfaithful. The baby, they said, was big and healthy, and in my eyes he was gorgeous.

My mother had a lot of trouble giving birth. She had a small pelvis and the posterior presentation of the baby's head made for a long and difficult birth. The delivery methods practised on her were primitive. Even the village women were surprised at what one of the midwives did (not Haj Nene). She sat herself on the floor, put her legs straight, sat my mother on her knees, drew them up with my mother sitting on them, and dropped them suddenly, jerking my mother vigorously. She did this twice before the baby was delivered. She took all the credit and had the honour of cutting the cord and wrapping up the baby.

The baby sucked well, but there was disquiet around the place. Both my mother and grandmother were worried. The baby hadn't passed urine, and he was now two days old. They said they'd take him to the doctor if he didn't pass urine by tomorrow. Tomorrow came, and there was much joy in the household and in the neighbourhood. I couldn't understand what the fuss was about a baby piddling. The next two days as well as the previous two, I had spent by the baby's side except when forced to leave. Grandma said I should be out playing, but I wouldn't go. Mother said, "Leave her. She will soon get tired of him." I was allowed to stay in all day. I talked to him, showing him a cardboard painted doll and waving it at front of his eyes. I wouldn't accept that he couldn't focus yet.

The baby was now seven days old, and I hadn't left his side. As soon as I was awake, I'd be by his side till the last thing at night. My mother and grandmother decided it was time for me to go play with the other kids. I stayed away for a while, but I didn't mix or play. I simply bided my time till I could go inside again. When I went in, I found my mother spoon-feeding the baby with expressed milk. The baby was taking it without any trouble. Both my mother and grandmother looked very worried. He looked fine to me.

The next day, as soon as the animals were tended to, they took the baby to the doctor, and I was sure he would make the baby well. The doctor was wise and all-knowing and had some nasty medicines that cured all kinds of horrible diseases, including scabies. Surely, he could make our baby better. I didn't worry. Mother and Grandmother came back later in the day with the baby still unable to suck. They said they had to take the baby back tomorrow again. It was the same routine: up early, animals fed, left us home in the care of the neighbours. "Call Soula if you have any problems." They started the nearly five-kilometre-trip on foot, taking turns carrying the baby; there were no prams in the village. They came back with the baby still sick. The doctor said if the baby was not better by tomorrow, they'd have to take him to Thessaloniki. It was a difficult trip, but not because of the distance. There was one bus a week from the village to the city at best of times, now it was worse because of the war.

The baby was getting worse by the hour, and an emergency baptism was arranged. The midwife's daughter, the one who'd delivered the baby, was the godmother. The priest was only too happy to baptise the baby on short notice. I remember him saying to the baby as he was dipping him in the water, "Don't cry, baby, don't cry. You will now get better." I fully believed him. The thought of the baby dying didn't enter my mind. He was named Damien, after my mother's brother who was killed at age forty by falling off the horse he was trying to break in. He'd secured his feet in the stirrups, the horse bolted, throwing him backwards. He'd been dragged over the rough, stony road, sustaining severe head injuries and died on the way to the doctor.

The baby was now twelve days old. They took him back to the doctor for the third time. I got worried. I had a terrible premonition that the baby would die without my father seeing him. I went inside, bolted the door, and cried for a long time. I was still sobbing when Yana came. "What are you doing?" she shouted. "Open the door." I did. "Why are you crying?"

"The baby is going to die, and my father is not here to see him," I sobbed.

She took my word for gospel and started crying, saying, "My father is not here to see him either." He too was away somewhere in the war; nobody knew where. We both had a good cry and then decided to walk towards town, to meet my mother and grandmother, who should be coming home anytime now.

We hadn't walked far before I was sure I heard my mother's voice. I froze for a moment. I looked at Yana and we started running. Just around the bend of the road, I saw my mother carrying the baby and wailing, "My baby! My baby is dead!" She repeated it over and over. I didn't want to believe her. No, she couldn't be right. The priest said he would get better—surely he wasn't lying? I looked at my grandmother, and she too was crying. Neither of them said a word to us. We walked home, Yana and I in silence and my mother and grandmother crying. The baby died in my grandmother's arms. When she got tired, she passed the baby on to my mother, who sensed that the baby was dead. She pulled the cover off his face and knew it. He had only died a few minutes before Yana and I had left home. My premonition was right. I cried for him before he'd died. I was shocked and stunned, and I couldn't cry anymore. The news of the baby's death went through the village quickly. The villagers came to commiserate, and many of them cried with Mother and Grandmother.

The custom was that someone had to stay with the dead and their family all night, but who took turns in staying up, I don't know. I don't know whether the baby was buried the day he died or the next. It was a blur. I wanted to give the baby something, but I had nothing to give him other than that cardboard doll. I didn't think it was good enough. I wanted to put some flowers on his little body, but there weren't any; the hot weather had killed just about everything. I walked around the village looking for some flowers, and in someone's yard there was a lone pink rose on the bush with a divine perfume. It hadn't occurred to me to ask for it. I went in and cut it. Later, I thought surely they wouldn't mind me taking it for my dead little brother. I went upstairs to the room where his little body was laid on the floor on a blanket; my mother sat next to him cross-legged. I knelt next to him feeling forlorn, sad, and miserable, but I was dry-eyed. I put the rose on the baby's chest and sat down next to my mother. That gesture was enough to make my mother and the other women start crying again.

My mother leaned over the baby, kissed him crying and said "You were born without a father, and you died without him." The other women wiped their eyes. I was looking at my mother when I heard someone giggling. I looked and saw Aunt Sassa and Ria (who was twenty) laughing as if they had heard a great joke. My mother and the other women looked at them, but they kept on laughing, making no effort to stop or to walk out. Oh, how I hated them then—and more so now that I understand the meaning of their amusement. Yes, my parents didn't get on, but that was no reason for those two evil witches to laugh at my mother's pain. The baby was buried that afternoon. No casket was made for him; someone carried him to the cemetery. The rose was wrapped up in his clothes, and his little grave was marked by a small tree growing at the head of it.

Years later, I realised that my baby brother had died of infantile tetanus. The midwife who'd delivered him had horses and was tending to them when she was called upon for assistance. Their knowledge of hygiene and germ transmission was non-existent. Most likely she went from the stable straight to the labour room. When I thought of that years later, I thought it was a blessing that only the baby died and not my mother as well. What would have my grandmother done with three young children in the middle of a raging civil war?

The death of the baby affected me terribly. For weeks, I'd dream I was holding him, only to wake up and realise he was gone. I would cry for hours, and nobody could comfort me. Three years later in Thessaloniki, I'd be dreaming that I had him sitting at the edge of the very deep well in the churchyard, but he'd slip from my arms and fall in the well. I'd wake up crying silently for him. I was nearly fifteen years old when I stopped dreaming about him.

Chapter 14

The Civil War Contentious

The civil war started soon after the Second World War ended. The Greeks were divided. Some supported King Paul and the government, and others supported communism. America and England supported the government.

Summer went by, September came, and school started. I had read the second-grade reader many times before. I felt a sense of pride and achievement at being in grade two.

September went by quickly, and it was now mid-October. One day after school, a small convoy of trucks and Jeeps pulled up in the village, and a soldier with lots of decorations on his sleeve got out of the Jeep, put a megaphone to his mouth, and demanded that everybody assemble in the village square to hear an important message. There were people everywhere, and we heard everything clearly. All the soldiers were off the trucks too; they looked big and bright-eyed. In a loud voice and without much ado, the leader said, "You must leave the village. The guerrillas come down from the mountains and take food supplies for themselves and their animals. We must starve them and their animals to death to stop the war." I thought of my much-loved cousin John, my father, and all others who were fighting in the guerrilla war. I didn't want them to die. When the guerrillas came to the village, most people were happy to give their loved ones knitted gloves, socks, fodder, and food. I wondered if he knew that.

"You have the choice of going anywhere in Greece from Thessaloniki to Athens, or you can cross the boundaries and go to Europe." There was dead silence, followed by a horrible mixture of children crying and adults wailing. I didn't know whether to laugh or cry. Eva stood next to me and was howling, tears running down her face I told her to shut up because I couldn't think while watching her cry. She yelled even louder.

A young soldier, who was watching us, picked her up in his arms and tried to pacify her. My mother had three-year-old Ellie in her arms. The soldier was saying to Eva, "Don't cry, little girl, don't cry. You'll be back as soon as the war is over."

Eva yelled even more, saying, "But I don't want to leave Toula! She's my friend! I don't want to leave her!."

While Eva was wailing in the soldier's arms I was going through periods of delight and despair. I wanted to travel, and I wanted to see Thessaloniki. Here was my opportunity. I was pretty sure that my mother wouldn't go to Yugoslavia or anywhere in Europe;. she was a Thessalonian girl. She always said how much she loved the city and how she regretted having come to the village. But I was madly in love with Demos, the mischievous, nine-year-old gang leader. I despaired when I thought of him. I wanted to marry him. What would I do? I had to think very fast, and I found a solution. I had it all worked out. I decided, *Yes, I'll go to the city, have a good look around, and come back to the village at the end of the war. Then I'll marry my sweetheart.* I was happy with that.

The only other regret I had was that I wouldn't see Vivika every day, but in my child's mind and plans, I said to myself, *When the war is over, we'll come back and play again.* Before the evacuation, a lot of the men went to fight against the government, and Michael went too. We heard that he was killed. Zizi didn't believe it, and when the villages were evacuated, she went to Yugoslavia in search of him. She never found him. Later, she ended up in Poland, where she remarried. When she did, she put Vivika in an orphanage. That didn't upset me because I didn't know anything about orphanages, but then I heard women saying that Zizi didn't visit Vivika much. When the other children were visited, Vivika would be sitting alone, waiting. That upset me. I wished I could go and bring her home. How could she be so heartless? I cried at night for her. I wished I could put my arms around her and tell her I love her. I still wish I could find out where she is now, whether she is happy, or whether she's still suffering the effects of the war—and the pain of rejection. Does she still speak Greek, or is she even alive? What a terrible, terrible thing war is. It affects people for at least three generations. Every time I think of Vivika, I get a big lump in my throat. The war caused devastation in our lives, especially Vivika's.

The civil war was in full swing, but we kids weren't aware of it, and I didn't understand its consequences till I was told that we wouldn't be going back to school because it wouldn't open for the rest of the year. The school in the next village would be open, and it would take pupils from all around, but there was no way my mother would let me go even though some of the older children went. I cried and promised faithfully to stay by the big kids and be careful while crossing the rickety bridge, but she was adamant. Stakos was nearly six kilometres from Peria. The distance wasn't the problem—the bridge was. We had to cross the river, which flooded and roared, rushing down furiously in winter. The bridge was narrow and rickety, had boards missing, had no rails, and was less than a metre wide. We had to take big steps to cross it while playing there in summer, before we left Rodia. After the war, when my grandmother and Ellie returned to the village, the children were playing there on a nice winter's day. Ellie was pushed and fell in the swollen waters. She would have drowned, but miraculously a log which was floating downriver, got under her just in time to lift her up high enough. She grabbed hold of the side of the bridge, pulling herself up enough for Eva and the other children to pull her to safety.

Soon the whole village was in turmoil. The people were divided politically. There was great animosity amongst those who, only a few weeks earlier, were friends and sat around the table playing cards and drinking ouzo despite their political differences. Now they were arguing about politics, and they wouldn't talk to each other. The village president, who was my father's close friend and the godfather of one his daughters, wouldn't talk to my mother or Aunt Soula because Kostas, my cousin, was a communist and a political prisoner, and his brother, John, aged nineteen, supported the opposition. He was killed in that war by a bullet fired by a fellow Greek. As my grandmother always said, "In this war, brother kills brother." Families were split by political ideology. My cousin Magda was arrested and taken to the village square along with other girls. They had their hair shaved to shame them because their families supported the opposition. Her beautiful black, long hair was trodden underfoot. The girls wore scarves to hide their shaven heads.

Everybody knew it wouldn't be long before the guerrillas would come down to raid the villages for food supplies. It was a beautiful day when they came. While they loaded their trucks, the female soldiers, all very young, danced and sang patriotic songs. I was so touched that I decided there and then that when I grew up, I'd go fight too. It didn't occur to me that the war would have to last at least ten years before I could carry a gun, but my mind was made up. Those girl soldiers looked beautiful while wearing chunky army uniforms, berets, bullet belts around their waists and across their chest, and guns on their shoulders. They looked formidable but feminine just the same.

My family was getting ready to send my cousin Magda to the city. She stayed with her paternal relatives. They said it was so that the guerrillas wouldn't take her away. I was sent to stay with Aunt Soula and keep her company now that she was alone. One night, we were woken by heavy steps coming upstairs and a lot of male voices. They didn't knock—they opened the door to the room where we were asleep and asked my aunt if there were any young people here. She pointed to floor where I was sleeping and said, "She is the only one" They looked at me, decided I was too young, searched the house, cleared it of all edibles, and took off, leaving us unharmed. We were all glad Magda had gone to Thessaloniki just in time.

Soon after that incident, the bombs started falling, and the mines started killing people. I soon knew the meaning of war, the dangers and the pain of it. One morning after a heavy night's bombing, we got up to hear that George, our ten-year-old friend, had been hit by shrapnel and killed. In the next few days, Thanos, my friend's seventeen-year-old brother, was blown to pieces by a land mine; he had been bringing the animals back from feeding with the herd. The whole village mourned for him. I was upset and angry at the soldiers who'd killed my friends. The raids got worse and worse. One night we were at Aunt Soula's place and sitting around the open fireplace. The bombs were flying over us, one after the other; there seemed to be no end to them. Suddenly a bomb flew over the house, the windows shuddered, the walls shook, and we put our hands over our heads. We thought the house was going to fall on us. It was a great relief when, looking up at each other, we realised we were all alive. The bomb fell in the village, killing a few more people.

Another night while I stayed with Aunt Soula, there was another heavy bombing. A bomb fell nearby. Everybody was expecting to count the dead again in the morning. Just as the sound of the bomb died down, my mother heard a terrible scream, and in the confusion and fear of the moment, she interpreted it as me screaming. She thought we were hit. She was panic and grief-stricken. But it was curfew from dusk to dawn, and she couldn't come to investigate. She and my grandmother spent the night agonising.

At first light, mother was at the door. We were still asleep. She dashed in the room yelling, "Are you alive? Are you alive?" She looked wild with worry and fear.

"Yes, why?" asked Aunt Soula.

"Last night when the bomb fell near the village, I thought it fell in your yard, and I heard Mallie scream. I thought you were both killed. We didn't sleep all night." As soon as she calmed down, they realised the "scream" she'd heard was a dog howling. She raced home to tell grandmother that we were alive.

After a few more rounds of bombing, I decided war wasn't a good idea. I wanted it to finish. I hated the sound of bombs and the fear it caused. I hated the look of guns. I gave up the idea of being a girl soldier and the idea of going to the mountains to look for my father, as my cousin John had done to look for his sweetheart.

Chapter 15

Evacuating the Village

The dreaded time came to evacuate the village. I had never seen so much comings and goings on that dirt road. It was as if hell, with all her fury, was let loose. People from the villages all around were coming and going to town several times, carting their belongings and food for winter. This took many trips. No food or fodder could be left around for guerrillas to take. The animals had to be sold. My mother took them to the market after transporting all our stuff, but nobody wanted to buy them because everybody else was selling their animals too. She sold them to the butcher for very little. There were no freezers, the butchers could only hold so much meat in their shops. We were very sad to see one particular cow, Marika, go. She had such a beautiful nature and was a hard worker. No matter how heavy her load, she always saw her job through. If the cart got bogged in the mud or stuck in a pothole, she wouldn't give up as most other animals would. She would kneel on her back legs, pushing, and with help from people pushing the cart, she'd pull. She looked so proud when the cart was pulled out and on solid ground. I felt like crying when I realised someone ate that beautiful animal.

My mother and grandmother decided to go to Thessaloniki. They both knew the city well. My mother grew up there, and Grandma often visited her sister Katerina, who lived there with her family.

While my mother and grandmother were loading the heavy things, we also had to help. We carried outside what we could, ready for loading. At last we were on the road to Adrea. We tried to take Irma with us, and she came a little way but turned back. She had her first litter of pups, which I wasn't allowed to play with—too young, they said. Irma is one of my saddest memories of the war to this day, and it will be till the day I die.

The road to Ardea was choked with traffic. It looked like a gigantic, slow-moving caterpillar. There were carts, animals, and people everywhere. We were the second to last cart on the road and were a long way behind. My mother led the cart, and I walked by its side. Grandma held Eva's and my hand. Ellie was securely tucked on top of the cart and wrapped in blankets. I don't know how it happened, but halfway to town, I veered to the left, and my left foot went under the wheel of the heavily laden cart. I winced! My grandmother looked worried; she had seen what had happened and had heard me wince. She wanted to put me on the cart for the rest of the way, about two kilometres, but I wouldn't have it. I told her it didn't hurt, and just then it didn't, but by the time we got to Ardea I was in agony. No doctors, no X-rays, and no treatment other than bathing and rubbing it with oil, which hurt when touched. I limped for what seemed months.

At Ardea, the town looked different. There was a wire fence around it and a gate, which hadn't been there before. I thought it was to keep out the guerrillas. The gate was shut, and a soldier with a gun guarded it. He told us we couldn't get in. We were too late—there was no room anywhere in the town. However, we could stay outside the fence if we wanted to. My mother said nothing. She calmly walked to the cart and from between some bedding pulled out a small parcel. I knew what it was; I'd seen her wrap it up and put there. I saw the knowing look on my grandmother's face. She walked back to the soldier, very discreetly put it under his arm, whispered something in his ear, and went back to the cart. Then she got the reins, the soldier opened the flimsy gate, they thanked him, and we were safely inside the wire fence.

The November night was cold but dry. Mother and Grandmother got the mattresses down and put them on the frozen ground in the open air. We all crawled under the covers with clothes and shoes on. I was so glad not to have to stand on my sore foot, which was now throbbing and swelling. No sooner were we were under the covers and warming up than a fine, sleety rain started falling. "What shall we do? We will freeze," I heard Granny say. I put my head under the covers and thought we'd be fine if we stayed under the blankets. Just then, the young soldier came. He pointed to a large machinery shed and told us we could sleep there for the night. If I have ever heard a heartfelt thank-you, it was then. They thanked that young soldier with tears in their eyes. They thanked God for shelter, food, and the safety of that open-fronted machinery shed. They got us up and put everything under the roof of the shed, including cart and animals. I thought it was a great luxury. Neither the wind nor the rain could get us now, and we were warm. Bless that young man's soul. In the morning, they woke us up early. We had something to eat and went back to bed to keep warm while my mother went in search of accommodation. We stayed in the shed for three days before she found us a place to live.

The day my mother came and told us she found us a place to live in Ardea, we celebrated by shouting. The kids jumped up and down on the mattresses. I couldn't jump because my foot was sore and swollen. Soon everything was packed up again and put on the cart. We were off, ready to settle in at our new place. What my mother didn't tell us was that it was one medium-sized room occupied by two other families with lots of kids. My poor grandmother cried. I wondered where on earth we would all sleep. There seemed to be no room anywhere. As it turned out, there were only nine other people there, including their kids, and the five of us made fourteen—in one room! The people seemed friendly enough and accepted us. The three youngest children were great; we soon became friends and played well together. One or the little boys never wore socks or shoes even though it was very cold. I noticed he had no foot, and I heard them say he was born like this. He limped as he walked. He was a jolly little boy and very beautiful, with blond hair and blue eyes. His skin was as fair as my mother's, and I thought he even looked like her.

The other people in the room rearranged their things to make room for our bedding. There were two beds where the adults slept. There was enough room for only one mattress on the floor, so Grandma and Mother slept together. All of us kids slept under the beds or on mattresses piled halfway up the wall. The kids who slept on top of the mattresses had to be helped up. We thought it was great fun!

Fortunately for all of us, the weather was good. There were sunny days with no wind or rain, enabling us to spend the day playing outside, out of the adults' way.

My mother went back to the village to bring the last few things which they couldn't fit in the cart, but she didn't bring Irma and her pups. "She will OK there," she kept saying. I trusted her and believed her because I had never heard her tell a lie to anyone. Irma and Vivika are my saddest memories of the war to this day, and will always be.

We lived in that little room for about three weeks. One of the families left for Yugoslavia before us. My mother feared for their safety because it was winter, and they were going through snow-covered mountains. We were ready to leave for Thessaloniki soon. I couldn't wait to get there. My childhood dream, the first one in my life, was about to be fulfilled. I was thrilled.

Chapter 16

Moving to the City

Everything that could be transported from the village was in Ardea. My mother hired a large truck, and she and Grandmother helped the driver load it. There were trunks full of wheat, rye, corn, and barley. There were large tins of cheese, oil, and pickles on the truck. We kids were told in no uncertain terms to keep out of the way. While the driver was organising things in the truck, we were rounded up to be dressed for the journey. I thought we were going to wear our Sunday best. We were dressed up all right, but we had to wear everything we owned—summer and winter clothes! Four pairs of underpants, camisoles, dresses, jumpers, everything. When I dared say I was warm enough and didn't need any more clothes on, I was told they had to stay on because there was no room in the truck, and Grandma wouldn't be able to find them if we took them off. They stayed on. We only wore two pairs of socks each, thick knitted ones, or else the shoes wouldn't fit; the rest were shoved in our pockets. I looked at my sisters and had to restrain from laughing. They looked really fat and couldn't put their arms down straight. They stuck out like real fat people's arms do. When I looked at myself, I realised I looked just like them. But we were warm.

They lifted us on the truck, which had a canopy. It was a luxury after my last experience. Grandma was helped up. The driver took the address from my mother, got into his cabin, and started the motor. I saw my mother pray, and Grandma cross herself. We were off! My mother stayed behind to sort out a few things such as selling the bullock cart, which nobody wanted, and the last two animals that were pulling it. We fell asleep sitting up amongst the load.

After what seemed hours of driving, the truck stopped, and the driver told us we were in Thessaloniki. It stopped at front of the Seventh-day Adventist Church. It was December 4, 1947.

I poked my head out of the truck but saw nothing, just a high stone wall and a huge iron gate, which the driver banged on with all his might. After a long time, a man opened it, and the driver drove the truck inside. The men and my grandmother unloaded and put everything in a huge room, which had a lot of other things in it, including church pews. Soon after, two women came out. Their hair was dishevelled, and they looked as if they had just woken up with a rude shock. One of them was carrying a baby, and the other one had a funny nose which made her whole face look silly. They looked us over, not too impressed or pleased. They spoke in Turkish. They helped my grandmother organise some beds by putting two church pews together, forming a cot for us kids, and putting a mattress in. Grandma was on the floor; she gave the man my mother's letter, but he told her to give it to Pastor Demos in the morning. We slept there for the night, which wasn't very long because we arrived there late and took at least two hours to unload.

As soon as it was light enough, we scrambled out of our cots and went outside to investigate our new surroundings. It was a strange place. It was surrounded by a very high, thick stone wall. From the inside, we could see the tops of the two-storey houses. The gate was in two segments, solid steel, strong, and wide. It was made of square pieces joined together by two-centimetre strips of steel, but some of them were missing, allowing us a view to the outside world. We squatted and took turns looking outside because the strip was not wide enough for all three of us to look out at the same time. The yard was large. There were two huge pine trees inhabited by a lot of pigeons and sparrows. There was a deep well close to the back door and a cracked concrete footpath leading to the gate.

At the back boundary were two tin sheds that were locked. The property was in the corner. We went down the side path, which was very wide, and from there we inspected the front of the large, stately home. A few steps led down to the front gate, which was solid steel halfway; the upper half was decorative wrought iron. It was a grey-blue colour, and the paint was flaking. I looked towards the house, and it was magnificent. There was a white marble staircase with beautiful, fancy steel balustrades leading to the front timber double doors, with side glass panels on either side. Later, I found out just how heavy they were, and years later I learned their true worth. I hadn't seen such a beautiful house before. The house was an old mansion which the church had bought. We didn't climb up the stairs.

We were getting hungry, and I wondered how Grandma would cook the trahana (homemade cereal) because she didn't have charcoal or a steel tripod, or a kerosene cooker. She was resourceful. She had put two bricks on top of each other, then two more opposite. She made a fire and was cooking our breakfast while talking to the other two refugee families. One was a family of four. His first name was Panos. (he was the one who opened the gate), his wife and their two children. The girl, Marta, was just a few months younger than Ellie, and the baby boy, Stratus, was about six months old. The other lady was Marah. She was a funny-looking woman. She had no nose, just a little bump in the middle of her face; it was more like a big, pink wart. She had nostrils, but they looked like slits placed vertically on her face, which was made worse by her very small, round, deeply set eyes. She was well built and was in her forties.

Marta was blonde with curly hair and brown eyes. She was standing by her mother and eying us, and we looked at them. Grandma introduced us, and we called them uncle and aunts, which was the polite way to address an adult in the village. It wasn't long before all of us kids played happily together. I got to love baby Stratus, who had blue eyes and fine blond hair just starting to grow. I carted him around, and before long, he'd prefer our company to his mother's; he'd cry when we'd leave. I adored him. I transferred all my love for my dead little brother, who would have been four months old now, to Stratus.

All the noise and running around woke up Pastor Demos, who was living upstairs with his new wife, Athena. He came down to investigate. I had never seen a more sour, angrier man. He had a sinister-looking face, receding hair, and a wrinkled forehead. He asked questions. "Who are you? Where did you come from? Who sent you here?"

My grandmother was frightened and gave him the letter my mother had given her. It was addressed to "Brother Alexander." This nasty creature was Demos Storidis! Brother Alexander had retired and returned to his home island, Chios. My poor grandmother was scared and intimidated by this man, who turned around and blasted Panos for taking it upon himself to open the gate and let us in. Panos very quietly tried to explain that this was war, and Christians had to help each other. Pastor Demos turned around and told my grandmother in no uncertain terms that, had he heard us first, he would have not let us in under any circumstances. "You cannot stay here long. You have to find another place." God must have anesthetised both him and his wife. By rights he should have heard us first. Their bedroom was upstairs and much closer to the gate than the bedroom at the back and downstairs, where Panos and his family were sleeping. The driver was banging hard enough and long enough to wake up the dead.

My grandmother cried, tears running down her face. She told Pastor Demos that she didn't want to be here anymore than he wanted us to be here. She didn't want to leave her home, her property, and her familiar environment, but she had no choice. He left angry, determined to kick us out. Later, we met his wife, Athena. She was very thin with fair skin, grey steely eyes, and fine, shoulder-length hair rolled upwards in the fashion of the forties. She inspected us, looking us up and down as if we were merchandise. She didn't offer a word or a smile. She simply looked, wondering what to do with this unwanted livestock delivered to her door.

Later on, we met the other family who lived upstairs in the huge house, shared with Pastor Demos. He was an old gentleman in his seventies, whom we called Mr Phillip. He had been a tobacco merchant, trading between Greece and Europe, mainly Germany. His wife, Jo, was a German lady thirty years his junior. She was very beautiful except when she opened her mouth to speak—she had no teeth. They had no children. We were used to toothless mouths because my grandmother and a lot of older people in the village had no teeth. My father had upper and lower dentures all made of gold, but he didn't wear them very often; I thought they were for Sundays only.

Jo would invite us up to her quarters, feed us, talk and play with us. We addressed her as Lady Jo, and we adored her. When we weren't upstairs, she would come down and talk to us. She had a very broad German accent, and after a while we imitated her. She taught us a few German words, which I still remember.

The only time Pastor Demos came and talked to us was to tell Grandmother to find another place. One day she plucked up enough courage and told him that she'd "Stay put till my daughter-in-law comes, and you can tell her." We didn't see him very often after that, and when we did, he never talked to us. I thought he hated us.

Brother Alexander was converted to the Seventh-day Adventist church in Australia, where he had migrated as a young man. The church sent him back to Greece to pastor the church. He baptised my mother when she was eighteen years old. When he found out that she was the daughter of one of the first Adventists in Turkey, and an orphan, he took her under his wing, he loved her. My mother always talked about him with respect and affection.

During the first winter in Thessaloniki, we lived in the huge hall which later became part of the church. It would have been big enough to hold about one hundred people. There was no heating in it. There were no bathing facilities, and the one and only toilet was outside and unconnected to sewerage; it had a pit. It was built beside one of the sheds and was used by the other refugees and us. The standard of the toilet was acceptable; it was kept clean by the combined effort of the two families and us. It was the old Turkish squatting style, but it had no hand-washing facilities. The thing that upset my grandmother most was that we had no privacy whatsoever. The house was built in the Edwardian style: a large hall where the doors of the rest of the rooms opened. It must have been awful for my poor grandmother, who had to wait for everybody to go to bed before she could have a quick wash.

And if during the night anyone had to go to the toilet, they had to go past us, waking us up. We children had our weekly bath in public view, and it was a major operation. The water had to be heated, and we sat in a tin basin which was also used for washing clothes. Panos seemed to have had diarrhoea or frequency during our bath time.

My mother came to Thessaloniki about ten days later. She came without Irma or the pups. She said Irma wouldn't leave her puppies and reassured me that they were all well. I was terribly upset but didn't show my emotions. Years later, I overheard her say that all the animals that were left behind had starved to death.

Now that my mother had arrived, we saw a lot more of Pastor Demos. The first time he spoke to her, he was civil. He told her we couldn't live here and had to go somewhere else, and he pointed out that it was no good for us here because we had no privacy.

"No," said my mother calmly. "We have no privacy. But you can open those two rooms there for us like a good Christian minister would do, and let us use them." My mother had been a regular churchgoer there before she'd gotten married, and she knew the outlay of the house well. That part of the house had a kitchen and a toilet connected to a sewage.

Demos was infuriated. The cruel, evil nature of that man became apparent to me even as an eight-year-old. He fumed, frothed at the mouth, yelled, and told her the rooms were full of tobacco which belonged to the merchant. Only one of the rooms had tobacco in it; the other was vacant.

He left in a huff, but not for long. He would come nearly every day and harass and upset my mother and grandmother so much so that my grandmother hated the thought of seeing him. She was a peace-loving person who could not cope with friction, unlike my mother, who would confront him and attack him like an enraged bull. Every time he'd come, Mother would tell him to open that room, and there would be another screaming match. We were terrified that he would hit her because he waved his fists very close to her face.

One day it happened. He got hold of her by the shoulders, pushed her against the wall, and was about to bash her head against it. She gave him a good kick in the groin, which he didn't expect. She broke free, looked him square in the eye, and in no uncertain terms told him, "I am not Margarita. If you think you can treat me in the same way, you are mistaken. Don't you ever raise your hand against me, or I will write to the General President in America and have you out of here before we go out!" He left, and we had a few days' peace.

Pastor Demos made sure our souls were well catered for, even if our bodies and minds were tormented by him. He told us where the church service was held and gave us the address. The church had not been renovated and had not been used as a church till after the civil war.

Aunt Soula and Cousin Magda, who came to live with us during the war, used to take us to church most of the time. They went out of fear and duty rather than love. My mother seldom went, and Grandma refused to go. One day halfway through the sermon, Magda grabbed our hands, got up, and walked out. I couldn't understand why, and I asked her. I liked reading the words in the hymnal while the congregation sang. "Because a hungry bear won't dance," she said curtly, and we were off. I can't say I was too upset at leaving. The sermons were boring for a child.

Another Sabbath, my mother took us to church. She liked going even though she hated Pastor Demos. He was preaching on love. That infuriated her, and she couldn't stand it any longer. Loud enough for others near her to hear, but not too loud to disturb the sermon, she kept contradicting him. I remember her saying, "You preach on love, but you don't practise it. Practise what you preach, you evil man." People looked at her as if she were mad. Years later, some church members told me that they now understood what she was all about. They too had experienced his cruelty and controlling spirit.

We lived in the hall all winter. One day early in spring, he came down with an alternate plan. He offered to make one of the sheds available to us. My mother gave a categorical no. He left, but not for long.

Chapter 17

Cousin Kostas

As if all this trouble between Pastor Demos and my mother wasn't enough, my cousin Kostas, Aunt Soula's eldest son, came to live with us. Now we were a happy family of eight! I wonder how Pastor Demos felt and whether he wondered if there would be an end to our relatives coming in dribs and drabs to live with us. Kostas had been exiled for years to a remote island, Macronisos, as a political prisoner. He was freed from exile without an explanation. I didn't remember him; he had left the village while I was still very young. He'd pursued with fanatical zeal his conviction that communism was the only regime for Greece.

I had heard a lot about Kostas. I had built an image of him of a demagogue, one who was as steady as a rock; nothing would make him renounce his convictions. I heard how he was tortured in that notorious island, but he was not moved—hence his nickname the Rock amongst the other prisoners and his political circles. Some of the tortures he and other exiles went through were horrible. They were beaten by the prison guards, put in bags up to their necks together with cats, and thrown in the water, letting the cats do the torturing. In winter, they would throw them in the sea till they were half frozen before they'd get them out. In hot weather, they'd starved them for days, and then they'd give them salty fish to eat and deprive them of water. Some of them would resort to drinking seawater, which would drive them mad. After a few of these treatments, most of them recanted—but not our Kostas.

Kostas was a distinguished-looking man: solidly built, average height, square jaw, wavy dark hair, and green eyes. When he spoke, it was quietly, slow, and with well-chosen words and great wisdom; everybody would hang on to his words. I stood in awe of him. Such a great, important, wise, courageous man! And he was my cousin! He was my hero. His name was mentioned many times in the communist newspaper. The government knew him by name and was scared to harm him because of repercussions. I was his disciple. I would fight tooth and nail for communism and couldn't understand why others didn't like it. It sounded very fair to me, even before I was ten years old. To me, communism was different than the civil war. There were no bombs.

We had plenty of time to listen to him expound the virtues of communism, and I distinctly remember my aunt saying, "Yes, we will win. We will win, and when we do, we will kick this bastard out of this house—and we will live in it." She shook her fists and gritted the few teeth in her mouth. The others nodded in agreement and looked forward, convinced that the wonderful day was just around the corner. I hoped it would be very soon so that the bastard wouldn't upset my grandmother and mother anymore.

We didn't go to school the first year we were in Thessaloniki. When I asked why, I was told that the year had already started, and we would be left behind. We would start next year, which would be the following September. I accepted it because I had no choice. We had plenty of time to ourselves to do things and get into mischief. One day, Eva and I found a red colouring pencil, and we decided to colour our nails, which we did with much difficulty. The colour wouldn't stick on, so we'd spit on the fingernails, scribble, and repeat the process till all of them were done, our toenails included. We thought they looked beautiful and went inside. It was a while before the others noticed. My grandmother smiled and said we looked like Turkish girls (they painted their fingernails red). My mother, with her Seventh-day Adventist background, looked disgusted. My aunt was of the same background and said we looked like prostitutes. Kostas was also an ex Seventh-day Adventist and asked us to put our hands in cold water. We thought that was harsh because it was the middle of winter, and the water was icy cold. Icicles as thick as a man's arm hung from the roofs.

I looked at my mother for defence, but none came. I knew my poor granny wouldn't be allowed to interfere; there was no point in going to her. Kostas asked again, and my mother nodded, so off we went to put our hands in a bucket of freezing water. We came inside, our hands red and aching from the cold. I thought that was the punishment for degrading ourselves, but no, not according to Kostas. The sin of cheapening ourselves demanded more. "Come here now," he said. "Give me your hands." We had no choice. He turned our hands palms down and rapped us on the knuckles with the sharp end of the wooden ruler several times. It was hard enough for the ruler to leave red marks on our cold, already aching hands. Before he let us go, he admonished us to never do it again. If we ever thought of wearing lipstick, he would chop off our lips from around our mouths, pointing with his fingers from where he'd cut: from under our noses to just above our chins. He laughingly said, "You will look as if you are wearing a permanent smile." They all laughed except my grandmother.

I believed he would do it. If he were cruel enough to punish us for painting our nails, I was sure he would cut off our lips for wearing lipstick. Eva and I were only seven and nine years old, respectively. My mother never interfered, and the incident was never mentioned again. I don't know how she felt about it. I know my grandmother never had time for my mother's relatives, and my father highly disliked Kostas, whom he thought of as lazy and shifty. Needless to say, Kostas fell out of my estimation, and nothing anybody said about his wisdom, bravery, courage, love for humanity, or steadfastness would make me respect him. From then on, I disliked him. Later on, when I was in my early teens, he gave me a good reason to loath him. After talking with my sisters later, I realised why they too hated him.

He was with us for a few weeks when the police came for him and imprisoned him in Thessaloniki without an explanation. I didn't miss him because I didn't want to lose my lips. In his defence, when some people are treated cruelly, they treat their fellow humans in the same way. They know no better. Others become forgiving, finding peace of mind and contentment in life. They refuse to obey the law of Moses, "an eye an eye and a tooth for a tooth," instead following Christ's law, "Love your enemies."

As the weather improved, we visited Kostas in prison. He was in a small, neat cell painted white. It had a window in the middle of the roof, where one could see the sky, which on that day and most others was blue and clear. He told us how one day, he was taken for a walk by two guards during the week, but they wouldn't tell him where they were going despite him asking several times. As they were walking past the houses, a woman came out the front door, saw the prison guards and Kostas walking towards the bush, and screamed, "They are going to kill you! They are going to shoot you! Yell! Get people out of their houses!" He said he screamed with all the power of his lungs. People came out from everywhere. The guards made a U-turn, took him back to his cell, gave him a good beating, and sent him back to Macronisos soon after that.

The reason for his release from exile became clear to us: it was a dirty way to silence the opposition. During the civil war, we often heard of people disappearing. Now we knew where they were. This was the dirty part of the war most people didn't hear about. We didn't see him till after the end of the civil war in the early 1950s.

The incident of the fingernails was forgotten, and with my enthusiasm for politics rekindled, I started corresponding with him till one of my letters encouraging and praising his virtues was intercepted. I never got another letter from him, and neither did I send him another. I forgave him for rapping us on the knuckles. Being persuaded that painting one's nails and lips was not becoming to a Christian, I was almost grateful for the punishment and for saving our souls from burning in hell and perishing forever. After Kostas was taken to exile again, Magda and my aunt left and lived with her husband's relatives. Now it was just the five of us living in the big hall.

The fights between my mother and Pastor Demos continued. He would come down every day and order us out of the church hall, and every day my mother would refuse to move. One day he came with a smile on his face, told mother he found us very good accommodation, and said we should move out before it was reallocated. "Oh, yes? And where might this place be?" asked Mother.

"In the Caravan Serai," he said, as if the place was a palace.

My mother looked at him through narrowed eyes and with venom in her voice told him to take his wife there. If he liked it, he could come back and tell her, and she'd think about it. My mother knew Thessaloniki and that place well. It was a high-rise block of flats where every family occupied just one room. They were all refugees. Sanitation was appalling, illness was rife, there was nowhere for kids to play, and the flats were in the middle of the city. Kids used to play on the rooftop. There were no high barriers, and there were accidents of kids falling twelve storeys down and ending in pulp.

The feud continued, and I wondered who was going to win or wear out first. One day a few days after the last offer, he came down with another offer. He again offered to empty out one of the sheds in the yard if we wanted to move there. My mother said she'd think about it and let him know. She talked it over with Grandma again, and they decided to accept. Lack of privacy was the deciding factor. They could put us in a tub and give us a scrub, but they couldn't do the same for themselves because they never knew when someone would walk through the hall.

The shed was a tin one, much like a tin garage. The door was in the middle. On the right side were two old-fashioned laundry copper troughs which were used to cook in during the war for the starving crowds. I suspect the outside toilet was built then. Part of the left side was built up to about thirty-five centimetres high. That was our living and sleeping area. The entire floor was dirt. We moved there in winter. The back wall was timber, and there were a few boards missing here and there, allowing the freezing winds to howl in. My mother organised for a man to come and line the sleeping area, ceiling, and walls with pitch paper. She couldn't afford to have the lot done. I looked at the room, thinking it was luxurious. The wind blew, making the paper move up and down as if someone mighty was sucking it in and blowing it out. But we were warmly dressed and slept well for a week—till the mice or rats, (they sounded more like elephants) found the place and used it as a racetrack.

The rodents would run up and down all night making a terrible racket. My mother, who was a light sleeper, couldn't sleep, and neither could I. She'd have a long stick by her side, and when the racket got too much, she'd bang the paper walls, cursing and swearing at the war but mostly Pastor Demos. There'd be peace for a few minutes, and the rat race would start again. To this day, I don't know which was worse, the rats racing or my mother banging and swearing. I reckoned I could have slept thought the rat race but not the banging. All through this, my grandmother was very philosophical. She would say, "Be patient, daughter. The war will not last forever. We will be out of here soon." My grandmother was happier living in the shed. She found a spot for her beloved icons, set them up, lit her little oil lamp, and was able to pray in privacy, which she hadn't done till now.

Eventually we learned to sleep through the rat race as well as the banging and cursing. Amazing what a few sleepless nights can do! We settled in the shed, and my mother started looking for work in the city, but there was no work anywhere. One day, a little old lady came to our shed. She was a "job-seeking agent" and said, "There are no jobs in the city, but if you wanted to, you could go to the country, approximately an hour and a half's drive, and work as a cook and housekeeper for some rich land owners." After a bit of discussion between Mum and Granny, Mum decided to accept the job, and Grandma would look after us. The money would come handy when returning to the village. They would buy some cattle, a cart, and things farmers need.

Chapter 18

Mother's Illness

Before Mother started working, she became sick. It started with a cough and a bit of fever and progressed to breathlessness and chest pain. It hurt her to move and breath. She was burning with fever, and the hacking cough kept her awake all night. She hovered between life and death for three weeks. My grandmother, Elena, and Marah took turns nursing and rubbing her back with homemade concoctions made out of kerosene camphor and olive oil. The neighbours would bring us food and ask if there was anything they could do. Lady Jo would bring hot fish soup. Grandma said it was a silly way to cook fish, but we got to like it after a while. Through her long illness, neither Pastor Demos nor his wife came down once to ask how Mother was and whether we needed anything, not even to offer a word of prayer for her recovery. Someone diagnosed her illness as pleurisy. Looking back, I reckon it was fully blown bilateral pneumonia.

With tender loving care from the neighbours and my grandmother, her strong will to survive, her previous good health, and a great dose of God's grace, she pulled through. By early spring, she was able to sit outside in a sheltered spot with her back to the sun, warming herself up. We had no heating in the shed, and the best the small coal brazier did for us was warm our hands. We played around our mother, glad she could sit up.

My mother became stronger each day, and by summer she was well enough to start looking for work again. The same old lady appeared, and guess what? The job offered earlier in the year was still available if Mum wanted it. The conditions were: cook for the workers, though she didn't say how many; keep house, she didn't say how big the house was; wash and iron; and provide separate meals for the boss, she didn't say how many bosses there were. Mum would have one Sunday off a month, but the lady didn't say "except the summer months." My mother needed to work in order to support us and save a bit of money to either buy a small place in Thessaloniki or buy some cattle if we returned to the village. She took the job.

My ninth birthday came and went without my mother. It was casually mentioned by my grandmother with the usual admonition. "You are now nine years old. You should be good." It was not customary to celebrate birthdays in Greece, and there was no present giving. The only celebration was the Name's Day—that is, if you were named after a saint. Because neither Eva nor I were named after saints we missed out. The Greek Orthodox Church prohibited baptising children unless they were named after saints, and there were plenty to choose from. But in the country, the priest who'd baptised us either didn't know, ignored it, or did my parents a favour. He was fond of my mother and would do anything for her.

Chapter 19

My Mother Starting Work

Nick Kalas, a young man engaged to be married, was the farm's truck driver. He lived just across the road from the church with his mother. He did his deliveries to the city, and on his way back to the farm, he picked my mother up to start work. Nick was my mother's main means of transport. She hugged and kissed us, gave Grandma a warm hug, said she'd see us very soon, told us to be good, and waved goodbye with a smile as the truck moved on. We watched the truck disappear in the distance with sadness. I had mixed feelings. I was sad to see my mother go but was glad she had a job; I knew how much she wanted to work. It must have been May when she started work.

Four weeks later, she had one day off. She came with the usual things an absent parent would bring their children: sweets and little knick-knacks. We were excited to see her. We stayed around her most of the day, chatting and telling her all the things we'd done and the games we'd played with the other kids. Monday morning very early, the truck driver, Nick, picked her up, and they left for the farm. By rights, she should be back again in four weeks. We didn't see her for three months. The three bosses, all brothers, refused to let her go, saying this was the busiest season of the year, and they couldn't do without her. She would have her allotted days off all together in September.

She was upset, protested, and cried, but she had no choice. When the driver came without her, we wanted to know where she was. He said she was too busy and wouldn't be back for a while, and he gave us the nice things she'd sent for us. Grandma was also upset and said, "It's not fair to the kids," but there was nothing they could do. Every time the driver came to Thessaloniki, my mother would send sweets and other things: fresh fruit, vegetables, wheat and corn in large bags, oil, eggs, and milk. Grandma made some of them into yoghurt. Mum also sent trahana and cottage cheese which she herself made as part of her duties. There was always plenty of wholesome food to eat. After shearing the sheep, she'd send wool. The bosses were only too happy to let her have anything she wanted as compensation for not allowing her to have days off. Grandma would spin the quality wool and knit jumpers, socks, and gloves for us, all in the same pattern. The second-grade wool she'd save for quilts, which were made by artisans, mostly gypsies. The patterns were intricate and the colours were in bright pinks, blues, and yellows. The material was always in satin. She had one made in hot pink; I remember her choosing the pattern and negotiating the price with the gypsy man. The gypsies would walk the streets, thread and needle in their bag, shouting, "Quilt maker." It was an art, and a time-consuming one at that. It would take a day to make a quilt. Even as a child, I wondered just how many quilts would a man have to make in order to make a living. Making mattresses was simple: make a bag the right size and fill it with wool till it was the right thickness.

Grandma was a good housekeeper and managed us well. With any spare cash, she'd save and buy gold coins. They called them Turkish Kokorakia because of the rooster that was imprinted on one side. Grandma would be considered rich by the standards of the day. I heard her say to my mother she had eight Kokorakia, enough to buy eight cows. Mother suggested they buy the small, two-room house just a little farther out from where we lived, but Grandma wouldn't hear of it. She wanted to go back to the village because she hated the city. Mum lived to regret it. We lacked nothing in terms of food or clothing, which wasn't always new. What with the American clothes distributed by the church, blankets made into warm coats for winter, and hand-me-downs from friends and neighbours, we had enough.

My mother worked hard on the farm, but my grandmother also worked hard in the city. Looking after three children aged four, seven, and nine years old was a job in itself, let alone for someone in her sixties. She had to bake bread, but she had to walk with a twenty-kilo bag of wheat on her shoulder about five kilometres to the mill and back before she could bake that bread. My mother told her several times to get the bus, but she wanted to save the fare. Our clothes were always clean. She'd line us up, comb our hair, clean our faces, and check our hands before sending us to school. She couldn't stand to see us dirty. My mother would say to her, "For goodness' sake, they are kids. A bit of dirt on their faces and clothes is not going to kill them. They can have a wash before bed."

Grandma would say, "It's shameful. Cleanliness is half a treasure." About three days a week, when we were at school in the morning shift, she'd do some housecleaning and save the money "for when we go back to the village."

She built a small chicken coop in the corner of the block with timber and a tin roof, where she put six chickens sent by my mother from the farm. We now had fresh eggs as well. In summer, she cooked in the open, on a steel tripod, and in winter she cooked inside on the coal brazier. We'd sit around it, warming our hands while watching and waiting for dinner to cook. She never skimped on food and prepared delicious meals. Cabbage rolls (dolmades) in winter and stuffed capsicums and tomatoes in summer were my favourites. Her chips were unrivalled. Afternoon snack consisted of homemade wholemeal bread and sugar, or olive oil with salt and herbs. We ate with gusto.

During our first summer holidays in Thessaloniki, we got to know the kids around us. Stephanos was a month younger than me and lived right opposite the church. He was the first one we got to know. He was an only child. His mother, Lady Katia, was a lovely lady and was very good to us. His father was a supervisor at a large tobacco factory. They lived in a nice brick house. It had a flat attached to the house which was rented out to a family who had a son, Kon, the same age as Eva and a baby daughter. All the houses in that street were brick, beautiful, and big.

Next to Stephanos was a family with young children, three-year-old Nicolas and five-year-old Katerina. Both were looked after by their grandmother. Both Nicolas's parents were fighting with the opposition in the war, as was Katerina's father. They were very sympathetic towards us and supportive of my grandmother. We got to know all the kids along the road, and because the church was on a corner, we got to know the kids opposite as well. Some of them were also refugees. We were a group of about eighteen. When we all got together, we made lots of noise, but nobody seemed to mind. We played well together and enjoyed our first summer in Thessaloniki, a long way from the raging civil war.

I had most contact with Stephanos. He had lots of books and was glad to lend them to me. I read *David Copperfield*, *Alice in Wonderland*, and a lot of Greek myths and tales. He was the only child allowed to come in the yard because Pastor Demos's wife was friendly with his mother. Stephanos got to like the bread Grandma made and became fond of olive oil and herbs. When Grandma baked bread, she always sent a loaf for him, and often his mother would send us a bought loaf, which to us was a luxury. I got to like Stephanos, and before long I realised I was madly in love with him. I forgot about Demos.

We hadn't seen our mother for three months. She sent word with the driver, along with many goodies, to say that she'd be coming on Wednesday by bus. We couldn't wait to see her. We waited all day, watching the road. She'd have to walk about one kilometre to get home. The day went, dusk came, and we still waited. With every figure who approached us we'd think it was her, but Grandma would say, "No, it's not her. She doesn't walk like your mother." We couldn't remember how she walked. Mother walked in slow, deliberate, and well-placed steps. In the semi-dark, suddenly Grandma said, "That's your mother coming now!" We ran as fast as we could. She seemed to be crying tears of happiness. Grandma told her we were good and she had no complaints. Mum was with us till Sunday. The driver picked her up Monday morning, and she promised to be back again next month.

Chapter 20

Starting School

The summer went by carefree and happy. We were told that we would be staring school this year. The school building hadn't been built as a school; it was a huge house similar to the church. It was two storeys with many rooms, a beautiful staircase, and polished balustrades. The yard was big for a house but woefully small as a schoolyard.

I was now nine and a half years old. I should be starting grade three. I was looking forward to going to school again. Stephanos led the way. Grandma came with us and talked to the headmaster and the teachers about our social situation. She enrolled us and left, taking Ellie with her, who was too young for kindergarten. I stuck by Stephanos, whose class I would be in. He took me under his wing, but even so I was nervous. I never gave poor Eva a thought. She was only seven years old, in a new school with hundreds of kids, and in a new city. She didn't know a soul in the school. The bell rang, and we lined up in long lines according to our grades.

Kindergarten and grade one were downstairs, and the rest were upstairs. We got in the classroom. I sat somewhere in the middle of the room not far from Stephanos. There were three rows of desks, three kids per desk. There must have been about sixty children in the class, which was small compared to other classes. The teacher, Mrs. Gounas, came in and sat at her desk, which was raised on a platform about thirty centimetres. She scanned the class without saying a word. The kids might as well have been statues; they didn't move. I got the feeling they were scared to death of her, which made me even more nervous. Her eyes fell on me, she studied me for what seemed an eternity. I was terrified and wished she'd stop looking at me like this, or at least say something. She never acknowledged me and never said a word to anybody.

Mrs. Gounas sat down, made herself comfortable, and said, "Get ready for work." The kids got their books out in a hurry. She gave the signal for the first kid to start reading. They'd read a paragraph each till the teacher said, "Next," and off they went. I had no books, no bag, and no notebooks. When my turn came, she said, "You. Read." I went red and dizzy. I don't know what I said, if anything. Later, I realised that school had started a week earlier, and the kids were already in routine. "Never mind, we'll sort you out later," she said. When everybody had a turn reading, she gruffly called me to her desk, gave me her book, pointed to a paragraph, and ordered me to read. I shook with fear and embarrassment. I looked at her and the kids. My eyes lingered on Stephanos; I needed his help. He looked worried. Sixty kids were looking at me and waiting to hear me read. I looked at the grade three book, the same one I had read many times before. I recognised the words, but no matter how hard I tried, I couldn't utter a word. I stumbled, gulped, and coughed, but not a word formed on my lips. I stoically stood there trying, all the time aware of the kids staring at me, especially Stephanos.

Suddenly she grabbed the book from my hands, shut it roughly, and in a very derogatory manner and hostile tone said, "You, in grade three? Who said so? You are not good enough for grade one. Sit down."

I was humiliated and upset, and I felt like crying, I wanted to say to her, "I can read. Give me a chance," but I could hardly find my seat much less speak. Next period, I was put in grade two, which was a bigger class. The teacher seemed kinder and softer. She looked at me, but I didn't feel threatened. By the end of the day, I relaxed. She gave me a book and told me to buy a notebook. Grandma made us some bags, and we started school. In two weeks, I caught up again and was one of the best readers in the class. The teacher liked me, and I liked her. Even though the class was big, the teachers soon connected Eva and me as sisters. Poor Eva was at a disadvantage. The teacher didn't have much time to teach because she had a big enough job trying to control the huge class of seven-year-olds, mostly refugee children.

We went to school six days a week. Three days we started at 8:00 a.m. and finished at 1:30 p.m., and three days we would start at 2:00 p.m. and finish at 7:00. There were another six hundred kids who used the school opposite shifts. It must have been very hard for the teachers because the civil war forced thousands of people from all over Macedonia to move to Thessaloniki, which was bigger, closer, and more central than other cities.

Schools were crowded. The smallest class was sixty to seventy kids. The rooms where Eva and I were, being larger, had more kids packed into them.

At recess, there was no room to run and play. There was no supervision either. Kids fared as best as they knew how. Usually the older kids took care of the younger ones and tried to stop fights. Two girls stood out above all the others. They were both in grade six. One was Stella. She had auburn hair, blue eyes, a square jaw, a space between her front teeth, and a determined look on her face. She was intelligent, caring, and motherly. The other girl who stood out in a thousand kids was Miranda Rose, a name as unusual as mine in Greece. They were often seen together, going around in the schoolyard and defending little kids from bullies. Miranda Rose had fair skin with dark eyes and brown wavy hair down to her shoulders. She was pretty and very gentle—a perfect little lady. I admired and adored her and wanted to be like her.

One day, Eva found a contraceptive condom in the yard. She picked it up and started blowing it unsuccessfully. I took it from her and tried to blow it up unsuccessfully. Stella came running, grabbed the condom from me, came close, and said, "This is not a balloon! Never put it in your mouths again. You will get very sick." She was like a good little mother: no laughing at our ignorance, no broadcasting it over the school, no ridiculing. I loved and respected that girl.

When the bell rang, we would all rush down together and the reason we didn't fall more often was that we were jam-packed together, moving down the wide staircase as one solid body. Somehow a little girl, Sophia, was left a bit behind the rest of us. She was still walking halfway down when another kid came running and gave her a push. She went flying down, fell on her face, and broke her four front teeth. There was blood everywhere! No ambulance, no doctor, no treatment whatsoever. The teachers did the best they could till the bleeding stopped. That kid stayed at school till the end of the day and went home, minus her teeth. I wondered how her parents reacted. She was without her front teeth for as long as I knew her. There was no dental care but for the very few elite.

Chapter 21

A Painful Memory

The new school year came. Eva was now in grade two, which was upstairs, and I was in grade three. One day a kid from Eva's class came to my class and spoke to my teacher, who in turn called me and told me to follow the kid. I went to Eva's class, which was bigger than mine, to find poor Eva standing at front of the teacher's desk and looking frightened and bewildered. The teacher told me that Eva didn't do her practice writing and could not read. She made me feel responsible for Eva's underperformance. Eva looked afraid and anxious, fiddling with her dress. She glanced at me. The teacher looked at the stick that was lying on her desk and pointed to it as if to say, "There it is—use it." I took that stick and hit Eva with it, wherever it landed—on her head, arms, back, and legs. Eva made no effort to defend herself, receiving the blows as her just punishment for failing to show her work. The more I hit her, the angrier I got and the more responsible I felt for her.

I caned her many times. That cruel, irresponsible, bloody teacher watched on without intervening, not even as much as to say, "Enough." She got satisfaction out of seeing me cane the poor, helpless child in front of the whole class. I put the stick on her desk. She looked at me with half a smile on her face and full approval in her eyes. She never said a word, not even to say, "Help her with her homework, or remind her to do it." I left the class and returned to mine shaken by the experience.

I never gave the incident another thought till years later. It caused me much pain, anger, frustration, and tears, which I can hardly control even now. The horrible, cruel, and cowardly woman! Why did she have to make me punish her pupil? Why didn't she do it herself? Why couldn't she tell me to help my little sister with her homework? I'd do it, if for no other reason than to please her.

The next few months at school didn't improve for Eva. She had trouble writing some letters more than others, especially the letter *b* in script. My grandmother could read but couldn't write, and so she couldn't teach her. This particular time, my mother happened to be on her three days off. She got it into her head to teach Eva write this letter. She held her hand, and together they traced over and over the letter, my mother gently encouraging and praising her at every step. Then she said, "Now you can do it by yourself," and gave her the freshly sharpened pencil. She watched Eva try unsuccessfully to write the letter. They tried together again, and then Eva on her own, unsuccessfully. My mother lost her cool, grabbed the pencil from Eva, turned her hand palm down, and in anger and frustration started puncturing that seven-year-old's hand with the pencil till it bled. I watched impassively; I was used to seeing this kind of discipline dished out to children and had heard of a lot worse. School wasn't easy for Eva, but neither was home.

Pastor Demos continued to be vicious. He started attacking us children in order to force us to move out. He'd look for every opportunity to hurt us. I managed to escape his wrath, but Eva and Ellie weren't so lucky.

One day, Eva was squatting by the front gate and was talking through the cracks to Stephanos' little dog, Bill. The dog, a little Jack Russell, was jumping up and down outside and barking with delight. Eva was just as delighted, encouraging him. They were having great fun, and no harm was done to anything or anyone.

Pastor Demos, who was watching from upstairs, came down. He picked her up and without an explanation gave her a savage beating, all for talking to the dog outside the gate. I was ten years old, and even then I thought it was unfair and cruel. My grandma was very upset and cried with Eva. But that was his whole purpose: to make life unbearable so that we would leave. The building wasn't used as a church at that time, it didn't belong to him, and there were three other families living there. One of the families had kids too, but he never touched them. Why did he take such a disliking to us?

Eva soon mastered the art of writing and had beautiful handwriting. She'd write on anything and everything she could get her hands on, including scratching on the ground. One day she got hold of an indelible pencil and scribbled her name and surname all over the cracked, concrete footpath, starting from the gate to the front door. One could hardly see it because the pencil blended in with the colour of concrete. The next morning, the dew made it stand out, and Pastor Demos saw it. We were both playing in the yard when he called her and asked, "Did you write this here?"

"Yes, I did," she said proudly with a smile, looking up at him and waiting for praise. Her smile alone would have melted an iceberg, but it didn't move him to mercy.

Without saying a word, he bent down, grabbed her, turned her around, and gave her a severe hiding. She was black and blue. When he finished with her, breathing like an angry bull, he said to her in between breaths, "Don't do it again." Then he went inside. I realised then that he was looking for opportunities to belt us.

Grandma cried again. "Lord, give me strength to bear all this and deliver us form this evil man," she'd pray. If at any time she was interested in my mother's religion, which was his religion too and his "truth," she lost all interest and clung desperately to her own. She wanted no part of his brand of Christianity. Eva, sweet as she was, seemed to always incite his wrath one way or another.

Eva was an animal lover. She always managed to bring stray animals home. This time she came home carrying a litter of six kittens cradled in her skirt, their eyes still closed. We found her sitting in a corner and all the kittens wrapped up and covered with her jumper to keep them warm. She told Grandma she was keeping them because she loved them all. Grandma tried to tell her they were too young to survive without their mother because their eyes were still closed, but Eva wouldn't listen and had it all worked out. She'd give them warm milk to drink, and they would be all right.

Pastor Demos, who kept an eye on us constantly, saw my grandmother talking to Eva. He came down, saw the kittens in her lap, got mad, and told her in no uncertain terms to take them and put them back where she'd found them unless she wanted another beating. She got up crying, and together we went and put them tenderly under the bridge where she had found them. We planned to go and see them every day, but when we went the next day, they weren't there. We concluded some kind person took them in, and we were happy for them. The truth is, dogs probably found them and ate them because they too, were hungry during the war.

A few months later, Eva found a litter of three beautiful puppies; their eyes were open, and they were fat and wriggly. She brought them home in her skirt again. We both wanted to keep them, but they were met with the same fate as the kittens: back under the bridge. We had to abandon them against our will and with much sadness. They were still there the next day, but they were gone after that.

Chapter 22

Unjust and Cruel

Ellie didn't escape the pastor's wrath either, and one event was the most unjustified and cruel act on the part of any human being, let alone of a man who professed to be a minister of God and had the gumption to stand on the pulpit and preach on love. He was Hypocrisy personified! Ellie was just four years old. The young people of the church had gone camping, and when they came back, Pastor Demos left the rolled-up tent right in the middle of the yard where we were playing. He could have easily put it in the shed where it belonged, just a few steps away. Ellie and Marta saw the rolled-up tent, climbed up, and took turns getting on and jumping off it. They were having great fun with an innocent, and harmless game. They weren't damaging the tent, and they weren't even getting it dirty because it was summer and the ground was dry. I watched the kids jump on and off, and then I sensed someone staring at me. I looked up at the window and saw Pastor Demos and his wife watching the kids play. He had half a smile on his face. I presumed it was OK for the children to play.

He opened the window and angrily yelled at them to get off the tent. They got off, but because they were very young, after a short while they were on it again, jumping with as much laughter and delight as before. He opened the window and again shouted at them to get off, adding, "Don't get on it again." He left the tent where it was instead of putting it away. Why didn't he put it in the shed where it belonged if he didn't want them to jump on it? A few minutes later, the kids were on it again. He came down and yelled at the kids, saying, "I told you not to get on it." He brushed Marta aside, grabbed Ellie, put her on her back on the ground, and mercilessly hit her with a stick on the soles of her feet. A cruel act of bastinado performed on a little child. Ellie screamed with pain.

My grandmother came running out and tried to rescue the child, but he was so angry that I don't think he was aware she was there. Grandma kept saying to him, "Why, my son, why? They weren't doing any harm," but he kept on beating the child. When he finished with her, Ellie couldn't walk. She crawled for days moaning with pain. My grandmother carried her around, and when she sat down with Ellie on her lap, she would weep silently. He did not as much as point the finger at Marta. She had also jumped on and off the same tent. You see, Marta had a mother and a father bigger than Demos, to defend her. We had nobody. To all intents and purposes, we were orphans and defenceless. I consider his wife equally as guilty. Even if she didn't encourage him, she didn't discourage him either. However, I dismissed that incident at the time.

****

During the civil war, the government provided one meal a day for refugee children. As such, we were entitled to the midday meal, but neither Eva nor I liked the idea of eating "other people's food." Ellie was too young to care. A child's wishes didn't matter when I was a child. Children had no rights; we did as we were told. The saying "Children should be seen but not heard" was literal and held strongly in Greece.

We were enrolled and waited for word to start. A few weeks later, we received a letter saying we were not eligible to be fed by the government because our father was with the opposition and fighting with the guerrillas. Eva and I were delighted because we wouldn't have to eat that food, and we wouldn't have to walk all the way to the feeding centre. Our mother was upset not because they couldn't afford to feed us but because of the discrimination. I can still hear her saying angrily, "These children are the innocent victims of the war. Suppose I couldn't afford to feed them? Should they die?"

There was another service for feeding refugee children. It was organised either by volunteers or social agencies. Willing families provided a meal three times a week. Two families offered to take us. The Athansiades family took Eva and Ellie; they had teenage children themselves. A widowed lady, Mrs. Karas, took me. We went against our will to start with, but we ended up looking forward to going not because of the food but because we got lots of attention. We also got lots of cod liver oil too. We heaved and belched, but we soon got used to it and took it without complaining. We even asked for another bottle when that was finished, but we were told it was in winter only.

While Pastor Demos was abusing us emotionally, physically, and psychologically, Panos took care of our souls. Every Friday night, he would invite us to study the Sabbath school lesson. I liked going for two reasons. First, I liked to listen to what adults were talking about. Second. their room was warm, whereas our shed was very cold.

One lesson stuck in mind, and I vividly recall it. Panos expounded the love of God towards His children, likening it to the love of parents towards their children. In all seriousness, he said to his little flock, "You love your children, but you shouldn't tell them so because they will take advantage of you." I couldn't work out the meaning of the "advantage" bit, but I concluded that our mother loved us but wouldn't tell us in case we took advantage of her. I supposed it was why people said God was like a father, and if that was the case, He had every right to punish His children. I had trouble for a long time saying "I love you." It bothered me. In my mid-thirties, I came to the conclusion that "If you love me and I don't know it, you might as well hate me if I didn't know it." It wouldn't make any difference either way. By the time I was a grandmother, I could tell my grandchildren, "I love you." Their reaction at hearing the magic words was so rewarding. Their faces brightened up, their eyes sparkled, and they were delights to behold. Sadly, it took me a lot longer to tell my own children I loved them.

Pastor Demos worked systematically to make my family's life miserable. First of all, he denied us access to water. There was a tap by the big gate, which he locked by removing the turning key, forcing us to use the water from the well, which was very hard. Grandma wouldn't use it to wash clothes in it. "It doesn't froth," she would say. She was a very independent and proud person and hated being under obligation. She declined the offer of the neighbours to give her water, preferring to walk half a kilometre each way carting water in heavy buckets. When the local council tap dried up, we'd all walk two kilometres or more carrying water according to our strength. Grandma hated that tap because it had no pressure, It was just a trickle. When that tap dried up as well, she had no choice but to swallow her pride and accept the water offered her by the kind neighbours, who professed no religion whatsoever. All the while, the minister of God, knowing the full extent of her travails—which he himself deliberately caused—did not relent and give her some water even if he had rationed it for drinking only. He even ignored Christ, telling him, "Even if you give a cup of cold water in my name, it will be considered as righteousness unto you" (Matthew 10:42). He did not succumb to the shame of the neighbours knowing our plight, our need for water the most essential part for life. He didn't relent. Despite of all this, I don't ever remember my grandmother criticising Pastor Demos openly, or even inferring that he should know better as a priest. But that wasn't all. There were more exhibitions of how low a human being could fall.

Grandma's chickens were laying. She was so pleased she had enough eggs from her chickens, and with what my mother sent us, we had enough. There was always plenty of food. She was thankful to God for it.

One day, Demos knocked on the door. We dreaded his visits because he always managed to upset Grandma. He looked his usual gruff self. Without much ado and not even a civilised hello, he told Grandma that he wanted some sort of payment for the electricity used by the night light shining on the footpath at the front gate. My grandmother was surprised because we never saw that light. The shed we lived in was at the back fence, away from the front gate. We had no electricity. She asked him how much he wanted. "Six eggs a week," he said. Grandma agreed to it; she had no choice. When he left with six eggs in his hands, Grandma sat down, sighed, rocked back and forth rhythmically in distress, and said, "Oh, Lord, what a mean person, what a mean person."

We paid for the electricity for as long as the chickens laid. They didn't lay in winter. He took the food out of the mouths of three war-stricken children and an old woman, all to feed his wife, who was "anaemic." She used to beat the egg yolks with sugar and eat them in front of us out in the yard in summer, saying it was to improve her blood.

Chapter 23

Jo and Phillip

We were not the only people Demos tormented and wanted to kick out of the building and out of his sight. Lady Jo and Mr. Phillip bore the brunt of his meanness and nastiness too. They had no children, but they had a dog, Molly, who was a white and orange Irish setter. She was their baby. They also had a black and white cat and loved her. They allowed the cat out in the backyard when nature called, but Molly wasn't allowed out of their sight. Molly had the best of everything, and Lady Jo hand-fed her, which amused us no end. We were used to feeding dogs bones and scrap, throwing them as far as possible from the family table, but here was Molly sitting at the table on Lady Jo's knee, being fed choice meats.

Demos hated the animals with passion. He couldn't stand them living in the same area as he, but there was nothing he could do about it. The way rental laws were in Greece at that time, Mr. Phillip had right to the house as long as he paid his rent, and Demos couldn't do anything other than complain and block his sensitive nose. He tried to kill the cat by putting broken glass in her meat. I overheard him tell his wife how the cat carefully picked the meat out and left the glass, which annoyed him. Later, he succeeded in killing the animal by poisoning it, and he was mighty pleased with himself. I saw him smile for the first time. "The cat won't dig in the garden again." There was no garden to speak of. There were two oleander bushes on either side of the stairs, a holly bush, and a yucca in the middle of the lawn on either side of the footpath. Lady Jo and her husband were devastated; Jo cried bitterly for days and cursed him with all the Greek curses and bad luck she had in her Greek vocabulary.

Pastor Demos harassed and upset the couple in every possible way he could. In the end, they accepted his offer to move downstairs in the rooms Panos, his family, and Mara had vacated a little earlier. He tormented them as well. Lady Jo would come, talk to my grandmother, and cry. She particularly disliked Pastor Demos's wife, whom she never referred to by name. She aptly nicknamed her the Duck because of the peculiar way Athena walked, and it stuck.

We all had a few weeks' reprieve. The civil war was still going on. Somehow the government caught up with Pastor Demos and enlisted him in the army. The Duck was devastated. Nobody could comfort her, and she cried every day for weeks. I heard Panos say to her, "It's all a mistake. He shouldn't be in the army, and he will be back soon," which he was. His brother, who was the president of the Seventh-day Adventist church in Greece, pulled a few strings and soon the American Big Brother had him returned "to take care of his little flock," who were glad to have him back, thanking God for answering their prayers for his speedy return. The Duck floated like a butterfly and wobbled her bum even more.

****

Our first year at school went well. We made friends and were happy. Monday mornings was health inspection day. The teachers checked us for lice, scabies, and clean ears, hands, and fingernails. The teacher stopped, looked at me with horror, took a step back, pointed at my hands, and without restraint shouted, "Scabies! You have scabies!" Everybody moved away from me, horrified. I was ordered to pick up my things and go home. Devastated, embarrassed, and humiliated, I felt dirty and unwanted. That was the worst feeling I had ever experienced in my short life, I cried all the way home. The next thing I knew, Eva was sent home too. During the war, lice were common. Most kids were infected by them, but scabies was the worst thing one could have. We scratched all night but didn't know what the problem was. We had been playing with Marta and Nikos, and they too scratched. Their mother didn't suspect anything till we were sent home. She lost no time. She took the kids to the baby health centre, where she was issued (free of charge) an ointment which was a grey-green, baby-pooh colour, and it smelled terrible! My grandmother refused to use it on her or us, preferring to make her own remedy. She used sulphur, which came in a solid, cylinder form. She crushed it into powder, and we had to eat a spoonful twice a day. Not the food of choice, but we got used to eating the gritty stuff without too much complaining. It was part of the treatment. "Better than scratching," Grandma said.

She made the rest of the sulphur into an ointment with olive oil, kerosene, and camphor. It looked better and didn't smell as bad as Aunt Leila's, but it was nowhere near as effective. She rubbed it on us three times a day after our bath. The treatment was terrible. Her ointment burned our scratched and broken skin, and we yelled with all our might. Ellie was by far the loudest. She'd take a deep breath in, puff out her chest, crane her neck like a rooster, and scream loud enough to lift up the tin roof off the shed. The neighbours behind us would throw stones on the roof, yell, and swear to let us know they weren't pleased with our disturbing their midday siesta.

Three days later, Marta and Nikos were clean and healthy. We weren't allowed to play with them or touch them. More than three weeks later, we were still scratching and missing school. It was a nightmare for poor Grandma, who had to cart the water from the public tap, heat it, and bathe three kids and herself three times a day. Pastor Demos knew of her plight, but he didn't let her have water even then. Aunt Leila offered Grandma the ointment, but Grandma stubbornly refused it every time. It was mid-May, and with no sign of our scabies clearing, she struggled three more weeks before she had to admit defeat. At last Grandma sent a message to Mother with the driver to come because she couldn't cope any more.

Mum came the next day by bus and lost no time at all. She got hold of Aunt Leila's ointment. Before she put it on us, she said she'd belt us if we as much breathed, let alone yelled. There wasn't as much as a whimper from us. The treatment was effective; within four days, we were all healthy and spanking clean. Oh, how I wished Grandma had used Aunt Leila's treatment. We'd have been back at school in a week, and poor Grandma wouldn't have suffered. More important, we wouldn't have missed a whole year of school. Because we were absent for the end-of-year test, which was compulsory, we had to repeat the whole year. I was ten years old and still in grade two. I was upset and ashamed at having to repeat.

Summer holidays were fun. We played hopscotch and skipped rope, and boys and girls competed as to who could make the most skips before getting tangled up. I wasn't too bad at that. But I was useless at games which involved running or aiming. Neither team was anxious to have me on its side. There was always a loud groan coming from the unlucky team which had to have me. "Oh, no, not her." It never bothered me because it was always said affectionately and in good humour. I knew the kids liked me; they simply doubted my prowess as a sportsperson. Most times I ended up keeping the score, which suited me well. In the evenings after the games, they'd all sit around me for a story. Even Stephanos would listen with his mouth open, and he'd have already read the stories. They were out of his books, but I had the ability to remember details and to embellish them. My childhood wasn't all gloom and doom despite the war. There were happy times playing, storytelling, and laughing.

Chapter 24

Little Sparrows and Red Sandals

Spring in North Greece is unpredictable. Some of the most fearsome storms I've ever experienced occurred in April and May, and this one was no exception. We were living in the tin-roofed shed when a terrible storm came from the north-west. Rain pelted down. The wind was fierce, uprooted trees, and swept away anything that wasn't well secured. The yard flooded. The birds' nests in the large pine trees were destroyed and the fledglings drowned.

When the wind abated and the rain stopped, Eva and I went out to see what had happened to the chickens. They'd all drowned because unbeknown to Grandma, she'd built the chicken coop where the drain hole was, blocking it and flooding the yard. Grandma was upset, couldn't bear the sight of her drowned chickens, left them there, and went inside. We waded in the knee-high water, gathering the dead birds and the chickens to bury. Amongst them, we found four little sparrows that were still alive. We left the dead birds and chickens, took the live sparrows, and waded as fast as we could. Inside, we dried and warmed them with our breaths, wrapped them up in towels, and put them in a box to keep them warm. We gave them some crumbs to eat, and in my child's mind, I saw us playing with them and making them our pets.

Aunt Soula and Magda were staying with us. They told us that the birds would die, but we didn't give up. We kept them in the box all night and were up early the next morning to check our birds. We were delighted to find them all alive and chirping. I ran and told Magda, and I ran back to the birds and put my hand in the box, feeling their soft, warm bodies. Magda came smiling, took my hand out of the box, and said, "I will show you how to hold the birdies so that you don't hurt them." I trusted her. She took one bird out of the box and held it in her hand. She put her closed hand on mine, and without letting me feel the bird, she let it fly away. I thought it was an accident and expected to hold the next one, but she did the same thing with all of them. I was so angry with her that I cried. To this day, I can't understand why would anyone do such a thing to a child. She was twenty-two years old and should have known better.

The other thing Magda did that upset me was to promise me a pair of red Roman-style sandals. I waited two years for them, but I never got them. I complained to Grandma. "My girl," she said, "some people's promises are like donkey's farts: don't take any notice of them." Grandma also used to say, "Promises made to a saint or to a child must be kept, or not made at all." Please don't disappoint children because they have long memories.

Chapter 25

Summer 1950

Winter was over, and it was good to feel warm again and to go to bed not shivering and shaking. Many times after a sunny winter's day, I'd sit in the corner of the north-facing wall (the same spot my mother sat to keep warm) till late at night because it was warmer there than in the shed.

Summer came, and the school year was over. It was a particularly hot night, and I asked Grandma if I could sleep outside. She wasn't keen, but I persisted. Eventually she relented, saying, "But only if the bed is right under the window," which was open. I agreed and slept on a canvas stretcher. It was cool and the bed was comfortable.

I was lying awake, looking up at the stars, and listening to my grandmother's peculiar breathing when sleeping. She would breathe rhythmically in through her nose and exhale through her mouth, making her lips vibrate with a peculiar sound, a sure sign she was fast asleep.

Panos must have wanted to go to the toilet. Before going, he stopped by my bed, sat on it, and very softly asked me if I were still awake. "Yes," I whispered.

"Let's talk for a while," he said. He got me out of bed and carried my stretcher to the farthest point of the yard, under the pine trees, away from the shed and my sleeping grandmother. Panos was a tall man with broad shoulders, a handsome face, and dark curly hair that was greying at the temples. He had a peculiar, dog-like smile, and he always kept his head lowered. He put the bed down. "We won't wake them up with our talking here." I thought it was reasonable. I sat on the bed, and he sat next to me. He put his arm around me in a fatherly manner, told me what a good and clever girl I was, and said that he liked me. I appreciated the attention and felt special. He kept moving his hands around my neck, shoulders, and gradually to my developing chest. He squeezed, and it hurt. I squealed with pain, which he ignored. He started breathing in a way which I hadn't heard before.

I became uncomfortable. I remembered my grandmother advising us, "Do not let any man touch you," and here was Panos fondling me all over. I tried to move away, but he held me there. After a while, still breathing heavily, he told me to go and see if Aunt Leila and my grandmother were asleep. I took the opportunity to run away. I pretended to be looking into the room where his heavily pregnant wife and children were sleeping. I could see nothing; the room was dark. Then I ran to the shed window and woke my grandmother up. In whispers, I told her everything.

She was shocked. "May fire consume him," she uttered, a common Eastern curse. I ran back to him and told him that Aunt Leila was asleep, but my grandmother was awake and wanted me inside. He sounded angry as he told me to go. I didn't feel angry or resentful with Panos. I had no idea of his intentions then.

Earlier in the year, we had a few visits from the police, talking to Panos and asking questions about him. When I asked my grandmother and Aunt Soula why the police wanted to talk to him, they told me that they wanted to talk to him about his "hobby of collecting used tram tickets." After a while, the police stopped coming around. Many years later, the collection of the used tram tickets and the police visits took on a new a meaning. I wondered how many little girls had suffered at his filthy hands. I was angry. I never mentioned the incident to anyone, and I don't know whether my grandmother told my mother. If she did, my mother would not be mincing her words; everybody would know.

About a week later, his wife had her baby, whom they called Theodora (the gift of God). When Leila came home from hospital, she would let me look after the baby. I was thrilled to bits to be trusted to look after the baby under the pine trees while Aunt Leila went around doing her jobs.

I was eleven years old and was getting cheeky and rude. We were big enough now to do messages for Grandma, the neighbours, and the families who lived in the church. Whenever we did anything for Lady Jo, she always rewarded us with something little: a sweat, a bit of bread and peanut butter (which we loved), and sometimes even ten cents. The others never bothered, and they didn't even say thanks.

One summer's day, it was so hot that even the cicadas had stopped singing. Aunt Leila asked me to go to the grocers to shop for her. I was hot and bothered, and I was also sick and tired of being used and abused. I plucked up courage and for the first time in my life I was rude and disobedient. I looked her straight in the eye and told her I wasn't going to go. "It is too hot." She tried to coax me, but I stuck to my guns. Encouraged by her reaction, I told her she could go, or she could send Marta. She threatened to tell my mother, and that worried me a bit, but I figured it'd be a long time anyway. She gave me a hateful look. Upon turning to go, she said something angrily in Turkish, which I didn't understand. I felt really good. For the first time in my life, I'd stood up for myself and did as I wanted, not as I had to do. I'm not sure if that was a good or a bad thing. From then on, I refused to do any messages for anyone except Lady Jo.

A family lived across the road from us: Anders and Dawn and their two children, Kon and a baby daughter. They used to have a roast every Sunday. The houses had no ovens those days. People had to take their roasts, cakes, and bread to the "common oven," and the baker would bake them for a fee. It was usually my "privilege" to take the roast to the baker's and bring it back after an hour or so, which meant a double trip. The aroma of the baked potatoes, herbs, and roast meat used to make my mouth water, but they never offered me a taste, let alone a small plate to take home. They never asked Stephanos to do any chores. His parents would not allow them to use him as they used us.

This particular Sunday, I wasn't around, and I don't know who took the roast to the bakers. Dawn asked Eva, who was nine years old, to bring it back. It was a large, round aluminium dish that was too big for me, let alone Eva. They gave her the money to pay the baker, and off she went.

She picked the delicious roast from the baker's and started on her way back. Not far from the baker's, she dropped the dish upside down on the dirt road. Frightened and confused, she picked up the empty dish and ran all the way home crying. She told Grandma what had happened.

My grandmother tried to pacify her, assuring her she wouldn't let them belt her. She took the empty dish and walked across the street, I at her heels wanting to know first-hand the outcome. In her polite, sweet manner, Grandma pointed out that the child was only nine years old, the same age as their son. The dish too big and hot for her to carry. They were both home, one of them should have gone to get it. They said nothing other than nod. I would have loved to have been a fly on the wall, watching them eat bread and cheese for both lunch and dinner. That dish was big enough for two meals for them. Needless to say, they didn't ask Eva to go to the baker's again. I became bolder and cheekier by the day, refusing to do jobs for them too. I enjoyed my new-found power.

The only trouble was I became too rude for words, and my grandmother became my next victim. I refused to do anything for her, I back-chatted I fought with my sisters, bullied them, and always managed to escape punishment. The odd time she caught me, the smack never hurt; she always used her hand, never a stick, and I used to laugh. She was at her wits' end. When my mother came on days off, Grandma told her just how bad I was, adding that she couldn't control me and that she let me do whatever I wanted to do. My mother looked at her in disbelief.

Chapter 26

Dream about My Father

The war was coming to an end, with the opposition losing ground (thanks to the Americans and the English). We hadn't heard a word from or about our father. We had no idea whether he was dead or alive. No one had seen or heard from him. We had heard that his brother, Minoas, was seen in Yugoslavia and went to Russia. He stayed there for many years after the war. Rumour had it that he lived with a Russian woman, and they had two sons. My grandmother refused to believe it, saying, "He loves Sassa too much to do such a thing." My grandmother prayed that she would live long enough to see him return.

We heard that my cousin John was killed, but we refused to believe it, and none of us grieved. I loved him, and I could not accept that I would never see him again. He was loving, caring, helpful, and unselfish. When my father was away in summer and busy in winter, John would be the only one to come and ask if we needed anything. He would chop wood and do other things to help. In winter while going to social functions, he would carry me on his back so that my shoes wouldn't get wet.

My grandmother would light her oil lamp, put it at front of her icons, and pray for my father and John's safe return. "The worse thing is the not knowing. I wish I knew one way or another," she would tell her sister.

When I was about eleven years old, I had a strange dream. I was back in Rodia, in the paddock where the cattle rested in the middle of the day. I saw my father from his shoulders up, walking in the tall bulrushes. He was holding a gun raised and chasing a huge elephant, intending to kill him. The bulrushes were slowing him down. He was a fair distance behind the elephant. Just as he raised his gun to shoot, the elephant stopped, turned back, and in an instant was transformed into a very beautiful young woman who said, "Don't kill me. I will help you." I didn't see my father's face at any time in the dream.

I turned around and looked to where the cattle bed was. Under the big plane tree, I saw a tap from which was running crystal-clear water falling on white pebbles and running away like a stream. I went to turn the tap off when I saw my grandmother in the distance, wearing her best clothes and shoes. She waved to me and shouted, "No, no, don't turn it off. Let it run."

The dream was so real and vivid that I was compelled to tell my grandmother as soon as she was awake. She listened very attentively, and when I finished telling her my dream, she asked anxiously, "Was the water clear or muddy?"

"Clear as crystal," I said.

She crossed herself over and over, praising and thanking God. She said in great excitement, joy, and conviction, "Thank You, my God. Alexis is alive and well, and we will hear from him soon" She sounded like a little girl receiving her most wanted present. I was amused to see her behave like this. I had never seen her as jubilant, prancing around like a child. I was glad my dream had made her happy, but I didn't put that much importance or faith on its interpretation.

About two weeks later, Grandma's sister Katerina came to visit as usual. When she came, she always brought us sweets. The first thing she said to Grandma was, "I have some good news for you. Sit down." I was more anxious to hear the good news than Grandma.

Grandma sat down on the little bench under the trees and casually said, "Tell me."

Aunt Katerina excitedly said, "We've heard from Alexis. He gave himself up. He is in jail at Yannena, and he'll be coming here in about three weeks."

"I knew we'd hear from him soon!" she said without surprise in her voice. She pointed. "That little Turk had a dream two weeks ago, and here it is. It came true!" She was glad. When the news sank in, she got so excited that she cried. The poor thing. For three years, she'd prayed every day. She'd faithfully lit her little oil lamp, never missing a day and never losing hope. She'd desperately tried to find out whether her son was alive or dead, asking people who came back from the war or anybody in the opposition. She would even have her coffee cup read, with no definite answer. Here it was now, as sure as it could be that her son was alive!

The reason my father contacted his aunt was that he didn't know where we were and whether we were dead or alive. So many people had crossed the border and gone to Europe, some as far as Russia. Many others, mostly older people and children, froze to death while crossing the mountains.

I told my sisters the good news; they had taken their sweets and gone across the road to play. They were excited. Ellie remembered him vaguely, because she'd been three years old. Eva remembered more clearly; she'd been six and I'd been eight. I had a clear recollection of him—both his good and bad points.

I hoped my parents wouldn't start fighting as they used to. I hated them fighting. I was scared that one day, Father might kill my mother, and that thought dampened my enthusiasm and excitement about his returning. But Grandma was delirious, and she kept thanking God all day long.

The day came when my father was transferred to Thessaloniki. Aunt Katerina came to tell us, and she added that Alexis needed some clean clothes. I can remember Grandma opening the truck with trembling hands, almost reverently taking out his clothes. His black suit (his best), another suit, shirts, some underwear, socks, and handkerchiefs. She had them ready the same day, just after her sister left.

The next day, we were up early, had a bath in the tub, dressed us up in our best, did our hair up more meticulously than usual, and took off on foot to see our father in the city, about four kilometres away. He was kept in detention at the police station before he was transferred to gaol, waiting for investigations of his activities during the war. We arrived to the place trembling with anticipation. A police officer brought out my father. My grandmother fell on his neck, and they wept in each other's arms, tears rolling down their faces. The police officer and we children looked on. After the initial weeping and howling, my father turned to us, still crying, and asked, "Mother, who are they?"

"Why, my son, they are your children."

With that, the policeman turned his back to us, and he too cried. I could see him taking his handkerchief out of his pocket and wiping his eyes. We didn't see the policeman's face till we left. What my father really wanted to ask was, "Mother, which is which?" Eva and I were the same height now and looked a bit alike—till she smiled and two deep dimples formed on her very pretty face. He hugged us all, tears still pouring down his face.

I don't know how long we were there; it seemed a long time. Then the policeman came and said, "Time's up. Come again tomorrow." All the way back on foot, we talked about our father. I recognised him, `he hadn't changed much. Eva said she recognised him from the lump on his forehead. He'd been stung by an insect when he was young, and the lump stayed permanently. Ellie said she recognised him from his missing thumb. My grandmother cried all the way home. She wailed, saying, "My Alexis, who was so clean he would not let a fly sit on his clothes. My meticulous, proud Alexis. How did he end up like a beggar? His clothes are patch upon patch and not even sewn properly. The patches are stuck together with wire. My Alexis, who would not touch food without washing his hands first. My Alexis, who would not go to bed without a wash. He looks like a pig without a shave, and his hair is so long! Oh, my God, how he must have suffered." She repeated this all the way home. The poor thing was too upset to think of all the hunger and the cold he and others had suffered for three winters, unable to light a fire to warm themselves up for fear of being detected by government troops.

The next day, we went to see my father again. He was clean, shaven, and wearing his clean clothes. He looked as I remembered him, and he even smelled like my father. They talked till the same young policeman came and said with a sad smile, "Time is up."

Grandma sent a message to my mother with the driver as soon as she could. Mum came to Thessaloniki about two days later. When she came, I couldn't say she was excited. There was an air of foreboding about her. We didn't have much to say to her because we were overwhelmed; even Ellie hadn't found her tongue yet. But when Ellie did, she was excited and told Mum all about how father still had his chopped-up thumb. Eva interjected. "And the lump is still on his head." Ellie gave Eva a scowling look for interrupting and continued about how filthy he had been and how the policeman was very upset about it and cried. I didn't get the chance to put a word in each way. The next day, we set out on foot to see my father as a complete family.

I was so pleased to see my parents hug and kiss. That was the very first and last time I ever saw them touch each other. I was sure that they'd made up and that there would be no more fights, yelling, or swearing. After yet another emotional greeting, we gathered around them. Ellie took over and chattered all the time. Up to this stage, my father hadn't asked after the baby, what happened, and whether it'd been a boy or a girl. My mother told him everything. He looked very sad because he really wanted a son.

Ellie listened very intently, and when my mother stopped to take a breath, she jumped in and matter-of-factly added, "And he looked just like you." Despite the sadness of the conversation, all the adults laughed, including the young policeman. As far as I can remember, nobody ever remarked who the baby looked like.

"Oh, the little Turk!" said my grandmother between fits of laughter and tears of sadness.

"Time's up," announced the young policeman. We walked home. My mother stayed two more days and then returned to work.

We visited my father daily while he was on remand, but soon he was transferred to Eidesah, to wait for clearance. It was too far to visit him. He was there for eight months, till the investigations were completed. My father had no political criminal record. Yes, he'd sided with the opposition, but that was no crime. He was taken by force by the guerrillas. He didn't carry a gun and only took care of their animals. Then he'd defected as soon as he could.

Chapter 27

My Mother's Workplace and Duties

While my father was in jail, my mother worked. I thought I worked hard, but it was nowhere as hard as my mother and grandmother did. Their hands were never still, never folded under their bosoms. Daytime was for working outside, doing the things farmers had to do, like looking after crops, animals, and a family. Half the night was for knitting, sewing, darning, or embroidery. Their brains and hands were only still when, after a hard day's work, they fell in a sweet, deep sleep brought about by a body having spent its last reserve of energy.

Mother worked in one of the largest farms in Greece; it was owned by three brothers and one sister. It employed sixty full-time workers year-round, including drivers, mechanics, a gardener, an accountant (Nikitas), two supervisors (Diamond and Stelios), and, up to the time my mother took over, two housekeepers. The house consisted of four floors. The ground floor was used as a storeroom. On the first floor was the kitchen, a huge dining room, a lounge room, and a very large bedroom where the housekeepers slept. On the second floor were four bedrooms, where the bosses slept. There were four more bedrooms on the third floor. Nikitas slept in one, and the other three were used as storerooms and to dry the trahana, which my mother had to make. There was no running water in the house, and the electricity was by a generator.

When I was eleven years old, I went with Nikos, the driver, to the farm to spend my school holidays with my mother, who was just thirty-five years old then.

Their sister, Lea, was married to another rich farmer and had one daughter, Vayia, a year older than me, and two ill-mannered boys aged six and eight whom everybody referred to as the beasties. Kostas, the oldest brother, was married to a beautiful, kind lady with olive skin, dark hair, and green eyes; they had an eight-year-old daughter, also named Vayia. Both girls were named after their dead paternal grandmother. Their son, Pericles, four years old. Both children were well behaved. They distinguished the two Vayias by calling the younger one Vaytsa (Little Vayia). My mother was fond of Kostas and his family. Kostas was the only one involved with farming. Even though he didn't need to, he was out with the workers early every morning and worked with them all day. He was much respected by everyone. He knew everything about machinery, and when they got their new, state-of-the-art harvester, he drove it himself and wouldn't let anybody touch it.

The other brother, Panos, was nicknamed by the workers "the Herring" because of his reddish hair and brightly coloured red moustache. He was also referred to as the lace boy, meaning sissy or delicate, not only because he didn't want to work but because he was also useless. The latter nickname came about when one day, he tried to show off by driving in a post. While the hammer was falling on the post, he'd bend his knees. The post refused to budge, he gave up and never tried again. He was Narcissus reincarnated. He'd spent hours before the mirror, and he'd only wash his face in water from one particular well because the water was softer and better for his skin. My mother had to make sure there was water in a pitcher for him to wash his face. He was illiterate despite going to school. He'd whistle for his coffee just as soon as his newspaper arrived, and he would take it to the veranda, where everybody could see him "read." Many times when my mother would take his coffee to him, she would discreetly go to his side and tell him, "The paper is upside down." He'd shift on his seat, put down the paper, take his coffee, and then pick the paper up the right way and proceed to "read," drinking his coffee with as much aplomb as he saw the men do in the cafenio. He treated everybody as inferior and with contempt, and he was good at it.

Vasos, the youngest, went to high school, to year ten. I held him in awe. I thought he was smart until one day on the fourth floor, I was rummaging through his high school textbooks and magazines. I found his reports and marks. They were all very low, and he had failed half his subjects. He fell in my estimation too.

Mother's duties were numerous. As far as I know, only once did she have help, and that was for six weeks from a lady who couldn't cope and left.

First of all, she had to look after the bosses. Two were there year-round, and all of them and their families were there during holidays, including the long summer holidays between June and September. That added to her already overloaded schedule. She had to cook, wash, and clean the two storeys that were used all the time. She cooked separate meals for the bosses and another one for the sixty workers. She made thirty litres of yoghurt every day. There was no running water in the house, she had to carry the water from the nearest pump, the only one which was operated by electricity. Occasionally the supervisors would carry a bit of water for her, but it wasn't very often.

She was expected to make trahana for them and the workers for winter. This had to be made in summer so that it could dry during the warm weather. She seemed to make tons of it. It was tiring and time-consuming, but she had to do it. She was expected to wash, "comb," and spin some of the best wool on a fifty-centimetre, comb-like machine with the steel combs, teeth fixed upwards, for their own personal use. (That was where I learned to spin wool.) She had to make butter and cottage cheese and use the by-products to make skim ricotta for the workers. The bosses wouldn't touch it. Another onerous job was to pound salt for table use. It was done with mortar and pestle, and that was my job when I was there. I sat on the floor pounding that bloody salt till it was fine enough for their lordships, who growled if it wasn't just right. Oh, how I hated it. Another duty she had was to look after the four cats, which I also did. Their job was to keep away the mice.

Many times, they'd catch snakes which came in to drink their milk. Watching them catching and killing snakes was terrifying.

It was a hot summer's evening, and everybody was dining out in the garden. Vayia and I decided to visit the village one kilometre away without telling anybody. We walked and talked all the way. We had no particular reason for going there; it was simply something to do. We didn't think of dangers. What we didn't know was that the dogs not only guarded their own territory but the whole village as well. The dogs knew everybody. When one dog barked, the whole pack would be alerted.

We hadn't quite entered the village when we heard a rushing sound. We didn't know what it was. We couldn't see in the dark, but we soon found out! A pack of vicious village dogs, as big as Shetland ponies, was upon us, barking like mad. I could imagine their big teeth and frothing mouths, ready to tear us to shreds. I screamed with my arms behind me, but Vayia, not knowing that moving anything in front of a dog excited him, was screaming at the top of her lungs, waving her arms madly and trying to ward off the dogs, which only came closer. I was sure we would be eaten alive. The villagers heard our screams and came out to investigate. They didn't have to ask us where we came from; they knew. There was no other place close enough for two kids to wander around at night. The bosses and the workers, who'd heard our screams and the dogs barking, came running to investigate. Trailing after them were our mothers.

They took us back. We were terrified and trembling. They reprimanded us, ordering us to tell them next time we went to the village. They didn't have to worry—we wouldn't dream of it. That was my first bad experience with Alsatian dogs. I refused to accept that the dogs were bad. I thought that had we gone in the daytime, the dogs wouldn't bark at us, let alone eat us up, but we didn't test the argument.

The summer holidays were nearly over, and the casual workers left. My mother was given her three days off and an extra one, and we returned to the city. We had three days together as a family. On her fourth day off, she went to clean Apostolea's house because that was the deal for coming home a week early and accompanying me home. The cruel bastards. She worked for three months without a break, doing the work of two people. Then they gave her four days off, but she had to clean their sister's house without payment. I went with her. I thought I'd read Vayia's books, but we decided to play outside instead.

We were outside the front door and still on the first step of the two-storey house. Their big Alsatian dog appeared from nowhere, dashed past Vayia, and attacked me without a bark. I screamed. They raced to my rescue, but not before it had the chance to sink its teeth into my thigh, which bled profusely, and tear off half my dress. My mother washed the wounds with salty water and bandaged it with strips from an old towel. She was upset. Apostolea looked on, emotionless. I had no medication, not even a Panadol. I was shaking and shocked, but mostly I was upset about my torn dress. It was my best, remodelled from the American parcels distributed by the church. It was bottle green with tiny white daisies, puff sleeves, and a belt that tied in a bow at the back. They never offered to replace it, but they gave me one of Vayia's old ones to wear home. After the house was cleaned, my mother returned to work. We enjoyed the rest of the school holidays.

At eleven, I finished grade three—two years behind everybody else my age.

Chapter 28

Evicted from the Church

One summer morning, there was a knock on the door. A young man appeared with a hand-written note. "From the police," he said, and he read it to my grandmother. It was an eviction notice, and because she couldn't read script (she only read print), when she heard the word *police*, she panicked. She didn't question the young man, didn't ask anybody else to read it, and didn't say, "Contact my daughter-in-law." She took it for gospel that it was from the police. Police were feared at that time in Greece. Looking back now, it was a ploy by Pastor Demos to try to kick us out of the church grounds, and it worked. The young man was not dressed in a police uniform; he was obviously hired by Demos to do his dirty, cruel work for him.

My grandmother was crying and in a panic. She asked the young man, "When do we have to get out by?"

"I don't know," he said. "I will ask Pastor Demos."

Demos came back with him and in a stern, cruel, and calculated way said to my grandmother, "Today. The war is over. You can't stay here any longer."

We were all panic-stricken. "But where will we go? We have nowhere to go."

"I don't know, and I don't care. Start packing," he said before he left.

We started. My grandmother put all the clothes in sheets and tied them in bundles. She put other things in pillow slips, and the young man carried them outside the gate and put them against the stone wall surrounding the church.

Pastor Demos went inside as soon as the first bundle was deposited on the pavement. I will never forget that cruel, evil smirk on his face as he walked away. The Duck was nowhere to be seen. Before long, another man came to help with the heavy stuff. The look of sadness and disgust was clearly written on their faces. Even as an eleven-year-old, I couldn't help but notice it. We cried all morning while carrying out our belongings. Grandma was beside herself. Here she was in her old age, with three kids, and in the streets with everything she possessed, little though it was. All the neighbours were out to watch the eviction happen.

With the last article out, the men left, and the gates were shut behind us. Grandma was still crying and squatted on the ground in her peculiar manner. She covered her face with her hand and kept crying. Kostas Laskaris, the man who owned the factory opposite the church and who was watching this happen, walked across, put his arm around Grandma's shoulders, and talked to her softly. I don't know what he said. The next thing we saw was all of Christos's workers outside, carrying our things into the factory. That was an unexpected surprise, a Christ-like, gesture, from a man who professed no Christianity. We couldn't sleep in the factory, but the neighbours came to our rescue again. A lady halfway down the street for whom Grandma did a bit of housecleaning offered to take her and one of the kids in, but they didn't have room for all of us. Her name was Vasiliky. My friend Anoula's mother, Mrs. Aurania, took Eva and me in, trying to comfort us. They too were refugees living in one room with their four children (three sons and one daughter). I had cried so much and so long that I ended up with a thumping headache, the first one in my life. I was scared beyond words and thought I was going to die. Mrs. Aurania got me to lie down, and with a mother's love she tried to reassure me that I would be OK. She said, "Don't be scared. It will go away soon." She sliced an onion in thick rings, put them on my forehead and temples, put a wet towel over them, and tied them around my head to hold the onions in place, all the while cursing Pastor Demos for his cruelty and sniggering at his professed Christianity.

The headache went away, and I stopped crying, but the tears still poured down my face because of the onions. I wondered which was worse, the headache or the onions. I don't know what cured the headache: the onions, the kindness and reassurance given to me by someone who cared, or the fact that I had stopped crying and felt safe with someone I knew. I dare say they all played a part. With the headache gone, I slept till the next day.

Grandma sent a message to my mother. We slept with Annoula for two nights before my mother came down. There were two beds in their room, which were placed end to end, and a little divan where Annoula slept. The parents slept on one, and all the boys slept together on the other double bed. When we were taken in, Annoula slept with her brothers, and Eva and I slept on the divan head to foot. Mrs. Aurania gave us breakfast, and we went to see how Grandma and Ellie were doing. They were well and had stopped crying too. We decided to go back to Mrs. Aurania's to play with the kids because that was home for us now. We had to go past the church, which was between Vasiliky and Mrs. Aurania's room.

The Duck saw us through the window, and she called us. We went upstairs. She was the sweetest I had ever seen her in the three years we'd lived in the church. She asked us if we were hungry because it was nearly lunchtime, and without waiting for an answer, she sat us at the table. She dished out a cold eggplant dish, obviously a leftover, saying all the time not to worry; we'd be OK, and God would look after us. Pastor Demos said nothing and just looked on. We ate that cold meal not because we were hungry but because we had to. As kids, we didn't know we could tell them to go to hell, which I felt like saying. We left as soon as we finished the meal. Before we left, Demos gave us a copy of the New Testament. Neither Eva nor I said a word to them. That same day, Grandma came to say that she was going to stay with Aunt Katerina, taking Ellie with her. We stayed at Mrs. Aurania's again.

My mother came to Thessaloniki late the second day, and of course she didn't know where to find us. The sensible thing to do was to ask Pastor Demos, "Where did you dispose of my family?" He told her where we were. My grandma and Ellie had returned from her sister's and were staying around Vasiliky's place, so Mum went there first, yelling and shouting abuses at Demos and his wife, whom she referred to as your Duck, all the way there and back with Grandma and Ellie to collect us. She was still shouting, and she didn't have to come to the door—we could hear her and went out to meet her. She was telling him he was not God's minister, he was the devil's representative and the personification of evil. With that thrown at him, he opened the window upstairs and said to her "if don't shut up, I'll go to the police and tell them that your husband is a communist and fighting with the opposition."

"You can go to hell!" she retorted, still yelling. "Everybody knows my husband was with the opposition. I don't care."

That night, my mother stayed at Aurania's. She slept on the divan and we children, all six of us, were on the double bed.

The day after my mother came, the third after our eviction, we moved into a one-room accommodation on the opposite side of the church. The room belonged to the driver's brother, Petros, who was living in Athens at that time. Their mother, Lady Eleni, was a lovely lady. She welcomed us, unlocked the room, and gave Mother and Grandma a broom and other cleaning equipment. She and the rest of the neighbourhood had witnessed the eviction and was glad to help us.

The room was built with mud bricks, and it had a ceiling and a tin roof. It was smaller than the shed but big enough to fit everything we owned. My mother bought some used furniture; a double bed, a divan, a small table, and a cupboard. Against the back wall, they put the double bed. At the end of the bed and under the window, they put the divan. Opposite the bed, they put a small linen cupboard and the table, on which they put the one-burner kerosene cooker, which we had to pump up before we could light, and we had to pump it periodically to keep it going. It was a very dangerous invention; many people were burned to death from the burner exploding and engulfing them in flames.

We thought it was the ultimate in luxury. I don't know what my poor grandmother thought of it all, but she never complained. "It's all in the hands of God," she would say. The large trunk with wheat in it stayed at the factory till it was empty. Everything else, which was precious little (cooking utensils and clothes), went to the new accommodation. My mother stayed with us that day. The next day, she returned to work by bus. We kids were happy. We were familiar with the area, our friends were nearby, Lady Eleni was good to us, and there was no Demos to upset our grandmother.

One day while Grandma was putting things in order, she found the New Testament Pastor Demos had given us. She put it aside. We didn't touch it again, till one day Annoula came to our place and saw it. She asked me where it came from, and I told her. "Oh, no, not from that evil man," she said. She picked it up and started throwing it up and down like a ball. We joined in, played and laughed, and made fun of his religion that mocked God. I loved books and would have normally treasured it not because it was part of the Bible but simply because it was a book. When Annoula mentioned "that evil man," that copy of the book became a reminder of cruelty and hypocrisy, and I didn't want to touch it ever again.

When school holidays were over, we enrolled in the same school shift again, but it wasn't long before the school found out (how I don't know, I suspect from Pr Demos) about the change of our address, and that meant we were now under a different catchment area and had to change school shifts. We had to go to school on the opposite shift with different kids, different teachers, different stages of the curriculum, and different classrooms—a complete upheaval once again. I missed going to school with Stephanos. Worse still, some of the nasty teachers, including Gounas and Eva's teacher, were still there. We had no choice. Ellie started kindergarten at the new school, and we soon made friends. A lot of faces were familiar, as we'd cross paths when one group of kids was going as the other group was leaving. The kids in the new school were mostly refugees whose education was interrupted, and they were much the same age as I was. That made me feel that I belonged there. We soon caught up with the rest of the students and did well. I was now twelve years old and still in grade four, whereas Stephanos was in grade six. I still saw him a fair bit and borrowed books from him. We still played together, and I loved him very much.

Grandma kept doing a bit of cleaning for four families and saved the money "for a few things and a cow when we go back to the village after the war." During the year, there was a teachers' strike (one of many), and we were off school. Grandma had to go to work for a couple of hours. It was the middle of winter. Before she left, she lit the coal brazier. When the coal was nearly burned, she brought it inside. I heard her say, "Leave the door open till all the coal is red-hot," and left. I went back to sleep. Eva and Ellie were cold and closed the door. The carbon monoxide produced by the half-burned coal was trapped in the small room. As it is heavier than oxygen it affected me sleeping on the floor, whereas they were sitting up on the divan playing.

While being poisoned, I had a dream. I was back in Peria, going for a walk in my favourite places. There was a heavy cover of snow everywhere, and as I was walking along the creek, I slipped and fell in it. I hated that creek, the one with the water snake in it. I shivered from the cold water. I desperately tried to get out, but there was nothing for me to pull myself up. I threshed about in the creek, getting up and slipping down again. Then I saw what I thought were tree roots. I got hold of them and tried to pull myself up when I realised they were black snakes! While I was having that nightmare and was dying of carbon monoxide poisoning, Eva and Ellie were watching me thrash about, get up, and fall down. They thought I was clowning about, and they laughed. When I fell down for the last time, my mouth and my nose full of froth and mucus discharge, Ellie, just seven years old, realised I was sick and started shouting for help.

The next thing I knew, I was outside, with the whole neighbourhood around me. I was still thrashing about while they were trying to pour black coffee down my throat. I was calling for my friend Annoula, whose mother was also there. I regained consciousness, but I felt pretty dopey for a while. All the people around me looked very worried. My grandmother came back soon after I regained consciousness, and the neighbours told her what had happened. Poor Grandma felt terrible. "I told them not to close the door. I was only going to be away for a couple of hours," she kept saying. She must have felt bad, guilty, and scared all at once. My mother heard of the incident through Nick, the driver. She was worried, and even though she had no leave, she told the bosses what had happened and that she was going whether they agreed to it or not. She came with Nick on his next delivery trip and the following one. I heard my mother reprimand poor Grandma, saying she should be staying home, looking after the kids. Very apologetically, Grandma told her what she had told the neighbours, adding, "Any money I get, I save to get us some cattle when we return to the village." My mother was with us for one day and one night, and she went back to work the following day early in the morning.

Chapter 29

My Father Back Home

All the research into my father's political activities was completed. He was released from prison soon after we were thrown out of the church. He too was angry at the treatment we'd received at the hands of "the man of God," and he threatened to do all sorts of things to him. "I want to kill him." Nothing ever happened, not even as much as Father telling off Demos. He completely ignored "the bastard," as he referred to him. The other thing that pained him was the state of our accommodation: just one small, crowded room. He couldn't get used to it, but he had no other option.

We were now a complete and "happy" family, for a while. Mother resigned and did some cleaning in Thessaloniki. Father and Grandmother were ecstatic. I hoped it would last forever. It was such a good feeling, thinking your parents loved each other and were at peace together. But a deep-seated fear marred my happiness even then.

My father told us some of the war horror stories and how they'd survived. Even now, I wish I had never heard some of them. They would hide in hollow trees or climb on them while the army was running after them. Later on, when the army realised what was happening because the guerrillas would attack from behind, they would machine gun any hollow trees, killing anybody inside them. My mother and grandmother would sigh in pain and would say, "Brother killing brother."

He told us how a woman soldier had her baby after a big battle, but the four-month-old baby wouldn't stop screaming no matter what the mother did. The army was pretty close, and if they heard the baby cry and found them, they would kill them all. They had no choice but to silence the baby somehow. He fell silent, gulped, lowered his head, hid his face in his hands, and said no more. My mother and grandmother wanted to know how they'd silenced the baby. After some hesitation and with pain in his voice, he said, "Someone took the baby from his mother's arms, went outside, and hit it on the head with the butt of the gun." My mother and grandmother gasped in horror. It was not the answer they'd expected. My heart missed a beat as he continued. "It was either the baby's life or all eighteen of us." He never looked up while he was telling this story. The pain was too much for him; he was ashamed of the whole thing.

My mother asked him about my cousin John. "We heard he was killed, but we don't believe it. Have you heard anything about him?"

He looked up at her, lowered his head, and almost hid his face in his hands. He sadly said, "Yes, I saw his body. He was killed." My mother looked at him in disbelief. I didn't want to believe it either. I loved John more than anybody else in my family.

None of us, not even his own mother, ever grieved for John properly. It is a horrible feeling to lose someone you love and be unable to grieve for him. There is no body to weep over, to see him buried and to put a closure to the tragic event. It is a horrible feeling of deep guilt which you cannot get rid of, a feeling of pain and shame mingled with hope. You feel as if you are emotionally crippled, inhuman. How could I know that John was dead and not want to cry? It was not normal. I only know that I can't cry and I feel bad about it. I haven't seen his body, and therefore I can't believe he is dead. I still think he might turn up from somewhere, sometime, and surprise us. They say hope never dies. I can understand how people whose loved ones disappeared feel. It's a hopeless and hopeful situation. It's one where you suspect the truth but refuse to accept it, and you live with an improbable hope. It is an unfinished business.

I can still see his freckly face and soft brown eyes. I don't remember his hair, whether it was brown or black, just that it was bushy and fell around his youthful face in an unruly manner. He was only nineteen when he was killed. Neither my father nor grandmother had time for my mother's family, but they both loved John. "He is different," they'd say. "He is just like his father: honest, loving, unselfish, and hardworking." John was all that and more. He loved people, and people loved him. Why must the best ones go first? I don't know, but then again, heaven has no favourites (the title of a book I read).

My father also told us how they would write songs and put them to music when there was a lull in the fighting. He sang some of them but very softly because they were political songs, and he was scared of being heard. That was the first and last time, I heard my father sing. He had a sweet tenor voice, which none of us inherited. All three of us had plenty of volume but no tune, just like our mother.

He told us how one night, they raided a nearby village's gardens for food. They only found turnips. They went in the house, and he saw a gold necklace on the table. He took it and put it in his pocket, saving it for me being the oldest. He said he felt bad about doing such a terrible, mean thing, and later on while swimming through a river trying to save their lives, he lost it. He said he was glad to rid himself of it; he recriminated himself many times, saying to himself, "Such an injustice, such a crime is beneath me. Why did I do it? That necklace might have had more than monetary value for those people, and I took it." He never forgave himself for it, and he hoped it would be forever buried in the depths of that river together with his wrongdoing.

My father got a job in a brick-making factory in Thessaloniki. For the first time in my life, I felt secure. We were happy, but the happiness didn't last long. My parents started bickering, a bit at first and viciously later. Arguments seemed to start over nothing and blew out of proportion. Worse still, they could start anywhere and at any time, and it was not unusual for them to fight in the middle of the night. My father had a habit of drinking water at night. Instead of getting it himself, he'd wake my mother up, to get it for him which infuriated her. One night she told him angrily, "I worked all day, and you woke me up to get you water? Get it yourself—and bring me some too. Don't you ever again wake me up to bring you water." A dreadful argument started.

Another time, we were returning home having been to the city. They were discussing the merits of city versus country living. They didn't agree, and a loud argument started in the middle of city on a busy road. The next thing I knew, Father left us, crossed the road, and walked all the way home on the opposite side. All the while, they threw insults and dirty looks at each other. I realised then that they wouldn't last long together.

We had a few days' reprieve because they wouldn't talk to each other. I didn't know which was worse, the arguments or not talking. I decided arguing was preferable to cold war.

He worked at the brick factory for about six months and hated every minute. While there, he got a spur in his heel, and he couldn't walk. He was in agony and groaned with pain. My mother took him to the hospital on the bus. It was lanced, and he returned home by the bus. He hobbled around for a while. When he got better, he decided to give up his factory work and go back to the village. They decided Grandma would also go with him and take seven-year-old Ellie. As soon as he could walk well, they packed up and returned to the village. It wasn't long before Eva wanted to go to the village too, but I refused to go and stayed with my mother in the city.

Some months later, Aunt Soula visited us for a few days and brought some fresh farm produce as usual. The two sisters sat down talking, and Aunt Soula told my mother all about my sisters and the village news. I started to talk about them, but I couldn't say anything because I was choking with tears. This was the first time we had been separated, and even though we fought, I missed them terribly.

It was still summer, and I had just finished grade four. I was thirteen years old and without my sisters. My mother kept doing housework. The money was pittance and the work was hard, but she had no choice. To give me something to do and keep me out of mischief, she talked to a young dressmaker across the road, who took me in as an apprentice till school started. I hated sitting down all day, pulling treads out of dresses, or putting them in. It was boring, monotonous, not challenging, and not stimulating. I had no choice but to stay and do as I was told. I got nothing out of it but constipation. I was so glad when school started again.

With school holidays over, I started grade five. The farmers my mother had worked for sent her a message with Nick, asking her to work for them again. The money was better than housecleaning, but that meant that I would be on my own in the city. Nick's mother offered to keep an eye on me. I was mature and responsible for my age, and our room was adjacent to hers, with just a wall between us. My mother trusted her, and I liked her. I addressed her as Lady Eleni. She was in her sixties with four grown-up, good-looking children and many grandchildren. One of her daughters, Erasmia, was in her forties, stunningly beautiful, and single. She worked as a nurse at the army hospital.

Lady Eleni was a gentle, loving lady and was good to me. She was born in Egypt, had lived all her early adult life there, and spoke perfect Arabic. Occasionally I'd ask her to speak in Arabic to me; the sound of languages fascinated me. She would, and when I'd ask her what she said, she'd say, "I counted to ten." Then she'd start again slowly: "Araf, one," she would say, and so on. I loved that old lady. She was wonderful.

There was an air of sadness about her, and she would often come out of her room crying, tears still rolling down her face. Nick, the driver, got married and had moved out by now. One day I asked her with all the innocence and inexperience of a thirteen-year-old why she was crying. She went on to tell me her story. When she came to Greece with her family, she lost her husband during the typhus epidemic, which devastated her. "We did everything together. We were never apart. He was my best friend, my support, and everything I had, loved, and wanted in this world. He was taken away from me suddenly and quickly!" She stopped to wipe tears from her eyes and continued with much pain. "But that wasn't all. Antonius, in his dying breath, told me not to cry for him. Holding two fingers up, he whispered, 'There will be two.' I asked him, Will it be me? He shook his head. He died without telling me who would be next to die. Exactly twenty days later, my seventeen-year-old daughter Maritsa contracted typhus, and she died too. How did he know?"

Maritsa was her youngest child. She had a very beautiful singing voice, and every time Lady Eleni heard the songs Maritsa had sung, she'd go in her room and weep for her daughter and husband. She found consolation in alcohol. She'd occasionally talk about her two sons in Athens: Petros, in whose room we lived, and her eldest son, Antonius.

The school year finished quickly, and I thoroughly enjoyed it. I was now fourteen and had finished grade five.

The next time Nick came to the city with his deliveries, he visited his mother. He asked me if I wanted to go to the farm for the holidays. I was excited. My last holidays there, I'd had a great time—except for the dogs, of course. "Good. We are leaving tomorrow morning early. Go pack up." I put my few clothes in a box and was ready in ten minutes.

Chapter 30

Mother's New Workplace

As usual, Mother had no help. I helped her. I was up at the crack of dawn, but she'd be up before me, and we wouldn't go to bed till midnight. Carrying the water was mostly my job. She'd wake me up and send me to get water from the power-operated pump. I'd be so tired that I'd go to sleep on the grass while waiting for the buckets to fill. She'd come and wake me up. She always woke me up gently and never scolded me for sleeping while she waited for the water. The other jobs I had was to make coffee for the bosses and the two supervisors, and go to the "good pump" with Herring to pump water to wash his none-too-pretty face. Once I was fully awake, there was no stopping for either of us till after dinner, which the Greeks don't take till 10:00 p.m. By the time we cleaned up, it would be 11:00. I was then allowed to go up to the fourth floor for an hour or so to read and to relax. Sometimes during the day, I'd hide a book or magazine in my pockets and read in the toilet.

One day, the youngest boss asked me to take his coffee to his opulent office. They went there with visitors to show it off. I took his coffee to him, and he gave me a very friendly smile. Politely asked me to look in the cupboard for some sweets, which were Herring's. The older Vayia and I would go now and then and help ourselves without his permission, so I knew exactly where to look and what kinds of sweets there were. I was surprised that the sweets were not there, and I started rummaging in the cupboard, thinking Vayia had hidden them somewhere. He got up and came to the cupboard, looking for the sweets and all the time making small talk. "Hope we find some. There were some nice ones here yesterday." He put his arm around me. My grandmother's words, "Don't let any man touch you," reverberated in my brain once again. I pulled away, gave him an angry look, and ran downstairs. He never tried that trick again or any other. I was fourteen, and he was twenty-six and in a position to abuse and exploit anyone he fancied, and get away with it. I didn't tell Mother.

This was one kind of abuse I and others suffered at the hands of rich employers. The other was verbal and emotional abuse. It occurred every time I went with Herring to the "good" pump in order to wash his flat, ugly face. If I weren't pumping fast enough, the flow would stop, and he'd have to wait till I started the pump again, which took a good while. Waiting irritated him, but the arrogant, narcissistic bastard would not start the pump himself, which would have been much quicker given he had more strength. Instead, he would stand there cursing and swearing while I tried to start that bloody pump. He'd call me anything that came to his idiotic brain, such as lazy, stupid, ignorant bitch, brainless creature, and dump sheep. The one I hated most was stupid calf, which implied that not only I was stupid and ignorant, but I was also completely mindless and brainless. All along, I was trying to bring the water up from the well. I wanted to scream at him, "If anyone is a calf, that is you, not me," but I knew my place and didn't dare endanger my mother's job—and being belted before being sent back to Thessaloniki.

It was in that place, seeing my mother work her butt off, that I learned to appreciate and love her more than ever before. She took a lot of verbal abuse from Herring but not from the others; the rest appreciated and valued her both as a person and as an employee.

At the end of summer, my mother and I went back to the city. Mum had a few days after three months of hard work. I would soon start school in year six.

We went by bus. I was sitting by the window with my elbow sticking out. A truck full of hay went to overtake the bus. I don't know what possessed me, but I put my arm out to get some straw. Fortunately,

I couldn't quite reach it, but the force of the wind current forcefully pushed my arm backwards. My mother was dumbfounded and the bus driver was angry. Another inch, and I would have been without an arm for life. The Lord was good to me again. I will praise Him day and night not for that incident alone, but also for the myriad of blessings right through my life. My faith in God never wavered even though my religious experience had its ups and downs.

Back to school. I studied hard, and to the very last day I hoped I would have a chance of going to high school. My mother said she couldn't afford it, adding that I would be over twenty years old before finishing high school. That made me feel embarrassed; most girls were married by that age. I well remember the last test we had to do before finishing grade six. It was an essay titled "What I'd Like to Do When I Finish School." I wanted to cry. I wanted to go on, finish high school, do medicine. I would have settled for teaching or nursing, but I didn't see the point in writing all that. Instead, I wrote a short essay of how I'd be a dressmaker and spend my day sitting at front of my sewing machine, enjoying the sound of the treadle." What a big lie! I finished my primary education and started my dressmaking apprenticeship in July the same year, not far from where we lived.

The following winter, my cousin Magda's husband came to Thessaloniki from another town looking for work; he was a carpenter and bricklayer. He stayed with me in the same room. He slept on the double bed, and I was on the divan. It wasn't long before Magda came down with baby Yiotis, who was just starting to walk. It was the second time I saw him; he was a beautiful baby with green eyes and curly blond hair. I loved him. Not long after that, my aunt came to Thessaloniki to see her daughter and grandson, bringing Eva and Ellie with her to see our mother, who also came down on days off. Aunt Soula brought two big baskets full of garden and farm produce.

It was seven of us and the baby in a small room again. The married couple and the baby slept on the double bed, my aunt (in her late fifties) was on the divan, my mother and the two girls were on the floor, and I was with the married couple and their baby, head to foot, four in a bed. That was OK because we had put up with a lot worse than that during the war. One night when everybody was asleep, I felt a foot coming close to me. I thought he was stretching in his sleep. The foot kept creeping onto my bosom. I couldn't decide whether he was asleep or awake. When I realised that the bastard was awake and what he was trying to do I gave him a kick and pinched his foot as hard as I could. In the morning, I kept giving him angry glances. I had to sleep with them for another week after that, but he never dared set foot near me. I never told anybody, especially Aunt Soula, who disliked him intensely and would love to have something to throw at him.

My mother went back to work, gave notice, and returned to the city before my aunt returned to the village. Ellie and Eva stayed in the city. Magda and her husband stayed with us; he was still unemployed. My mother did cleaning and washing and earned very little, but we shared what we had. Mother never complained. She was an eternal optimist, was generous to a fault, and loved Magda. Any eggs or milk went to her. We often thought she came first. Later, I realised Mother was worried about Magda's health. As soon as the weather warmed up, Magda and her family went to live at his mother's house, a few kilometres from us. They struggled financially. They went back to the mine, where he worked as a carpenter and bricklayer.

Mum and we three girls now had a whole room to ourselves. I thought it was a luxury. Stephanos's father, who was a supervisor at a tobacco factory, found work for Mother there. It was seasonal, started in June, and went for four months only, but the money was better. When it closed, she worked as a housekeeper for a German tobacco merchant's family. The money wasn't as good, but it was regular. My mother's health had been good since early in the war, when she'd had pleurisy and nearly died. We never heard her complain again.

One day, Ellie came to my work. I was at the end of my apprenticeship. She asked me to go home. "Mum is sick," she said. I went home to find Mum in bed looking sick and worried. She had passed blood in her urine—a bucketful, it seemed. The doctor was still there, and his face was sombre. He said nothing and just looked at me sadly. I was only sixteen and didn't think to ask. I didn't know what questions to ask. I was concerned, but I didn't realise the gravity of her condition. The doctor and I left and walked for a short distance together in silence. He headed to his business, and I went back to dressmaking. I was sure she'd be better soon. She got over it in a few days and went back to work—no special diet, no treatment, no medication of any kind, and no rest either.

****

Just after my mother got over her illness, my cousin Kostas came to Thessaloniki. He stayed with us in our small room. The civil war was over, and he was a free man and much respected in the communist circles. His release and his name was splattered over the front page of the communist newspaper. Pastor Demos offered him a job during the church renovations, but Kostas declined, preferring to work in the building industry as a labourer. Aunt Soula came from the village to see him because she hadn't seen him since he'd been taken back to exile three years earlier.

He was now thirty-nine, free, and eligible. He had many proposals for marriage. Amongst them were well-educated girls with responsible positions. One of them would visit us, and she would read and interpret the English Bible Marah had given me a couple of years earlier. This girl offered to teach me English and said, "In no time, you will be reading Shakespeare." I had no clue who Shakespeare was, but I hoped they'd get married and that she would teach me. I was disappointed when it fizzled out, but Kostas didn't seem to mind. Aunt Soula, who was the matchmaker, and my mother went over three girls (in his absence), rejecting each one for various reasons.

Eventually they settled for a girl from the village. She was thirty-five, a good dressmaker, and a hard worker. Aunt Soula figured out she'd have a few Kokorakia, and therefore she was a good catch. She was of the same political persuasion, an extra bonus. The proposal was put to Kostas, and he accepted. Aunt Soula went back to the village and spoke to the girl, whose name was Marina. She accepted, and they were soon engaged. Kostas stayed with us, working while they were engaged.

He eyed me in a way that made feel uncomfortable and angry. I felt like shouting at him, "Take your eyes off me." He was smart enough to avert his gaze when he realised I was aware of his stares. One hot summer's day, my mother was at work. He was lying on his bed, and because Mum wasn't there, I was lying down on the divan, nearly asleep. I became aware of him being restless in his bed and making noises I hadn't heard since Panos, when I was eleven. I turned around to see what was wrong with him, and to my horror, there he was red as a beetroot, his hands under the sheet fondling himself, looking at me lustily and without any shame. I got up, looked him straight in the eye, and said, "If you ever do that again in my presence, I will tell my mother." Not that she would believe me had he denied it; Kostas could do no wrong in her eyes. After that, he ignored me. Years later, both Eva and Ellie said that he'd exposed himself to them as well; Ellie was seven years old, and Eva ten.

My mother's dream was to own a house, no matter how small or humble. She saved every cent she could. Things improved. Mum was working, Eva at fifteen worked in a weaving factory, and Ellie at thirteen started work at a food factory; they had falsely increased her age by two years, which the village secretary was happy to do. I was still doing my dressmaking apprenticeship, which I hated and wanted to give up. I would have preferred to work in the factory too, but my mother said, "Keep going, learn it. Because you can read and speak French, you can go to France and come back a fully qualified dressmaker. Perhaps you'll start a small business which you can manage, and others can do the sewing for you." That appealed to me. I didn't think about how I would get to France, where I'd live, and the rest. In eighteen months, I finished my three-year apprenticeship. Despina didn't exploit me. She taught me all I had to learn, as soon as I could learn it. I finished my apprenticeship and started working for myself. There was enough work to keep me busy, but most people didn't pay, and I refused to sew anymore. I told my mother if I were going to starve, I'd rather do it sleeping than sewing.

Eight years went by since we'd left the village, and even though both Eva and Ellie went back, I hadn't. Aunt Soula visited again, and she suggested I go back with her. I had missed my grandmother and wanted to see her, but I didn't care about the village; city life suited me fine. While my aunt was with us, she gossiped about the villagers. I didn't know them and didn't care. Then she started talking about my father and his misdemeanours. She charged me with the responsibility of telling my grandmother about my "father stealing the flour from the mill," but she didn't say when or how. I was surprised because I always thought of him as an honest and upright man. I looked to my mother for verification or otherwise. She said nothing and kept knitting, half nodding to please her sister.

My aunt was hell-bent in poisoning me against my father and grandmother. My mother never defended either of them; she never stood up to her sister even when she knew her to be wrong or untruthful. My aunt kept running my grandma and father down and all the time, watching my reaction to her stories. I listened but said nothing.

One day she said that my grandmother, in her mid-seventies now, was threshing beans, and a bean had hit her in the eye. My heart sunk within me, and I wanted to cry. I was thinking of my poor grandmother working hard in her old age. I became aware my aunt was staring at me and waiting for a reaction. I knew what the old crow wanted to hear, and with as much pretence as I could muster, I said, "I don't care." My mother looked up, surprised. Another time, my aunt said that my father was kicked on the hip by the horse he was breaking in, and he limped for weeks. It hurt and upset me again because I felt for my father. That wicked woman waited for my reaction again. I told her what she wanted to hear: "Serves him right. He should know better. That end kicks, and the other bites." She laughed heartily.

She always found fault with me. Either I didn't wash the dishes properly, didn't dry them well, ate the visitors' leftover sweets, was a smarty, or was rude. Eva could do no wrong. I had too many faults, and she never missed an opportunity to criticise and belittle me, but I loved her anyway, admitting to myself I was a very naughty child and a difficult teenager.

Time came for my aunt to return to the village, and I went with her. I stayed with my grandmother and father, but I visited her practically every day just for something to do. By the time I'd get up and walk the nearly five kilometres to Peria, it would be nearly lunchtime. Instead of getting some lunch for us, the old crow would say, "Wait for a while. When it's nearer lunch, we'll go visit so-and-so today. They'll have to give us some lunch too."

I was ashamed, but I didn't have the courage to say, "Aunt, that's not nice." After a couple of times of this, I made sure I went to see her after lunch, and eventually I stopped going every day.

What my aunt said about my father stealing the flour played in my mind. I decided to find out for myself. One day my father told me to go to the farm with Grandma while he went to Peria. "Not unless you come too," I said. We had an argument, He went to Peria and left Grandma and me to go to the field while he did unimportant things. I was fuming and blind with anger. Grandma went to the field on her own. She worked all day and came home just before sunset. She cooked a meal, we ate, and we waited for Father to return from the cafenio. I was still angry with my father and said to my grandmother, "Not only is he lazy, he is also a thief."

My granny was astounded and couldn't believe her ears. She was sitting on the floor, unravelling loops of wool, making them into balls ready to start knitting for winter. She looked at me, tears rolling down her rosy cheeks, and said, "It's not true." Then she pled with me to not upset her. "I've had enough upsets in my life. I don't need you to add to them."

I felt terrible. I felt mean and nasty for doing that to my saintly grandmother, who I'd never heard speak evil of anyone, including nasty Aunt Soula. I regretted the whole incident and wished it had never happened. I felt angry at my aunt, who'd deliberately lied and twisted things to get me to upset my much-loved granny. I wonder what pleasure she got out of it all. I also held my mother guilty for not correcting her lying sister, who manipulated and controlled her all her life.

The story of the stolen flour, according to Grandma and other villagers, goes as follows. My father took grain to the mill to be ground. When he went to pick it up, the miller was busy. They shouted at each other over the racket of the grinding mill stones, and the miller shouted, "Your flour is by the door." My father loaded the bags on the bullock cart and went home, not realising it was not his. No harm done; others had made the same mistake before. The flour was exchanged, but the guy whose flour my father took jokingly said, "Alexis stole my flour," knowing full well that nobody would take him seriously. It was then that I lost all respect for Aunt Soula and didn't want to have anything to do with her. She simply liked creating sensation by telling tall stories.

I had good times and bad times at the village. I argued with my father, who would ask me to go to the field with my grandmother while he went to the cafenio. Grandma would go on her own as she always did. She would work all day in the field, and only God knew how hard she worked. What pain she suffered, both physical and psychological, all without complaining. My grandmother said one day, "Don't feel bad. I've been going to the field alone for a long time. Your help wouldn't make much difference." Temporarily I felt good because at least grandma wasn't angry with me, but after a while I felt very sorry for her and was even angrier at my father.

Chapter 31

A Painful Memory of a Photo

One day I went to Ardea with Noppy, the girl we collected lilies with before the civil war. She went to the dentist, and afterwards we had a look around town. We stopped at a photographer's studio, looking at the display. The photographer came out and invited us in, trying to persuade us to dress up as gypsies to photograph us for free. Noppy declined. He turned to me and asked sweetly. Reluctantly, I agreed. After all, he said it would be free. I got dressed, put on a scarf, lipstick, and had cards in hand. He took some photos, adding, "They'll be ready next week." We walked home. The weather was lovely, and as girls can talk, time passed quickly.

There were parties and dancing in the village. I wasn't much good at modern European dancing, but the boys still asked me to dance. At night was corn husking or thrashing. There was singing, stories, jokes, and mimicking. There was a young man there, Lambos, who was very funny and a good impersonator. He would take on my dead grandfather so well that I couldn't help laughing. By rights, I should be dying with embarrassment or disappearing with shame at Grandpa's disgraceful conduct, but he looked so funny.

The week went by quickly. Noppy and I returned to town to pick up my "free" photograph. At the shop, I looked in the window, and lo and behold, there I was in all my glory, beautifully framed and in colour!

I was scared. What if my father saw it? He'd belt me half to death! First of all, only prostitutes wore lipstick as far as he was concerned. Second, only cheap women were photographed like this and displayed for everyone to see. I couldn't take that photo out of the window quickly enough. I went into the studio and asked him to give me the photo. He looked at me and said, "That's mine, and it's for display." He gave me a small black-and-white one, the free one. He'd enlarged and hand-painted the one in the window.

I nearly cried. "You can't display it!" I said. "My father will kill me, and you too. You must give it to me."

"OK, that will be one hundred drachmas," he said.

I nearly fainted. This was an exorbitant amount of money—it was a week's wages for an adult. Where would I find that amount of money? I felt upset, angry, tricked, and betrayed all at once, and I didn't know what to do. I had no one to turn to. My aunt was out of the question; she'd take much pleasure in telling me I'd acted like a slut. My father would be angry. I could talk to my grandmother, but where would she find that much money? I felt so bad that I wished I was dead.

Noppy stood there very quiet; she must have sensed the turmoil I was in. We walked back to the village almost in silence. We parted, having found no solution to the problem. I said nothing to my grandmother and suffered for two days.

On the third day I walked to the room upstairs, and at front of the pile of rolled and folded bedding, I saw some money on the floor. I knew immediately it was Grandma's; she always put it amongst the linen, whereas my father kept his on him. It must have fallen out of the folded quilts as she was putting it back or while taking some out. My first reaction was to give it to her. Then the thought of the photograph came to my mind. I was in a terrible bind. I wished I had never put myself in that situation.

I agonised between giving the money back to Grandma and keeping it to get that bloody photograph. I stood there motionless, crying inwardly while trying to decide what to do. Fear overcame honesty. I decided to keep the money and get the photo. The very next day, I went on my own, picked it up, and hid it somewhere out of sight. I justified my action to myself, saying, "I found the money I did not steal it." I lived to regret it. To this day, over sixty years later, I can still see my grandmother rummaging through the linen looking for that money. I wish I could have the chance to throw my arms around her, confess my wrongdoing, and tell her how much I loved and respected her and what a wonderful person she was. I wish I had just three minutes with my beloved grandmother to tell her the truth and ask for forgiveness.

A few days later, she found the photograph and commented how nice it was. She asked where it was taken, but she didn't ask how much it cost or where I'd gotten the money from to pay for it. She didn't have to—she knew, and to the day she died, she never mentioned the money she had lost. Years later while talking with Ellie about it, she said, "Grandma knew who took that money, but she didn't want to upset you, so she said nothing to you." I felt like crying then, and I'm crying now.

She never accused me for taking that money, and only she and God knew just how long it took her to save that amount again by using her deft little hands to crochet curtains for others, sell eggs from her chickens, and vegetables from her garden for a bit of cash. I hate the photo with an undying passion; it brings back the pain I caused my loving, forgiving grandmother.

I was still in the village on August 15, 1955, the big religious holy day. My grandmother bought me a piece of material, floral on an apple green background, to make myself a dress to wear to the fair. I liked the material and color, she had good tastes. I made myself the dress and wore it with pride. It was at that fair that I danced the popular Greek dance Zebekico, which impressed the villagers.

Noppy, her cousin Kyriacos (older than me), and I went to the fair. He asked me to dance, and I accepted, but in the crowd and my embarrassment, I lost sight of him. I looked around and saw this young man who looked like Kyriacos, dancing on his own. Thinking it was Kyriacos, I joined him, and we danced. The Zebekico is a dance you can dance with or without a partner. Poor Kyriacos. When I realised what happened, I apologised profusely. He accepted the apology, saying he too danced. He was a perfect gentleman, mature for his age, and good-natured.

My dancing with a stranger caused furore. My cousin Yana's grandmother and mother told my father, who wasn't at the fair, that I did not conduct myself like a lady and shamed the family. They embellished and exaggerated the whole thing. My father waited for me to come back from the dressmaker's place, where I was helping out, to belt me. He was enraged at my disgracing him, as they'd put to him. Noppy's mother saw him angry and asked him what the problem was, though she already knew. When he told her, she calmly told him how it all was, how well we'd danced, and how proud he should be. She pointed out it was their jealousy that prompted them to tell all these lies, and it would please them no end to see me black and blue. She said he should think again. He didn't touch me. In fact, he never asked me about it, and I wasn't aware of what had happened till many years later, when Ellie told me about it.

Chapter 32

Building the Shack

My mother continued with her dream of building a little place for us. She reasoned, "Now that Petros is back in Thessaloniki, sooner or later he'll want his room back." For the moment, he was living with his mother. Petros was a lovable rascal. He drank too much and chased women—or more accurately, they chased him. Often he'd come home with a black eye after a drunken brawl, but he took it all in his stride. He spent his spare time flying his racing pigeons. It was gambling, but I didn't know it. Every Sunday there would be a dozen men aged sixteen to forty-five in the yard racing the pigeons, getting excited, shouting for joy one minute, and cursing the next. Petros sang like an angel, and no matter what I was doing, I'd drop it to listen to him sing. I fell in love with that voice, and I understood what people meant when they said his seventeen-year-old deceased sister Maritsa could sing.

Mother started making plans to build a little one-room "house" for us on common land, which was the usual thing. All the places in that area were built illegally. The man next door, Pantelis, was a handyman, and amongst other things, he built three two-bedroom houses on his land, without permits. He gave himself the title of "builder" but he had no formal qualifications. My mother talked to him, and they laid down their plans. They would build the walls and the roof in his yard, and everything would be cut to size. As soon as it was dark, they would move them over the little creek and assemble them on the land. While some would be putting the Masonite on the walls inside, others would be putting the cane and the mortar on the outside. They hoped that nobody would alert the authorities, or else the builder would be spending a few nights in the cooler. He started on the walls, and Mum went around recruiting the neighbours to help assemble the shack. Everybody was happy to lend a hand. My mother was always happy to help others in any way she could. Pantelis had it all done in three days.

They chose a full moon night to put it up. They would be able to work without lights, not exposing themselves to passers-by. The right night came, and as soon as it was dark enough, the whole neighbourhood were there to help. They carried the prefabricated walls and roof across the dry creek bed and bolted it together. As planned, some worked inside with a kerosene lamp, and others outside. Women, including my sisters and I, were allocated to putting the mortar on the outside while the men put the cane walls on. The dirt floor was covered by the loose boards we had in Petros's room, and it was all done before dawn. They helped us carry our few belongings and then went home. We made the bed and the divan and hopped in, but we were too excited to sleep. You couldn't wipe the smile off my mother's face with anything, not even if you had smeared cat pooh on it. She looked ecstatic! We waited for the police to come and start asking questions, but nobody came. Had the police come, we were advised to say, "It's been here for a long time." (Three months was the minimum; any less, and the council could order us to pull it down). The police were always sympathetic, and as long as they heard the magic "three months," they'd write it down and leave.

We were in our little house, as mother referred to it, when it rained heavily. Our shack proved to be waterproof, but Petros's room, the one we'd moved out of just three days earlier, collapsed. The roof and the mud brick wall caved in. Had we been there, someone was bound to have been hurt badly or killed, because the wall collapsed at night on the side where the bed had been and fell inwards. Everybody in the neighbourhood said that God held the rain back because He knew we had nowhere else to go. It really was a miracle that the place hadn't collapsed before. It too had been built illegally and in a hurry.

There was one disadvantage with the position of our house, as we soon found out. The tin-roofed shack was put at the bottom of the hill about three metres down, from the road above it. It was too much temptation for kids to go past and not throw a stone or two on the roof. It made such a racket that we'd all jump up in unison, and when my mother was there, she'd yell on top of her lungs. I couldn't decide which was worse, their throwing rocks or her yelling and cursing the little blithers (who got double the enjoyment, first the thunderous bang on the roof and then scaring us half to death). She'd run outside, shaking her fist at them, but they'd run away laughing at her, which would infuriate her even more.

She got sick and tired of three brothers throwing stones on the roof, and one day she followed them home. They lived very close to us in a "proper" house. Still fuming, she shouted for their parents to come out. We could hear her yelling at them. The poor people weren't too proud of their sons, with all the epithets she hurled onto them. To make sure they wouldn't do it too often, she threatened to see the school headmaster, who lived just across the road from them, if they did it again. As it turned out, only the youngest one was throwing stones; the other two were good kids.

However, it worked. No more stones on the roof. But the youngest one, a fair little bastard, started throwing stones at our little dog, Azor. One day when Azor was with me while getting water from the public tap, the boy threw a stone which hit him on the eye, bursting it and pouring it on the ground. I was upset beyond description. My stomach still churns with anger as I think of that moment. We nursed Azor back to health. We cleaned the eye socket with the only thing we had, salty water. The poor animal suffered a lot of pain.

Another disadvantage with our new "house" was that we had no toilet as yet. The kitchenette and the toilet were planned for later, and in the meantime we had to go to the back of the shack between the back wall and the hill. There was not much privacy, but if we timed it off peak walking hours and were quick, most of the time we evaded prying eyes. If anybody cared to look down, there was nothing to hide us from their view. And of course, nature's outputs are not always regular. They sometimes depend on input. It was on one of these occasions that I looked up instinctively before I had finished, and lo and behold, a young man was looking down at me peeing. I still feel the embarrassment keenly.

The worst disadvantage was still to be discovered. What neither we nor the builder knew, when we'd chosen the spot, was that there had been a dam there into which went all the waste water from the army hospital, which was above us on the other side of the road. When the site for the shack was extended by digging the side of the hill and spreading the soil, the wall of the dam was weakened. When the three months were up and the council wouldn't bother us, the kitchen and toilet were built there. Kostas brought a second-hand toilet seat. It was blue and cracked, but they were hell-bent on using it. It was sheer madness because there was no running water in the place. They connected the toilet seat onto the pipe and planned to dig a pit later. It was a disaster! Everybody was banned from using it. After they thoroughly cleaned it, that area was used as a pantry—with a blue toilet seat smack in the middle! But the kitchen had a brand-new concrete sink and a dish rack, Turkish style, made by my father's cousin many years ago. It was sheer luxury.

There was another disadvantage about the location. At the bottom of the hill ran a creek which dried in summer. People threw their rubbish in it. In spring during a heavy downpour, or when the snow would start melting on the mountains, it would flood, making access to the shack impossible. It cut us off from our neighbours; We had to go all the way around if we needed to contact them. Fortunately, it didn't affect our access to the bus stop or to the tap. We cleared around the shack, and my mother planted trees not just around the house but all up and down the hill. She had a vision of them growing and shading the old shack, which was as hot as hell in summer and as cold as the grave in winter.

We were in our house for about a year. It was early spring, and I had finished my apprenticeship and was working for a dressmaker not far from us. Hortiats, the mountain in the west, looked dark and menacing. Everybody knew there was going to be a big storm. It poured by the bucket for what seemed hours, the roads flooded, we and couldn't go home. All three of us employees stayed at the dressmaker's place that night, and Eva stayed at the factory where she worked. I wondered how my mother and Ellie fared and how high the creek got to, but there was no way of finding out. When I got home after work the next day, the story I heard horrified me.

Just before the storm came, my mother needed something from the shop and asked Ellie, who was twelve years old, to go get it. Ellie had twisted her ankle the week before and was still limping. She looked outside and, as gently and pleadingly as she could, said, "Mum, it's going to rain. Can I go after the storm? It will also rest my sore foot."

My mother hesitated, and rather than say, "Do as you are told," which would have been her normal reaction, she said, "OK, go later." Two minutes later, the rain started pelting down, and a hissing sound was followed by a torrent of water racing down the dry creek bed. The creek flooded and overflowed to the front door. My mother and Ellie just managed to scramble out of the house and onto higher ground, on the side of the hill where another family had built two rooms on higher ground a few months after us. They hadn't even gone inside the neighbour's house when another gush of water came out of the side of the hill behind the kitchen, throwing mud and lots of other rubbish in the air with a terrible bang. The torrent of water flowed at an angle, just missing the corner of the kitchenette. Had the water come straight, as it should have done, it would have taken the whole kitchen with it. When I looked at the gaping hole where the water had gushed out from, I was amazed that the kitchenette wasn't swept away, but that wouldn't have been the tragedy. The real tragedy would have been that had my mother insisted on Ellie going to the shop, she would have been swept away by the torrent of water and taken out to sea. We would have been lucky to have found her body.

The people who had built a shack just a bit farther up at the same level as us were flooded out too. Water rushed into their room, and they narrowly escaped drowning by climbing on the bed.

For a long time, my mother was in shock as to what could have happened had she insisted on Ellie obeying her word. She kept thanking

God for listening to her inner voice telling her to let the child be. When the place dried out, we went in through the opening the water had made, and we were amazed to find a hole about three metres high by five metres wide by ten metres long. There was no reason why the water had exited at the angle it did. All the neighbours wondered and asked why the water hadn't gone the way it should have gone and taken everything with it. We thanked the Almighty for his mercies and for yet another miracle in our lives. "He orders the waters and the winds and they obey him!" (Mark 4:41).

My mother had another haematuria (blood in the urine) early in the second year we were in our new house. We were young and ignorant of the nature of her illness and the consequences, so we didn't worry too much. We were sure she'd get over it as she had last time, and she did.

After the house was built, Aunt Soula suggested she go to Xanthe, north-west of Greece, to visit their relatives—and that I go with her. There were lots of them there. I had never been to Xanthe before, and that was a good opportunity for me to meet my cousins and second cousins on my mother's side of the family. They made a fuss of me, were glad to meet George Haj George's granddaughter, and weren't offended when I told them I didn't eat pork, which made it very difficult for them. They slaughtered their own, and it was plentiful. I met my first cousin Aria. She was married with two beautiful children: a girl, Yana, about nine with beautiful, big, blue eyes just like Aria's, and a son, Theodore, about six, a handsome boy with dark hair, like his father.

I met my first cousins, including Magdalena's children. Michael was about twenty, and I hadn't met him before. I knew his sister Sophia; she had come to Thessaloniki looking for a job, and she'd found one as a nurse. She stayed with us while working in the city. I met their paternal uncle, who was a shepherd. He had meningitis as a child and was left with a mild intellectual disability. When he was told I was Magdalena's niece, he started weeping uncontrollably, calling out, "Magdalene, Magdalena, the saint!" He went on to tell us how, when Aunt Magdalena was ill and dying from the cholera epidemic, she'd crawled out of her bed to wash his clothes on her knees and hang them around the fireplace so that they would be ready when he went back to the fields to tend the sheep. Then she would crawl back in her bed. He cried for a long time, calling her name saying there wasn't a kinder, more considerate person on this earth than Magdalena. At that time, I didn't realise—or I would have told him just to comfort him—that my sister Ellie, who was the image of Magdalena physically, also had her kind, loving, generous, and unselfish nature. I love Ellie for this.

Magdalena died aged twenty-seven, leaving her two children, Michael (seven) and Sophia (three), at the mercy of their uncaring, weak-minded father. He remarried soon after and brought his new wife into the house. She took over, refused to do anything for her shepherd brother-in-law, and neglected his two children. When their own child was born a girl, she moved Michael and Sophia to the stable. "Not enough room in here," she said. He never said a word to her in their defence, and if it wasn't for the neighbours caring for them, feeding and washing them, the kids would have died of neglect and starvation. Other than this saddening story about my cousins, I had a good time in Xanthe.

Chapter 33

Polly on the Scene

When I was seventeen years old, a family moved just across the road from us. The parents were a fair bit older than my mother. The lady, whose name was Elena, was in her fifties. She was tall and very good-looking. Her husband, Jordan, was in his mid-sixties, though he looked older and sounded very sick with asthma. They had two children, a married son who lived elsewhere and a daughter, Polly, about three years older than me. She was single and lived with her parents. She was a short, square girl with a mop of beautiful red hair, which I envied; it was her crowning glory. She had beautiful brown eyes. she was clean, tidy, and hard-working. My mother idolised her, and many times when she was angry with me for not cleaning and tidying up, she'd say, "Why can't you be like Polly? She is such a wonderful girl." And she was.

Within a few months, our friendship deepened and solidified. I'd confide in her and she in me. We'd talk for hours as young girls do, and I received a lot of information on the facts of life. At sixteen, I knew the basics, which the lady next door explained because my mother wouldn't.

It was Easter 1956. My mother cooked the traditional Easter soup, Magiritsa. We had the Easter meal in the traditional way and the Easter spirit, and as usual there was plenty leftover. Mum always cooked more than needed "just in case someone called in." We went to bed, and because it was Easter Sunday, we girls slept in.

I got up about 11:00 a.m. and went looking for something to eat. My mother suggested I have the usual breakfast, which was a glass of milk and bread. "I don't want milk. I want some of the soup," I said. The fact that I dared disobey infuriated her. Her blue eyes sparked, her face went red, and she ordered me to drink the milk. "No, I don't want it. I am not hungry."

"You will drink the milk," she said in her military tone.

"No, I will not!" I retorted, and I walked out and sat outside.

She followed me with a piece of firewood in her hand, and in full view of all the neighbours, mother has belted me. I didn't move and made no effort to defend myself out of respect. I had made up my mind not to cry. I was not going to humiliate myself even more than being belted at seventeen—and out in the front yard! She had a habit of belting us till we cried, or else the belting was not effective. She belted me till I was black and blue, and all because I wouldn't drink the milk. She wouldn't stop. "Enough!" I screamed. Then I got up and went inside.

The neighbours could see and hear what was going on, and when the storm was over, Polly came across. She looked concerned and didn't ask any questions. "Get dressed. We are going for a walk by the beach. It's Easter today." I was too dazed and too upset to think straight, and I did as I was told. My mother didn't object. We left the house and walked silently towards the beach, a distance of about three kilometres.

We went past a photo studio, and she said, "We are both dressed. Let's go and have our photo taken." I looked very sombre and couldn't bring myself to smile, hard as I tried. She asked for the reason of the beating, she thought it was harsh.

We continued our walk, and as the fresh air hit me, my mind cleared and I collected my thoughts. I said to Polly; "This is the last time my mother has belted me. I will not stand for it anymore." She nodded, saying nothing. The last time she'd belted me worse than this was the previous year for daring suggest I polish the cutlery next time I do the dishes. We used ash to polish them. I had just cut and polished my fingernails with clear polish (red was forbidden for modesty reasons). I thought they looked good for once; I always thought my hands and legs were the ugliest parts of me.

My mother inspected the cutlery and said, "You didn't polish the cutlery."

"No, Mum. I will do them tomorrow."

"No, you will do them now," she said in her usual tone. I pled with her and promised faithfully, but she wouldn't budge. It was the fact that her authority was challenged, and the fear of losing control, that made her wild.

I saw the anger, the determination, and the fury in her eyes, and I too became angry. I felt the helplessness of being controlled, and I resented it. "No," I said with resolute and determination. "I will do them tomorrow." I turned to go.

I didn't get very far. She came after me, grabbed me by the hair, pushed me on a chair just outside where I was doing the dishes by the kitchen window, and with a hunk of wood beat me on the head and shoulders in full view of everybody. I didn't want to cry, but my head would have split. My shoulders were sore. I cried from humiliation more than from pain. When I cried, she was satisfied that she'd done a good job and let me go.

Polly listened without saying a word. Having recounted and recollected this unfair beating as well made me all the more determined not to take anymore.

We walked by the beach for about an hour and returned home. My head was sore and swollen, and my shoulders were sore and bruised again. I went in the kitchen / living room. She was sitting there and greeted me as if nothing had happened. I was still angry and felt humiliated at being treated like an animal. I greeted her back, and as calmly as I could, I said, "This is the last time you have raised your hand against me. If you ever try it again, I will retaliate."

She sniggered, smiled, and looked me straight in the eye as if to say, "Try it if you dare." I said nothing.

A few months down the track, we had another confrontation. Basil and I were running a platonic friendship. I told Mother about it and asked her not to tell anybody, because I wasn't sure about it. One day soon after I told her, she went to visit Magda's mother-in-law, Tammy, and told her about Basil and me. She returned quoting Tammy, who said

"I should end the friendship". I'd confided in her, and she'd betrayed my trust. I questioned her action, which infuriated her. She came to hit me. I put up my hands and told her to stay where she was. I reminded her that I wouldn't stand for it anymore, but to no avail. She grabbed my hands. I gave her a push, which sent her reeling away from me. She fell on the divan, more surprised than hurt.

She was upset, and she cried out of frustration, shouting abuses and telling me what an ungrateful and disrespectful animal I was. "And you claiming to be a Christian!" This hurt me and made me sombre. "Honour your mother and your father, says the law (Exodus 20:12), and you have pushed me over. I will tell Pastor Demos and see what he says!" she howled.

I reminded her, "The same book also says, -Parents do not provoke your children to anger-' (Ephesians 6:4), and you have been treating me like an animal and worse." I left the kitchen.

She didn't talk to me for a week, and I was determined not to talk till she did first. It was hard for me because I forget quickly and don't hold grudges. By the end of the week, she tentatively said something unimportant, just to make conversation. I responded amicably. From then on, we became best friends. We developed a mutual respect for each other and confided in each other. Together, we organised and saved money for the materials to build a small house. We enjoyed an excellent relationship that only a few mothers and daughters enjoy.

Chapter 34

Basil

I met Basil when I was nearly seventeen years old, nearing the end of my dressmaking apprenticeship. In order to go to work, I had to go past the church. One day as I was going to work, I noticed a young man watering the church garden instead of Pastor Demos. I looked at him, he looked at me, we acknowledged each other, and I kept going. I became curious. Who was he? Was he a hired gardener? Where did he come from? Why was he watering the garden which Demos created and cared for tenderly? For a few weeks, we kept greeting each other with a nod or a quick hello. Curiosity overcame me and surpassed my disdain for Pastor Demos and his Duck. There was only one way to find out, and that was to go back to church. I told Despena I wasn't going to work next Saturday, but didn't tell her why.

At church the next morning, I was very surprised that people remembered me even though I hadn't been to church for six years. They were glad to see me.

It wasn't long before I was introduced to this young man, who was from Athens. He was helping Pastor Demos and was preparing to enter the ministry himself. He was four years older than me. He had brown eyes, brown curly hair, fair skin, rosy cheeks, a protruding brow, and rounded shoulders. He was very thin and walked with a forward stoop.

But when he started speaking, all I could see was that beautiful, self-assured personality and a perfect expression of language.

As I got to know him better, I realised he had a brilliant mind. He was articulate, eloquent, and well-versed in the Bible. He was an excellent speaker and an interesting person. I admired his biblical knowledge, his quick wit, and his ready, well-thought answers on any subject in the Bible. Not even Pastor Demos, himself an excellent speaker, could match Basil's knowledge and understanding. I took a liking to him, and we soon became friends. One day he said something to Ellie in French, which she spoke fluently. She told me in Greek that she was teaching him French and English, that he was talking to her about her mother, and that he was practicing just in case I thought he was talking about me. She added that he made a grammatical error. "Yes," I said, "he should have said 'a sa votre mere,' not 'a sa mere.' Ellie was surprised and asked me where I'd learned French. I told her at the French academy, where I'd gone for three years and also told her that I couldn't continue because the fees were too high, and my mother couldn't afford to pay them anymore.

She asked me to join Basil in her class, if I wanted to. I didn't need to be asked twice. The following day, we went to her place by bus at the other side of the city. We had the French lesson first and English afterwards. I used his English books, and during the week I bought my own. I didn't need any French books because I had plenty. I couldn't wait to start using them. I didn't do much in the way of French, not because I didn't want to but because Ellie didn't have the time to teach us both French and English. She asked which language I'd prefer to continue with. I opted for English because I'd wanted to go to Australia since I was twelve years old. At that time, a lot of Greeks were migrating there, and amongst them were two of cousin Magda's brothers-in-law. That was where I hoped to go.

I got to know her father well. He was not a Seventh-day Adventist, and neither was her brother. It was against his will that his wife and daughter were baptised in the Seventh-day Adventist church. He was a very likeable gentleman, a retired army officer with a friendly face and a dignified, imposing look. I liked him a lot. Years later, Ellie said that Basil and I were the only two Seventh-day Adventists to set foot in their house. I felt honoured. Mother Economou was a rare gem, a true Christian. She was humble despite her relatively high station in life. She was loving and caring, the closest I've come to a Christ-like person—other than my grandmother, of course. It is people like them who restore one's faith in religion and make it a living faith.

Many times, we had lunch with them after the lesson. Often Ellie would take us to the restaurant they owned, which was next to their house on top of the hill. Occasionally, the young people of the church would come to our shack, and we'd have a good time talking and joking.

I soon took office in the church, helping Ellie with the children. There were about twenty, and most were about the same age. I enjoyed being with them. My spirituality awoken and was baptised by Demos in the Seventh-day Adventist church in October 1956, much to my mother's pleasure—and my grandmother's pain, in that I denied the Orthodox baptism they'd given me as a three-month-old baby. Now, I am so sorry for the pain I caused her, but I'm not sorry for being baptised. All she said was, "Why did you do it, my girl? Have you forgotten his cruelty?" No, I hadn't forgotten, but he was not Christ; he only pointed me to Christ, and as he said in one of his sermons, "Some people are the scaffolding which helps to complete the building, and it is discarded when the building is finished." *He* was that scaffolding for me, unless of course he saw the error of his ways and changed course.

I became involved with the church and held office in Sabbath school. I was Sabbath school secretary, was asked to take lesson reviews and felt very important, I was all of seventeen. I made friends with the other members, got to know and love the children, and loved being Ellie's assistant.

During the second year I started going to the church, there was a youth camp in Athens. I was asked to go as an assistant. I felt honoured and important and couldn't wait to get there. I made some new clothes for myself, including a white see-through blouse, which was fashionable at that time but which raised a few eyebrows. I wore it anyway. The day arrived for us to leave. We boarded the bus and were on our way. There was Antonia (ten), Desi (eight), and Dinah (five), and their mother, Gena, who had a very strong and tuneful alto voice. The other child was ten-year-old Hanna, a very pretty girl. They could all sing well. We were very happy to be going to Athens, and we had decided to sing all the Sabbath school songs and church hymns as a witness to our faith.

The bus was full. We sat together in the middle of the bus on the left side. My enthusiasm and love for my church and faith surpassed my ability to sing by miles. I sang out of tune with my powerful lungs, throwing everybody off tune. I received a lot of glances and stares, but I interpreted them as admiration—till I saw a few people giggling and Gena leaning over from behind, telling me to drop a few decibels. I still blush with embarrassment. That was the last time I sang other than in a whisper. It wasn't long before we were all carsick and flat out vomiting, especially Hanna. I thought she was going to die before we got to Athens. After a long, bumpy, winding trip, we arrived at our destination. We were picked up by the church minister, an American-born Greek who picked up the Greek language quickly. His American wife couldn't speak a word of Greek at that time. There was another American Greek couple who were sent "to build up the church" in Greece. All they managed to do was to increase the membership by four, and later by their three children, which Nick and his wife Ramonahad. Greece is the hardest place on earth for Protestant churches to work.

We were taken to the church in Athens. We were accommodated at the two American ministers' homes and at the Greek minister's eldest brother's place. We got some rest, and the next day we were at a meeting organising the running of the camp. The children were playing in the front yard of the house with the gate open onto the busy street.

Suddenly we heard brakes screech, children scream, and a terrible commotion outside. After the initial shock, we ran outside to see a truck stopped just past the gate. The driver was holding Dinah in his arms and putting her in the cabin of the truck. Before we knew it, he was off, shouting the name of the hospital he was taking her to. From the kids, we learned that Dinah was chased by another child. She ran on the road and into the side of the oncoming truck. I saw no blood on her or on the road. Given the little I knew of injuries, internal or otherwise, I was hopeful that she would be all right. She was my favourite little girl and a delightful child. One of pastors drove the mother and me to the hospital. The other children were locked inside the yard.

We found Dinah lying on a bed unattended, a nurse somewhere in the distance. She was deathly white down to her ears, which looked stretched and transparent; No medication and no intravenous fluids. She looked terrified, having been hit by a truck and separated by her mother. When she saw us, she brightened a little. Her mother hugged her, and then I gave her a hug. She clung to me and wouldn't let me go. I sat by her bed, holding her little hand and praying all the time she would be OK. She seemed content to lie there with me next to her. Her mother cried, being more aware of the gravity of the situation than I was.

I stayed with her while her mother went back to the church to ring her family. It was a very trying time for all. Her mother stayed with Dinah that night, and in the morning we heard she was still alive and out of danger. She was discharged from the hospital in the next three days. Her father demanded they return to Thessaloniki to see with his own eyes that the child was still alive. Needless to say, no one prayed as long and hard for three days and nights for her as we did. We thanked God for the miracle of her being alive. We were thrilled and relieved to see her back with us again. She could hardly walk, and she was bruised around the hips and legs, but thankfully there were no internal injuries, no brain damage, and miraculously no broken bones. Gena took her three children and returned to Thessaloniki.

Camp started. I was given six girls to look after. Five of them were between the ages of eight and ten, and one was a thirteen-year-old with an intellectual disability. We lived in tents, and I ran the group strictly. No nonsense, no fun after lights out, and a lot of shouting on my part during the day. I thought I did a great job—till someone gently pointed out that I didn't have to yell so loudly. Someone else came to my defence, saying, "She has powerful lungs, and it's her manner. She is not growling at the kids," which was true.

In the evenings, there were stories and singing, which I enjoyed, but I didn't sing after the bus incident. Everybody had to take turns in telling a story. We were given thirty to sixty minutes to tell it. I told them a story which I had recently read. It was translated from French and took an hour and half to tell, but nobody said, "Time's up." After the story, the cook came up and said, "I heard you had the gift of the gab. You are even better than I thought." I didn't know whether it was a compliment or a reprimand. Her voice had an ominous tone to it. She then introduced herself as Basil's mother. Basil was at the camp too.

While there, I earned the nickname of 'Monkey' because of the ease with which I climbed trees. Some other "monkey" took a kid's belongings and put them up on highest tree branch, which upset the child. When the meeting was over, I climbed the tree, got the child's belongings, and gave them to him, not realising I was being watched.

Next to the religious camp was an army camp, and when our camp's religious singing stopped, the soldiers started their own singing of patriotic and popular songs. Their singing surpassed ours. They seemed handpicked to sing. One voice amongst them sounded angelic; I had never heard a voice like that before or since. It was a tenor's voice, clear and sweet, resonant and tuneful. I wanted to jump the fence and look at the person who produced such a heavenly sound. Many times, I thought it was a great loss to the world—a great talent "buried in the ground," never to be discovered.

Soon after camp, Basil was called to serve his national service. I don't know where he started, but he returned to Thessaloniki. We became friends went out a couple of times. We talked about the church and its controversial beliefs, such as diet and the law of Moses. He asked, "Why do we only keep part of it? If all the Bible is inspired, we should adhere to the lot, shouldn't we?" I enjoyed those discussions, and they challenged my thinking. He was transferred elsewhere for the rest of his service. We were still friends, but we didn't correspond. I was nearly eighteen years old now.

The new minister, Kostas, and his wife, Ellie, were the new ministers of the Thessaloniki church. Ellie was my mother's childhood friend. When they found out about my friendship with Basil, they objected to it. Kostas announced he would not marry us so that he would not be held guilty before God, knowing what he knew about Basil. I had no idea what it was, but I thought it must have been pretty bad. At that time, marriage had not entered my mind. I had no desire to marry Basil or anybody else. We were simply friends.

Vasilis planned to go to France to do his ministerial course there, after he finished serving in the army. I was to follow. I wanted to go to France to finish my dressmaking career, return to Greece, and start a business, as my mother had suggested. By now, I came across to a good bra patterns which proved to be popular, and I hoped to be able to combine the two skills and be successful. I thought it would be a good idea to keep the friendship going on platonic terms, as it had always been. I hoped he'd be able to help me find accommodation and start me on my way. But I gave up the idea because it was all too hard. Before Basil finished his service, I knew that he was homosexual, though I had no idea what it all meant.

While Basil was serving in the army, another young man, Michael, was associated with the church in Athens. He was not a baptised member but finished his national service with the navy, and he returned to Thessaloniki, where he and his family lived not far from us. His name was mentioned with warmth and excitement at his return. We were introduced, and when he got to know me, he said, "I've heard so much about you. I thought you were a grown-up lady, but you are only a kid." I was eighteen years old, and he was twenty-six.

Theo, whose family was also Seventh-day Adventist, had finished his national service at about the same time as Michael, and he returned to Thessaloniki. At this time, another single girl about our age came to the church. Nicky was a Bulgarian-born Greek, and she stayed with her Seventh-day Adventist aunt. We had great times going out together as a group—Nicky, Eva, Michael, Theo, and I. In the summer, we would go to the beach either by ferry or by bus. We enjoyed swimming, picnics, climbing rocks, and socials. Michael was a real gentleman who was polite and generous. He always insisted in paying our bus and ferry fares, including Theo's. He was an electrician. I got to like Michael because of his generosity and consideration, but we were just friends.

One day, Eva decided she wasn't going to come with us anymore. I was peeved because if she didn't go, I wouldn't be allowed to go either.

My mother said, "Either you both go, or you both stay home." She thought we might "get into trouble," and so we chaperoned each other.

Every Saturday night, Eva would put an act on. "I'm not coming tomorrow. I don't feel well."

I'd plead with her. "Please come. Why not? We are going to have a good time! What's wrong? You will be all right by tomorrow." But the more I pleaded, the more stubborn she became, refusing to come without giving a reason.

Sunday morning, the pleading and the refusing would start again. Mother witnessed this without a comment either way. When the others were at our place to pick us up, Eva would start the same thing all over again, with everybody pleading with her. She'd change her mind, and having wasted an hour, she'd decide to get ready while we were waiting for her. After two weeks of this, I got sick and tired of her game. One Saturday evening before she started her usual tune, I approached her in front of my mother. In no uncertain terms, I said, "Tomorrow, we are going to the beach. Don't start your 'I'm not coming' or 'I'm sick,' because whether you are coming or not, I'm going." I turned to my mother, pointed my finger, and said "And you, try stopping me if you can." To my surprise, my mother didn't say a word. I expected at least a reprimand for rudeness, if not a wallop. Sunday morning, Eva was up and ready before the rest of the group came to pick us up, and there was no more trouble.

I don't know how, but the people in church knew about Michael's feelings for me before I did. He had never asked me out by myself. As soon as he was baptised, he asked me out, and his words still ring in my mind. "I like you. I don't promise you great luxuries, but there will always be bread and cheese on the table." That was good enough for me; luxuries were superfluous for me, even as an eighteen-year-old.

The pastor's wife was upset about it. "No, not Mallie. She's not educated. Tania would be more suitable for you." Tania was her niece.

Michael would take me out with his friends and their girlfriends to restaurants and all around the country side. We'd go out on our own too. While we were going out with his friends and work colleagues, I realised that he drank alcohol, and I didn't like it. As a little girl seeing my father drunk, I decided that when I grew up, I would not marry a man who drank. Also, one day he was very upset about something. He pulled a packet of cigarettes out of his pocket and started smoking, saying that he was too upset and that he doesn't always smoke. This incident was another blow to our relationship. I didn't want to marry a man who smoked, but I said nothing at that time.

After the incident with Basil, I decided not to tell my mother about my relationship with Michael. If she suspected, she didn't questioned me. I was nineteen and he was twenty-six. I wasn't sure about him. His father was a heavy drinker and his grandfather was an alcoholic. When we got to know each other better, I asked Michael to explain homosexuality to me. He did the best he could, but it didn't sink in. I asked if these people can have children? he smiled at my ignorance.

Chapter 35

Preparation to Build the House, 1957

While Eva and I worked at the tobacco factory, Mother found work in a restaurant washing dishes outside the city in the pine forest, just over two kilometres from where we lived. It operated mostly in the warmer months.

Word got around the factory (most likely from Eva) that I was a dressmaker, made bras, had a special pattern that augmented small bosoms, and also had a supportive one for heavy ones. One wouldn't think there is such a thing as a Greek woman with a small bosom, but there is! They came for enhancement of their natural if meagre endowments and also the big, watermelon ones. I'm not sure which ones I preferred to sew for, the enhancing or the reducing ones. I hated them both. However, we needed as much money as we could make to upgrade the house. My mother's dream was to rebuild in brick a two-room place, a lounge room and a bedroom. She'd use the existing room as a kitchen till she could afford a better one. As before, there were no plans, no surveyor, and no licence—just tell the builder what you want and leave it with him.

We worked a full day at the factory. When the girls asked me to make them bras, I didn't miss the opportunity. My measuring tape in the bag with my lunch, I would take the measurements during lunchtime, cut them at home, try them on the next day, and finish them during the next night. I sewed under the light of a small kerosene lamp till 3:00 a.m. Then I was up at 6:00, and we'd walk four kilometres to the city and catch the bus to the factory, which was about ten kilometres away. By the afternoon, I'd be very tired and bored. Eva, who could sleep anywhere, anytime, and under any circumstances, had the same problem even though she got a full night's sleep.

One day I looked up at her to see why she wasn't sorting the leaves; she was sitting next to me. I looked at her sideways, and there she was with one eyelid propped open with a matchstick, and she was trying to prop open the other one! I laughed so long and loud that half the factory workers stopped to see what the joke was all about. When they saw Eva's eyelids propped open with the sticks, they roared with laughter too. The supervisor couldn't miss hearing the uproar, and he came to investigate. When he saw Eva (who was enjoying the reaction she got) sitting up pretending to be asleep with her eyes propped up open, he cracked up too. The rest of afternoon went quickly, and nobody slowed down. That endeared Gloria to everybody. She had such a quirky sense of humour, and even many years later, far in her dementia, she'd come up with some things that would make me laugh and then cry all the way home on the train.

When the work at the tobacco factory finished, I answered an ad in the paper which my mother's boss saw and thought I was suitable for. It read as follows: "Wanted: presentable young woman 18–24 years old, able to use a sewing machine for factory work." It didn't say what sort of sewing, and we presumed it'd be a dress-making factory. I applied for the job. What the ad didn't say was that the sewing involved patching hessian bags used for what they called marble powder for rendering walls, a similar thing to cement only lighter, finer, and much dustier! I took the job. Because we were preparing to build the house, it had a double advantage. The money came in handy, and we could get the marble powder and other building materials at cost because the boss had connections with the building industry. He deducted the cost out of my wages. I worked there for nearly eight months. It was a dirty and dusty job, constantly breathing in that fine dust. There were no masks around at that time. I was covered in it from head to foot. I couldn't go to bed without a bath, and that was easier said than done. We didn't have a bathroom or running hot water. In summer, we'd put a twenty-litre container of water in the sun before leaving home. By the time we returned, it would be hot enough to bathe with. In winter, we'd have to boil it in a pot and use a little trough to wash in.

The other problem was going to and from work during peak hours on very crowded buses. There would always be some bastard who would stand behind me and fondle me—or worse, try to copulate on the bus. I got wise. I gave them the appropriate look, which stopped most of them—for a while, anyway. If that didn't work, I quickly learned where to pinch or punch. When one got to know me, he'd leave me alone, but there was always another bastard to take his place. It was a constant game, which I learned to play well after a while. I couldn't very well go to the police and say, "He touched me inappropriately, sir," because they would laugh at me. They would say, only in different words, what Peter said to Jesus: "But Lord you are pressed on every side and you say someone touched me?" (Luke 8:45). Or, "If you don't like the crowded buses, young lady, just walk." Either way, I had no leg to stand on. I quickly learned self-defence.

By October 1958, we had all the materials needed for the two-room house. The bricks were nicely stacked outside, and the timber materials were inside with us, to protect them from the weather. We were ready to go, and Mother was delighted. She couldn't wait for spring to come to start building. She'd go past the bricks and would look at them as if they were gold nuggets. She'd talk about it every chance she got and to anyone who would listen. The neighbours encouraged her no end. She used to say, "It won't be as hot as hell in summer or as cold as the grave in winter." I could see the pleasure in her eyes at seeing her dream slowly materialising. We too shared her joy and her dream.

We all worked hard. Mum and Eva saved as much as they could, and even poor Ellie worked at a canning food factory aged not yet thirteen. The poor kid came home one day, her hands all wrinkled up, red, and dry from chopping vegetables, especially tomatoes, all day. She put her hands out and said, "Look at my hands." My mother looked at those hands, and her face clouded. Her forehead wrinkled with empathy and pain.

My heart ached, but I pretended it was nothing much and said, "So what?" I wasn't going to admit I was soft. I always presented a tough front, even when my heart was breaking and bleeding. I will never forget the look of those hands, I will never forget how my heart shrunk inside me, and I will never forget how I pretended I didn't care. My mother was doubly hurt: because her thirteen-year-old child had to work hard and suffered pain, and because of my apparent callousness.

One day in the early autumn Despina's husband came to our house with a sad story of his need and want, and he asked my mother to lend him some money. With tears in his eyes, he promised he would pay it back, and soon. My mother was sympathetic, kind, generous, and well acquainted with need, and gave him what he asked for, two thousand drachmas, half of our savings for the building project. No sooner he had left than Despina's fourteen-year-old son, Aris, came running out of breath to tell my mother not to lend him the money, but it was too late. The boy said there was no great hardship, and he had no intention of paying it back. Later, when she got over her anger at being deceived, she philosophically said, "Consider it as payment for Despina for teaching my child a trade. The Lord will provide in some other way." She never mentioned it again. My only grudge was that he didn't teach me dressmaking. Despina never benefitted from that money.

My mother was still working at the restaurant washing up, Eva was at the weaving factory, and Ellie was at home, her seasonal work over. We managed to save and get back most of the money my mother had lent to Despina's husband. While working, I took up my study of French again, but not as a full-time student because I couldn't afford the money. I did it three times a week at night class in the city, and I studied during lunch. I shook the dust off my clothes and hair and walked to my class after work.

Chapter 36

Mother's Final Illness

I got home one day after work. Aunt Soula said that Mum was in hospital. "She passed a bucketful of blood in her urine." I wasn't overly concerned. Mum had been sick before and gotten better. She would this time too, I was sure. As far as the bucket of blood went, I dismissed it. Aunt Soula never told a truth in all her life; she always exaggerated. When the Russians sent Sputnik into orbit, she got scared. In all seriousness, she said, "I'm scared this world is ending soon. I promise I won't tell anymore lies." But the poor devil was a compulsive liar, and when the world didn't end, she took up her old hobby of misleading everybody by strangling the truth with delight.

The private hospital my mother was in was very close to where I worked, and had I really wanted to, I could have gone to see her during lunch or on my way home. However, I didn't think she was that sick. I was sure she was going to be discharged soon, and so I used my lunch time to study. I hadn't visited my mother for two days even though I should have done so. On the first day of her admission to the hospital, I didn't know she was in. On the second day, I went to my French class, walking past the hospital where she was without visiting her. I lived to regret it. I castigated myself for years afterwards, unable to forgive myself and find peace.

When I went to see her on the third day, my second cousin John and Aunt Soula were there. The doctor took us all aside and talked about her condition, but I still didn't realise how ill she was. My aunt told me plainly, "Your mother is going to die." I didn't believe her. The doctor told us that she was going to be transferred to another clinic. The other clinic was for palliative care, but I didn't know it then. Aunt Soula, having stayed with my mother for and two nights without sleep, asked me to stay with her for a while, which I did.

Mum was transferred to the new clinic that day. I sat on a chair by her side, day and night, for three days, napping here and there. In the afternoon on the second day, I asked her if I could go to my French class for two hours. She indicated no, She couldn't speak. Later, I realised her tongue was swollen, but she still recognised me. She also recognised the doctor who came to see her; she had worked at this clinic some years ago.

On the third day, when the evening meal came, the nurse tried to feed her. Mother tried to swallow, but the soup dribbled out of her mouth. The nurse hit my mother on the face. I was stunned, and Mother looked mortified. I was young and inexperienced, and at that time in Greece, doctors were gods and nurses were demigods. I said nothing, but I was very upset. The nurse realised she had done the wrong thing, but she poured oil on the fire by growling at my mother, telling her, "You are upsetting your children, you are." I felt as if I could attack her and maul her to death. She looked at me as if to say, "I only did it to protect you." She didn't get my approval or my understanding. She knew my mother was dying, and to hit a dying person is the most inhumane thing one can do. After that incident, she was softer and more careful.

I was so sure that she would be going home, and even after having seen her swollen tongue and her inability to pass urine, I still didn't think she was going to die. Pastor Kostas and his wife visited and arranged for a church member to come and stay with me. She came on the fourth day. By now Mum was losing consciousness on and off, but I thought she was sleeping because she was restless all night. This was how she was when the lady arrived. I didn't like that woman. She was a typical legalistic person who pulled me up for wearing sleeveless dresses while she wore very low-cut necklines showing her well-endowed bosom. The first thing she did was to pray for recovery when she knew my mother was dying. She sat by me for a few hours talking incessantly, which frustrated and wearied me.

At this stage, cousin Kostas came, having taken leave from the hospital, where he was convalescing form major surgery. Early in the afternoon, my mother improved tremendously and became lucid, as people do before the final battle with death. She sat up in bed with help and tried to talk. She took notice of her surroundings and noticed a young visitor doing some tatting (needlework). She riveted her eyes on the girl's hands. I said something like, "You can learn to do this when you are better." Kostas looked at me disapprovingly; he knew that she was dying, but I didn't. Mum recognised Ellie when she came to visit. She hugged her with tears running down her face, and she wouldn't let her to go. I always wondered what she wanted to say. Her tone and look was now urgent, but we couldn't understand a word. I wonder what final advice she wanted to give us and what her concerns were.

The lady, upon seeing the improvement, said, "Your mother is getting better. I don't need to be here. I'll go and will be back tomorrow." I was pleased because she couldn't do anything anyway, other than talk of God's love and how He would take care of us. I never doubted that, but I didn't want her reminding me in her superior, patronising manner.

The lady, my sister, and Kostas left. I stayed with Mother. After a while, she lost consciousness, and it was then that I realised that she was going to die. In a very short while, she went into the death rattles, which I came to recognise so well later.

I sat on the floor holding her deathly white hand and praying earnestly that God would cut short her suffering. For a moment, she stopped breathing, I got up and stood over her, my face very close to hers. Suddenly she took a deep breath in, held it for a moment, and breathed out a long and slow breath—her last one. That breath hit me in the face. Her eyes were open, blue, and glassy; her mouth was open; and her palms were turned upwards and open. I closed her eyes, crying. Right to the last minute, after Marika and everybody else had left and just before she lapsed into her last coma, I didn't think she would die. She died about six hours after everybody left, at 4:00 a.m. on December 19, 1958, aged forty-three. She was young and very pretty. Her illness lasted just one week.

I helped the nurse (the one who'd hit her) take her off the bed and put her on a mattress on the floor. Together we dragged the mattress in another room. I then sat on a chair and wept, telling my dead mother all the things I would have loved to have told her when she was alive. The nurse came and sat with me, listening to my rumbles and the outpouring of my grief. We wept together. I told my mother that she'd sacrificed herself on the altar of love for us. She worked hard to feed us, clothe us, and supply our every need, and we did nothing for her. After a while, the nurse went about her business, her eyes red and her nose running. I can still see her intense, steely blue eyes, her square jaw' the space between her front teeth, and her fair curly hair. I hated her then, and for a long time afterwards, for hitting a dying person, my mother. I don't hate her anymore. I feel sorry for her, because she too probably had to live with that mistake, just like the rest of us.

The nurse organised the undertakers to bring the coffin. They were at the clinic at about 6:00 a.m. The coffin was too small. They looked at Mum's body and quietly and respectfully said, "It's too small." They left and returned with a larger one. They lifted her off the mattress, and I noticed that rigour mortis had already set in. They took her body home. The sun was up, and the morning was cold and crisp. Fourteen-year-old Ellie was very distressed, crying, and asking, "Mum, have you gone to heaven? Have you gone to heaven?" The question hadn't occurred to me; I only knew that she was gone forever.

They placed the coffin on two chairs in the middle of the only room we had. The undertakers left. I remember sending a telegram to my cousin Magda at my aunt's suggestion. I remember my aunt asking me for money to buy a couple of things for my mother's burial. I gave her three hundred drachmas out of the savings we had for building. It was a lot of money, but I wanted the best for her. She came back with a pair of slippers, a white sheet, and some flowers—fifty drachmas total. She justified spending the rest "a bit here and a bit there." I knew she was lying, but that was the least of my worries. She never gave us the change. Later, Ellie said she'd given it to Kostas, who was sick and not working.

When Magda came in, she threw herself onto my mother's body and wept, saying softly, "You took all my secrets to the grave with you, just as you said you would, Aunty. All my secrets!" She kept repeating herself over and over.

Her mother heard her say that, and a few days after the funeral, she said, "What secrets did she have? Why didn't she confide in me? I'm her mother, after all."

I am sorry to say I didn't send a telegram to my father. I honestly didn't think of it, and if I had thought of it, I would have been inclined to think that he didn't care. But I didn't think of my grandmother, who loved my mother and thought of her as a daughter more than a daughter-in-law.

To this day, I don't know who organised the funeral, who notified all the relatives and friends, and who paid for it. I only know that Michael paid for the taxis for the family. His sister Violetta, who was a nurse, gave Eva and Ellie a sedative injection. I got nothing. I felt nothing.

Despina was sitting opposite me and looking at me sadly. At one stage, she looked at me and said in all honesty, "I will give you the money back. I promise." Poor woman. She must have felt bad because she too was destitute now that her husband wasn't working having had a stroke.

At one stage, I looked at my mother's arms and noticed she had gone all goose pimply. I jumped up, excited, and said to Despina, "She is not dead, she is not dead! Look, she feels the cold—look!" Despina started crying at my plight. She held me, trying to calm me down. I sat down and fell silent.

By lunchtime, there were people everywhere. How did they find out so quickly? There weren't many phones then. The people kept coming. I sat silently by my dead mother. Despina was still sitting opposite me.

Suddenly, I felt like laughing. A hollow laughter, empty of all emotion, just an unearthly sound, came out of the depths of my pained, distraught soul. I laughed and laughed, all the while telling my mother "what a stupid thing to do. She should have listened to me". Two people, one on either side of me, took me away. I felt scared and didn't know where they were taking me to. I recognised Michael, and that gave me some reassurance. I don't remember who the other person was. Despina followed me to the door, crying. I was taken to the church where they made me lie down in the lounge—the same room we were thrown into during the civil war just twelve years earlier. I pulled the blanket over my head and didn't want to see anybody. My hearing became very acute, and I heard them whispering the funeral arrangements. Someone asked whether I should go to the cemetery. I threw the blanket off my face and with deadly determination told them, "I am coming." They then moved to another room and carried on their discussion where I couldn't hear them.

Soon after that, they brought my mother's body to the church, which was upstairs. I was led upstairs to the church as if I were a robot. The church was packed to capacity, and there was no room inside. A lot of people stood outside. I remember seeing the boss's uncle in the church. He was looking at me crying.

I vaguely remember the hymns being sung. I remember someone asking me, "Which was your mother's favourite hymn?" Even though I knew it—she sang it all the time at the top of her voice and out of tune, its words and tune ringing in my ears—I couldn't tell them. In the end, they sang "I Surrender All."

My cousin Kostas made a speech, the contents of which I don't remember. I remember getting angry when he turned to the coffin and said, "I promise to look after your girls." He, looking after us? He couldn't even look after himself! The cemetery service was a blur.

As time went by, I thought of my aunt keeping the money I'd given her to buy the burial things. I became disgusted with her and despised her. How could she, or anybody, do that to her sister's orphaned children when she knew that we were struggling to put some money together and keep a roof over our heads? And on the day her sister died! What a despicable thing to do! How could one stoop so low? These were two people my mother loved and in whose eyes could do no wrong. Oh, how I despised their kind.

Aunt Soula stayed with us. She felt she was protecting us and taking care of us. I didn't mind her staying; I didn't like her, but she got on well with Eva. Soula spent her time visiting the neighbours and talking. A week or so after the funeral, a neighbour called me to her house She looked upset and angry. I wondered what I'd done wrong. "Listen," she said in a firm tone. "Your aunt goes around to all the neighbours gossiping about you, saying you are of low morals and that the two boys who visit you from Xanthe are not your cousins, they are boyfriends. We know this is not true; your mother told us they are the sons of her first cousins. Your mother wouldn't lie."

I wasn't moved. I was still too shocked and numb to feel any anger, love, hate, or pain. I said nothing. The neighbours knew us and our mother since we were little kids; they knew us better than my aunt did.

She continued. "What do you keep her for? Tell her to go, or I will. I already told her off for spreading tales about you. None of us want her in our homes."

Two weeks later, I told Aunt Soula she could leave if she wanted to; we would be OK. A week or so later, she left for the village because there was nobody left to gossip with. After she left, the neighbours told us she said she'd kept the money because we'd only waste it.

My mother's death was a shock to us, but I didn't realise it then. When people expressed their shock and sadness, I couldn't understand it. I was on the bus one day going to work soon after her death, and a friend of hers saw me wearing the mourning black armband and asked me who died. Unemotionally, I said, "My mother."

She was shocked and horrified, put her hands on her head, and cried aloud, "I don't believe it! What happened?" I felt angry at her reaction and refused to tell her. I figured if I was not upset, why should she be? I was sure she was acting.

I returned to work a week after her death. At times during the day, I'd become aware that my mother had died, but it meant nothing. I felt no loss whatsoever. I was like this for nearly six weeks. On day forty-two, a full six weeks to the day, just before lunch the reality of my mother's death suddenly hit me. I felt paralysed with grief, pain, and loss. I broke down, and for the first time after her burial, I sobbed uncontrollably. The boss in the office and his uncle in the yard came running in, wondering what the matter was. All I could say was, "My mother died, my mother died." They looked at me sadly. There was nothing they could do or say. They silently and slowly left the workroom and let me cry.

After her death and as soon as I got my wits about me, I made an application with the immigration department to migrate to Australia. At last, my childhood dream was on the horizon with a high possibility of materialising, but I didn't tell anybody. My mother had refused to let me migrate by not signing my application because I was still under nineteen.

Nightmares plagued me frequently for the first year after her death. I'd wake after dreaming that she was buried alive, half out of the grave and calling me to pull her out, but I wasn't able to extend my hand to help her. I'd go to the cemetery after work, and all I could do was to stand there paralysed, half waiting for her to come up and talk to me. Those horrible nightmares are still vivid in my mind fifty-seven years later.

Time went by. I worked and paid for all the building materials. One day, the boss, who was the image of Robert Mitcham minus a few gaps in his mouth, came swaggering into the sewing room all smiles and very friendly. With a flirting look on his face, he asked me to go out with him, making no secret as to what he had in mind. With my usual lack of tact, I told him I had no intention whatsoever in going out with him or his young mate, and I reminded him that he was married with a family. He gave me a hateful look and took off like a dog being growled at. The following Friday he gave me my pay and told me there was someone else coming to do my job on Monday. He wasn't obliged to give me two weeks' notice. I was upset, but there was nothing I could do. I knew I wouldn't be able to get another job till June, when the tobacco factories opened; it was only March. I didn't know where the money would come from to live on.

Chapter 37

Building the House

Spring came, I wanted us to build the house. It was my mother's dream, but it was ours also. I hoped that one day soon, I'd leave this lice-ridden country for a better place, and that my sisters would have a better place in which to live. We now turned our attention and directed our efforts to building. Eva was still working at the weaving factory. Ellie and I were unemployed. We started building our small house in April. My cousin John came from Xanthe to do the building. A neighbour, Charis, who was a bricklayer and builder, offered to help. John was glad for any help he could get. Charis had hurt his back at work, and my mother had massaged him several times till he got better. She refused to accept payment. The builder who'd put up the old shack also came to help. When my girlfriend's husband, Kriton, saw them digging the foundations, he too came, bringing his own pick and shovel. The four men had the foundation for the two-roomed house finished in one day.

The next day, they started the building and poured concrete. While it was drying, they cut the timber for the roof, all by hand. The next day, they did all the brick work. Kriton mixed the mortar. Ellie and I were the brickies' labourers. We borrowed the water hose from church; Pr Kostas, the new minister, was glad to lend it to us. We connected it to the public tap, which was about a hundred metres from the house, but it only reached one-third of the way. We filled the buckets and carried the water the rest of the way to Kriton for the mortar. Between carrying water, Ellie and I took the mortar and the bricks to the builders in buckets. The three bricklayers finished the brickwork in one day. The third day, they started the roof.

They were busy working when a policeman called in. He wanted to see the permit and all the other legalities, of which we had none. He asked to speak to the builder. John presented himself and answered all the questions. Ellie and I were passing roof tiles to the builders, which the policeman noticed. John explained our situation. "Three orphan girls all alone in the city. Please let us finish the work!" The policeman was touched. He said he had no choice but to take him to the police station because a neighbour had dobbed us in, and the notification had to be investigated. He told John to say that he was doing repair work, not new building. They got on the bus and went to the station. John said what he was advised to say. He was allowed to go with a warning to not do any new work. John wanted to know who the dobber was, and the policeman said it was the neighbour just above us, the last ones to build. My mother had gone out of her way to help them during their illegal building. As far as we were concerned, we were friends. Why would they do such a thing? We couldn't understand. The other neighbours were disgusted.

Michael, my boyfriend, did the electrical wiring. They finished the rendering in a day, and the whole project was done in just under five days. We moved in against advice before the rendering and the concrete floor were completely dry, but we were so thrilled with the new house that we couldn't wait. We even put some flimsy curtains on the windows (all two of them) and the half-glazed front door. The neighbours rejoiced with us, and they too were sad that our mother didn't live to see her dream materialise. We felt a mixture of joy and sorrow; her death was still raw in our hearts. She died only five months before the house was built.

After building the house, at seventeen Eva, became engaged to Theo and went to Athens to stay with her in-laws for a while. Ellie went to the village to see our father and grandmother. I stayed in Thessaloniki on my own.

Soon after my mother's death, my father was diagnosed with tuberculosis. He came to Thessaloniki and told me he was on his way to the sanatorium to get treatment. I hadn't seen him for two years, and I was glad to see him. I was sad and upset, even though I wasn't close to him and hardly knew him as a father. During my formative years, he'd spent long periods of time away from home working in the mountains. His absence during the three years of the civil war added to our estrangement. I gave him a drink, and we sat down together. He looked at my mother's photo on the wall. With genuine sadness, he said, "Why didn't you let us know? I would have liked to have come to her funeral." I was surprised because I thought they hated each other. He was admitted to the sanatorium, and as soon as I had some money for the bus fare, I visited him empty-handed. I had no money to buy him a little gift, not even a packet of cigarettes.

Soon after my father's admission to hospital, I got a lovely surprise. My grandmother arrived at our place. I was thrilled to see her again. I hugged her and held her tight, and we cried in each other's arms. She wanted to visit my father in hospital. She brought a few things such as butter, cheese, and fruit. We sat in our newly built house, she looked at my mother's photo. The sadness in her face was palpable. She wept and kept saying, "So young, so young. Why didn't you let us know?" They truly loved each other. Mum was the daughter my grandmother had lost, and to Mum, Grandma was the mother she hardly remembered.

I took Grandma to the bus depot, told her where to get off, and put her on the bus. She went on her own. I don't remember why I didn't go with her. I have a feeling I didn't have money for the fares, and I had seen him only the week before. She managed well, returned on the same day, stayed overnight, and went back to the village the next day to look after the farm and the animals. She was eighty years old. When I visited my father again, he was amazed at how Grandma had found her way around. Obviously, he underestimated her love for him, her intelligence, and her determination to see him. They were very close.

I visited my father at the sanatorium as often as finances would allow me. He complained about the food, he couldn't stomach the frozen meat. He wasn't a big meat eater anyway. My grandfather, with his enormous meat-eating habit managed to cure the whole family from meat eating. Father stayed in the hospital for two months and discharged himself, saying, "They can't do anything for me anyway." He went back to the village.

The saddest thing was that the villagers avoided him for fear of getting tuberculosis. The barber refused to cut his hair. When he was too weak to shave himself, his beard and hair grew long. It brings tears to my eyes knowing just how meticulous he was about his appearance and how neat and clean he always was. The villagers referred to him as "the cleanest man under the sun." It must have been heart-rending for my grandmother to watch her impeccable son end up like this.

In the cafenio, people avoided him, so he stopped going. According to Ellie, there was only one family in the village who would open their home to him. That was Sophia and her husband, Jehoachim. She would make him a cup of coffee and give him water in the same cups and glasses as they used. She didn't make him feel discriminated against. When he'd leave, she'd wash his cup and glass separately and would put them aside for his use only. What a thoughtful, considerate, and caring person. She was a true child of God in anybody's religion. Every time I think of that kindness shown to my father, I cry not just because he was my father, but because he was another human being. The kindness shown brings tears to my eyes every time.

Chapter 38

Hard Times

I found it very difficult to recount my next life's story. It held me back for over seven months. But when I decided to tell my story, I had promised myself to tell it all or nothing.

I was unemployed and couldn't find work anywhere. Jobs were scarce, and with Sabbath keeping, it was impossible to get a job. The food we had in the cupboard was nearing an end. I walked to another suburb five kilometres away, where one of my customers lived. She owed me some money for sewing for her. Had she paid me, I'd have enough to live on, economising till the tobacco factories opened. The girl was married at fourteen and had three little boys by the time was eighteen. She had no money to give me. No matter how much I told her I was desperate, she insisted she couldn't pay me. They too were poor; they too were struggling. I had no choice but to walk all the way back home empty-handed.

I was living in the city alone. Ellie returned to the village to stay there for a little while, and Eva went to Athens. I had no family near me and no one to turn to. By this time, there was practically nothing left in the cupboard, and I was hungry most of the time. I had bruises on the back of my hands and legs without bumping into anything. My skin was dry and flaking, my hair fell out in handfuls while combing, and my abdomen was extended. My diet had been poor for months.

I had gone without eating anything for three days, and I was having hunger pangs. I went looking in the cupboard for something to eat for the tenth time, but the cupboards were empty. I looked in boxes and in every tin, and at last I found some flour in a paper bag. I was glad. I mixed it into a paste and made some gruel for myself. I closed my eyes and thanked God for it. Only God knows how thankful I really was.

I had taken about three mouthfuls when I noticed something black in the gruel. I looked closely. To my disgust, I realised it was mice droppings! I can't put in words how I felt. There was a mixture of being let down, being disappointed, angry with God. "Lord, how long are You going to test me and try me?" I asked. I looked at that gruel again. I felt a bit like a hungry man shown a delicious meal, allowed to smell and taste it, and then take it away from him. I wanted to throw it away, but I could not bring myself to do it. I didn't know how long it would be before I would get another meal. I remember looking at it for a long time in disgust and anger. A terrible battle between disgust and hunger raged within me. Then hunger won; it always does. People ate dogs, cats, and rats. Mothers ate their own children; read it in 2 Kings 6:25, 30.

I carefully removed all the shit out of the bowl and ate the gruel in anger. I finished the last mouthful of the last food in the house. I prayed and said, "Lord, please give me faith." Half in anger and half in resolution, I added, "Though He slay me I will trust in Him" (Job 13:15). I remembered Pastor Demos preaching a sermon on faith once. With a smug look on his face, he said, "Faith starts when the food in the cupboard finishes." Here I was in exactly the same situation, with nothing in the cupboard to sustain me physically. I had to hold on to my faith to sustain me spiritually as well as physically. I would rather die of hunger than go to the neighbours and ask for food. No, not after what my grandfather had done to shame my father and shame the family. With all the determination I could muster, I said. "I will never beg for food. I will work for it. Lord, please help me."

This experience was the final blow that made me hate Greece even more than my grandmother did. It made me more determined than ever to leave Greece, and to that end I directed all my energies. I kept studying English with Ellie, who taught me free of charge. I'm ever so grateful. I also kept going to the English classes offered by the immigration department, which were compulsory and free of charge.

About three days later, it was Sabbath. Gena, the mother of Dinah, invited me to lunch after church. I was glad to accept because I had had only a couple of meals with friends since the gruel. I know only too well what it feels like to be hungry and not know where the next meal is coming from. But I also knew that God was in control. I prayed again. "Please, Lord, test me and try me, but not beyond my endurance."

It wasn't long before June came, and the tobacco factories opened. Eva returned from Athens, and we both started working at the tobacco factory. If we didn't work on the Sabbath, we didn't get paid. While working at the tobacco factory, Basil pointed out to me that as Christians, we didn't smoke, and therefore we shouldn't be working at places where cigarettes were manufactured. Because he was so sincere and well-meaning in what he said, I said nothing. I looked at him long and hard, making sure his gaze didn't escape mine. He dropped his eyes. I didn't have to say anything; he got the message loud and clear.

After the closing of the tobacco factory, my mother's former employer offered me a job. I went for the interview. She showed me the house, explained my duties, and proudly showed me her new twin tub washing machine. I remembered my mother's delicate hands, all red, cracked, and swollen from the constant use of soda and harsh bleaches. I tried very hard not to cry. She must have noticed my reaction and gently asked, "Will you take the job?" In a choked voice and with a shake of the head, I indicated no. Mrs. Schultz looked at me, surprised at my refusal of such a good position. I was sure she couldn't understand my behaviour; she had no inkling of the turmoil and the agony I was going through just then.

Truth be known, the woman offered me the job out of love for my mother and pity for us. But I could not bear to be constantly reminded of my mother's hard lot as a servant all her life, the jobs she did, and the care she gave those two little children, four-year-old Thomas (whom she adored) and one-year-old Elke. Several times their parents would go away for a week at a time, leaving them with her, knowing the kids were safe and in good hands. They trusted Mum utterly and completely because she was trustworthy and hard-working. I would not be able to fill her shoes. Most important, I was not going to follow in my poor mother's steps. I did not want to be a house servant for the rest of my days. I hoped and believed there was something different, something better for me in life. I left the German lady with my spirit crushed and my heart broken. A thousand sad thoughts raced through my clouded mind. My poverty and uncertainty of the future confused and bewildered me.

The first group of migrants in my group left for Australia. I wasn't amongst them, and I wondered why. I feared that for some reason I was rejected, as another girl had been. I didn't know whether they took us alphabetically by name. Maybe it was because they had to investigate my father's political affiliations during the civil war. I was disappointed and afraid.

A month later, I got a letter from the immigration department giving me the date of my departure by plane on April 11, 1960. I was delighted and couldn't contain my joy. At long last, my childhood dream was about to materialise! I had nearly two months left in Greece. I didn't tell anybody—not the neighbours or anyone in the church. I felt there was still plenty of time for that. I had worked at the tobacco factory the previous summer, and I still had a few customers coming to me to make bras for them, so there was a bit of money coming in, which I managed carefully. By now I had broken up with Michael; his smoking, drinking, and womanising were the deciding factors.

Part 2

Chapter 39

Time to Leave

The time came for me to leave Greece for Australia. I went to say goodbye to my father and grandmother. We all knew this would be the last time we saw each other on this earth. I arrived in the middle of the day in early April. The sight of my grandmother sitting on the bench and peeling vegetables in her peculiar way, one leg folded under her and one leg bent at the knee in front of her, is vivid in my mind. She didn't hear me walk into the yard. I watched her for a moment. She looked lost in her thoughts, she looked sad, beaten, and defeated. I'm not one given to tears, but it was more than I could bear. I burst into tears, weeping uncontrollably as I threw my arms around her and held her tight. Not expecting me, she didn't recognise me.

My father heard the commotion from upstairs, where he was lying down. He wanted to know what the trouble was. He wasn't strong enough to negotiate the stairs. I went upstairs and gave him a hug. It was like hugging a clothed skeleton, he was thinner than he looked. I was still crying at having seen my grandmother, and I cried some more. I told him I was leaving Greece in two weeks. He already knew; he had signed my application to migrate because I wasn't twenty-one when I'd applied to migrate. He gave me his blessing, wished me well, and said, "If you do well, send me a little money to buy two calves to put on the land." I cried in pain. (When he was admitted to the hospital, Grandma sold the animals.) Here was my father, dying and unable to walk, and my grandmother at eighty-one years old—and he still thought he could work the land. It was a heart-rending experience. The only other thing he asked for were some tablets for his TB. I felt sad and helpless. I left the village crying all the way to town, where I caught the bus for Thessaloniki.

The preparation for the journey to Australia was simple. There was nothing much I wanted to take with me, and I owned very little in a way of clothes. I had enough time to make some clothes for myself. I bought the material on credit. I made two suits and gave one to Eva. I made a couple of skirts and two pairs of pyjamas; the pants were three-quarter length because I didn't have enough material. As I was packing my few things, Eva watched me and asked, "Won't you take any cutlery with you?"

I looked at her and said, "He who will provide the meal will also provide the cutlery," believing God would. She left for Athens two weeks before I left Thessaloniki by train.

I went to say goodbye to the church minister, Kostas, and his wife, Ellie. I also talked to some of the church members, but not Michael; I didn't feel obliged to. On the day of my departure, there were a few friends at the railway station. Just as the train was about to leave, I spotted Michael running. We had less than one minute to talk. He was upset, shaking, and out of breath. "Why didn't you tell me you were leaving?" he kept asking. I simply looked at him and ignored the question. I'm sure he'd have a good idea. He handed me a large box of chocolates and wished me well in my new country and new life. I thanked him politely, keeping my distance. He hopped out of the train without a goodbye kiss.

At Athens, Eva and her sister-in-law to be, Katia, met me at the train station. I stayed with them for three days. Katia took Eva and me to Parthenon. As I looked around from the top of the hill down at Athens, I felt a hate for Greece and all it stood for. I hated her politics, her poverty, and the lack of opportunities for the poor. The lavish lifestyles of the rich stood out in stark contrast in my mind. They had everything while my poor mother struggled as a washer woman and cleaner to keep us fed and clothed, and there was no way she could break the poverty cycle. Unfairness, corruption, and injustice reigned supreme in that miserable country, and the epithet my grandmother described came ringing in my ears: "this lice-ridden country" was an apt description now, more than ever before.

I hated the place of my birth with an undying hate. The last sight of it is still vivid in my mind. The Parthenon standing there, mauled and broken as a witness of the tyranny of war, pain, and suffering. The dearth, the lack of green grass, the dust, and the dry clay reminded me of the reason my grandmother hated Greece. Only a few bay leaf trees were unmindful of her poverty and dearth, and even they couldn't shake the dry dust off their leaves. I looked at the ground, which was strewn with broken stone, marble, and dirt.

I picked up three stones and cleaned the dust from them. Eva and Katia looked at me, thinking I was going to take them with me as souvenirs. "No," I said. "I am going to take an oath." In the Greek custom, I threw the first stone over my left shoulder and said, "This is my first oath: I will never come back to this country unless the political regime changes." I threw the second one over and said, "I will not marry a Greek, even if I'm left on the shelf." I threw the third one over and vowed with determination, "I will get an education." I kept all three vows with no regrets for the first two, and with a sense of achievement for the third.

I spent a bit of time with the Greek-American minister, Nick, and his family. He wrote a letter of recommendation for me to take to my future employer. I was invited to lunch by Pastor Demos. They were most friendly, and he even asked me to say something in his new tape recorder "so that we can remember your voice." I said something like, "I am looking forward to leaving this place and never coming back." The Duck tried to tell me just how hard it would be living in a new, strange country "without friends, without anyone you know." I told her it couldn't be much harder than it had been here, and I nearly said, "And you didn't make it any easier for us," but I managed bite my tongue.

On April 11, Pastor Nick, Eva, and Katia took me to the airport. I was glad to be leaving Greece. The excitement of my first flight on a plane faded to nothing at the thought that I was going to Australia. Once the plane took off and the first excitement died down, a deep sadness overcame me which I could not define. There was merriment on the plane. Some of the girls became very friendly with the plane stewards or with the male migrants. There were ninety-one of us travelling to Australia from all parts of Greece. The young man sitting next to me tried to cheer me up by throwing some perfume on me. It hit me in the eye, which watered for a few hours. It failed to cheer me up.

The trip was long and tiresome. We stopped in a few places to refuel. I was not interested in any of them. My destination was Australia, and that was where my sight was fixed.

We stopped at the Delhi airport. From inside the plane, I saw some people working on the tarmac. One man caught my attention. He looked old and thin. He had no hat on, and his Indian outfit hardly protected him from the hot sun. While I was looking at him, he collapsed. I and the others who saw him gasped, but there was no way we could go out to help. The steward, who spoke very little Greek, was unconcerned and said, "Escase," which means 'to burst or busted, like a balloon. He was corrected by the girl sitting on his lap and managed to twist his tongue around the Greek word for *fainted*. Meanwhile, two men ran to him from nowhere and dragged him by the arms. They didn't even have the decency to lift him in a stretcher and take him inside. That incident upset me so much that it coloured my impression of India to a degree, and I have never wanted to go there. The suffering of that man was equal to, if not worse than, that of the Greek people. "Lord," I said, "how long will Your children suffer? How long are You going to put up with us? Please come quickly and take us home." That has been my prayer for a long time now.

The plane took off again, and we were told the next stop would be Darwin, Australia. We were all very tired and quiet. The girl sitting next to me was crying. She said, "How stupid I am. I left my home, my mother, and my relatives for a man. How could I do it?" She was born when her mother was in her forties. All her siblings were married, she was the only one living with her mother, and now she had second thoughts. The young man she was in love with had left for Australia a year earlier, and she'd left Greece to marry him.

In Darwin, the plane stopped to refuel and took off after a short stay. The next thing I knew, we were in Melbourne late in the evening on April 14, 1960. Some of the migrants were picked by their families from the Essendon airport. The rest of us were taken by bus to our accommodations. As the bus drove, I looked out of the window and liked what I saw. Nice wide streets, with trees in the middle of the road! Beautiful buildings with plenty of plants and trees around them. Then we went through a street planted with tall, straight palm trees, which I had seen in pictures. They took my breath away and looked majestic in the light of the street lamps. *What a beautiful city,* I thought. I fell in love with Melbourne there and then.

We were taken at a hostel for migrants. We were orientated to the area by the hostel staff. There was a shower block with running hot water, and there were toilets that flushed! *What luxury,* I thought. We were then shown to our rooms, which were clean and comfortable, and settled in for the night. I was too excited, emotional, and unsettled to sleep. In the morning, we were taken to the cafeteria for breakfast. We served ourselves; food was plentiful and good. Eggs and bacon, porridge, Weet-Bix, baked beans, and toast. We could eat all we wanted. After the financial struggles I went through and the scarcity of food, to me it was refreshing and reassuring to come to a country of not only beauty but also of plenty. I fell in love with Australia and was convinced that this land was God's own land, the land flowing with milk and honey. I was still at the hostel after everybody else left. I knew nobody.

Chapter 40

Getting a Job

I was at the hostel for three days when I was called to the office. My prospective employer came to pick me up. I was to work as a housekeeper, which I had signed for when I applied to migrate to Australia as an assisted passage immigrant. The contract was for two years, after which I could return to Greece if I wanted, fares paid. I was to work for this family with three young children. Two girls, Lily (eight) and Donna (six), and eighteen-month-old Harry. The lady's name was Ruth, and her husband was Bill. They were Jewish, and he was a businessman.

I was shown to my room which was neat, clean, and carpeted. It was a sleep-out in the backyard, next to the house. I felt like a lowly servant, an outcast if not like a dog. Ruth must have noticed my reaction and asked, "Don't you like it?"

I understood the question. "It is good," I said, but I couldn't work out where the "don't" bit fitted in. It took me a long time to learn that particular Anglicism because it made no grammatical sense.

I put my case inside, and she said to me, "You start work in the morning. You get the children ready for school, clean the house, do the dishes, tidy up outside, and polish the children's shoes. I cook the meal and serve it." I was grateful I didn't have to cook as well, but I'd have to set the table. I was to have all Saturday off and half of Sunday.

Dinnertime came. She prepared the evening meal as I set the table. She dished the meal out for the family, served mine last on a different plate, put it on the kitchen table, and said, "You eat here; we eat in the dining room," emphasising the *we* and *you*. I sat at the table on my own in the kitchen and looked at the food dished out for me on an odd plate. It was then that I became keenly aware what discrimination felt like. I felt discriminated against. I ate mechanically, and the full meaning of the word *servant* slowly but poignantly became clear in my mind. I thought of my poor mother spending her life working as a servant. She started working aged eleven. She was treated like a servant, like a dog. I felt like howling, but I managed to control my tears. I vowed there and then that I was not going to be a servant to anybody ever again. Of all the verses in the Bible, the one I hate most says, "As the eyes of servants [slaves] look to the hand of their master, as the eyes of a maid look to the hand of her mistress" (Psalms 123:2). This verse conjures up for me an image of someone feeding his dog. I thought of it a million times, having had dogs all my life. Oh, how I hate seeing people depending on others! For me, the most precious asset one has is not good health or wealth. It's not high intelligence, noble birth, good looks, honour, or anything else you can think of. To me, independence and freedom is the most precious thing of all, and when I lose this one precious asset, I want to die. Life without it would be worse than death for me, and hell for those around me.

The first week at my new job went by quickly. I was still jet-lagged and found it very hard to wake up in the morning. A couple of times, my mistress came to wake me up. She wasn't happy and made it known. I hated being a housekeeper. My capabilities as such did not meet her expectations. I hated doing dishes, polishing shoes, dusting, and mopping. There was one thing I liked about the place: there were plenty of kids' books. I read every opportunity I got. One day while my mistress was feeding Harry, I came across the word *swallow*. I didn't know the meaning and asked her. She looked at me and demonstrated the meaning by a fake swallowing motion, which I understood. Then she said, "Swallow is also a bird with a scissors-like tail," and she indicated with her fingers the motion of scissors. I also understood that and could identify the bird.

The week went by, and I told her I was a Seventh-day Adventist (which she knew) and that on Sabbath, I wanted to go to church. She had other ideas about my day off. Yes, I could have it off, but only after breakfast, and only after I cleaned the kitchen—which would make it impossible for me to be at church on time. However, she contacted the church headquarters, which at that time was in Hawthorn, and arranged for someone to pick me up the following Sabbath. The nearest church was in Hughsdale. A couple in their early middle years came to pick me up. They knocked on the door, and she told them to wait for me. They waited in their car, and I could see them through the large lounge window. The dishes weren't done, and halfway through them she came to me and in a curt, irritated tone said, "Go. They are waiting for you." I didn't wait to be told again.

We were late for Sabbath school. The couple introduced me during the church service. I stood up and bowed to the congregation. The church was full, and there were a lot of people my age there. I was invited to someone's house for lunch and was dropped off back home in the afternoon because I didn't know my way around. The same thing happened for the next two weeks. I couldn't finish my work any earlier because their breakfast was at 8:00 a.m. She was obviously annoyed at the inconvenience I caused her, but after all, she was Jewish and the Sabbath was a rest for all—masters, servants, animals, and "the stranger in your house" (Exodus 20:10). I was supposed to have Sabbaths off.

After the second week at her service, I took off to orientate myself in Caulfield and get to know the public transport. I got on a tram and went far. I got out and had a look around, and on the way home I asked the tram conductress to let me know when I was near the stop I wanted to get off. My English was very poor. She became impatient with me, turned to go, looked back, and angrily said, "I will tell you." I became anxious because I didn't know the way back. I was not sure she'd remember to tell me, but I was too embarrassed to remind her. A little way down the track, she came to me and said something like, "The next stop." I got up to get out of the tram. She shouted for all to hear, "No, not this one. The next stop!" Before the next stop, she came and in a condescending and angry manner ordered, "Get out here," pushing me out of the tram. It was not a good feeling, but that made me all the more determined to learn English and learn to find my way around on public transport. From then on, whenever I got on a tram, I would mark not only the stop and the tram number but the name of the nearest street as well.

While still working as a housekeeper I was invited for Sabbath lunch to Pastor Thomson's place. They had a daughter, who was newly married; a son, Barry, who was engaged to Desi; and a sixteen-year-old son Ben, a good-looking lad just like his father. The pastor's wife had multiple sclerosis in the late stages. She was bedridden, frail, and looked old, but I could see Barry was the image of her. Pastor Thomson introduced me to her. I didn't understand the relationship and asked, "Your mother?"

He said, "No, my wife."

I felt bad and tried to justify my blunder by saying, "The mother of the family?"

"Yes," he said. "The mother of my family." Mrs. Thomson smiled.

The next week, my fourth in Australia, Pastor Thomson invited me to their home again. His sister and her husband were visiting from Perth. I don't know whether she took pity or liking to me. She suggested I go to Western Australia with them to attend the Seventh-day Adventist college there. The thought thrilled me, and I agreed. After lunch while doing the dishes, she asked for a towel. The paucity of my English and her accent made it impossible for me to understand what she was asking for. She went to the bathroom, took a towel, and patiently and slowly pronounced, "Towel." I asked her to write it down, which she did, and that day I added one more word to my vocabulary. Every word counts.

The following week, a Greek girl came to visit my employers. She had been their previous housekeeper, and they talked privately. The housekeeper and I talked. She asked me about my plans. I told her that I planned to go West to study there. She told Mrs. Schultz. The next week, my fifth in Australia, Mrs. Schultz told me in simple English,

"Someone else is coming to work for me here." I understood because she always spoke slowly and clearly to me.

The following week, the Thomsons kindly invited me to dinner again. I told them that from next Monday, I would have no job and nowhere to stay. He said, "I will see what I can do for you." I prayed he would. He rang the Sanatorium Health Food factory and organised a job interview for me. He rang me at my employers' and told me. I rang him later from a public phone for the address and directions to the factory. This might sound easy, but for me it turned out to be a nightmare. My English was poor, and I did not know where the place was. The problem was compounded by my lack of sense of direction.

It is one thing speaking to someone face-to-face, and it's another thing on the phone. When speaking face-to-face, you see expressions and gestures, which give you a clue as to what is being said. On the phone, you are blindfolded. Worse still, I confuse my lefts and rights. I must have been on the phone for at least ten minutes trying to get directions from Caulfield East to Windsor, but it wasn't sinking in. I could hear the poor fellow sighing with frustration, and I'm sure he could sense my desperation and agitation. To make things worse, there was a man outside the phone box banging on the door, indicating with his hand that I was only allowed five minutes; I had been in the box more than ten. By the time I finished, I was no wiser as to where I was supposed to be going than before I'd started. The only thing I understood was Union Street, Number 118, Windsor. Where Windsor was and how to get there, I had no idea. I worked out the best way to start was from the city. Now I had to learn how to construct a question, which to a non-English-speaking person is no mean task.

The *does*, *do*, or *did*, made absolutely no sense in a question translated into Greek. In French, Spanish, and Greek, the question was asked by the inflection of voice. Simple. But "Where do I catch the bus from?" or "Why did you do it?" or "Where does the bus for Winsor leave from?" made no sense. It was all back to front, and I struggled with it for two years. At that time, the best I could come up with was, "From where leaves the bus for Windsor?" which I interpreted from Greek to English. I was told which tram to catch. On the tram, in fear and trembling, I told the conductor slowly, "I want to go to Union Street." With a smile on his face, he nodded and said, "Yes, certainly." I was so surprised at the different treatment between the two conductors. I wanted to believe it was not the norm to be ill-treated on public transport in Australia.

As the tram approached Union Street, the conductor came to where I was sitting and quietly and politely said, "Next stop for you," which I understood, having heard it loudly twice last time from the nasty conductress.

Once off the tram, it was much easier than I anticipated. Yes, I still had no idea where the Sanatorium Health Food factory was, but at least I was in the right suburb and on the right street. I asked a man who pointed to the right direction. I was shown to the office and spoke with the manager, Mr. Williams. He had a son working there, who was a younger version of his father. I introduced myself and produced the precious recommendation letter which Pastor Nick had given me before leaving Greece. Mr. Williams read it and looked me up and down. I passed inspection. No make-up on, though maybe the skirt was a little too short. He nodded, saying I could start next Monday or Thursday. I chose Thursday, only a few days away.

Back in Caulfield, I told Mrs. Schultz I would be leaving at the end of the week. She asked where I was going to work and live. I told her. She nodded saying nothing. In the meantime, I contacted my cousin Magda's in-laws, whose phone number and address I'd had before leaving Greece. They lived in Bentley. I arranged to live with them till I found accommodation closer to the factory. I said goodbye to my employer, expecting to get paid. She said, "I can't pay you today. Come next week," I was disgusted. She owed me seven miserable pounds, which she could well afford to pay. First, she sacked me; second, I told her a week in advance when I would be leaving; and third, she was paying me less than half of basic wage, which at that time was ten pounds a week. She deducted five pounds weekly for my board.

I had no choice but to return the following week. Fortunately, I still had ten pounds left—enough to keep me going till I got paid again. With all my belongings in my small suitcase, I left. I was not sorry. I found my way to Bentley East and shared a room with Allana, paying two pounds a week in rent. The Bovas had three children. Allana was sixteen going thirty. She was mad about Elvis Presley. Their ten-year-old son James, and their four-year-old daughter, Mary, who was adored and spoiled. Her parents were very conservative, country folk who kept the Greek tradition of keeping their daughters under control—tin pants and chastity belt on, and under lock and key. Allana had other ideas which they knew nothing about. When she realised that girls didn't live like this, even in Greece, she rebelled even more. She demanded to go out with her friends, wear short skirts, and do all the things girls her age did. Her parents were dismayed. She argued with them constantly. The change in her behaviour was blamed on my influence on her.

The Bovas home was a four-bedroom house. One room was used by the parents. The second was used by the two younger children. Allana and I shared one, and the fourth was let to a newly married Greek couple. The young woman's name was Malama. She was a lovely girl who tried to teach me English, but hers was just a little better than mine. They were giving me a lift one day when we faced a "danger" sign at an intersection. She pointed at it and said, "That says *dahnguer*," pronouncing it much like a German would.

I should have shut my mouth, but I said, "That's pronounced *danger*," as correctly as I could pronounce it myself. I think I embarrassed her. Later, I found out she had only been in Australia for two years. Two weeks later, I was asked to find somewhere else to live. The reason was I was too old for Allana, nearly five years older, and there wasn't much room, which was true. Her parents thought I might be corrupting Allana. The truth was I learned more from her than she did from me. I didn't get upset because I was looking for accommodation close to the factory anyway. As it turned out, a room came up with another Greek family. I took it, and I moved out in the next two days with no hard feelings. I wasn't happy living with the Greek family simply because I had to speak Greek constantly, to the detriment of my English. At that stage, I was attending English classes for migrants in Melbourne. People had a lot of trouble pronouncing my Greek name, and so I took my nickname Estella, which was given to me by the young people at church in Greece.

Working at the factory was a young Yugoslavian girl who was looking for someone to share a room with, close to the factory. There was one in the home of an Italian family. I accepted only because I'd be forced to speak English. Rada and I moved in together and shared a room, which had problems of its own. Rada was very untidy, and sometimes she'd come home late at night, waking me up. However, that was better than speaking Greek at the expense of English. The landlady's name was Philomena. They had a four-year-old daughter Rosetta, who was minded by an Australian lady while her parents worked. Rosetta spoke perfect English and perfect Italian, and I took advantage of that. I spent as much time as I could talking with her.

The house was a three-bedroom place. The main bedroom was used by the owners, the second by a Polish couple, and the third by Rada and me. Outside in the bungalow lived Alberto (Alto), an Italian bachelor in his mid-forties. He was a staunch Catholic with an unshakable faith in the infallibility of the pope, which I didn't know. I found out by bitter experience. One day while discussing religion and Catholic beliefs, I dared say, "He is only a man, after all."

Alberto banged his fist on the table with all his might. His eyes bulged, and he looked angry while shouting, "He is holy, he is holy!" I wasn't one to give up an argument easily, but that time I knew I was beat. I never again challenged the pope's infallibility with Alberto. Philomena and her husband giggled quietly.

Chapter 41

Freddy

Rada and I shared the room peacefully. We got to know the landlords' friends and relatives well. One of the frequent visitors was a twenty-six-year-old, single Italian man named Freddy. He was as wide as he was tall, but he had a handsome face and a beautiful voice. He took an interest in Rada and me and asked us out, which we accepted. He took us out in his car, an old Morris. I chose to sit at the back, and Rada rode in front. He showed us around Melbourne. The next time, he took us to the country somewhere and parked the car. I got out and looked around. Rada and he stayed in the car, being very amorous with much giggling and caressing. I gave them a wide berth. I looked around, admiring the beautiful plants and trees that were new to me. About an hour later, I went back to the car and said, "I'm ready to go home." They reluctantly disembraced, I got in the car, and he dropped us home.

The following weekend, he took Rada out by herself. She came back glowing and said they had a lovely time. Freddy looked like the tomcat who'd eaten the cream. Then Freddy said to me, "Your turn next time." I didn't commit myself one way or another, I said maybe.

I worked at the printing room with Mr. Brady, who also operated the guillotine machine; Mr. Lewis, Allana, and another lovely lady, Allana. We distinguished them by referring to them as big Allana and little Allana. Both mature ladies were good to me. We tied Weet-Bix boxes into packets and talked as we worked; mostly I, asking them to explain the meaning of words and told them, "Please, correct my English."

I took the opportunity to tell them of the invitation I'd received from Freddy for next Sunday, but I didn't know what to do. Little Allana looked at me and said, "Say yes, but only if he behaves." Big Allana nodded in agreement. I did not understand the full inference of the expression so I wrote it down, practised it in front of the mirror, and made sure my facial expression was congruent with my determination. I said it till I thought I had it perfect.

When he visited the following week, he asked in front of his friends if I'd go out with him next Sunday. Having practised my answer for three days, I innocently and decidedly said, "Yes, but if you promise to behave." Well, I didn't expect his reaction.

He went red on the face, his eyes flashed with anger, and he shouted at me "What do you think I am? I am a gentleman." The others giggled.

"OK," I said, "I'll go out with you."

We did so, and he was a gentleman. He corrected my English as I asked him (and others) to do. We had a lively discussion about the correctness of the expression "if I was" versus "if I were." I didn't persist because his English was very good. He took me home and asked me to go out with him the next Sunday. He said he'd show me a bit more of the countryside, which I agreed to.

At work the next day, I asked Allana of the correctness of the above-mentioned expression. She thought for a minute, pronounced it a couple of times in both ways, but she couldn't make up her mind. She asked big Allana, who couldn't decide either. At the end, little Allana said, "I'll ask Mrs. X in the office at lunchtime. She was a schoolteacher; she should know." After lunch, she said, "It is correct to say 'if I were.'" I learned a new sentence.

I continued with my English classes and enjoyed them. By this time, I had been in Australia for three months. Mr. Fred Brady was in his mid-forties. He was tall and beautifully built, with a handsome face and greying wavy hair. He and his family lived in East Bentley. The other gentleman, Mr. Lewis, lived in Ballarat and was close to retirement; he worked part-time. He was quiet and gentle and always had a smile on his face. They were all good to me.

Big Allana turned out to be a very good teacher. She patiently explained words of abstract meaning and corrected my expressions, but she was no match for Mr. Brady. He had the gift of teaching, and because I was an avid learner, we clicked. At one stage, I asked Big Allana the meaning of the word *optimist*. She tried the best she could, but I couldn't get it. Little Allana wasn't any more help. They asked Mr. Lewis, and he too made a valiant effort, but I was none the wiser after all that. In the end, they suggested I ask Mr. Brady. When Mr. Brady returned, I asked him. He silently picked up a bit of scrap paper from the guillotine, took a pencil out of pocket, drew a face with a happy look on it, and said, "Happy, everything will go well." He bent over towards, me and added quietly, "Optimist, like little Allana." Then he drew a face with a sour look on it and wrote down the word *pessimist*. "Unhappy, nothing will go well, everything will go wrong." Again he bent over and even quieter said, "A bit like big Allana." He knew them better than I did. Mr Brady wasn't one to put people down; he was simply very good at making a point. I had no trouble understanding the meaning of those two words. Fifty-five years later, I still remember that lesson, and I fondly remember the teacher.

The next Sabbath, Mr. Brady invited me to his home for lunch, and I met the rest of his family. I had met one of his sons, Peter, nineteen years old who was also working at the Sanatorium Health Food factory. He was a nice young man who was polite and very cheeky. Mr. Brady's son James was a schoolteacher. He was the image of his father not quite as tall, but he was well-built. I also met James's lovely girlfriend. They also had two daughters, Fay (eleven) and Shirley (nine). His wife Elsa was a gem—bright, warm, and jovial, and she was the best cook of her generation. She had a feast prepared with all sorts of delicious vegetarian dishes. They made me feel welcome, and the little girls were so sweet; they talked incessantly, which was just what I needed to practice my English.

Mrs. Brady asked me how long had I been in Australia, and I told her nearly four months. "Only four months? You speak English so well."

I would have liked to have said, "Yes, thanks to your husband, who is such a good teacher," but at that time I didn't have the skill; it would have taken me too long to have constructed the sentence correctly. I was grateful for his patience and willingness to teach me. She gave me her recipe of her famous cream puffs, but I was a lousy cook and never got around to trying it. The Brady family was one of the loveliest families I've met, and I count myself privileged to have known them.

By this time, I was attending the East Prahran Seventh-day Adventist church. I used to go by tram, and I hadn't met anybody my age yet.

The following Sunday, Freddy and I went out. He'd promised to be the gentleman he said he was, and so I was happy to go out with him and see a little more of the countryside, which I loved. We walked and talked about Australia and all her merits. I told him how much I liked being here and added that I had no intention of returning to Greece, even though my fare would be paid by the government if I wanted to return. We walked for about an hour. After a while, he suggested we go back to the car for a rest. We walked all the way back to the car, and he suggested we sit at the back seat. "More comfortable." I had no objections and no suspicions. We talked, and he kept teaching me or correcting my English.

After a while, he started showing signs of being amorous, touching my hand or wanting a kiss. I ignored him, but he didn't notice. I said no, but he ignored me. He came closer to me and put his arm around my shoulders. I tried to move away but couldn't. I didn't realise just how strong he was. With a yank, he pulled me close to him, grabbed me by the scruff of the neck with one arm, and shoved my face into his lap. His fly was already undone! I tried to yell. I struggled vigorously, but he held my head fast, facing down. I had to think fast. I stopped struggling and let him carry on with what he wanted to do. He would anyway, but not without me teaching him a lesson first and getting my sweet revenge. I felt his penis close to my mouth. I felt sick in the stomach and was disgusted, but I couldn't move my head. I opened my mouth to heave he forced it in my mouth. I did the only thing I could under the circumstances: I bit him. Admittedly it was not as hard as I could have, but it hard enough to make him yelp with a blood-curdling shriek like a dog being kicked in the ribs with a steel-toed boot.

"You bitch!" he yelped, letting go of me. He threw the car door open, returned into the driver's seat, and took off in a fury. I don't know if he even did his fly up! He turned around, looked at me with a hateful look, and called me a bitch again. I thought the epithet was appropriate, all things considered. I dare say in the future, he'd think twice before sticking his dick in an uncooperative woman's mouth, especially if she has a good set of teeth. I wonder if he is still alive, and if he remembers me? He never asked me out again. He never visited his friends while I was still living there, and I didn't see any more of the country side for a good while. At work the next day, I was glad I wasn't asked about my outing with Freddy. I didn't want to lie, but I wouldn't tell them the truth either.

Chapter 42

Meeting Edward

I was still living with the Italian family. Rada had moved out, and I started feeling very lonely. I went to church regularly and met a lot of young people who were friendly. I tried my best to make conversation. Amongst them were David and his girlfriend, Mary, both university students of medicine. They were approachable and humble despite their high status in society. His brother, Larry, did law, and Larry's girlfriend, Nora, who was studying physiotherapy. Nora used to wear huge hats. In order to see under them, she had to lift up her head, which gave the impression that she was looking down at me, but it wasn't so. I also met Gladys, a nice girl. She always acknowledged me and smiled.

I noticed a young man of unusual appearance; he was not exactly handsome but was distinguished and attractive in his own way. He went about his duties at Sabbath school in a reverent and assured manner, but I hadn't met him. After church, I went home, and for the second week I felt very lonely. I used to close my door and study English, and as usual I prayed, saying, "Dear God, You know just how lonely I feel. Please send someone my way, someone I can talk to and share my life and my interests with." I'd leave it at that. During the coming week, after prayer I got a distinct, powerful, and convincing feeling that I was going to meet someone soon who would be my friend, but I had no clue as to who, where, or how, or whether it would be a male or female. I didn't care—I simply wanted a friend.

Sabbath came again, and as usual I looked forward to going to church. I've always had a strong need to commune with God. With Sabbath school and church over, that strong feeling of meeting someone was overwhelming but unfulfilled. I started making my way home but decided to go to the bathroom before catching the tram. On the way to the bathroom, at the corner I almost bumped into an older lady, Mrs. Swanson, whose face I can still see. She stopped, said hello, smiled, looked behind me, and beckoned to someone. I turned and saw the same young man I had noticed going reverently and quietly about his duties the week before. He came to her, said hello, and smiled shyly. She asked him if we two had met and proceeded with the introduction. "This is Edward, and this is Estella." We shook hands.

I went to the bathroom and then caught the tram home. I had a strong feeling I was going to get to know this young man and said to myself, *He is not handsome as such. I must remember he has a rather large head and a pronounced nose. He is short, but there is something very attractive about him.*

During the week, he came to the factory to say hi. He asked me if I'd like a lift to church next Sabbath and if I'd like to go out with him sometime, to which I said yes. We went to church together. After church, we went to the botanical gardens. During conversation, which was halted and strained because of my English, he asked me, "How long have you been in Australia, Estella?"

I said, "Four months tomorrow." He remarked that my English was good for the time I had been here. At the botanical gardens, it was easy to make conversation. We talked about the plants, which I loved; there were so many I hadn't seen before. The lake and the general beauty of the gardens enthralled me. I had a great day and thanked him for it. He took me home. As we were saying goodbye, I looked into his face and for the first time noticed that he had the most beautiful green eyes and a broad, friendly smile—a common feature of Edward's family, not to mention the mop of very curly hair.

Next, he took me to the war memorial, to the zoo, to the beach, and later to Sale to meet his parents. I also met his sixteen-year-old sister, Jan, a very sweet girl. His parents were friendly, down to earth, and easy to talk to. His father was a breeze to talk to, and we even talked about politics and economics. When he asked me, "What made you come to Australia?" I told him of the joblessness, the poverty in Greece, and of my wish to travel. We spent the weekend at Edward's place, and I was made to feel welcome by his family. His sister, Jan, had a very contagious laughter, she was light-hearted and happy. She and Edward were the image of each other, except her eyes were big and blue. She was genuine and good-natured. She was tall and thin like the rest of the family except for Edward and Ellen, who were shorter.

On Sabbath, we went to church. The people were friendly and welcomed me in style during the church service, and the majority of them came to say hi after the sermon. We went to Seaspray and around town. On Sunday afternoon, we returned to Melbourne, where Edward was finishing his teacher training at the end of the year. We kept company, went out together, and got to know each other.

Three months later, Edward proposed. I accepted on one condition: That if he ever hit me, he would never see me again. I was not going to hang around for him to do it twice. He was shocked at my answer and said, "I would never do that. I would never hit a woman," and he didn't, well not exactly, later about it.

Soon after I met Edward, a room became available with an Australian family. I moved in with them because it was closer to work. The biggest advantage was that the family spoke English. Geoff also worked at the factory. His wife, Naomi, was a schoolteacher but stayed home to look after their three gorgeous and well-behaved children: Gary, four; Marilyn, three; and Ruth, just eighteen months old.

By now my English had improved a little. Speaking with the children helped a lot. Mr. Brady kept me supplied with the off-cut paper from the guillotine as well as private coaching. Big and Little Allana contributed and occasionally Mr. Lewis. How could one not learn with all that coaching? I kept up the weekly English classes for migrants.

My sister Ellie wanted to migrate to Australia. By now, my sister Eva and Theo were married, and they decided to migrate too. I started proceedings with the Immigration Office to bring Ellie here as an invited immigrant. This would entitle her to come to Australia, fares paid, as long as I guaranteed her accommodation and living expenses.

I kept working at the health food factory. I made some good friends there, and Mr. Brady and his family were my best friends. The Williamson family was very kind to me, and I will never forget them. I tried to find them years later but was unsuccessful. I wanted to say a big thank-you and tell them just how much I appreciated all they did for me. May God reward them abundantly.

My and Edward's engagement was announced in the local paper in Sale, and the Williamsons gave us a party and invited a few people from work. It was an enjoyable surprise, something neither Edward nor I expected. We will never forget it.

Chapter 43

The Wedding Date Set

The wedding date was set for Sunday, April 2, 1961, at 2:00 p.m., eleven and a half months after my arrival in Australia. Mr. Brady gave me away, and Sienna, his little girl, was the flower girl; she was only ten but was tall for her age. Jan was my bride's maid I made the dresses for all the wedding party:, and my mother-in-law's. Corry's outfit was white satin. I gave it to Ellen to take home till the wedding day. Edward's mother did the catering for seventy or so guests. Some of them were from the factory where I worked. The reception was held in an old, almost dilapidated hall somewhere in Sale, which was made to look remarkably good with flowers and sheets covering the mess. I kept a piece of white satin to make a little bag for Sienna to carry instead of flowers

The day of the wedding, early in the morning, I opened the sewing machine to make Sienna's little bag. Ellen came in and said, "I left Corry's pants at home. What do we do now?" There was only one thing to do: either keep Corry out of the wedding party or use the material to make pants instead. Sienna didn't know about the bag, and five-year-old Corry was excited about being a page boy, so I made a pair of short trousers instead of a bag. Both kids were happy.

Edward had a funny haircut first thing in the morning, given to him by his brother, who was neither a hairdresser nor a barber. Things were hectic. Everybody was racing around and running late. A few minutes before Edward left to go to the church, he took me aside and said to me, "When the minister calls your name and asks you a question, you say, 'I do.'" There was no time for explanations as to the meaning. I could be saying "I do" to anything, from being hung to being showered with precious jewels for all I knew. It took me years to realise to what I was saying "I do."

I got dressed, and we were at church on time. The only person of Greek extraction was Hanna Bovas, related to my cousin Magda by marriage. I can't honestly say my wedding day was a happy one. I thought of my mother, dead for two years; my sick father; my aging, much-loved grandmother; and my sisters. I felt very sad, but nothing compared to the turmoil and ambivalence I felt about marrying Edward.

While walking down the aisle, it hit me that I didn't love Edward enough to marry him. I walked down the aisle holding onto Mr. Brady's arm and thinking to myself, *Yes, I like him, and I respect him a lot. But if he doesn't treat me well, I will divorce him.* I didn't know the meaning of the "I do" then. That day I felt I was a horrible, dishonest, and sad person.

After the wedding ceremony, I caught sight of Hanna Bovas. She was crying, but I didn't know why. Ron, a work colleague, brought Hanna to Sale, and he took her back. The poor fellow got into trouble for being late; her parents had no clue where Sale was, how far it was, and that the reception took three hours.

We spent our honeymoon in Edward's rented room in Morwell, and we spent the next two days by the beach. Edward started teaching at the technical college and returned to work after the Easter break. We soon moved in with Mrs. Crofts, who let us two furnished rooms of her three-bedroom house. The move was very easy. Neither of us had anything other than wedding gifts, which were at Sale, and my sewing machine, which was the first thing I'd bought when I came to Australia. The other was a steam iron costing eleven pounds, just a little over a week's wages for me. How things have changed! One can buy the same thing now for less than three hours' basic wages.

Mrs. Crofts was a lovely lady sixty-two years old., She been widowed for two years. She was annoyed that George, her husband, had dropped dead at home and not at work. Mrs. Finlay's husband dropped dead at work, and Mrs Finlay had gotten compensation, but Mrs. Crofts missed out. A fair enough grudge; I would feel the same. The old fellow should have been a little more considerate. He'd die anyway—why not do it in the right place and save her the shock of finding him dead? Also, then she wouldn't have missed out on compensation. Other than this, she loved George dearly and talked about him with fondness. They had two sons, two daughters, and at that time five grandsons.

As winter came, she allowed us to put a solid fuel heater in the spare room. We bought it second hand, and Edward installed it. It worked without burning down the house. I tried to get a job, but there was nothing available, and if there was, single women were given first preference. I was getting bored doing nothing. We decided to start a family, and I fell pregnant quickly.

My pregnancy wasn't easy. I got evening sickness and had fainting spells when standing. Edward had bought a ten-acre block of land in Newborough, which he could pay from his savings, but then the credit squeeze of the 1960s hit. The credit union wouldn't release his money. He had also bought two blocks of land in Narre Warren (a new subdivision), as well as his car. I had no option but to do something to help with paying the bills if we didn't want to lose anything. We put an ad in the local paper for dressmaking.

Some people recognised the address and asked if Mrs. Crofts had started sewing again. She was also a dressmaker and had sewn for many years; she was well-known around the area. The work started coming in fast just as I started getting sick. Mrs. Crofts was very good to me. She'd ring the customers and cancel the fittings, saying to me, "You are not well enough to work today." I sewed and earned enough to help with everyday expenses.

Chapter 44

Smacked in the Face

Edward and I had been married for about two months and were having a bath together. The water was nice and hot just as I like it. We talked about paying the debts off and what we'd do with all the money we would have. We scrubbed till our skin was red. I got out first and dried myself. He got out too, pulled out the plug, and was drying himself while standing under the over-bath shower, complaining that the water was too hot, that he looked like a cooked lobster, adding that that it boiled his eggs. On and on he went.

The imp in me woke up. I thought, *Well, if he is hot, I'll cool him down*. I turned the big, old-fashioned shower full on, gushing ten gallons of freezing water in ten seconds on his nicely dried, warm back. "Ugh!" he yelled, his face horribly contorted. He turned around to turn off the shower tap, only to have the cold water hit his front as well. His arm flew and caught my face. It was more of a reaction than a calculated action. I ran to the bedroom wailing and went straight to bed, my pride hurt more than my face. The poor bastard. I'd have done the same thing and worse. In the middle of winter and after a hot bath, to be showered with a blast of cold water when he least expected it—that was no small annoyance. He came to the bedroom in his pyjamas, all contrite and apologetic promising never to do it again, and he never did. I purposely ignored him, letting him believe he was wrong, but I didn't blame him;

I'd started it all. Poor bugger! Needless to say, he refused to have a bath with me ever again, saying, "The water is too hot. I don't want my eggs boiled." Whenever we'd have eggs as a meal, and I'd ask him how he wanted his eggs. He'd politely and with a cheeky look on his face would say, "Left as they are, thank you." This became our private little joke.

Chapter 45

Dream of Grandmother

My mind was preoccupied with my father's and grandmother's plight. Day and night, I'd think of them. The image of my grandmother as I saw her for the last time, sitting on the bench peeling apples, and of my father in bed upstairs coughing tormented me. I prayed fervently, "Please, please, dear God, take them together. No matter who dies first, the other will suffer." If my grandmother died first, there would be no one to look after my sick father; the villagers would not go in for fear of getting TB. If my father died first, my grandmother would be heartbroken, and her life wouldn't be worth living. She never got over losing her twenty-four-year daughter. Twenty years after her death, she'd be rocking three-year-old Ellie, singing to her the songs her daughter sang with tears rolling down her face. She and my father were very close, and she would have suffered at his death as she had suffered at the death of her beloved daughter. I could not bear the thought. I kept praying, knowing God heard and answered prayer.

One night I had a dream, vivid and in colour; it was more like a vision. I wished some artist would paint it for me. I only had four dreams like this one, each with a very special meaning. Three have been fulfilled to the letter, the fourth is pending.

It was a sunset of extreme calm and beauty. It surpassed the most beautiful sunsets in real life. The sun had just set behind a gentle hill.

The glow of its golden colours was as beautiful as only God could make them. As I admired the silent beauty, I became aware of the dark and silent valley to my left, where my father was, doing nothing in particular. I wondered why. He was always busy doing something. My attention was drawn to the front of the hill, which was covered with scrub, lots of bushes, and small trees not quite tall enough to reach to the top of the hill, which was bare. I could only see the outline of the trees because the light was behind the hill.

While watching, I heard my grandmother's voice coming from my right. I turned and looked at her direction. She was running and nearly on the crest of the hill. She was waving her right arm and shouting earnestly and loudly, as if she were going to miss the last train to an important destination. "Alexis! Alexis, wait! Wait for me! I'm coming too, I'm coming too." I woke up still seeing her arm waving. I was too stunned to think or work out whether I was dreaming, I was in the actual place, or I'd had a vision. It took me a few moments to get my wits about me. Was God telling me that He'd heard my prayer and answered it? It became clear to me, that yes, God, my personal and loving God who always heard my prayer, led me every step of the way, was saying to me, "Hush, child. I have heard you, and I will do as you have asked of Me." A peace came over me—the peace that passeth all understanding, and which I felt many times before. I sat up in my bed, put my head down, and with gratitude and humility said, "Thank You, dear God. You have heard my prayer, and You have answered it. I will not worry anymore." From then on, I neither worried nor prayed about it. I simply thanked God every day for answering my prayer. I knew God had everything under control. By now, I was about four months pregnant, still sewing to supplement our income and pay our debts.

One afternoon after school, Edward said, "Tomorrow, I will go to the block straight from school and do some clearing up." It was OK by me. Tomorrow came, and he went to the block in Newborough. I prepared the evening meal, which was paltry as usual. It was getting dark, and there was no sign of him. I waited a while worrying all the time. Eventually I went to Mrs. Crofts', wondering what to do. We had no way of contacting him by phone, and Mrs. Crofts didn't have a car. I was worried. It was then that I realised just how much I loved this man I'd married only because I was lonely.

About six weeks after the dream about Grandma and my father, I got a letter from Ellie. I opened and eagerly read. "Dear sister, Grandma and Dad died together." No gentle breaking the news, no preamble, no "This letter contains some bad news," no preparation at all. It was as I wanted to hear it. I burst out crying, half sad and half grateful. I was sad they'd died, my father at only fifty-nine, and my grandmother eighty-two but healthy and spritely, her memory intact, just her hearing failing. I grieved their deaths, more deeply hurt for my grandmother, who'd had so much sadness in her life. She'd brought us up and played a bigger role in our lives than my parents did, who because of circumstances were away for long periods of time during our formatives years. I grieved for Father just the same. I had a good, long cry and reopened the letter. Between sobs I read the rest.

Ellie went on to say that the villagers had found them dead on Friday morning. Dad's body was washed and wrapped in the white sheet which Grandma herself had woven and crocheted around the edges. She kept it for her own burial. She told us never to use it for anybody else or for any other purpose.

Grandma's body was next to Father's, her arm over his chest. I wiped more tears off my face as I struggled to read on. Ellie stated that Grandma had baked bread on Wednesday, which was a big job. She had to fire the big, outdoor Turkish oven. She normally baked fifteen loaves, enough for them and to return "the borrowed."

The custom in the village was that the women would take turns in baking bread, keep some for themselves and return what they'd borrowed from each other. This way they always had fresh bread. On Thursday, she went to the market, three kilometres from the village. She took a basketful of vegetables from her garden to the chef in Ardeaa, whom she was supplying. Mostly beans, cucumbers, and zucchinis. She bought some meat, oil, and a watermelon because hers weren't ready, and she walked all the way home. Each way, she declined the offer of a lift. She carried the basket on her shoulder.

At home, she cooked a meal. My father was too ill to eat. In the morning when Yana's husband went past and didn't see grandma around or hear my father cough, he went in to investigate. He found them dead. It was summer. My father was sleeping outside under the covered veranda of the Turkish-style house when he died. Apparently, Grandma couldn't drag his body over the door ledge. They were both lying in front of the door, my grandmother's arm on his chest. Ellie and Eva were both in the city working, and they were notified by my cousins. They left immediately for the village, but the priest was too impatient and didn't wait for them to arrive. They arrived as the mourners were returning from the cemetery, the priest leading the way. Ellie was upset, grieving and furious at the priest for not waiting just another hour. She attacked him, grabbed his long beard, and shouted curses at him, refusing to let him go. She reckoned she would have killed him if the villagers hadn't intervened. Years later, when we were talking about their deaths, Ellie said that our cousin's husband thought that Grandma might have tripped over the ledge as she was dragging my father's body in, and she may have fallen backwards and fractured her skull. That was his theory. The description of their deaths was detailed in the local paper.

The details of how they died and how they were found are irrelevant to me. The important thing is that they died together within an hour of each other at the most. It wouldn't have taken my grandmother much more than an hour to sponge his body and wrap him in the sheet, even when allowing her time to weep over him. Thinking on the scene, I still have mixed feelings of gratitude and sadness, and I struggle to hold back tears. She must have suffered untold pain, sitting by his side, watching him dying, but not for long. I'm grateful for this. Her life was full of pain and suffering; she buried five of her children. My father was the last one she cried over. Her four daughters died between the ages of nine months and twenty-four years. She died with her wish to see her son Minoas return from Russia unfulfilled; he returned two months after her death.

During the years, my religious experience had its highs and lows, but not once did I doubt that God is, that God hears, that God knows, and that God "holds each one of us in the palm of His hand." I firmly believe that the supernatural communicates with the natural in a way we can understand according to our beliefs, culture, and depth of spiritual experience. To those who discount that God communicates with us in dreams and visions, I say, Go to your Bibles, Korans, Torah or whatever scriptures you believe in and tear out every page that mentions dreams and visions... See how much you have actually removed. You will be surprised.

"God spoke in times past in dreams and riddles." God doesn't change, and I believe that God still communicates with us regardless of our religion and our beliefs, in a way that we can understand. God speaks to humans, not to religions. If our spiritual ears are open—if we are tuned in, as it were—we will hear Him. Putting it simply, the way I understand it is that if we want to listen to a particular radio station or watch a particular TV channel, we must first tune in. If we are not tuned in, no matter how loudly that channel broadcasts, we will not be able to hear it. It is as simple as this. Tune in, and you will hear God's voice loud and clear.

Chapter 46

A Home of Our Own

Edward had applied for a commission house with the State Electricity Commission, in the Latrobe Valley where he was teaching at the time. As such, we were eligible to rent in the town near the school where he taught. All the houses were owned by the State Electricity Commission. He came home after school one day and said, "The Housing Commission has allocated us a house in Latrobe Valley till they have one closer to the school for us. Do we want it?" Of course, we did. It was a two-bedroom house with large windows. It was light and airy, sat on the crest of the hill, and had a beautiful view of the valley. We had no furniture except my sewing machine.

We got a table painted sky blue from Edward's father's garage and two timber chairs in natural varnish, though they were old and dusty. We cleaned and scrubbed them, and they did the job. We bought a bedroom suite from the same second-hand dealer who'd sold us the heater. The little gentleman who ran the shop was old and bent over, was lame, and walked on a stick. He took us around and proudly showed us his stock, of which there was plenty. He gave us a bit of his wisdom and advice. "Why buy new stuff if you can get second hand?" We agreed. We bought a bedroom suite with two wardrobes, two bedside cabinets, and a dressing table with a large, round mirror. They were presentable, but the springs of the bed were old and sagging; even with tightening, it was still no good. We paid thirty pounds for it, just over a week's wage for Edward. We went to Sale, and out of Dad's garage, Edward got some planks. We bought a new mattress, and as far as we were concerned, we were set for life. We used that old bedroom suite for many years. We had enough crockery, cutlery, and glassware from wedding gifts. We set up house and put newspapers on the windows, and as soon as we had some money, I went to Sharps to buy some curtain material.

We couldn't afford what I liked. I didn't want to spend a lot of money on a temporary place. In the end, the saleslady showed me a roll of material which was on special, two shillings and six pence per yard. It was a yellowish background with penguins in pairs—some dancing, some back-to-back, and some facing each other kissing. In cursive was writing above each pair, which I couldn't read. The colour was OK, and so was the price. I bought the whole roll, enough to cover two large windows. Now we had furniture as well as privacy. I made the curtains, and Edward bought the rods and hung them. We took five steps back to admire the effect. I was waiting for a comment. He burst out laughing. I asked him what the joke was all about. He laughed even more, pointed to the writing above a pair, and swinging his bum recited the writing in a rhythmic, singing manner. "Penny loves Pete, cheek to cheek " pointing to the penguins with their bottoms touching. I didn't know that buttocks were also referred to as cheeks. No wonder the salesperson smiled wryly when she sold me the whole roll of material. I learned two more words that day.

I was still having evening sickness at nearly five months. One day, I fancied a glass of milk. We had some in the cupboard; we had no fridge. I drank some, kept it down, and was thrilled because I was convinced I'd be sick to the end. Money was still tight., We used to scrounge around in Edward's boxes and were delighted when we found sixpence. We'd walk down to the shops, get an icy pole each, and lick it all the way up the hill, feeling content and very lucky.

We just managed to survive, mostly on spaghetti, rice, and potatoes. We had vegetables when we visited Edward's parents at Sale. My dear mother-in-law would give us lots of vegetables to take home. She was such a wonderful lady, and I loved her.

The house had a gas copper trough to heat water, and a double concrete trough to wash in. I thought it was a great luxury to have all that hot water to do the washing. I even boiled sheets in it! We didn't have a washing machine, but I didn't miss it. You don't miss what you have never had. We didn't get one till after the baby was born, from the same old gentleman in Trarralgon, who assured us it was a good one and would last forever. With a bit of maintenance, I'm sure it would have. It was a green Simpson wringer, the first invention and the first one to come out of the production line. We kept it for three years, and it never missed a beat. I thought it was the ultimate in luxury.

We struggled financially, and we had to budget to the last penny. I still did some sewing even though I had terrible backaches. I had no choice but to keep going. I looked forward to the time when I wouldn't have to sew any more.

We had been in the house for two months when Edward came home one day and said, "There are two Housing Commission houses available. Do you want to go and have a look at them?"

Off we went. They were both on the same street. The first one we looked at was vacant, a two-bedroom place and well appointed. I liked it. The maintenance men were working there. One of them asked, "Do you like it?"

We said, "Yes, it's OK, but we'll go have a look at the other one and decide."

"Good," he said. He picked up a sledgehammer and attacked the kitchen benches with all his might, smashing them and doing a perfect demolition job in less than three minutes. "Here," he said with great satisfaction. "You will have a new kitchen too. They wouldn't let us put a new one in otherwise, and this one is too old." The kitchen wasn't A1, but it would have done us. The other one was about the same and much better than the one in Greece.

As we walked away, Edward looked at me half surprised and half amused and said, "That's how you get a new kitchen from the SEC!"

The next house was in a corner up from the police station and close to the high school. It was a three-bedroom house with a large lounge room and a big block of land which was in three levels. In the backyard were two huge fig trees, a nectarine tree, and a lemon tree. The house was built on the side of the hill. There were four steps to get to the front yard and three steps to the house. Around the house was a narrow, flat area cut out of the side of the hill. The laundry was built on the second level of the block; there were fifteen steps to get to it. The two fig trees grew behind the house, keeping it dark and damp. There were six steps on the third level to the garage, which was accessible via the back lane.

Mr. and Mrs. Salisbury lived in it. He was the deputy principal of the high school. We were greeted by both of them. Meeting them made a deep impression on me. He was a tall, imposing man who was quiet and pensive, bordering on depression. He sucked on his pipe, which he moved to the left corner of his mouth when speaking. He had very little to say. Mrs. Salisbury was of medium height. She wore a pink dress that was reasonably clean, but it had a big chunk torn off it, as if a vicious dog ripped it off. She was wearing a dark apron, perhaps to hide the missing dress, which failed to do so. I tried not to stare at it, but my gaze didn't escape Mr. Salisbury's attention. He shifted on his chair and looked away. She was unaware and kept talking, praising the graces and advantages of the house.

There were the curtains on the windows, which they were taking them with them. I was glad because they were ancient. "The blinds cost us thirty pounds." Only the Lord knew how old they were. There was a rusty rotary clothesline which cost twenty pounds. There was the garage with no door and a lot of planks missing from the walls. She valued it at eighty pounds. That made a total of £130. We looked at each other, shocked. Mr. Salisbury looked at us, took the pipe out of his mouth, and in a decided monotone said, "Fifty pounds will do." We thought that was much better. We briefly talked about it in private and decided to take it. We paid two weeks' worth of wages for an old Hill's clothes line, five black worn-out Holland blinds, a garage that was falling down, and the kitchen lino. We were both too young and inexperienced, and neither Edward or I realised that we could have told them to take everything and go.

When we moved in, the lino had big holes on it. There were no other floor coverings left in the house; thankfully, they'd taken them.

We ripped out the old lino, and good old Dad came to our rescue again. In his shed, he had a roll of lino salvaged out of a bank being renovated. It was a light brown and was heavy-duty. "It has a lot of wear in it yet," he said, and there were no holes. Edward laid it down, and after a scrub and a polish, it looked good. It took me a week to clean up the place. The kitchen wasn't much. It had a sink and a bench big enough to put a jug on. There was a wood stove and lots of grease and dirt. The bathroom had a wood-fired hot-water system, a bathtub, a hand basin, and lots of dirt. It wasn't easy cleaning it because I was seven months pregnant. I didn't think to ask Edward to help. That was not a man's work.

We bought a second-hand carpet from Melbourne and brought it home in the VW. Some sat on the roof and some went in the back seat. Edward did a good job laying it. We had no underlay. It covered the lounge room and the hall. It was green, thin, and worn-out, but we were thrilled. We bought a red lounge suite from Myers in Melbourne on hire purchase. I made curtains, and the place looked pretty good.

We moved our little bit of furniture in, and I finished my last bit of sewing for Gladys, a lovely lady for whom I had sewn before. She had no children of her own, and when I told her I was having a baby, with longing she said, "I would have given my right arm to have had children." Her husband was also a lovely man. They were the first ones to bring me a gift for the unborn baby, a yellow cot blanket with a satin trim. She picked up the dress and kindly said, "You should start thinking about stop working. You may not go full term." I didn't think of that, I presumed I still had two months to sew for the baby. I had to sew for an hour and rest for an hour to ease the backache, but I had no choice. I had nothing for the baby except two dozen flannelette nappies, which another customer had given me. I bought some white material to make some nighties for the baby. I bought four singlets and everything the hospital specified in the "to bring" list.

Chapter 47

Cleaning Job

Jack had a cleaning business in Sale. As a kid, Edward had helped Jack during school holidays. Edward knew the job. Jack left Edward to take care of the business while he took his family to the annual church camp. This year, we needed the job. We went to Sale to take over Jack's business. We cleaned banks, the Sale radio broadcasting station, and a number of shops. Edward's eldest sister, Ellen, her husband, and their three children were also visiting their parents during Christmas.

We were cleaning this particular bank. Not knowing that the manager was still there, I asked Edward, who was at the other end of the room very loudly, "Where do they keep the money?" I wondered where the safes were kept. Out of nowhere appeared this big man with an even bigger scowl on his face, looking at the potential robber. Edward looked at me with an even bigger scowl. The manager, feeling safe, retreated to his office. We were cleaning the Sale radio station, and Edward told me, "Shut up—they are broadcasting." By the end of the day, I was very tired and glad to be off my feet. I greatly appreciated a decent meal prepared for us by dear Mum and Jan. The poor things had six extra people to cater for, but they never complained.

Time came to clean Dalgety's. That was a long room with seventeen desks, and under each one was a big, heavy mat. At the far end were four offices. Edward thought he'd give me the easy job of taking the

mats from under the desks and shaking them; he'd sweep, and I'd put
them back again. I agreed. By the time I came to the last desk, my back
was aching. I said nothing and put all the mats back. That was easier
because I didn't have to jerk my back while shaking them. I didn't I
think to say, "I'll sweep, and you do the mats." I did as I was told—a
habit that went back to my childhood. We went home. I laid down on
my back on the dining room floor, where we were sleeping on a thin
flock mattress. All the bending, lifting, and shaking mats was too much
for my already painful back. I thought I was going to either die or be
crippled for life. I couldn't feel my toes. I called out to Jan, who came
in and looked at me, worried. In between moans, I asked her to help
me turn onto my side. She called Mum, and the two of them turned
me to my side; the pain eased a little. Mum whispered, "A couple more
days, and you can sleep on the bed." Ellen and her family used the two
spare rooms.

With camp over, Jack and his family returned. He paid Edward,
He got more for ten days cleaning than teaching. He jokingly said, "I
should take over Jack's job. The money is better and the responsibility
is less." He would have, except that Jack wasn't about to retire. We paid
a few bills.

We lived in the Valley for seven years. For the majority of them,
I cooked on a two-burner gas camping stove—a luxury compared to
the kerosene one in Greece. Financially we were still struggling, but we
were happy. I wasn't used to luxury, and at least we had food on the
table. There was enough space to start a garden, but it was overgrown
with blackberries and weeds. Edward tried to burn them and nearly
set fire to the whole town; the flames went close to the electric wires.
He tried to put it out with a garden hose, he was terrified. He pranced
around putting the hose now on top of the flames now at the bottom,
he looked funny as he ran around, I laughed. Neither of us thought of
ringing the Fire brigade.

Chapter 48

The Baby's Arrival

About two weeks before the baby was born, my backaches stopped. I thought that no sewing and getting some rest was the reason for it. Sunday afternoon, we were lying down resting. Suddenly I felt my back ache a bit. "Oh," I said, "the back ache has started again." The baby wasn't due till March 17, so I had more than two weeks to go. The backache wasn't as bad as the ones I'd had before, and so I ignored it. The school where Edward taught was at the end of the street, and so he walked home for lunch every day. On Monday, I prepared lunch for him, the back pain still coming and going, but I ignored it. I went to the toilet and saw some pink stain, but I didn't know what it was. On Tuesday, he came home for lunch. I didn't say anything about the back pain. At times it was so bad that I was crawling on all fours and taking aspirin, which gave me some relief. I don't know what quantity I consumed because the aspirin was not in tablets, but in a roll about two centimetres in diameter. It was given to Edward as a sample when he took a group of students to some pharmaceutical company. I'd take big chunks of it more often than I care to admit. To compound things, I had a roaring urinary tract infection. I thought the frequency and burning was due to the pregnancy and the backache. I didn't know what it was.

On Wednesday morning, I struggled out of bed and prepared Edward's breakfast as usual. Wednesday at lunch, I told him to get his own because my backache was unbearable. I spent my day either walking or crawling on all fours, taking aspirin to relieve it. When he came home and after he had dinner, I said to him, "I can't put up with this anymore. Could you ring the doctor and tell him I have had backaches? I saw some blood last Monday." He went to the public phone up the hill and returned running within fifteen minutes. My doctor wasn't there, but the one who answered the phone told him to take me to the hospital immediately. The doctor rang the hospital, warning them to expect us.

A lovely nurse received us, put me in a bed, and asked, "Have you been taking aspirin?" I said yes. "How much?" she asked.

"I don't know. I've been biting big pieces when the pain got too much."

She said nothing, put the foetal stethoscope on, listened intently for a minute, and with a serious look on her face said, "He is still alive." I didn't know what she meant. I thought this was the normal thing to say. I told Edward to go home, not expecting anything to happen for a long time—a couple of days, at least. It was too early, as far as I was concerned. Edward left the hospital at about 9:30 p.m.

The nurse turned around to leave the ward. I called her back, saying, "Sorry, I wet the bed. I couldn't help it."

She knew better. "Come with me," she said. "The other bed is clean." I didn't realise she took me to the labour ward at Latrobe Hospital. As the labour progressed, I felt lonely and asked for Edward. She reminded me that I'd told him to go home. We had no telephone, and he didn't ring, thinking as I was, that it was too early. Neither of us realised I had been in labour since last Sunday.

The backache was as bad as ever, and I complained. "Here," she said gently. "This is better than aspirin, and it won't hurt the baby." She put a mask on my face. "Breathe in deeply." I fought it to start with. After a couple of breaths, I went floating somewhere up in the sky, and it felt good. Not long after that, Dr. John White arrived, and he too asked about the aspirin, which I verified. He shook his head but said nothing.

I wondered what the fuss was all about. "If you have pain, that's what you take, isn't it?"

A couple of hours later, a man put another mask on my face. The smell was horrible, and I fought with all my might, but his strong hands held it on. The last thing I heard was, "It won't be long now." Nobody told me that I was having an anaesthetic and a forceps delivery. The baby was born at 11:00 p.m. Coming out of the anaesthetic was a frightening experience for me. I could see a long, dark tunnel in which there were small squares coming towards me very fast, growing bigger and bigger as they approached my face. Just before they crashed on me, they flew away, just missing me. Suddenly I realised I was alive, and I remembered where I was and why I was there.

I wondered if the baby had been born yet. I remembered the male voice saying, "It won't be long now." Now a female voice said, "You had a little girl. At that very moment, I couldn't care less whether it was a baby or a pup. I was still groggy from the anaesthetic and exhausted from the four-day-long labour. I had lost a lot of blood due to the effect of the aspirin and a large placenta. When I was fully awake, I wanted to see my baby, but there was nobody around, and I didn't know I could ring the bell and ask them to bring her to me. I didn't think it polite to ask in the middle of the night; they might be cross with me for disturbing them. I was awake most of the night, waiting for them to come, but nobody came. They brought her the next morning at about 6:00 a.m.

The sister who'd admitted me wheeled in the clear plastic bassinet with the baby in it. She gently pulled the blanket down to the baby's neck so that I could have a look. I was pleased but too shy to show my thrill and pride. Instead, I said, "Oh, what an ugly baby she is." Just as I said that, the baby vomited a frothy lot of sputum.

"She is not," said the nurse emphatically as she wiped the sputum off the baby's face and took it away in a hurry. I was expecting to see a baby with blond curly hair and a pink ribbon. This poor little thing looked like a cross between a pug and a porcupine, and it was painted purple! I wondered why it was all over her—behind her ears, half her cheeks, and her clothes. When I asked why they'd painted the baby purple, the nurse said, "It is gentian violet. They put it on her grazed skin, caused by the forceps." I had never heard of, nor seen such a thing before.

On Thursday morning, the hospital rang Edward at school to give him the news. He came straight away and saw the baby first. He looked very pleased and said, "She isn't that bad. She has nice gums. She yawned, and I saw them."

Oh, well, at least she'll have a nice mouth on her, if nothing else, I thought.

They told him of my reaction to the baby and how low we both were, and they advised him not to stay too long for that day. Sometime later, he said, "The way they talked, I thought you'd be half dead." Truth be known, I was close to it.

Next time they brought the baby to me, she looked a bit better and didn't have all the colour around her. The nurse gently but tentatively said, "Here is your baby. Would you like to nurse her?" I nodded. She helped me sit up, tenderly took the baby out of the basinet, and handed her to me.

The feeling of holding my baby for the first time is something that words cannot describe; it was a mixture of joy, pride, anticipation, fulfilment, and anything else one can think of. The nurse sat next to the bed, watching my every move in silence; I thought it was the normal thing to do. "Would you like to breastfeed or bottle feed?" she asked.

"I'll breastfeed," I said. She nodded and said nothing more. I put the baby to the breast, a familiar action to me. Every mother I knew except one had breastfed her baby. I saw it as far back as I could remember, and I didn't need instructions how to breastfeed; you could say it came naturally with the pregnancy. The baby latched on with no problem whatsoever. The nurse stayed with me till the baby finished feeding. She took the baby back to the nursery without asking if I wanted the baby in the room too. All the other babies were in the room with their mothers. I wondered at the discrimination but said nothing. I didn't question their authority. I thought they had their own rules and exceptions to them.

The next morning, another nurse with a heavy German accent was on duty. She came in and asked me when I'd had the baby. "Yesterday," I said.

"Have you been out of bed yet?"

"No."

"Ah. You must get out of bed today. You can get up now for a shower."

I did as I was told. I struggled out of bed, feeling dizzy and light-headed with every step. I felt as if I was wetting myself and looked down on the floor. There was a pool of blood, and it kept dripping, getting faster by the moment. "Oh, oh! Back to bed," she said in a hurry. I went back to bed.

On the third day, the matron came in and said, "Today, we'll get you out of bed."

"I have already been out," I said.

She looked at me with a scowl on her face. "You were supposed to have been on a three-day strict bed rest. You had a big haemorrhage. Who told you to get out of bed?"

"The nurse—I don't know her name. She wore a white uniform," I said. That wasn't helpful because they all wore white uniforms. She wasn't happy but didn't ask anymore questions.

As anywhere else, breakdown of communications causes most of the problems. Hospitals are no different, except they cause deaths there. For the next three days, no matter which nurse brought the baby to me, she'd sit next to me and watch. I noticed it was not the case with all the other mothers, but I didn't know why. Years later, it occurred to me that they thought, "Here is a rejected baby and in danger of its life. Watch it."

Some of the nurses were lovely and chatted while sitting with me. Others sat there with an impatient look on their faces. One of them asked, "What's the baby's name?"

"Rose," I said with some pride.

"Hmm. She looks like one too," she said with a tone of ridicule in her voice.

One day the matron asked me to come to the nursery so she could teach me how to bathe my baby. I needed no teaching. I was always where a new born was, watching the mothers handle, bathe, feed, and change them. I got enough practice handling, bathing, and bottle feeding Concetta, Despina's baby. I was sixteen years old when she was born. The matron showed me to the sink, where they bathed the babies. I was feeling light-headed, fearing I would faint and drown the baby, but I didn't tell her how I felt. I hesitated, she noticed. In a gruff manner, she said. "Come on. What are you waiting for?"

I said nothing. I figured out that if I didn't put too much water in the tub, the baby wouldn't drown if I fainted. She looked at the basin and just as gruffly said, "Give the poor baby a bit more water!" She leaned over, turned the tap full on, and filled the tub.

"I'm too scared I might faint and drown the baby," I said timidly, looking at the full tub. "Don't worry. I'm here," she said peremptorily. I wondered how she'd manage to stop me from cracking my skull on the floor and at the same time stop the baby from drowning; there was nobody else around. She didn't ask why I thought I might faint.

I stayed in the hospital for ten days. Before I was discharged, the doctor saw me and asked if I had any help for a few days till I got stronger. I said no. "What about your mother-in-law?" he asked.

"No," I said again, without explaining that she cared for my father-in-law, who was wheelchair-bound due to multiple sclerosis. He asked no more questions, presuming that we didn't get on, which was far from the truth.

I went home with a new baby. I felt constantly tired and dopey all day, barely managing to look after the baby. Edward coming home for lunch added to my work, but I felt it my duty to prepare lunch as a good wife should. I dragged my feet and couldn't sleep at night. The moment I'd lie down, I'd be wide awake. Questions raced through my head to which I had no answers. I was obsessed with finding out what happened when I was under anaesthetic, how long I'd been under, what the placenta looked like, whether the baby cried straight away, and a hundred other questions. Some were relevant and reasonable, and others not but just as important to me. I cared for nothing and no one, including the baby. I looked after it out of duty because I knew if I didn't, there was no one else to do it. I felt no love for the baby; I had no interest in her. I was devoid of all emotion, negative or positive. I can only describe myself as an empty shell, doing things mechanically.

Many times, I looked at that baby and felt guilty because I could not love it. I thought back to when Despina had her baby Concetta, how thrilled I was, how much I loved and cared for her, and how implicitly Despina trusted me to look after her. Yet now that I had my own, the one I'd hoped and waited for since I was a little girl, I could not love. I would have gladly given her away to others if I were sure they'd love and take good care of her.

These feelings made me feel terrible. I considered myself unworthy of being a mother. I could not understand or explain my feelings, and I didn't care whether I lived or died. Edward had no idea what I was going through, and I was too ashamed to tell him. The thought of hurting the baby never crossed my mind.

Mrs. Hardy, the pastor's wife, came to visit. She chatted away, and I listened and understood part of what she said. It was not so much because of the poverty of my English but because I couldn't concentrate long enough to listen. The only thing I remember her saying was, "Can I see the baby?" I went to the bedroom and wheeled out the borrowed bassinet. I was too scared of fainting and dropping the baby. I put it next to her as if it was a can of cold baked beans. She looked at the baby and said, "Wait till she gets all her curls!" Her forehead was still badly pushed backwards, and there was a pronounced ridge where the forehead and the cranium bones met. She had a large haematoma, which made her head look like an egg. Mrs. Hardy left, and I don't even remember what the gift was or if I'd offered a drink. I was not all there.

I'd always wanted a boy first to call him Damien, after my baby brother, but during my pregnancy I had a feeling I was going to have a girl. I accepted it and was happy with it. But now, even the baby's gender was an issue. I was bitterly disappointed. Fortunately, the baby was very placid, fed, and changed she'd sleep day and night, which saved me the worry and frustration of a crying baby.

The time came for the six-week check-up. I went to the doctor, and he asked me how I was and how the baby was. I started to tell him how I couldn't sleep and wanted to ask him a few questions. He cut me short, went to his desk, wrote a script, and coldly but with authority said, "Take one or two tablets before bed." He gave me the script and escorted me out of the surgery. "We will see you in three months." That was it. I left the surgery disappointed and angry. I got the tablets and took two tablets that night, having no idea what they were or what they did. I had never taken any medication other than paracetamol and aspirin.

The next day, I walked around like a zombie, too scared to sit on the chair to feed the baby in case I dropped it. I figured out if I sat up in the middle of the bed to feed it and fainted, went to sleep, or died, the baby would be safe on the bed.

Years later, I realised I was taking Nitrazepam (Mogadon). Even half a tablet would have knocked me out, but I kept taking two every night for about four nights. I decided they were making me too drowsy and it would be better to be tired and sleepless than dopey and dangerous. I stopped taking them.

Rose was seven weeks old when the SEC painters came to paint the house. I asked them if they could leave my bedroom last, and they did. There were three of them there painting for ten days. When I took the baby and her things out of the bedroom for them to paint, they were surprised. "You have a baby in the house? We haven't heard it cry!" said one of them.

"It's a good baby," I said, not realising then that Nitrazepam was affecting her too.

Back to the doctor in three months' time for the final check-up. I heard Dr. White say, "Her haemoglobin is low, but it will get better." He put me on iron tablets. They gave me constipation, and so I stopped taking them. Our diet was poor. It took over four months for my physical and mental health to improve. After four months, I started feeling better. My thoughts slowed down, and questions stopped racing through my head. I still felt tired and faint when standing. Many years later, I realised I'd gone through a terrible stage of post-natal depression, which neither the GP, Edward, my in-laws, nor I had recognised. It was about six months before I became interested in the baby. I spent time with her and caught up with lost time, talking and playing with her every minute I had. What's more, I thought she was beautiful. Thankfully, maternal and child health care has improved since then.

Edward was a proud, loving, and caring father from day one. He cared so much that he even suggested the baby should be on cod liver oil, to help her grow up healthy. He bought a bottle of Hypol, and we stuffed it down the newborn's neck. It didn't do much harm. His enthusiasm knew no bounds. He photographed the baby regularly and developed the photos himself.

With the baby starting to focus, he said, "We shouldn't miss this wonderful stage of her development. We should start recording it." Edward's hobby was photography. He had all sorts of cameras, including an 8mm movie camera. He hadn't used any of them because we had no money for films. Now we had a choice to make. Should we spend the money on films and cut down on essentials? We decided to do without necessities in order to buy the films. Rose was filmed and photographed left, right, and centre. It was fun, and I'm glad we did it then. She was a placid, happy baby and spoke her first words clearly at nine months in Greek: *yiayia*, meaning grandma, and John, which she heard often enough from us reading to her the book *John and Betty*, the grade one reader. It was more for my benefit than hers. She walked and talked early. She was independent. She'd sit on my knee only so long, and then she'd push me away and go do her own thing.

We had no high chair, and so she'd sit on my knee long enough to be fed. As soon as she learned to manoeuvre a spoon, she preferred to sit on the floor till she learned to sit on the chair. She fell a few times but quickly learned to balance on it. I'd missed out on the first six months of her babyhood, and because she was very independent, I didn't have a baby for very long. By the time she was two, she had an amazing command of both Greek and English. She'd take a message from me in Greek and would translate it accurately to her grandparents. She could read and recite many rhymes and poems in Greek before she was three years old.

One day with my baby sitting on my knee, I thought of Pastor Demos beating three-year-old Ellie. The enormity of his cruelty hit me with great force, crippling me emotionally. I wrestled with hate, anger, helplessness, and frustration for a long time. I stayed awake many nights, wishing I could tell him how I felt. It was more about the injustice than anything else. I felt I couldn't forgive him, and I couldn't bear to hear his name without getting upset. Many times I thought of writing him a letter, but I'd be even angrier if he denied wrongdoing. I'd pray that God would forgive me for being unforgiving, and if God saw it fit to allow Demos on the earth made new, I'd say, "Please, Lord, put us on different hemispheres. I don't want to see him ever again." I prayed that God would give me the strength to cope with my feelings against that monster.

I don't know if God gave me the strength I asked for, but He certainly gave me the wisdom I needed. One day while struggling with my anger, and aged twenty-three, I asked myself, *How is this anger affecting me? Who is it hurting more? I sit here being angry and losing my peace of mind, and he doesn't even know it. If he knew, would he care? Please, dear God, help me understand this and get over it. I leave him with You to deal with.* After a consistent effort and much prayer, I managed to completely get over my anger. I forgave him and found peace. They say forgiving benefits the forgiver more than the forgiven, and this is very true. When Ellie went to Greece forty years later, she reminded him of the incident. The sad thing was he denied he had ever touched her, but I was there, a silent witness to his cruelty and injustice, which I'd felt keenly even as a nine-year-old. They say children have an exaggerated sense of justice and a long memory, and they do.

Rose was four months old when my sister Ellie arrived from Greece. Ellie was just seventeen years old. She was thrilled with the baby and thought Rose was beautiful. Ellie played with her a lot. I was glad to have my sister with me. She stayed with us for a few months and then with Edward's parents for a while. She had to speak English only and so learned very quickly. She was able to get a job at the local hospital as a machinist, where she met her Dutch-born husband, Tinny. They were married within a few months of their meeting and moved to Melbourne, where they both worked hard and established themselves. They bought a house and later farming land near Whittlesea, which was Ellie's dream. They built a house on it and lived there for many years. She had three beautiful children, a son, Jack, and two daughters, Annabel and Ellie junior. I loved them very much.

Rose was thirteen months old when I fell pregnant again. I wanted a boy so I could call him Damien. One day I was praying for a boy. I didn't know then that a child's gender is determined at conception. While on my knees praying, I felt faint and nearly lost consciousness. When I regained my senses, I prayed again and said, "Dear God, give me a boy who will grow up to love You and honour You." As I was praying, the name Timotheos flashed through my mind. The name is two Greek words, meaning God and honour. That was enough for me. In my simple, childlike faith, I knew God heard my prayer—and yes, I would have a boy! When Edward came home, I met him at the door, and before he even said hello, I said to him, "It is going to be Timotheos."

He laughed and said, "You are not even sure that you are pregnant yet!"

"It is going to be Timotheos," I said emphatically. He laughed good-heartedly at my simple faith and didn't argue with me about the gender or the name. All along, I had a strong conviction I was having a boy and settled for the name Timotheos, middle name Milton, after the English Poet.

Christmas 1963 came, and I was eight months pregnant. Jack asked Edward to take over his job again while they went camping. Even though we were much better off financially, Edward accepted. We went to Sale for Christmas. My in-laws were very good to me. They didn't allow me to even wash the baby's diapers; either Mum or Jan would wash them. After Christmas we returned home, and in mid-January Edward took Rose and went back to Sale. He was to start Jack's job, and Rose would stay with her grandparents until the baby was born. By this time we had the telephone on; if I needed to contact them, I could ring the neighbours, who would take a message to my in-laws. I waved Edward and Rose goodbye. A deep sadness overcame me. My little girl was going away for the first time, and for all that I knew, it could be three weeks or more before I saw her again. I wasn't due till early February.

Chapter 49

Foolishness

I made up my mind that this time, nobody was going to rob me of the privilege of being awake when the baby was born. I was determined to have the baby at home and on my own, as so many women did both here and in Greece. I read up all I could find on home birth and preparation, and I made sure everything was ready and within reach: newspapers, bunny rugs, tape, and scissors, all boiled and wrapped in clean cloths and everything else the book said. I started labouring at 9:00 p.m. on January 29 and I got everything in place. I dragged the dressing table with the mirror at the end of the bed, and everything was within my reach. Alas, even I had to give in. 5:00 a.m. I realised I was in trouble. I got up and in between contractions, moved the dressing table back in its place, and got rid of all the evidence, not wanting people to think I was mad. By now it was 6:00. I rang my in-laws' neighbours, who took the message to Edward. Then I rang the taxi. The driver was a friend, and he came quickly and took me to Latrobe Hospital. An hour later, Edward came.

By late afternoon, I realised I was in trouble. I said to the midwife, "I wish he'd hurry up and give me a caesarean. I've had enough of this." By 7:00 p.m., I had no strength left. The baby's heartbeat slowed down. I was transferred to Trarralgon Hospital, where we were greeted by the same lovely midwife who'd attended Rose's birth. She greeted us with, "You are in trouble again, Edward?"

The baby was born by caesarean section at 9:00 p.m. As I was coming out of the anaesthetic, I heard them say, "We'd better not ruin all her veins." They were trying to put a cannula in for a blood transfusion. I heard the midwife say, "She lost more blood than this last time; she didn't get a transfusion then." They ended up doing a cut down on my foot. That blood I received was literally life-saving. No fainting, no dizzy spells. and most important no depression.

In the ward when the anaesthetic wore off, I was told I'd had a little boy. I didn't see the baby till the next morning; He had a cut on his left cheek bone about two centimetres long, which was stitched with the same thick, black, string I was stitched with. The scar and suture dots are still visible on his face. I was told "it was an accident, easy to do." He too looked like Rose with his forehead pushed back, but not as bad. I would have loved to have seen my baby. During the night, while lying awake I could hear different babies cry, but when one particular baby cried (and it cried a lot), something in me stirred. I was sure that was my baby crying, and I would have loved to hold him, feed him, and comfort him, but no one came to ask me if I wanted to do so. I still didn't know that I could have asked. I stayed awake worrying.

In the morning, the nurse brought the baby to me still screaming. I tentatively asked the nurse, "Why did my baby cry all night?"

"He was hungry and wouldn't shut up till we fed him," she said. You'd think they'd come and ask me if I wanted to feed my baby, but they didn't. They might have thought I needed a rest, which I didn't get anyway.

After the blood transfusion, they gave me intravenous fluids. When they finished, they clamped the urine indwelling catheter (IDC) and left me without saying anything to me. By the time the afternoon shift came on, I was restless, had abdominal pain, and felt anxious. I didn't know what the problem was. An older nurse came in, sat by my bed, looked at me, pulled the blankets back and said. "I see,". She left and returned with a basin and a jug. I had no idea what she was going to do. She proceeded to unclamp the catheter, which drained furiously.

I glanced at the jug before she emptied one thousand millilitres. She allowed it to drain three hundred more, clamped it again, and left, saying, "You will feel better now." I did.

When my catheter was out, the next day I was transferred to Morwell Hospital. I was treated like a second-class citizen by some nurses. I rang the bell and disturbed their morning tea. I asked if I could go back to bed. having sat out on a chair for two hours, my back was aching, and so was the incision line. The majority of the nurses were good to everybody, but there were a couple who were nasty. You need only one nasty staff to ruin the reputation of good establishment.

I was in the hospital for a week when my in-laws visited. I hadn't seen Rose for three weeks. Our meeting was the most awkward one I have ever encountered. To start with, I couldn't believe how much she had changed. She looked grown-up! I saw her running down the street, Jan running after her, and I couldn't believe it was her. I was sitting outside when they came. I got up and went to meet them. I said hi to the adults. Rose looked up at me with those big, expressive green eyes. She studied me for a moment, put her head down, and stood perfectly still. I myself didn't know what to do or say, and I stood frozen. Edward looked on, most uncomfortably. In a tone of frustration, pain, and impatience, he said, "Pick her up!" The scene of a little toddler standing in front of me, not responding, has been etched in my memory forever. I squatted and gave her a hug, she responded, and I was so glad.

My father-in-law was walking with difficulty now, using two walking sticks due to his MS. They sat outside on the veranda. The nurse gave my father-in-law a white gown to put on. She brought the baby out and put him on his lap. He smiled proudly. "Tut, tut," he said. "He is beautiful." By this time, he was seven days old and looked more like a human than fish.

"He is so tiny," said my mother-in-law.

"Mum," said Jan, "he is eight pounds five ounces. That's a big baby!"

"I suppose so, but he still looks tiny to me," she said. Having a twenty-two-month-old around made a new- bornlook small. I made that mistake myself many times, expecting too much of Rose. I thought she was grown-up.

Before I was discharged from hospital, Dr. J. White asked me again if I had help at home, to which I said no. He didn't ask any more questions. I dare say he remembered we'd had the same conversation twenty-two months earlier. He organised with the council to get me help for a few weeks. When I was discharged, we went straight to Sale, picked up Rose, and returned home.

Ellie and her husband visited the day after. She thought the baby was beautiful and wanted to know what the name was. "Timotheos," I said with pride.

"Timmy!" she said, smiling.

"No," I said emphatically. "Timotheos." She was one of many I had to correct about his name.

My in-laws thought the name was funny, and Edward asked if we could change it. "No," I said firmly. "It is Timotheos. Change the middle name if you want to, but not the first." He was named Timotheos Edward, and they were happier with that.

Mrs. Lazos came to help for a few weeks. She was lovely, and I was fortunate to have met her. She was with us for six weeks. I wished she could have stayed forever. Her husband worked with the SEC. One day, Mr. Lazos called in to see his wife about something. She showed him the new baby and said to him, "This is the first baby I have ever heard to laugh and giggle at five weeks old." Timotheos actually laughed aloud in response to my talking to him. As a toddler, if I had to reprimand him or growl at him, he'd laugh, put his hands on his fat belly, and in his deep voice say, "My belly makes me laugh!"

I bonded with the baby and was over the moon. He was placid and easy to care for. Rose was a perfect big sister. She would sit by my side while I fed him, gently stroking his head saying, "Lothely Tsimimy." It was closest way she could pronounce his name.

One day, I left the seven-week-old baby on the couch to go to the kitchen for something. On returning, I saw her trying to pick him up. I yelled at her in panic, "No!" and my yelling frightened her. Her attempt to pick the baby up terrified me, remembering my dropping

Eva when she was six weeks old. Many years later, when I was watching *The Thorn Birds*, I ran out of the room howling after watching the same scene where Fiona's older daughter tried to pick up her baby brother.

I have many regrets about Rose's upbringing. Far too many. One day we were having lunch, and Mrs. Lazos sat with us at the table. Rose, not two years old, picked up a piece of beetroot. She didn't like it, leaned over her plate, and spat it out as a two-year-old would do. That was a terrible thing to do as far as I was concerned. I promptly gave her a smack across the forehead with a sharp "No." I looked to Mrs. Lazos, who seemed shocked.

Edward said in a low, defending voice, "She is only a baby," and she was, but to me she was grown-up. That action of mine has cost me more pain than I can describe in words.

Another day, Rose was playing in her cubby house. I called her, she didn't come. Whether she didn't hear me or was disobedient, I don't know. I gave her a belting with a leather strap. The neighbour across the road watched in horror. That was bad enough, but it didn't have as lasting an effect on her as when, just a few months later, at the shop she asked for something little. Instead of me saying no, she got a whack across the face. To this day, she is reluctant to ask for anything. I feel terrible about it and blame myself for her difficulty in asking. I find it difficult to justify my treatment of her. I did not know how to say no to the child. Oh, how I wish I could turn back the clock to the first seven years of her life to rectify all the wrongs she suffered at my hands. I swear I'd make it all up to her, but it is too late now.

I don't have as many regrets about bringing up Timotheos. He was the second child and didn't have to be perfect. He didn't have to learn to read; he could learn at school. He had a different temperament, and I was two years older, which made a lot of difference to my maturity and thinking.

A few months later, when Timotheos was about eight months old, I had him sitting in a low potty chair outside on the veranda while I was doing the washing. Rose played in the lounge room and was able to go in and out. She came to me and said, "Mummy, the baby is crying." I could hear him, and I told her so. She went away and didn't come back, but the baby was still crying. I ignored him. He stopped crying, Before I took out the washing. I had a strong impulse to check on him. I panicked when I saw him slumped across the chair, his neck jammed between the backrest and armrest in a space of about ten centimetres—big enough for a baby's neck to be stuck. I freed him from it, he was limp. I didn't know if he was asleep or unconscious. I shook him, he opened his eyes, and I breathed with relief. I can still hear that concerned voice of that thirty-month-old saying, "Mummy, the baby is crying." I thanked God for the sudden prompting to check the baby. Had I put out the clothes first, who knows what the consequences would have been?

As parents, we only get one chance at child-rearing, and if we muck it up, there is no going back. We have to live with it. It is true that we only bring up our children slightly better than we have been brought up ourselves. The only difference between my upbringing and my children's was that they knew why they were punished, whereas half the time I had no idea.

My life has been a life of prayer. Sometimes more intense and consistent than others, but never more so than before the children were born and during their growing years. Before they were born, my prayer was, "Please, dear God, endow them with wisdom, intelligence, and good health, and bring them to this world safely." Later it was, "Lord, just for today, I leave them with You. Please take care of them." It was a mother's simple prayer, stemming from a simple, childlike faith, which God honoured many times.

A lot of things happened then for which I have no explanation. I didn't realise their significance till years later, when I recounted the incidents to the kids or to the family. Two of these are clear in my memory.

Before Rose was three years old, I did a home nursing and a first aid course offered by the local hospital. Amongst other things, we learned how to make beds the hospital way. The blankets, sheets, and bedspread were tucked under so tightly that if one threw a coin on them, it'd bounce. I was so proud of my ability to make them well. I made all the beds at home the hospital way, sheets tightly tucked under so that one would have to lift the mattress to pull them up. Edward complained, saying that if he had to sleep in this bed long enough, he'd get gangrenous feet. "That's how I'll have to make them when I do nursing, and I have to practise," I told him.

This day, I put Rose to bed for a midday rest, and the baby was in the cot. I sat down to do some sewing. Both kids were sleeping peacefully, but suddenly something urged me to go and check them. Normally Rose would get out of bed and come to the lounge room, and the baby would stand and rock the cot sides. This time all was quiet— no crying, no banging, and no Rose coming. I ran to the bedroom, and there was Rose at the end of the bed, facing down and fighting desperately to free herself from under the blankets. I ripped them off and pulled her out. She looked at me terrified. Many years later when I mentioned the incident, she said, "I had just woken up and was trying to get out. I had no time to cry." I don't know how she ended up at the other end of the bed. One thing I know is that God sees, God hears, God responds, and God answers our sincere prayers.

A few weeks later, Rose was playing outside in the backyard, and the baby was sleeping. There were a few diversions to occupy her there: the stairs, which she liked climbing up and down and from which she fell a few times; a second-hand tricycle; and a swing which Edward had made. The swing was stable enough. He hung the seat with chains but put one hole on either end of the seat instead of two.

I was inside, sewing and absorbed in my work and thoughts. Suddenly I got an urgent impulse like a kick in the gut to check on Rose. I threw my sewing on the floor and ran straight to the swing, which was slightly to the side of the house but visible from the back door. What I saw horrified me. Rose was hanging upside down, still sitting on the swing, her thumbs stuck between the seat and the chains. I lifted her up, she was alive. She looked at me as if nothing had happened. I thanked God yet again for His care and protection and for hearing my prayers. I heard no cry and no calls for help, and I wondered why. Years later, when I recounted this incident to her also, she said, "Mum I remember that. I had just tipped over. I had no time to cry. You were there as soon as I tipped." In both incidents, the warning I'd had was before the child was in trouble, and I got there just in time. Try telling me there is no

God who hears prayer and no guardian angels who protect us. You will not convince me. There have been many incidents like this and many near misses in my life, including near drownings of my children both at home and at the beach, but either I, or someone else was there just in time.

Chapter 50

Eva and Theo Arrive in Australia

Eva and family arrived in Australia in February 1965 for a better life with more opportunities, as did thousands of others. Georgina was four months old and one of the prettiest babies around, with big blue eyes, dark hair, and olive skin. She was petite like a doll. I was very glad to have them stay with us. I was sure they'd make the most of the opportunities this country had to offer. Theo was sure of his abilities and was confident he'd get straight into his trade as a welder. He was even more confident of his grasp of the English language. He had a job interview at the SEC and was sure he'd understand the language, but he returned humbled. We asked him how it all went. He shook his head and said, "I thought I could speak English, but I felt as comfortable understanding it as sitting on the sharp end of a fencing post with no pants on!"

I knew exactly how that felt. When you learn a language from non-English-speaking teachers or from a book, you don't understand it when spoken by native speakers. Compared to other languages, English has a poor vocabulary. There are too many words spelled the same way but with different meanings, or words spelled differently but sound the same. For a long time after I came to Australia, I had to ask people to write down the word because the pronunciation was hard to understand.

Despite the difficulty with English, Theo was offered a job with the SEC, he was ecstatic. He got up early for work, eager and thankful to have a job. We waited with anticipation for the end of his first day, wondering how it went. We saw him walk up the hill slowly with his head down, and we thought he was tired. When he got home, he looked terrible. We fearfully asked how it went.

In a low, despairing voice, He uttered three words, "Pick and shovel," as if he were ashamed. My heart ached for him. Here was a young man, a well-qualified, A-grade welder who worked with stainless steel supervising men in his country. He was proud by nature and hoped to get a job in his line of work. Instead, he was given a pick and a shovel and was told where to dig. His big pride was wounded, and I could have cried. But he kept working with pick and shovel, and he set his mind to learning English. Within a year or so, he sat for his exam. His qualifications were recognised in Australia, and we heard later he was one of the best welders the SEC had.

Eva and Theo stayed with us for three months till they were given a commission house of their own. Eva got a job at a local factory in her line of work. Their neighbour looked after Georgina.

Life was busy. I was learning English, running a home, keeping a garden, and doing a bit of sewing for the kids. On top of that, I wanted to have some birds. Edward was always eager to please me. He built me a large aviary more than one metre wide, three metres long, and high enough for him to stand in. We went around the place buying budgerigars. We had all colours. It was such a thrill to watch the birds fly around, breed, feed their young, and grow feathers and colours. But of course, they were extra work, which I hadn't thought of before. They bred so well that within a few months, we had fifty birds. It was a constant round of cleaning and feeding. When I lost a white budgie in a separate cage because I forgot to feed it for a day, I decided it was time to call it quits.

Edward and I were happy together. He was a peace-loving man who avoided friction at any cost. I liked a challenging discussion. (I still do.) Sabbath school was the place I found it. Learning English was put to the test there. The Bible study and the lesson pamphlet were a rich source of vocabulary, which I reviewed when I got home. I also memorised next week's memory verse, all from the King James Version, which was helpful in that it was grammatically similar to the Greek, with "*thine, thou, and thee*". The hymn singing was the most helpful of all. Not only could I hear the words in slow motion, as it were, but it gave me time to read them, and because it was poetry, it was easy to remember. I loved the King James Version. For me, the psalms lost their poetic beauty when translated to modern English, especially Psalm 23. I wished they had left that one in its original, or put in both.

My whole social life revolved around church and its activities. We'd pack up the kids and attend mission meetings to help swell the numbers. I had two sleeping kids, one in the back seat of the VW beetle and the other in my arms. Nothing was too much trouble. Timotheos would be in the pram, Rose would walk, and we'd do the rounds, delivering church advertising papers or collecting money for overseas missions.

There was one thing that cast a shadow on my happy life, and that was my health. I felt constantly sick with indigestion, vomited very often, and had terrible halitosis (bad breath). The GP diagnosed it as gastritis and put me on milk, cakes, a low-residue diet, and antacids three times a day. After a week on this treatment, I felt ill. I was sure I was dying from cancer of the stomach.

At the same time, I had a terrible spinal pain around the T3–5 area. It was so bad that the only way I could stand was to twist my torso to the right side. The doctor couldn't find anything wrong and so couldn't offer any treatment. I'm sure he thought it was all in my head. I was miserable and short-tempered. One morning I got up to get Edward's breakfast as usual. I was trying to put on my firm corsets, which gave me some support. I felt dizzy, and before I could sit down, I fainted and fell forward, hitting the edge of dressing table and cutting my upper lip.

The thud of my body hitting the floor brought Edward running in. When I regained consciousness, he was trying to lift me up, my leg stuck under the bed. I saw him through a mist, he looked worried. He didn't go to school that day. Dr. Sweeney from the health centre came. He put me through all the exercises, lifting my arms and legs, pinching and pushing them, and declaring me fit. "Nothing wrong," he said.

"You are OK." No suggestions for X-rays, no physiotherapy, and no support. I spent the day in bed. The next day, I dragged myself out of bed to resume my duties as a mother, housekeeper, and wife.

That week, I did very little other than feed the kids and go back to bed. Edward had to get his own breakfast and lunch for a whole week. The following Sabbath, he took the three kids (Joanne was with us at that time) and went to church. I stayed home to get some rest. He fixed a stretcher bed for me outside under the thick shade of the fig trees, took the kids, and left. My back was still very painful. While lying there trying to make myself comfortable, I felt as if someone touched my back very gently, enough to make me aware of the touch. The pain went away instantly! I was amazed and thrilled. I got up, went inside, and looked at the clock. It was about church service prayer time, and I knew they had prayed for me. I thanked God for yet another miracle in my life. I folded the bed and put it away. I couldn't wait for Edward to come home from church to tell him and praise God with him. I heard the VW chug up the hill, I looked out to make sure it was him and not the guy next door. Just as they got to the door, I was standing there to meet them.

My face said it all, I was beaming with joy. Edward was stunned. "Well!" he uttered.

"I know you prayed for me at church because the pain went away at about eleven o'clock."

"Yes," he said. "Prayer was offered on your behalf."

I can't help but be a great believer in the power of prayer. I don't care what anyone else says. I stood up straight that day, but after a few days, I felt uncomfortable standing up straight. By twisting my torso to the right, I felt OK. The strange thing was that the next time we went to see my much-loved in-laws, Dad asked if we were in trouble of any sort. When Edward told him what had happened, he looked to Mum and said, "What did I tell you? Didn't I tell you they are in trouble of some sort?" She nodded in amazement. Apparently, he had had a bad dream about us. I wish I had asked him about his dream. At the time, I didn't think to do so. I walked sideways for a long time, but the pain was gone, and I thought I'd walk like this for the rest of my days.

I did not realise then just how close I came to breaking my neck. It was years later, when I applied for a permanent position at the local hospital in Canberra, that the X-ray revealed a hairline fracture of C1 and C2 and the damaged disk between T3 and T5.

This particular Sabbath, we went to church as usual. Theo and Eva were there, and a visitor, a young woman in her early thirties. We invited them to lunch. She noticed I was uncomfortable and asked what the matter was with my back. I told her the story. She said she was a student of naturopathy in her last year of study. She asked if I'd trust her to give me a manipulation, which I gladly accepted. Anything to be able stand up straight! As we went into the bedroom, I glanced across to Theo. He looked worried, and Edward's mouth hung open.

I laid down on the bed, and her fingers ran up and down my spine. She said she felt the offending spot and firmly but gently pressed down, simultaneously turning my shoulder. She told me to stand, asking how it felt. I felt free and able to stand straight. If a student of naturopathy could achieve a "miracle" with one treatment, what would the master be capable of? I didn't have to say anything; my posture said it all.

I ran to the lounge, stood at the door, jumped with joy, and shouted, "I can stand up straight, I can stand up straight!" I was so thankful to that girl, and I wish I could remember her name. She was Dutch with a heavy accent. She gave us the name and address of the practicing naturopath in Latrobe Valley, a Mr. Van der Mullen, whom I visited soon after. He took over the treatment of my back, as well as my stomach. He put me on his medications, and within two weeks I was a different person. He suggested no dairy products for me. I faithfully took his medications, and the halitosis was completely gone. The next time we went to see my in-laws, Dad asked Edward, "What happened to Estella? She looks better." Edward told him the story. He interjected, "I told you it was the milk, didn't I?"

To this day, I prefer to see a good naturopath before I see a GP. My colleague Elaine says, "I see a doctor to tell me what's not wrong, and I see the naturopath to fix what is." Both sciences have a place in restoring health; they should be working together, not against each other.

We spent the rest of the afternoon talking. Joanne sang for us a Sabbath school song in a sweet, soft, and tuneful voice. Poor darling. How proud would her mother have been! By this time, her mother had been dead for three years. Joanne could barely remember her mother's face. One Sabbath, a lady came from Melbourne to tell the kids a story. At home, Joanne said, "She looked a bit like my mommy." There was a thrill in her voice. I can remember hearing my mother say with the same thrill in her voice that she saw her dead mother's face in the clouds. I feel the pain of those words more acutely now than I did then.

Chapter 51

Joanne

What can I say about Joanne? I shed many tears and spent many sleepless nights thinking of her.

Joanne's mother died of breast cancer three weeks after Edward and I were married. When we went to church a week after our wedding, the church was praying for her mother's recovery. The third week, her death was announced, leaving John with four young children aged between the ages of four and eleven, two boys and two girls. Joanne was the youngest, Rosanne was the oldest, and Paul and Jack were in between. I felt sorry for John, but being just twenty-two years old myself, I could not perceive the enormity of his loss and the responsibility he had in bringing up the children on his own, or the effect on the children of losing their mother. I would have loved to have been able to do something for them, but what? I had no idea.

Soon after her death, I heard that her mother offered to move in with John and help him look after the children, but he refused, fearing she might give them meat to eat. I thought he was being a bit silly, but we were in the same environment, had the same mindset as everybody else in the church and as strict vegetarians thought he had a point. Looking back now, I feel like kicking him, shaking him, and screaming, "Stupid, stupid, bloody stupid! Millions of children eat meat, they neither die nor go to hell." But he too was caught up with the fanaticism, the brainwashing, and the narrow-mindedness of the church. A vegetarian diet is good, but not when it becomes a religion which overrides or blinds reason. We almost believed that a vegetarian diet was a direct passport to heaven. I feel resentful now. Benjamin Franklin said, "It is good for reasonable man to be reasonable," and he ate the fish.

It wasn't long before the family was split up. John kept the three older children. Joanne was sent to stay with a Seventh-day Adventist family somewhere in Melbourne. They had a twelve-year-old son who had cerebral palsy. Joanne was there for about three years. One day, John mentioned to Edward that the lady couldn't look after Joanne any more and that she was coming back home. My heart ached for Joanne. I asked Edward if we could look after her. By this time, we had gotten to know all the church members, and John and Edward had a very good relationship despite the fifteen-year gap in age. He spoke to John about letting Joanne stay with us for a while, and John agreed. We went to pick up Joanne from Melbourne. The lady who was looking after her seemed to be very gentle, but she couldn't manage any longer and said, "This is an answer to prayer." I have no idea what it's like to have a disabled child around or what the issues were. I dare say it wouldn't have been easy for her. Of her treatment there, I know nothing. Joanne never mentioned anything good or bad.

On the way back home, I tried to engage Joanne in conversation. She smiled but appeared shy and reserved. We went straight home. John was pleased to have Joanne closer to him. He and the kids would come and have lunch with us some Sabbaths. It was on one of these occasions that John said as gently as he could in front of Joanne, "I hope she is going to be a good little girl for you. Sometimes she tells fibs, and she can be disobedient." I felt more uncomfortable than Joanne did. Even then, with the little experience I had with children, I didn't think it was necessary for him to say so in front of the child.

Joanne settled in with us soon. I gave her the option to call me what she wanted, Aunty or Mum. she chose Mum. We often talked about her mother, how we would meet her one day again, how she was now in the care of God, and all the rest. She never tired of hearing this.

Rose and her got on well. As she got used to us and felt free to be herself, a few minor problems emerged, mostly usual seven-year-old childish behaviour. Bed-wetting was another little problem. It was never an issue for me. Eva was a bed-wetter, and I can still hear my grandmother saying, "Well, she's not going to be wetting the bed forever." She was about the same age as Joanne. All I asked Joanne to do was to put the wet clothes in the bathroom for washing, but she never did it. It frustrated me to find them hidden in all sorts of places, including under the mattress. No matter how hard I pled with her, and no matter how much I told her I didn't mind her wetting the bed, it made no difference. Later, John said he'd make her take a cold shower after wetting, whether it was summer or winter. No wonder the child was loath to admit she'd wet the bed. She started school at the local primary school, settled down quickly, and did well.

The one thing that upset me most and brought me to tears was the fibs. They were about childish, unimportant things, but with my upbringing and my religious beliefs, that was a big issue. I'd sit pleading with her not to tell lies. "No matter how bad the things you do are, they are not as bad as telling lies. It's a sin, and God is not happy to hear us lying. We want to meet your mummy in heaven, don't we?" We'd both be sitting and crying, I from frustration and she from pain or guilt. Today, I would do it differently. Edward was critical of her behaviour. He too was young and inexperienced, and he too was brought up in the same environment, with the same values and beliefs. I didn't have the courage to tell him to leave the child alone. We were harder disciplining our own children, especially Rose.

The lies continued. I was at my wits' end, and one day I said to Edward, "Maybe we should give her a smack for lying." I was hoping against hope that it would fix her. He agreed. I took Rose and Timotheos for a walk, not wanting them to witness Joanne being smacked. That was a terrible, terrible mistake. Tears still well up in my eyes. To start with, Rose perceived what was going to happen and in distress asked, "Is Joanne going to get a smack?" I didn't answer. I walked back within five minutes, figuring out two to three smacks on the behind would be enough, and it'd be done and over with. Joanne would understand that lies were bad, and she'd be settled by the time we got back.

As we were coming around the back, I could hear Joanne scream, "No, no, no!" I ran, leaving the kids behind, and threw the door open. He was belting the child with the leather strap teachers used to have in the old days. I was beside myself. He stopped when I got in, and he was visibly upset and angry. "I meant a smack on the bottom with your hand, not with a belt!" I blurted. I had used that belt on Rose once, but I put it back in the drawer, vowing to never use it again.

I didn't know what a thrashing that child got till the next day, when the kids were in the bath and I saw the bruises on her little body. I closed the bathroom door, and as he was going to the bathroom, I said to him, "Did you see what you did to the child? We said a smack, but not like this." I was still very upset and angry with him, which gave me courage to confront him for the first time in the five years we were married. "Please, Joanne, forgive us both. I am so sorry this happened to you while in my care," is all I can say now. The literal rod was not spared on my children's back either. I didn't have the wisdom to distinguish between bad behaviour and childish behaviour.

With a horrible feeling in my stomach and pain in my heart, I recall how a while later for two nights, I made her wear a nappy in the hope it would either shame her or help her remember to get up at night and go to the toilet. It didn't work. I'd get her up at night and take her to the toilet, sometimes on time and sometimes too late. Many times I cried silently, sorry for her and angry at myself and the world. You can't teach a young child to be dry. You have to wait for their bladder and brain to make a connection, as it were, and shut down at night. You simply have to be patient. I'd love to be able to hug her now and tell her how sorry I am for the wrongs she suffered at our hands.

Joanne lived with us for nearly eighteen months. John took a job in Cooranbong, New South Wales, with a Seventh-day Adventist establishment and moved there with the three older children. The house they lived in was an old weatherboard place. Soon after they moved in, it burned to the ground along with everything in it. Nothing was saved, but thankfully nobody was hurt. John was upset at losing photographs and family records. Soon after the fire, John met Lin, whom he married, and Joanne left us to live with her family. Lin was a lovely lady and a good wife and mother to her ready-made family.

I haven't seen Joanne in years. She got married and moved to New South Wales, and we moved round a lot. I hope she has grown up to be mature and forgiving. I hope she understands that we too were young and inexperienced, and we interpreted E. G. White's writings on child-rearing with our own understanding and from the wrong angle.

E. G. White spoke on disciplining with love, not belting, but for both Edward's background and mine, disciplining meant belting. "Spare the rod and spoil the child" had a very literal meaning. This is a justification I try to hang on to. It doesn't make me feel any better. I will take my failure as a parent to the grave with me. How glad I am that in that glorious day, all of our sad, bad, and embarrassing memories will be wiped away. Here, I would like to mention an experience I had many years ago, which makes me sure that the statement in Jeremiah 31:34 is true: "For I will forgive their wickedness and will remember their sins no more." I find that comforting and believe it is literal, and here is why.

I must have done or said something to someone at some time which gave me much pain and many sleepless nights for many years. One night in July 2001 or 2002, I woke up dreaming about it. I sat on my bed and said, "Dear Lord, I know You have forgiven me. Why can't I forgive myself? Please help me forgive myself." I went back to sleep. Once again I woke up with the same dream, still upset with whatever I'd done or said to whomever it was. I got up, sat at the edge of my bed, and once again I asked God to help me forget the incident.

In the morning when I got up, I tried to remember what the offence was. I could not recall it. I wracked my brains in vain. I can clearly remember being upset and asking God to help me forget it, and I have. Nobody in the world will dissuade me of that. God means what God says, and that includes the above statements. Over the years, I tried in vain to remember the offence that gave me so much pain. It has been wiped from my memory forever, just as our wrongdoings will be wiped out off the mind of God.

Chapter 52

First Rough Patch in My Marriage

I was flat out with the three children, my studies (by now I was doing year eight maths and English by correspondence), home, and garden. I had also started a sewing class for the women in the neighbourhood. Mrs. Brown had asked me to teach her sewing, and three other women joined us. We had a weekly class, which we all enjoyed. A year or so later, Mrs. Brown and her family left town, and the class was disbanded.

Edward was flat out with school work. He had the load of two and a half teachers. For a time, he taught electrical engineering, a subject he hadn't done himself. He had to study it before he could teach it. If he wasn't teaching, he was setting exam papers and correcting them. We were both overworked and overstressed, and we had no time for each other. Any spare time Edward had was spent at church meetings. I felt alone, emotionally neglected, and physically exhausted. All my social dealings were with the church, and other than the dressmaking class, I had nobody to talk to. I longed for some adult company and communication. Occasionally I'd talk to the neighbours, or I would visit the Greek family, Anders and Kathleen, across the road, but it wasn't very often because we didn't have much in common other than the fact that her little boy, Steven, and Rose were about the same age.

One afternoon while I was preparing the evening meal, Edward said, "I need to talk to John [Joanne's father], I won't be long. I'll be back for dinner." John lived a few kilometres from where we lived.

"OK," I said.

The meal was ready, and we waited for a while. At 7:30 p.m., he was still not home. The kids and I ate, and we waited for him for the evening prayer. At 8:30 I put the kids to bed and waited. I was too tired to do the dishes, and the kitchen was left in a mess. At 9:30 p.m., Edward was still not home. I was upset, angry, and lonely. I felt like crying. By 10:00 I could not hold back my tears and anger. I kissed Joanne and Rose goodbye; they were both sleeping peacefully. Timotheos was sleeping in the pram in the lounge room. When I went to kiss him goodbye, he was awake, and he started laughing and kicking his fat little legs. That undid me. I started howling while stroking his face, tears pouring down my face and falling on his.

Then I heard the VW engine sound and knew it was Edward coming home. I was in a terrible state of mind. I didn't think to wait for him to turn the corner, and then get out of the door and run. I ran out of the front gate just as he was driving past. He saw me get out.

By the time he drove to the garage, he found my note saying, "I've had enough. Take care of the kids." He checked the drawer, saw the missing money, and realised I was serious. I was down at the bus stop. He found me sitting at the bus stop crying. He was apologetic and profoundly sorry. I told him, "I am not coming home. It's school holidays. You can look after the kids for a week. I need a break." He asked me where I was going to go. I didn't tell him I was going to a motel for a few days. He would not go home without me and said so. The kids were at home on their own. I figured out I couldn't get away now. There were no buses at that time of the night, anyway. I decided to go home. We walked home around midnight. He was contrite and promised he wouldn't do it again. I hoped he'd learned the lesson I wanted to teach him. He soon forgot.

I felt as if I didn't matter in his life. I felt neglected and unloved, a piece of necessary furniture around the place. I was someone to cook, wash, clean, and look after the kids. I felt more and more envious of

Valerie, a friend from church whose husband, Graham, was helpful and tender and showered her with attention. I wished Edward could show me a bit of love and affection, but he either didn't love me or was incapable of showing affection. Either way, I felt alone and unloved.

Valerie and Graham and their daughters went to the same church as we did, and we often visited each other. I enjoyed going to their place for a meal. Valerie would say, "We are going to have this or that. If you don't mind it, please join us for lunch/dinner." Knowing she hadn't gone to too much trouble just for us, I felt comfortable and enjoyed whatever she put on the table. More accurately, what Graham put it on the table., The kids set the table and did the dishes. While watching Graham go about his job organising the meal and the kids, giving Valerie a break and time to talk with us, I developed a respect and fondness for him. He seemed capable, considerate, and loving towards his wife and children. I longed for some recognition and love.

There were a couple of other families in the church we'd visit and be visited by, and we'd have a meal together, but it was not very often. I liked asking people to lunch on most Sabbaths, but Edward didn't share my pleasure. One day he said, "Can we not invite anyone for a while? I want a break." He didn't need interaction with other people as much as I did. He worked and interacted with others, but I didn't. I was shut in the house with the kids. There were no mothers' groups those days, either in the community or within the church.

Edward and I had no time together, and our relationship deteriorated. I felt neglected, with no one to turn to. The only people we socialised regularly with were Graham and Valerie, and once a month with others at church socials.

Timotheos was a great mimic. He would take on Graham perfectly. Rose was Valerie while playing. He would sit semi-reclined, stretch his right leg out, put his hand in his right pocket, and rest his chin on his chest. Rose would chat away, pretending to be Valerie. She'd tell him about the house, the kids, and how this and that should be. Intermittently she'd ask, "Isn't it, darling?" Timotheos would respond, "Yes, dear" or, "No, dear" in the exact intonation, stance, and attitude as Graham talked to Valerie. We tried not to laugh, pretending we weren't listening.

I liked Valerie a lot; she was intelligent and kind. However, I was attracted to Graham in a way that scared me. I tried to show indifference. The thought of making a mistake terrified me. There were five young children and four adults whose lives would be changed forever if I wasn't very careful. I started suggesting to Edward that he should start looking for another job, that he worked too hard, and that we had been in this place too long (seven years), all of which were correct. He was receptive to my suggestions. He looked at teaching positions within the Seventh-day Adventist school system. There was a teaching position advertised in Mildura which he was qualified for, and he decided to apply for it. Before he did so, we wanted to go and see the place first because neither of us knew it. We didn't want to take the kids with us. We needed a break on our own—the first one since we were married.

We left Rose with my sister Eva. We explained to Rose what was going on. She was four and a half, understood, and didn't mind staying with her aunt. We left Timotheos with his grandparents and Jan. He was two and a half years old. We knew he was going to be well cared for and spoiled. We all thought it'd better if we said nothing. We didn't think he'd understand, and we didn't want him crying. Big mistake! He didn't cry then or when he asked where we were. He was told, "They went on a holiday. They will be back soon." We intended to stay in Mildura for up to a week.

We arrived at the caravan park late in the afternoon and booked a spot. We were both tired and slept in the station wagon that night—not the most comfortable bed. The next day, we looked around the town. By lunchtime the heat was unbearable. We didn't even look at the school—the place too hot for us. We stayed overnight, and early in the morning we were on our way home, cutting the holiday short by five days. I missed the kids. Timotheos occupied himself as usual; he was no bother and he didn't ask much after us. We got to Sale mid-afternoon, and Mum came out to meet us. She looked as if she was seeing a ghost and had a look of disbelief on her face.

"What's the matter, Mum?" I asked.

"He told me you were coming home today. I said, 'No, Mummy is not coming today.' But he looked at me and emphatically said, 'They are coming today. I know they are.' There was no way he'd accept no for an answer!"

Timotheos was happy enough to see us. We left Sale later that afternoon, picked up Rose from my sister's place, and were glad to be home. The idea of moving to Mildura was rejected and forgotten.

I didn't realise then how my absence had affected Timotheos. If I had to go outside, he'd cry and wouldn't leave my side. He became clingy and nervous, and he behaved like that for over a year.

Timotheos started kindergarten when he was nearly four years old. He wouldn't get on the bus without me. He wouldn't play unless I was within his sight. When he started playing with the other kids, I'd hide. When he became anxious, the teacher would bring him to me, and once he saw me, he was OK. It took over six weeks to settle down, play with the other kids, and get on the bus on his own.

We loved visiting my in-laws. They welcomed us, fussed over the kids, and spent time talking and playing with them. Timotheos wasn't quite three when we visited them one weekend. He was on the floor, playing with his little cars. Rose talked with her grandfather. He dared refer to Timotheos as Tim, and she knew I didn't like it and corrected him. They argued about the name back and forth. "No, it's Timotheos." "No, it's Tim." Rose got frustrated and angry, and Granddad enjoyed teasing her. Timotheos was seemingly oblivious to the situation. After a minute or so of this, Granddad said to her, "Anyway, his name is Timotheos." she looked up at him, lost for an answer.

Timotheos looked at her, then at his grandfather, and in his deep voice he said, "Yes, Grandpa, but that's in Greek."

Grandpa looked surprised and burst out laughing. "And I thought he was oblivious to what's going on around him! He doesn't miss a trick!" He was very proud of his grandson.

That was the last time we saw him alive. A week later, he died from a massive heart attack. We saw him at the hospital before they switched off his life support. I was so glad I insisted on going to Sale that weekend. We hadn't seen them for a few weeks before that. Edward was "too busy" with his church work, and he kept putting off visiting his parents. Timotheos' last memory of his grandfather is "helping Grandpa push his wheelchair into the garage." He was a lovely man, and I loved him. They were the loveliest people one could wish to know, and they were true children of God. Grandpa was miles ahead of his time in terms of his thinking about the church, its teachings, and everything it stood for. We didn't give him credit for it then.

Chapter 53

Moving to Canberra

I dislike writing about this part of my life. When I think about sitting down to write, all sorts of other "important" issues and excuses come to my mind, including a painful hand which becomes worse when I have to make an entry into this diary. Right now it is giving me hell. I'll make me a hot drink and will force myself to write.

My restlessness and dissatisfaction with my marriage became more intense. Edward was a good man, a man of peace, and a good husband and father. He was gentle, generous, honest, and very mature for his twenty-nine years. I had control of the finances, and he never asked what I spent the money on. He didn't refuse my requests and went out of his way to please me. I loved him—so why was I unhappy?

He wasn't demonstrative with his emotions. He seldom told me he loved me or paid me attention, but he was good to me. Why was I so unsettled? Why was I withdrawing from him emotionally? Was I mad? I concluded I was mad and made an extra effort to be more caring and loving towards him. I focused on the positives of my life and counted my blessings. I was infinitely better off than millions of women on this planet. I wasn't physically abused, I had two beautiful and healthy children, and he was helping me with my year ten English and year nine maths studies that I attended at night school. What else did I want? There was nothing more, as far as I could see.

Despite my efforts to dismiss Graham, my attraction to him grew. I began to actively avoid contact with him, be it at church or social functions, but that didn't change my feelings. I began to more actively push for a change. Fate would have that there were changes to the technical educational system, and Edward would have to teach in the junior school. His words were, "I am not looking forward to teaching fourteen- to sixteen-year-old boys. I don't like disciplining them. The thought upsets me." He kept an eye out for a new job, and as is the case, if you search, you will find.

One day he came home with a cheeky smile on his face and the *Age* newspaper under his arm. He didn't often buy a newspaper. He said, "How would you like to go to Canberra? There is a job advertised for which I'm qualified." I was excited for two reasons. First of all, I wanted to see Canberra because I hadn't been there before. My gypsy soul woke up, and I wanted to move, and move quickly. Second, Canberra was far away enough. I wanted to put as much distance as possible between Graham and me, which pleased me even more. I encouraged him to apply. He said it wasn't a teaching position, but he needed a change anyway. He applied for the position, which was an analytical chemist with the Department of Works (as it was known then). His duties would be to collect water from all the dams at different depths and at different times of the year and then analyse it. He thought he'd like it and applied immediately. Within two weeks, he was going to Canberra for an interview. We arranged to rent a little cottage at Seasperay, a very old place where we had stayed before. We drove to sale, saw Edward's family, and went from there to the beach. We settled in the cottage, and Edward left the next morning for Canberra.

The children slept inside. I put a mattress outside and lay down, looking at the stars. It was a cool, clear night. The sky looked immense, and the stars shined brightly. It was peaceful. I thanked God for my blessings and the privileges He bestowed on my family and me. My life was heaven compared to my last few years in Greece. At that moment, I missed Edward terribly. I wished he was there with me to share my moment of happiness and peace, a happiness he contributed to by being in my life. I realised then just how much I loved him. I wanted to spend the rest of my days with him. I cried that night half from fear of losing that happiness, and half because I missed him. I went inside, took his pyjamas, and put them next to my pillow. The scent of his body comforted me, and I slept deeply and peacefully, the sound of the waves lulling me to sleep.

Edward returned early the next afternoon. I was so happy to see him, and he was glad to be back. I hadn't seen him so animated for a long time. His face beamed, and his green eyes sparkled with happiness. He was very pleased with the interview. He was asked how soon he could start if he was successful, and he said, "Any time. I only need enough time to give notice to the school principal." We were hopeful. Within two weeks, he got a letter to say he was successful in his application, and he could start work in October. That gave us three weeks to organise a move, get some money together to put a deposit on a house, and start life in Canberra.

Rose didn't mind moving. Timotheos didn't want to move. He didn't want to leave his kindergarten, his house, the shops, his friend Ernie, and everything that was familiar to him. He lacked his mother's gypsy spirit. He preferred to stay in his familiar surroundings and was more like his grandparents, who were happy to spend their lives around Gippsland.

We had a bit of money, but not enough for a deposit on a house. Still, we had a brand-new car paid for, a Ford Falcon, which we could sell to make up for the rest of the deposit. We'd keep the old Austin A40, which I used to drive around. We weren't sure that we could sell the car on time, and in case we didn't, we asked Theo, my brother-in-law, for a loan of approximately eight hundred dollars, promising, "As soon as the car is sold, we'll pay you back."

I will never forget the look of superiority and self-importance when he heard the request. He put his hands in his pockets, puffed his sizable chest, and looked at us as if we were beggars. He raised his head and in an air of self-importance and mightiness said, "You want to borrow money?" He had a tone that said, "Poor things. I feel sorry for you." It was then that I wished we hadn't asked.

"Yes," said Edward, "but only if we can't sell the car on time." I felt humiliated. Theo had a way of emphasising his self-importance. Thankfully, the car was sold within a week, fetching more than we expected.

Before we sold the Ford, we bought a second-hand Mini. A friend did some work on it and I re--upholstered the seats, and it looked like new. It was more reliable than the Austin and went like fury. I didn't realise just how fast it went till one day I was driving it to the junior technical school for my maths class. Timotheos stood at the back, put his head between the front seats, and said, "Mummy, I like you driving!"

"Why?" I asked.

"Because you drive fast!"

I looked at the speedometer and was horrified. I was doing seventy-five miles per hour, more than double the allowed speed limit!. I was careful about driving that little beast after that.

We didn't have much time. The story of my life, "never enough time". We organised to leave the children with their grandmother while we went to Canberra to look for a house. This time we told Timotheos, who was nearly five years old. He liked staying with his grandparents. We left Sale early in the morning and were in Canberra mid-afternoon. We booked our accommodation at a caravan park in Fyshwick and met the real estate agent, a lovely fellow who showed us around several houses. Some of them were very nice around Woden and elsewhere. One house in Mawson suited us well. The price ($13,500) and size were right, but above all I liked the location. It was a little off the main road in a cull-de-sac, just opposite the park and the primary school. The block next to the school was owned by the church, on which the Seventh-day Adventist school was going to be built later. It couldn't have been better had we ordered it. We paid the deposit and left it with the agent to complete the legalities. The house was bought, and there was nothing more to do in Canberra and plenty to do at home. We decided to leave that evening and take turns driving. Edward drove while I rested at the back of the Mini. I'd wake up every time the car freewheeled, wondering if Edward had fallen asleep at the wheel. I'd talk to him to make sure he was awake and go back to sleep. Time came to change drivers. By now, it was the early hours of the morning. He was tired and fell asleep quickly on the back seat.

There were no freeways. Driving from Sydney to Melbourne on the Princes Highway was a challenge for any driver. The roads were twisting, turning, narrow, and one lane. This particular stretch was cut into the right side of the hill, a steep cliff on the left. I was going fast. On a curvy stretch, smack in the middle and at front of me was a big wombat; dead or alive, I didn't know. It was a split-second decision to veer to avoid it and risk going down the cliff, cross over to the wrong side of the road and risk a head-on collision, or go over it. I decided to go over it. I straddled the wombat all right, but when the Mini hit it, the car left the road, flew up in the air, and landed with a crash and a bang on the other side of it. Edward went up in the air and came down with a thump as the car hit the road again! With his heart between his teeth, he asked, "What happened?" I told him I'd straddled a combat. "You straddled a wombat? In a Mini? And we are still alive?"

"We are more alive than we would have been had I tried to avoid it," I said. It was a miracle the car stayed on the road and did not roll over or go down the hill. That was the end of Edward's sleep. I knew I'd have to soak his underwear. He drove the rest of the way very alert—watching for wombats, I'd say. After getting into the driver's seat, he admonished me, "Never, ever again straddle a wombat, and especially not in a Mini. They are too low to the road." Later, he said, "You have to be very careful. They come out early in the morning and early evening to feed." I learned another Australian nature lesson. Years later, whenever he saw a wombat dead or alive, he'd remember the incident, the poor bugger!

We only had about two weeks to pack. I left the bare minimum to keep us going. Edward organised the truck, and I concentrated on getting all my dahlia tubers from the garden. He brought a large wooden box from school that was half the size of the Austin A40. We put all dahlias in it, about two hundred of them; they were different shapes, sizes and colours and weighed down the car. Edward was a bit dubious of the safety of the box up on the roof racks, but there was no way I was going to leave my precious dahlias behind. It was a dangerous thing to do; the car could easily roll if the wind caught it.

The box was high and top heavy, but I had no sense of the danger. My physics failed me, thankfully. We filled the car with the last few bits and pieces, squeezed the kids in, and left as soon as the truck did. Why we didn't we put the tubers in the truck too? Stupid, I suppose. We got a few quizzical glances from other drives on the way. I didn't know why then, but I do now.

We arrived at Canberra in late September 1968. Rose finished grade one at the local primary school. The pre-school year in Victoria is called kindergarten, but I didn't realise and enrolled Timotheos in kindergarten, which is the first year of school in the Australian Capital Territory. He had a lovely young teacher who took him under her wing and made him feel safe and welcome. Rose had no trouble settling in. The kids liked their new school. I continued with my studies, maths year ten and English year eleven. Edward started work mid-October, and we settled in quickly.

We were welcomed into the church, which used the local primary school for meetings till the church was built. We met our neighbours. Our house was situated in Mawson. Yohan, next door, was in the process of building his house. On the left was another young couple, Leo and Bernadette, with two children, Christina (three) and Peter (nine months). Christina used to spend a lot of time with the kids. Bernadette was very sick, and I looked after Christina till Leo returned from work. Sometimes it was late, but I didn't mind. My kids would be in the bathtub, with Christina standing out and playing with the water. When Bernadette went to hospital, I looked after Christina, and her mother took the baby.

One of the kids' favourite games was playing doctors and nurses. Rose was influenced by the kids song "I Want to Be a Missionary Nurse." She was the nurse, Timotheos the doctor, and Christina was the patient. They'd occupy themselves for hours, changing their clothes and swapping roles.

One day, Leo came to my place after Christina went home, and in his heavy accent he angrily said, "Christina is not allowed to set foot in your house ever again, and she will not be playing with your children either." His eyes flashed.

"Why? What's the problem?" I asked.

"Christina said they have been playing doctors and nurses. She is too young to know that Timotheos is a boy and Rose is a girl. They must have been taking off their clothes. Bernadette is too sick to be getting upset like this." Then he stormed off. I was stunned. We were all upset for different reasons. He was right: Bernadette was sick, and she didn't need to be upset. Edward was as stunned as I was. I didn't know what to do. I thought about it all night, and the next afternoon I decided to see them and try to explain.

After dinner, I went. Leo came to the door. As calmly as I could, I said, "I want to explain a couple of things to put your mind at peace. First of all, Christina has been at my place a lot. She has been in the bathroom while my kids were bathing, and when Bernadette was in the hospital, she too had a bath with them. Second, she is old enough to know the difference between a boy and a girl. She has a brother, and she must have seen Bernadette changing his nappy. I want to assure you that Christina has not been abused by my kids in any way, shape, or form. That's all I wanted to say. I won't bother you again." I wished them a good evening and left, still feeling upset and shaken. I was sure there would be no more neighbourly interactions between us.

The next day, there was a knock on the door, I answered. It was Leo. He looked very quiet. In a very contrite manner, he said, "I came to apologise. Bernadette, being sick, misinterpreted what Christina said, and I was too tired to think it through. We are sorry."

"It's OK, Leo. I understand. Apology accepted Imagine it never happened." He left with a smile, and I was happy. Christina was allowed to come to my place and play with the children again.

Chapter 54

Grateful Forever

While in Canberra, I had the worst experience in my life so far, and I hope it is the last. I got up one morning to get the kids ready for school. While they were having breakfast, I went to their room to get their clothes ready. In Rose's drawer, I found some small pieces of coloured chalk. I asked her if she got permission from the teacher to take them. She looked sheepish and guilty and didn't say yes nor no. I presumed that she'd stolen them. I told Timotheos to go to school before dealing with Rose. My own upbringing, and my mother's way of disciplining us for dishonesty, seized me. I didn't know of another way of dealing with it. I belted her, all along telling her stealing was a sin and that I'd kill her if she did it again—as if killing was a lesser sin. As always, she would not give me the satisfaction of crying. I kept belting her till she cried, and when she did, I felt that the message got through. She cried for a good while, and when she settled down, I sent her to school.

I stayed in the front garden, looking at the plants and scratching around, feeling upset myself. I noticed a green station wagon going past very fast, and in two seconds I heard the breaks screech. I froze. I could not move for a few seconds because I knew Rose would be at the crossing about now.

I stood up and could not move. I could hear no commotion. I didn't want to go look, fearing the very worst. Then I ran like mad. There was no accident. The car was gone, and Rose was not on the road dead or alive. She had gone to school by the time I'd gotten the courage to have a look. The shock over, and the reality of what could have been got hold of me. I felt undone. I walked back home very slowly, each step a great effort. The school crossing was only two houses away from ours, but it felt like a mile.

My whole day was affected, and I felt terrible about punishing her so severely for such a triviality. I felt cruel and too self-righteous. The pieces of chalk were no more than a couple of centimetres long, and they were useless to the teacher. In my ignorance, I'd wanted to teach her that stealing was bad and lying was worse. Oh, how I wish this had never happened. How I wish I could erase it from my memory. Forty-nine years later as I am writing this, I feel sick in the stomach. It is more painful now that the years softened me. My fiery nature subsided, and experience taught me differently. I saw the futility of severe punishing, and I felt bad. I thanked God that day for sparing her life, and every time I think of it, I thank Him over and over again. Had she been killed that day on the road, I know I would not be able to live with being responsible for her death.

When the kids came home from school, Rose innocently said, "Mummy, a car nearly killed me today." My heart missed a few beats. I cried inwardly but said nothing. Then I thanked God silently for sparing her life. The teachers knew of the near miss. How, I don't know, and I am too ashamed to ask her. There were no attendants at school crossings those days.

The fear of that near miss, and the thought of losing her, stayed with me. I will take it to the grave with me. When I think that she could have been killed on the road, going to school with a smack instead of with a hug and a kiss, it upsets me and fills my eyes with tears even now. My gratitude to God is undying; no words can express it. God spared me that pain because He knew I would not have been able to bear it. Life would be worse than death for me. Thank You again, my loving God.

****

Edward enrolled at the ANU for an advanced chemistry course, but he didn't think it would be of any use to him, and he didn't enjoy it. He said, "I would be happier somewhere on some land with some chickens on it." I left him to decide. I kept up with my studies, doing maths year ten and English year twelve at night.

Not seeing Graham, I found myself thinking less and less of him, which pleased me immensely. I wanted to forget him and only think of him as a friend. However, I was still not satisfied with the state of my relationship with Edward, who seemed to be withdrawing from me. Every time I tried to approach him about the state of our relationship, his standard answer was, "I'm happy. What's wrong with you?" No matter how hard I tried, I couldn't work out why I was unhappy and what was lacking in my marriage. I had everything I needed and a lot of what I wanted. By now, we had paid all of our debts, we only had a very small government loan on the house, and we had no difficulty in meeting the payments. I was free to pursue my studies. We bought an old ute, which I sometimes drove to night school.

One day, Edward came home from work with the newspaper under his arm and a challenging, cheeky look on his face. I wondered what he'd found in it this time. "Do you want to go to New Guinea?" he asked.

I had heard a lot about that land, both at school as a kid and from missionary reports at church. My gypsy feet tingled. "Why are you asking?" I said.

"There is a teaching position advertised in here." He went on to read it. "What do you think? Would you be happy? Should I apply for it?"

I said. "Well, you only have a five-cent stamp to lose. If you don't get it, you don't get it, and that's that."

That night, a year after we moved to Canberra, he sat down filled in an application form, put it in an envelope with his resume, licked it and, with a quizzical look on his face said, "Let's see what comes out of this." Two weeks later, he got a reply asking him to ring for an interview, and a couple weeks later a letter arrived congratulating him on getting the job. He could start teaching at technical school at the start of the school year. I was thrilled and jumped for joy. He stood in front of me, scratching his head. All he could say was, "It's all too fast for me, it's all too fast. I need time to think about it."

"If you stop and think about it for too long, you'll miss the boat," I said, and I didn't want that to happen. Once again, I reminded him of the old Greek saying: "By the time the wise man thought about it, the foolish man had two kids." He laughed at the saying again, and because I was packed and ready to go, he wrote back to say he accepted the position. We now needed to tell the kids. Rose, being seven years old and well versed in missionary songs and stories and putting all her money "for the children in the mission lands," was pleased. Timotheos hated moving, put his head down, and didn't say much, the poor little bugger. I dare say he thought it was decided, and he accepted whatever would be, would be; there was no point in complaining. We asked the kids not to say anything because it was still too early to tell anybody yet. This was late October 1969, and we would be travelling in January 1970 sometime.

At school the next day, it was show and tell time, and Rose volunteered, "We are going to go to New Guinea, but we are not supposed to tell anybody yet because it's too soon." I dare say the teachers had a bit of a chuckle amongst them. I wonder if the show and tell time wasn't designed to find out the real story in each child's home life. Teachers will tell you they hear all sorts of things from kids of this age group.

We didn't have much time—again! My first consideration was my garden. How naïve I was, thinking people would look after it as I did. I got it looking beautiful, and the lawn was immaculate. Marigolds were in full bloom, my trees were well trimmed and sprayed, and it looked a picture. My one little regret was leaving it behind. Edward sorted out his teaching notes and put the majority in boxes under the house—a good source for a fire and a plentiful supply for rats to build nests. I packed our personal items. Furniture was supplied by the education department, and we were ready to leave on January 17 (which happened to be on the Sabbath) if we wanted to travel as a family. If not, we'd have to travel separately because there were not four seats available for the next two weeks.

When Edward told the brethren at church that we were leaving next week and flying out on the Sabbath, the brethren—in their wisdom, ignorance, or fanaticism—told him we shouldn't travel on the Sabbath. He was upset when he told me. I said to him, "They can all jump in the lake. We are travelling together, and that's that." When they asked him for his decision, he told them we were travelling on the Sabbath. I would have loved to have been a fly on the wall and seen the expression on their faces. I dare say they feared we would burn in hell.

Chapter 55

Life in Papua New Guinea

The kids were excited to be flying. I looked forward to seeing this new land I'd heard so much about. We were met at the airport by Education Department personnel and were taken to our temporary accommodation. The house was typical of houses in the tropics, built on stilts about 1.5 metres off the ground. It had three bedrooms and was furnished with the basic necessities.

Our baggage arrived four weeks later. Rose silently watched me unpack till I opened the box her doll, Rosemary, was in. She picked her up eagerly, cuddled her, and left me to finish. Over thirty years later, she told me just how much she wanted to take Rosemary with her on the plane, but I'd packed it without asking her. I'd discouraged her from asking, as a good Greek mother should, and so she didn't ask for her doll. Neither did she ask for a Barbie doll, which she always wanted. She will never know just how terrible I felt for denying her the pleasure and comfort of taking her doll with her. I too can sing with Frank Sinatra: "Regrets I have a few." Perhaps I have a few more than he did, and I can blame my culture and upbringing for most of them.

When I was a child, good children were supposed to be seen but not heard. We were not allowed to ask for anything, and we got what we were given. Our wishes and feelings did not exist as far as adults went. I don't ever remember asking for anything or being given a choice, except when I was about ten years old and was asked to choose between two dresses. I had that privilege as the oldest. I can still remember Eva looking with longing at the dress I liked best. Without saying anything, I picked my second choice. It was the one torn by the Alsatian. I still find asking difficult, and I can't say no easily, but I have come a long way with much effort.

We settled in our new home, and in the next few days, we met our neighbours, who were very nice. They came to ask if they could help in any way. Both our neighbours were schoolteachers. On one side lived an Australian couple with two little girls, school-age Christina and three-year-old Julie. Their parents, Jim and Fiona, were expecting their third child in a few weeks. They had a daughter, whom they called Ella. Later, they had a son.

On the other side was a Canadian couple, Wayne and Kathrine. She was lovely young woman who looked just as stunning dressed in her finery as in a man's old shirt. They had two children, a five-year-old-boy, Austin, and a cute three-year-old girl, April.

We inspected the tech school, which was nice and clean with lots of tropical trees. There were intricate flowers I hadn't seen before with an intoxicating perfume. The school the children would go to was by the beach, and it was well kept. Not far from the school and on the beach was the Seventh-day Adventist church. Everything was new to us—the way local people dressed (or rather didn't dress), their customs, and their food. We made friends with a lot of local people whose company and meals we enjoyed.

We had a look at the local market, and it was a sight to behold! The vendors, mostly women, sat on mats on the ground, displaying their goods, veggies, fruits, and fish of all sizes and colours. I hadn't seen many of these vegetables before, and I developed a taste for them, especially abica, cooked with fish and coconut in underground "ovens." We had a look around the neighbourhood, and I was shocked at what I saw. I thought our house in Greece was wanting, but at least it was stable enough to withstand strong winds and snowstorms, and keep out the rain. Here in Papua New Guinea, the houses were more like hovels. They were flimsy, and one could push them over without too much effort. They were made of corrugated iron sheets at varying stages of rusting, and they were patched up with plywood or cardboard nailed together to keep outprying eyes more than to protect from the elements. The sight of such poverty made me feel guilty of my own good fortune. I thanked God and wondered what I could do to help, but I felt powerless at the degree of such misery. It took me a long time to come to terms with it. The human mind quickly gets used to good or bad, beautiful or ugly.

I hated the great waste of money by the different churches and denominations preaching their own dogma with fanaticism, forgetting to preach Christ and "Him crucified". By my thinking, it would be infinitely better if the churches pooled their resources together and, with the government's help, tried to improve people's lives, but that was easier said than done. The churches would lose their identity, and that would never do. We humans as nations, families, and individuals don't like losing our identity. If we did, there would be no racism, no wars, and no starvation. We would consider ourselves as one. But the motto of the power of greed and evil says, "Divide and conquer. Subdue your fellow man, exploit him. Keep him uneducated, ignorant, and hungry, and he will have no choice but to serve you while you get richer and more powerful." Oh, how I hate it.

In defence of the churches, they built schools to educate a few children even though those kids had to get up at dawn and work in the school gardens to grow their own food before they went to school. Even then, they had only two meals a day. How could those kids manage to concentrate is beyond me. And I mustn't forget to mention that the churches provided some health care even though it was hard to access. The roads were bad and the terrain was difficult even for a bicycle to accommodate. The health care system was overloaded, and dental care was worse than that of Greece and Australia for that matter, even now. To make things worse, a lot of the local people chewed betel nut, which made their beautiful teeth black and gave them oral cancer. The youngest person with oral cancer I saw was a five-year-old boy brought to the town's hospital from one of the villages; it was too late for help. It was painful to watch him cry with pain, unable to relieve it because of the lack of suitable analgesia. I can still see his little face, his big brown eyes full of tears looking at me pleadingly. I wanted to cry then, and I am crying now. I felt sick in the stomach, frustrated, angry, and helpless, and I wanted to die myself. All I could do was pray for Jesus to come and put an end to all of this pain and suffering, which I desperately wanted to help but could do nothing about. I could not see how else we selfish humans could fix it. It is impossible for us to fix.

The first Sabbath we were at church, we met a few of the brethren, who were friendly and welcoming. A week or so later, two women came to us after church, and one of them said to Edward, "We were wondering where we have met. Have you been to Avondale, College?"

He laughed, saying, "No, we haven't met before, and I haven't been to Avondale, but my sister Iris has been there." There was a bit of a chuckle, and a conversation followed. Edward's clan all look alike; if you saw one, you saw the lot. We also met Naralie, who worked at the food factory office when I was there. We became good friends and socialised a lot, and the kids loved her and her famous chiffon pumpkin pies, which she'd make and bring to our place for Sabbath lunch.

The school year started. The kids were at primary, and Edward was at the tech college. I went to the local high school to see the principal, a tall, thin man, with a light-coloured beard and hair, and blue eyes, I wanted to apply for entry. He looked me up and down, thought for a minute, stroked his beard, and scratched his head, and said, "I don't see the harm in it. It might help the students realise the importance of education and prompt them to study." I enrolled, started the next school day, and did five. year eleven subjects with sixteen-year-old kids. I did geography, economics, maths, science, history, at the High School and Greek by correspondence.

The history was the period of the English industrial revolution, and I could not cope with the pain of it. The last straw was when the teacher said, "They used six- and seven-year-old children as chimney sweeps, and of course their lives were cut short from lung disease." Rose was about that age at the time. I couldn't bear the thought and dropped the subject. I didn't do English because I had already passed year twelve English in Canberra, and I didn't think I needed to do it again. I enjoyed economics and did it in both levels one and two; it was a breeze, and I could understand it. Greek took most of my time because I hadn't done Classical Greek before, and I had to put a lot of time into studying it.

I wasn't at school very long before I got a visit from someone who wanted to talk to me about my attending high school at my age; I was thirty years old. I told him I didn't go to high school in Greece because my father didn't think girls needed high school education; all they needed to learn was to read and write, and above all to cook and sew. I didn't realise he was a journalist and the father of one of the students in the class. He broadcasted the interview without telling me. I was very surprised when it came on the news on the radio all over New Guinea.

Soon after that, we got two more mature students in the class. One was a twenty-four-year-old married girl who was six months pregnant; she dropped out just before the baby was born. The other was a twenty-year-old married girl who continued for the two years but failed to get a year 12 certificate. Once again, I was the oldest in the class. When everybody else was coming, I was going. That was my way of doing things.

The time came to apply to sit for year twelve final exams. I was told that I wasn't eligible to sit for the exams because I didn't do English, which was a compulsory subject. Unless I did English, I couldn't sit for the exams. This was July, and the exams were to be held in October or November. I started attending English classes, read all the books I needed to read, and sat for level three English, which was the lowest level. I didn't want to sit for higher level in case I failed. I sat for science, economics, and geography at level two. I was kicking myself for not doing level one economics. The paper was up my alley and very easy, but I figured a lower level with a pass was better than a higher level with a fail.

At exam time, I didn't realise the Greek exam papers had arrived from New South Wales. I didn't get the letter of notification. When I found out about the exam date, it was too late. Fortunately, they allowed me to sit anyway. I was glad because I didn't want to waste the year. When the exams results were published, we were on holidays in Australia. Many times I wondered whether I had passed my exams. When we returned to Papua New Guinea, Naraly gave me the paper with the results and her congratulations. "You have passed everything," she said. I had to read it myself before I sighed with relief.

We brought my niece Georgina with us to Papua New Guinea. Ellie had her second child and couldn't manage; Eva and Theo were divorced, and Eva had nobody she trusted to look after Georgina while she worked. Georgina was seven years old and excited about going to Papua New Guinea. She too was well versed with the missions and missionary songs. For me, one more child aged seven wouldn't be any trouble, and I loved her very much. She'd go to school with Rose and Timotheos.

We had moved into the tech school grounds a few days before going on holidays. As soon as we got home from the airport and put down our cases, I got the kids together and told them not to get on the swing at the front yard. I explained that the chains looked rusty, dad would check them. If safe, they could swing.

I especially turned to Georgina and said to her, "Don't go on the swing before Uncle Edward checks it first. Do you know why?"

"Because the chains are rusty, and it might break," she said. I was glad she understood.

Ten minutes later, I heard this creaking and squeaking. I looked out of the window, and there was Georgina flying as high as the swing could go! I called her, she stopped swinging and came. I asked her, "What did I tell you about the swing?"

She looked at me with those big, beautiful brown eyes (they had changed to soft brown before she was three). She repeated to me the reason word for word, looking at me as if to say, "Because I wanted to." I took her inside, told her that in the future I expected her to do as I asked her, and in the good old-fashioned way gave her three hard pats on the bottom with the wooden spoon. We had no more problems with disobedience from then on.

There were two other little girls Georgina's age living in the compound close to us. Georgina would play with them, but she'd come back within fifteen minutes upset, saying, "They won't play with me. They don't do what I want them to do."

"Well," I'd say, "you do as they ask you to do. After all, you are in their house."

It wasn't long before she learned to play well with other children. Across the road lived a couple, Jennifer and Byron. They had three children, two boys older than Rose and a younger daughter. Timotheos would spend a lot of time playing with the boys and more so with their big boxer dog. They were churchgoing people (not Adventists) and were very nice. Jennifer had the most angelic soprano voice that was equal to if not better than Mrs. Ashworth's. When she sang, I'd stop what I was doing to listen. Usually sopranos singing irritate me, but not those two women. Their voice was needle sharp, but it came out of their voice box with ease, and I could have listened to them for hours. Pity that such talent was enjoyed by a privileged few.

The school year started. With the kids at school, I started work as a clerk with the aeronautics facility at the pay office. After I underpaid a few big bods, I was transferred to the claims section, which was less stressful for me. I didn't need to work, but I wanted to. It gave me the opportunity to get to know people, socialise, and be financially independent.

My life was busy. I didn't have too much time to spare. Neroli suggested I get some help, which was readily available. A young man came recommended to help clean the house, do the washing, and cut the lawns. After he did the first lot of washing, mixing everything together, I decided to do the washing myself. He'd bring it in for me, which was a help. After he had been with us for a little while, one day I found him cleaning the toilet bowl with face towels. I explained to him the difference between face towels and cleaning cloths. He indicated he understood. I showed him the toilet cleaning cloths and hoped he didn't mix the two. I shudder thinking how many times we washed our faces with toilet cloths!

The students at the college and the house help boys liked Timotheos. They cared for him, which was good. What I didn't know was that they took much pleasure in teaching European children to smoke, they thought it was fun. I was horrified when I caught him under the house, aged seven, smoking like an old man. I tried very hard to stop him, but I didn't succeed. He knew it was bad for him. As a three-year-old, he'd carry a health book under his arm, the hard cover worn out and the pages all curled up. He'd flip the pages to the picture of the blackened lungs of the dead smoker and would say to anybody who would listen, "Look what happens to you if you smoke." His favourite "preaching spot" was the front gate. The house being on the corner, he had a good audience, catching the traffic of both roads. I thought he would be the last child on earth to take up smoking. I didn't realise then that both his grandfathers had addictive personalities and had smoked till they died. We can escape many things in life, but sadly we cannot escape our heredity. Nature beats nurture, hands down every time.

I didn't have too much trouble with the kids, but kids will be kids. One day I went shopping and took Georgina and Timotheos with me. I went to the supermarket, gave them one dollar each, and told them to buy some toys and wait for me there. The money wasn't enough for toys, and I knew that, but I figured out by the time they asked the prices of each toy and considered their options, I'd have finished my shopping. "We don't have enough money," they'd say. Then I'd suggest an ice cream, which they would be happy with, and we'd go home after that.

That was the routine for a while, and I was lulled into a false sense of security that it was how it would always be. Of course, with time they learned their way around town and where the other toy shops were. This particular day, they decided to go to the other shop to check the prices without telling me. When I went to collect them, they weren't there. I called out, looked nearby, went outside, but they were nowhere. They'd vanished! The traffic was as heavy as always, with no pedestrian crossings or traffic lights. The worst possible thought crossed my mind. There was no accident, I concluded they were abducted. I felt sick in the stomach. I crossed the road and went to the other supermarket, heading straight to the toy section. There they were at the front counter, asking toy prices. Relief never felt as good as this. After relief came anger. I felt like killing them both there and then. I made a superhuman effort to contain myself. "What are you doing here?" I asked not very sweetly.

"We couldn't buy anything at the other shop, and we came to see if we could buy something here," Georgina innocently said. I ordered them into the car, skipped the ice cream, and told them I'd fix them when we got home. Never have two kids sat in a car as quietly as those two did that day.

I drove slowly to give myself time to calm down. At home, still fuming, I took the shopping in and put it away. When I cooled down, I went looking for them, but they were nowhere to be seen. I called them. They came out of their rooms, walking slowly and looking like wet cats. I got hold of Timotheos first and then Georgina, and I gave them a few well-placed pats on the bottom with the wooden spoon, which bounced back. I realised then what they were doing in their rooms. They had put on every pair of underpants they owned! Georgina, wearing a dress, didn't look very different, but Timotheos' trousers bulged, and he walked to his room as if his pants were full of pooh. I was still too upset to laugh then, but I did later. They remember the incident and laugh too. After that they asked before going anywhere.

The kids did well at school. Rose got a prize for "most improved" from Mr. Somare, the first prime minister of Papua New Guinea. Things were going well till Georgina started having seizures. Eva didn't tell me that she had neurological problems. When she was four years old, they'd had a car accident. Thankfully nobody was hurt badly, but Georgina said, "I just got a few bumps on the head." One night after we went to bed, Rose came to our room and said, "Georgina is funny. She is shaking." I ran to find her fitting. I called out to Edward to bring the wooden spoon just in case I needed it to pry her jaw open if she was biting her tongue. That was what people did those days. Luckily, I didn't need to use it.

We took her to the hospital. The emergency department was crowded. I was upset and worried. She was semi-conscious. At the back of my mind was Eva. How would I tell her without alarming her? We were there half the night wandering around the emergency department with her in my arms, whimpering. I was beside myself.

Halfway through the night, she improved. They gave us the details of a paediatrician, a Dr. Gander. She was a lovely lady in her mid-forties and reassured us that Georgina would be OK. We could do some tests for epilepsy when we went back to Australia. Fortunately, that was the only episode of seizures while we were in Papua New Guinea. Eva was worried. At the end of the school year, which wasn't far off, we returned to Australia for the holidays. Eva was glad to see her child again, and even though we were happy to take Georgina back, Eva decided to keep her home because she missed her. The lady next door to them, Mrs. Luca, looked after Georgina while Eva worked.

On the whole, I enjoyed living in Papua New Guinea. I loved the first three years, and I enjoyed visiting new places by plane, by car, or walking. We walked for miles, visiting bush churches and worshipping with the local people, who always welcomed us. What I liked most was their singing. They had no accompaniment, but they didn't need one; their voices were pure, tuneful, and powerful. Singing God's praise came from the depths of their hearts. I wished I could have joined them, but I silently thanked and praised God.

When I get to heaven I'm going to ask God to give me the best of angelic voices, because I have so much to thank and praise Him for. It will take me an eternity of singing, and then I will start all over again. I will never tire praising God for leading me every step of the way and blessing me above millions of people on this earth. We humans have a lot more to thank and praise God for than all the angels in heaven. We have redemption to thank and praise Him for, the angels don't.

Chapter 56

"Peace That Passeth All Understanding"

One hot, humid Sabbath day, we drove as far as we could to visit a bush church. We parked the car and walked for an hour to get there. There was no road, just a rough dirt track. Sometimes we had to go through puddles, over tree stumps, or around rocks. After worship, we went over the same obstacles, which was the least of my problems. Because of the humidity, I started getting a headache. By the time we got to the car, my head was throbbing. At home, I felt nauseated, with lights flashing at my peripheral vision. I told Edward and Naraly that I felt sick and they'd have to look after themselves. With Naraly there, I didn't worry; she was a good organiser and an excellent cook.

I went to bed, but the headache got worse. My head thumped and felt like bursting. I was sure I was getting a stroke. I was still nauseous and still saw flashing lights. I had never experienced a headache like this one before.

I was lying there, unable to move. I prayed fervently that God would touch me and take this headache away, believing that God heard me and was able to heal me. Then a miracle took place—one more in my life.

As I was praying, I felt being lifted from my bed by unseen hands about one metre up. I don't know how long I was suspended there. Then very gently, I was lowered onto my bed again. The headache was gone, vanished! A peace seized me. That peace was heavenly and paralysed me. It was a peace I cannot describe in words; it can only be experienced. I can only repeat the words of Jesus to describe it: "a peace that passeth all understanding." I don't know how long that peace stayed with me. A few seconds? A few minutes? I did not move, wanting that peace to be with me forever. It eventually passed, I felt normal again but very weak.

As soon as I could, I went to the kitchen, where Edward and Naraly were preparing lunch, and said with as much strength as I could muster, "A miracle just took place. My headache is gone, and I know it will never come back again." It is over forty-five years as I am typing this, but I haven't had another headache like that, not even in the remaining three years we were in Papua New Guinea with all its humidity. Praise God for hearing our prayers and answering them. "He who promised is faithful" (Hebrews 10:23) to keep His promises to us if we believe, take Him at His word, and above all challenge Him.

During our third year in Papua New Guinea, Edward got a promotion. He was working at the Education Department head office, not far from my work. I hated the sedentary work as much as I hated dressmaking. At least at the office, we had tea and lunch breaks. There were people around me, and I could even walk to the beach at lunchtime. The first year as a clerk wasn't too bad. There was a small challenge learning the job, but during the second and third years, I counted the days, ticking each one off, for two reasons. First, the job was repetitive, sedentary, and uninteresting. Second, I was unhappy within myself. No matter how hard I tried to tell Edward I was not happy, our marriage was under threat of breaking. He'd look at me and say, "What's wrong with you? I'm happy. Everything is OK." That was the end of the conversation. He was oblivious to the signs of a cracking and dying relationship.

I made an effort to spend a bit of time with him during lunch. He came a few times, and we walked up and down the beach holding hands. One morning he rang to say he had too much to do and could not come for a walk with me any more. I felt like crying. He couldn't even spend half an hour with me. I felt let down, alone, and unloved.

The harder I tried to make him realise what was happening to me, the more distant he became.

I did not realise it then, but I went through a terrible depression. I could not sleep, my appetite went down, and I could never get enough air no matter how deeply I breathed. I felt as if I was suffocating. I'd sigh a lot in an uncontrollable way, trying to get air in my lungs. At times, especially while driving, my sighing would annoy him, and he'd tell me in an irritated manner, "Stop it."

When he was driving, I had a habit of putting my hand on his knee. Often I'd ask him, "Do you love me?" He'd ignore the question. One day while driving to work, after having dropped off the children at school as usual, my hand was still on his knee. I rephrased the question and said, "You don't love me, do you?"

He hesitated. Without looking at me, he softly said, "No." I took my hand off his knee, feeling upset but not surprised. I made up my mind to not give up, and I didn't, hoping and praying that one day he'd see sense. I had recurring nightmares of losing my teeth, racing to the dentist with my hands over my mouth, trying to stop them from falling out. Every time, either the dentist wasn't there, the surgery was closed, or they had moved and the place derelict. I'd wake up in a cold sweat. Because I used to have the same dream just before my mother died, I thought someone close to me was going to die, which added to my depression and anxiety. Years later, my sister Ellie said the same dream could mean a divorce or a breakdown of a relationship. The other recurrent nightmare was, that I was flying high at great speed and without control. The setting of the dream was either at dusk or dark, sometimes landing in a field with no one around, and sometimes in an abandoned warehouse flying down long, narrow staircases with nowhere to land; the place was full of broken furniture and other useless household wares.

The dream of flying was so real that I was convinced I had actually been flying; I had to make sure I was awake. It was weird. However, depression or not, sleep deprived or not, I'd drag myself out of bed, organise the kids, and go to work, putting on a brave face. Going to work was the best thing I could have done; it kept me busy and helped me forget my misery.

The other major stressor for me was my inability to connect with Rose. The mild disappointment I felt years ago at having a girl came back to me, only more intense and with more guilt. Not being able to confide my feelings to anybody, together with my state of mind, exacerbated my feeling of distance from her. A typical sign of depression is bluntness and an inability to feel emotion, positive or negative. I loved her dearly and was terrified at the thought of losing her. I'd make sure she was sitting at the back seat of the car in case of an accident, because I felt as I would never be able to forgive myself. However, I could not express my love and affection to her. I know she sensed my distance. She was quiet, almost withdrawn. She was a very sensitive and intelligent child. She would see much of everything going on around her, including the favouritism I showed towards Timotheos and my unwillingness to deny his requests, most times denying hers. She said nothing.

I tried to analyse my behaviour and treatment between them. I realised that half the problem was the way the kids asked. Timotheos always asked expecting to receive. He was very surprised whenever he didn't get what he wanted. Rose always asked timidly and only when she absolutely had to, not expecting to receive. She was surprised when her request was granted. You see, Timotheos wasn't smacked across the face for asking, but Rose was. By the time he came along, I had learned it was OK for kids to ask and OK for parents to say no. I cry with regret and pain every time I think of that day over fifty-two years ago. I still see the shocked expression on that three-year-old's face, and I wish I were dead.

Chapter 57

A Dream of Eyes

It has taken me almost six months to pluck up the courage to tell the story where I left it last, but if I'm going to catch up with the rest of my life, I'll have to confront my reluctance and deal with that particular event.

I kept praying that somehow God would enable me to connect with Rose, to somehow be able to show her my affection and tell her just how much I love her, but nothing changed. I felt unjust and inadequate, a horrible mother and an unfair person. It was depressing and stressing me. Her withdrawal from me was upsetting and increased my guilt feelings.

I was at my wits' end till one day. It was a day I will never forget for as long as my memory is intact, a day like any other day. Up, school, work, home, bathe the kids, dinner, and bed. Edward was out that night. I cleaned up, the kids were still up doing their own thing. I went to bed early to rest and read. I was reading a series of nine books titled Angelique. They were a mixture of fiction and fact and were gripping. I'd often be reading till 2:00 a.m.

No sooner had I gone to bed than Timotheos crawled into my bed without asking. He presumed it was OK. I looked at him not pleased but said nothing. I kept reading, ignoring him. Rose finished her shower, and she too came in. She looked at Timotheos lying next to me and then looked at me with an unmistakeable but unspoken request: "Can I come to bed with you too?"

I simply wanted to read, and because it wasn't hard to refuse her, I said to her, "You can go to your bed," emphasising the *you*."

She looked at me with those big green eyes full of sadness, but she accepted without a word of complaint. She gave me a good night kiss and sweetly said, "Good night, Mummy." I said good night, she went to her bed, and I continued reading.

I don't know what time Timotheos went to his bed, or what time Edward came home, and I wish I could not remember the whole incident, which gave me so much pain over the years. It still does. I see those sad green sad eyes, that little face badly hurt to see her brother in bed with Mum—but she was sent to her own bed. I cry when I think of it. How unfair can a parent be? I loved her as much as I loved Timotheos, and the thought of losing either of them terrified me equally. But I know in my heart that I was much harder on Rose, and I expected much more of her than Timotheos.

That night I had a dream that shattered and shocked me, but at the same time it changed my relationship with Rose. The dream was a short one, a continuation of last night's incident, of her bending over to kiss me good night. But in the dream, I could not see her body; her facial features were blurred. All I could see clearly were those beautiful green eyes full of sadness and love. No anger, resentment, or accusation. I focussed on those eyes for a few moments. I woke up with my heart thumping, and a load of guilt descended upon me, crushing me. I flew out of my bed and ran to her room, bawling my eyes out. She was fast asleep. I threw my arms around her, got her out of her bed, and sobbed like a child. I told her I loved her. She didn't say anything then, and to this day I don't know what she made out of the whole incident, or even if she remembers it; she would have been about eight years old. That night I slept on the floor next to her bed. It is forty-seven years later as I am typing this. I have to stop and dry the tears running down my face.

For a couple of weeks, I felt worn out and raw inside, as if someone had kicked me in the gut. I thanked God for that dream, which woke me up and gave me the courage to tell Rose just how much I loved her. I thanked God then, and I do now for that painful dream which changed her whole life and my relationship with her. I now have a great relationship with a wonderful daughter, who is also my best friend and confidante. I know it will be so till the day I die. I dread the thought of what would have been had things continued the way they were. That painful dream changed everything. The Lord works in weird and mysterious ways His wonders to perform. I will always be thankful for the difficult and thorny paths He led me through, and for the lessons He so poignantly taught me. I don't want to think of the times when, in my depression, I resented having had a daughter and not a son so that I could call him Damien in memory my little brother. Then again, fate would have it that I ended up with a ready-made son named Damien who is much loved and very dear to me.

That's life. We all have our regrets, and I'm sure we'd do it differently if we had our time over again. Unfortunately, we only get one chance with each child. We have to live with our regrets and mistakes. I often think of Jacob, the patriarch. He too made the same mistake and was unfair in the treatment of his children and his wives. He too suffered many years of grieving and pain because of it. He made no secret that Rachel and Joseph were his favourites. When preparing to meet his brother Esau, he placed Rachel (who was pregnant) and Joseph at the back of the vanguard, not knowing Esau's reaction at seeing him again, having deceived him twice. But it is never too late to go to them, throw our arms around them, and say, "So sorry I have hurt you, but myself I have hurt even more."

During Rose's growing years, we had some ups and downs. Later on, when she went to England to do her paediatric nursing, I was able to write to her and tell her how I felt, and I asked her to please forgive me. Her childhood wasn't an easy one, I know, and it hurts me more than any other hurt I've had in life. It is a pain I cannot assuage, and I will take it to the grave with me, but it is a little easier to bear knowing she has forgiven me and does not hold a grudge against me. Here, I must say we find it easier to forgive others than to forgive ourselves, and it is easier to be kind to others than to ourselves.

She wrote back and said, "Looking around me, I would much rather the way you brought us up than some other kids. Thanks, Mum, for the vote of confidence. You were too young to know any better." She is so loving, forgiving, and understanding, and she's much loved and respected by those who know her best.

We as parents cause more psychological damage and more physical hurt to our children than anybody else in their whole world. A psychiatrist and author whose name I don't remember said in his book in the opening chapter on child-rearing (and I am paraphrasing), "We as parents are pretty good at F ... our children's brains." Where I work, I see it practically every day. But this does not have to be so forever. When we recognise our failure to have done a better job in bringing them up, usually many years later, we need to humble ourselves. It's not easy. Go to them and humbly and sincerely say, "The job I thought I did so well wasn't so good after all. "from my poem "A Parent's Regret' The apology will heal them, even though we won't forgive ourselves. Knowing they have forgiven us, it is easier to carry the burden of guilt. And remember that forgiving benefits the forgiver more than the forgiven. It helps our children heal.

Chapter 58

A Difficult Decision

November 1972. The school year was over for me, and there were only four weeks left for the children. We decided that the children and I would leave for Australia before Edward.

I wanted a break from the home situation, and I also wanted to work at a Psychiatric Hospital for experience. When I said that I would only be available for six weeks, they wouldn't employ me. They offered me a position as a student, which I couldn't accept at the time. We stayed with my sister Eva in Melbourne for a couple of weeks. The kids went to the local primary school. Timotheos hated the concrete jungle, but he never said a word about it till years later.

I wanted to do something. Ellie said she could find us a job in "the rag trade." We went to a clothing factory. The supervisor, Pauline, never asked for any references or any experience we might have had. She simply sat us at front of a sewing machine next to each other, gave us the thread, and said, "Thread the machine." I could thread any machine from the old hand-operated Singers to treadles and the new electronic ones; they were much the same.

I threaded mine while the supervisor watched. I glanced across to Ellie, who was struggling to thread hers. She owned a sewing machine, but it was different than this one. I leaned over to help her, but the supervisor intervened and looked at me, shaking her head. I felt bad for not being able to help my sister, especially when she looked at me and quietly called my name as if to say "help me". Regardless of the difficulty Ellie had, Pauline employed us both, and we worked there for about four weeks while Eva looked after my two kids and Ellie's son, who was four years old. When the school year was over, I decided to go to Sale and stay there till Edward came. Mum was in a nursing home because of a stroke she'd had a while ago.

Ellie pleaded with me to stay with her, saying, "If you don't want to work while the kids are on holidays, you can stay here and look after the kids while I work a bit longer." I was torn between staying with her and helping her out, or going to see my sick mother-in-law. I asked Ellie to let me take Jack with me for a short while, but she wouldn't. I reluctantly decided to go to Gippsland.

The fact that I didn't stay to help my sister, especially when she went out of her way to help me every time I needed her, has bothered me, and I still feel guilty now. Many times I wish I had stayed with her.

We went to Gippsland before Christmas. The house had been empty for some time; it looked abandoned, sad, and dismal. I cleaned the dead leaves from the back veranda, trying to hold back tears. This had been a happy place for me, where people welcomed me and my children, a place full of happy memories. Now it was silent. The ghosts of people who made it happy were in every corner and in every room. One day I had stupidly asked Dad why there was a mirror opposite the toilet seat. With an impish look on his face, he said, "I look at it, and when I start going red in the face, I know I need a Ford pill!"

I smiled sadly. I saw Dad sitting on the toilet with the door open, shaving. His voice came back to me from somewhere in the distant past. I saw Mum standing at front of the wood stove, stirring the porridge, and baking her famous wholemeal bread rolls, whose aroma filled the whole house and made my mouth water. I saw her washing the kids' nappies as if it was the greatest privilege in the world for her. I wished she was here to hug her, to tell her how much I appreciated every little thing she did for me and my children, but she was not. She was sitting on a chair in a nursing home, watching everything that went on around her, unable to speak, and unable to use her right hand—the hand that had helped everybody. I couldn't help feeling resentful and angry at the cruel fate of such a saintly person.

I didn't say much to the kids that day. I kept my pain hidden in my heart, nursing an unseen but deep wound. The kids ran around visiting their old haunts, asking, "When is Grandma coming home?" All I could say was, "For Christmas."

Mum was home for Christmas, with her two sons and two daughters and their families around her. She beamed with happiness. Iris was in the United States.

With Christmas holidays over, Mum went back into care. Ellen and Jan and their families went home. We stayed on and visited Mum every day. What amazed me was that even though she had lost her speech and couldn't utter a word in conversation, she could recite whole verses from the Bible as well as sing hymns. Her favourite verse was, "Let not your heart be troubled … in my father's house there are many mansions … I go and prepare a place for you … and I will come again … to take you with me" (John 14:1–4). Her favourite hymns were "Shall we meet beyond the river where the surges cease to roll" and "When all my labours and trials are o'er … that will be glory for me." She would either forget the rest of the words or mix them up. She would sing or recite with a glint in her eye. She also loved Psalm 23 and would recite whole verses of it. "The Lord is my Shepherd; I shall not want." She would muddle it up and paraphrase. "If I walk through the valley of death, I will not fear." Both Mum and Dad were lovely people, and I loved them both.

That year, 1972, we attended church camp just for the weekend. We saw friends and relatives, including Graham and Valerie. Their daughter, Jane, and her husband, John, were there. Their little boy, Marc, was nine months old and had just started walking by hanging onto furniture. He was a beautiful baby, and the main feature of his face was his eyes, which were big, blue, full of expression with dark, long eyelashes, just like his mother.

Seeing Graham and Valerie interact, Graham seemingly affectionate and attentive, made me feel cheated. Once again I felt alone, sad, and angry, and I wished I could be in Valerie's boots. Graham was always polite and attentive towards me. My feelings for him stirred again. All I wanted to do was to get away from him. I felt vulnerable and was scared to death of the consequences. We ended up (or rather, Edward did) inviting them to visit us in Papua New Guinea. I was both hopeful and fearful they'd accept.

A few months later, we received a phone call from Jan to say that Mum had died after another massive stroke. I was sad and upset at being unable to attend her funeral. Edward was given compassionate leave to attend his mother's funeral, but not me. After her estate was sorted out and Edward's share came through, he suggested we go for a holiday. "No," I said. "We will invest it in another house. We are getting enough holidays as it is." During the August and September holidays, I went to Canberra and bought a house in Canberra North, a three-bedroom place whose kitchen window looked over Canberra. I liked it better than the one we were in, but I never lived in it.

Valerie took us up on our offer and came to New Guinea. Graham didn't come even though later he said he could have. I wondered why not. Valerie and I had great times together. We went to the beach regularly after work while Edward looked after the children. We caught the boat to the island of the Lepers, swam topless in its clear tropical waters, and talked about all sorts of things. Valerie talked about Graham, praising his job, his position, and all the important functions they went to; she said she was looked upon as very privileged and important (not her exact words). I did not care about his job and all the glory it brought her. All I cared about was one warm, loving hug. I wanted to feel loved, to be appreciated, nothing else. I felt envious, rejected, and angry. I felt as if I were not worthy to be loved. I blamed myself and felt more depressed. Often Edward would take Valerie out, I would choose to stay home, using the children as the excuse.

Anger and self-pity filled my soul. My eyes would fill with tears, and I wished he'd roll his car down the cliff, killing them both. Then I could have Graham. It was a thought that made me feel good momentarily, but soon I'd be overwhelmed by a terrible feeling of guilt, which was much worse than all the depression, anger, and rejection put together. Guilt, keenly felt, is the hardest of all emotions to bear, and if we only understood its potential to destroy the human spirit, we would never ever make our children feel guilty. We would try to take that feeling away from them at any cost. Then another feeling even worse than guilt would descend upon me: shame.

I would feel ashamed for my horrible, murderous thoughts and would wonder what kind of person I was to allow such thoughts enter my mind, and still professe to be a Christian... With bitter tears, I would fall on my knees and ask God to forgive me and to protect Edward and Valerie, bringing them home safely.

Valerie was with us for nearly three months. She was no trouble at all and was a pleasure indeed to have around. Graham came to Papua New Guinea for a few days to stay with us and to accompany Valerie back to Australia by boat, as a holiday for them.

I was, and still am, angry with Edward, who didn't repair our second car for them to drive around and see the place. They were my guests, and according my culture, they should take priority over everybody else. At that stage, I wasn't eligible for holidays, and so I couldn't take time off to be with them.

I had loved Edward and his mannerisms. I had loved the way he put his tongue in his cheek, the way he moved his hands, and the way he walked. I had loved his gentleness, his generosity, his quietness, and his bright mind. He was a thinker who never offered an opinion unless he was asked. I used to pray, "Dear God, take days out of my life and give them to him." But all that was gone. I was consumed with Graham and his display of affection, and all I wanted was to be loved by someone.

I became obsessed with Graham again. I often found myself signing his name during lunchtime at work. I had lost all sense of reality. I was living a delusion, a dream which was not likely to ever come true. It was during one of those times that I promised God that if He ever brought Graham my way, I would stand by him through thick and thin, through poverty, sickness, difficulties, and anything else life cared to throw at me. That delusion kept me sane. Edward was happy and completely oblivious to my pain and torment. Everything in his life took precedence over me. His work, the church, and board meetings kept him busy. I came to resent them all.

The people I worked with were very nice. Through them, I got to know a lot of other people, including the commodore of the town's sailing club. I became a member. Edward was not interested in joining, and I didn't want to go on my own, but Graham had a boat and had mentioned he'd like to come back to Papua New Guinea sometime later. I spent time imagining myself sailing with him. It kept me sane and was something to look forward to.

Sometime during my second working year, we got a letter from a friend Ernest, who was a church member saying that Graham was going to Japan on business, and he was going with him for a holiday. On the way back, they would stop at Port Moresby, and he asked if they could stay with us for a few days. We were pleased to have them, and I was delighted. We could all go sailing and spend time together. I was looking forward to seeing Graham again. I held Ernest in high esteem; he was one of the loveliest, most mature, wholesome people I knew.

The time came to pick them up from the airport, but Graham wasn't there! Ernest said Graham had decided at the last minute to fly directly to Melbourne for family reasons. I was disappointed. Ernest stayed with us for a few days and returned home. His contagious laughter and thigh slapping is still vivid in my mind.

Independence for Papua New Guinea was looming, and there was a general unease amongst the expatriate population. Nobody was sure how it was going to turn out. Was it going to be a peaceful transition, or a riotous one? A lot of expatriates were sending their families home just in case of an uproar. Edward had to stay in Papua New Guinea to finish his contract. The kids and I returned to Australia. The main reason was to give each other space and to try to sort out our marriage. The other reasons were Rose's education (she was in high school now), and I would be starting nurse training, for which I'd worked long and hard. I had been accepted to do my nurse training at the local hospital in Canberra.

We arrived at Canberra airport on January 5, 1975. I had a terrible lot of mixed feelings. I was glad for the break from a miserable marriage, and I was sad at the way things were. I would have given everything we possessed and would have lived in a tent if I could be as happy as we were fifteen years ago, when we were struggling to pay off debts.

Kids enrolled at their schools, I had my interview at the hospital with the director of nursing and her deputy director, both single women and former nuns. I was so excited about the interview that I even had my hair done at the hairdressers for the first and last time in my life. I looked ridiculous in that high, starched style of the seventies.

I started nursing in February 1975. I looked forward to becoming a nurse—something I'd wanted to do since I was fourteen years old. My passion was teaching, but that was impossible in Greece, and it was not possible in Australia either.

I had nearly two weeks before starting nursing, and I spent it looking around for another house that was a little bigger. With the kids growing up, the extra bedroom would be useful.

I went around to the newer suburbs and spoke to builders and agents. Prices were around four hundred thousand dollars. Only five years earlier, we had paid $13,500 for ours. I realised that if we wanted a bigger house, the only way we'd get one was to extend. I phoned around and settled for a Cape Cod with a company specialising building upwards. The extension would include two bedrooms, a bathroom, and a small study upstairs, with some alterations downstairs. The plans were drawn, and I signed the contract. There was a bit more mucking around than building in Greece. The building went ahead without hassles and finished on time.

Rose started at the local high school, and Timotheos started year six at the local Seventh-day Adventist primary school down the street. The academic year started for all of us. The kids went back to school a week before I started nursing. I loved nursing more than I imagined. It was a refreshing change from sitting at a desk all day. I loved talking to people and doing things for them.

The first year flew by, and I still kept praying and hoping that my marriage would be salvaged. I did not want it to break down. During the September school holidays, we went to Port Moresby for two weeks. I can't say I was glad to see Edward. I seemed to have grown away from him and was happy living on my own. I thought maybe we needed a bit more time away from each other.

Edward came down for the Christmas holidays, and together we went to Melbourne. Eva was in trouble again and had nobody to look after ten-year-old Georgina on permanent basis. The lady who looked after her could no longer do so. I suggested that Georgina come with us to Canberra for a while. She was excited at the suggestion, and Eva reluctantly let her come. One more child wouldn't make that much difference. Rose was a very responsible teenager. She took half the responsibility of managing the house, and at fourteen she was a better cook than I was. When Timotheos was twelve years old, he was allowed to cut the large lawn, relieving me of the responsibility. Rose spent her pocket money on fabric and made her own clothes. She made her first dress all by herself when she was twelve years old. I don't know what Timotheos spent his money on.

The second year of my nursing started with three kids, more study, more responsibility in the wards, and working shift work, which was tiring. The philosophy of the director and her deputy was, "Your work comes first, and then your family." Not knowing any better, I tried to apply the rule, and it was very hard. To make things worse, they believed, "It's nice for the patient to see the familiar face they saw before they went to sleep, first thing in the morning again." We had a lot of afternoon shifts followed by mornings. The afternoon shift didn't finish till 11:00 p.m., and we seldom ever got off on time. By the time I got home, it was midnight. I then had to get up at 6:00 a.m. to get ready for work, and I regularly wouldn't see the kids for twenty-four. hours Rose worked hard too. She studied, cooked often, and organised the kids when I was at work. Without her, I wouldn't have managed.

The way the rotating roster system worked was barbaric. We'd work five days on, two days off, six days on, two off, and so on till we worked ten days straight. Then we had four off, and the schedule started again. It was horrible! A lot of people took sick leave regularly, and the management complained and asked us to dob our colleagues in if we knew they weren't really sick.

I still get angry when I think of those days and the conditions those two old maids imposed on us. We had no voice and no right to complain. It was exhausting. I'd go home after a late shift followed by an early one and make a cup of coffee to wake me up, but I'd be asleep before I'd finish the coffee.

It was after one of those horrible "ten days straight" shifts that Rose asked if we could go to the shop to get linen for her new bedroom. I agreed. She navigated. I felt very tired and hoped she already knew what she wanted; then I could pay for it, take it home, and be done. She was excited. At the shop, she wanted to show me all the things that were on sale. The salesperson was just as willing to show us because there were no other customers around. In anger, frustration, or whatever you want to call it, I shrieked, "I didn't come here to see what the shop has. Take what you want, and let's go home. I'm tired."

Oh, how I wish I could forget the look on Rose's face! The excitement of shopping for her new bedroom vanished instantly. Was it fear, shame, or disappointment? I don't know, and I don't dare ask. The look on the shop assistant's face was easy to read: "What a bitch of a mother!" She was right. My behaviour warranted the thoughts it evoked. To say I am sorry now would be a great understatement. Being sorry doesn't change facts, but hopefully it changes behaviour.

As I think of the scene in that shop forty-three years later, tears well up in my eyes. I wish it never took place. I wish I could forget about it, or better still, wipe it from Rose's memory and replace it with a happy one. Every time I look at the quilt cover she bought that day, I remember my reaction and stop to catch my breath and wipe away tears. I looked at that quilt cover many times over the years. I wanted to throw it out, but for some mysterious reason I couldn't do it. It is now folded and wrapped up at the back of the top shelf of the linen cupboard. It can stay there till I die; they can wrap my corpse and bury me in it.

Edward finished his contract and returned to Canberra, where he worked at his old job. The kids went back to school. I started the third and final year of my general nursing. I wasn't involved with the children's education because I was flat out with my own. I didn't have the luxury of visiting schools on open days. Now, I feel as I've missed out on something very important (more to them than to me), and I am sorry. Life was hectic. Study, full-time shift work, keeping house, and a garden was more than enough. Edward was more work than help. Coming from a family of girls and a capable mother, he didn't even know how to make a cup of tea.

The third year was hard work both at the hospital and at home. I had to fit in study here and there, and having to study in a foreign language made it more time-consuming. In 1977, I had been in Australia just over sixteen years, and presenting essays took me longer than most students. But the hardest part was changing hats. At work, I was a student. I had to follow instructions, learn new procedures, and be supervised. At home, I had to literally take off the student's cap and take on the roles of mother, housekeeper, and organiser. It takes mental and psychological energy swapping from one to the other. Many people don't realise that.

My nurse training on the whole was a very rewarding and enjoyable experience. I worked with all sorts of people, some of whom were happy passing on their knowledge and experience in a respectful and constructive manner. Some did so in a superior and bigoted way that made me feel belittled. Some saw the problems and difficulties of mature students (there were three of us in the class) and appreciated the problems and sacrifices we made. Others were completely oblivious and treated us as rejects who, as a last resort, decided to try our hand at nursing. It was frustrating and hard to take, but we had to tolerate it and ignore them.

It was during my second year of training that one of the nursing sisters criticised my report writing. At the end of a very busy shift and in front of the whole team, she said that my report writing was not up to scratch and I should do something about it. I was tired, and that was the last thing I wanted to hear in a demeaning manner. My quick temper, straightforwardness, and lack of tact (mostly by choice) got the better of me. I told her it was her duty to take me aside, point to the shortcomings of the report, and teach me a better way of doing it, not just sit back, read the report, and then tell me it was no good. As was telling her this, another mature student standing behind her was nodding her head, vigorously encouraging me on. The other students were smiling. I was furious

From then on, my reputation as a big mouth preceded me to every ward. I didn't mind it, and at times I even took advantage of it. I wouldn't let them push me around too much.

I was in my final year of training and was doing my last placement in a surgical ward. We were extremely busy and short-staffed: just a registered nurse and me to look after over twenty patients. One of the patients was just down from the recovery ward and was bleeding. I was working with a big Tongan nurse who was slow moving and phlegmatic. I was running around, doing dressings, and answering bells while she sat at the desk doing what I thought was administrative work. I glanced across the desk from behind her and noticed she was reading a magazine. I said nothing. At 11:00 a.m., the supervisor came in, saw I was on my own, and sent a nurse from another ward to relieve me for morning tea, an hour late.

While I was away, the nurse washed the bleeding patient, reinforced the dressing, and made her comfortable. I went in to take over. I had no time to clean up the mess of bloodied towels and water. The Tongan nurse came in and in an authoritative, superior tone said, "Why haven't you cleaned up yet?" I tried to explain that I'd just come back from my break and was about to take over from where the other nurse left. She cut me short and in her manly voice said, "Don't you backchat me," looking at me in a threatening manner. I told her I was simply trying to explain the situation. Shaking her head and pointing her finger at me, said "Don't talk like that to me, or I'll give you a bad report."

I saw red. I was run off my feet, and I was angry at her sitting at the desk and reading magazines, not caring about the patients or me. I lost control. I looked up at her (she was a foot taller than me and three times my weight). In anger and frustration, I said to her, "I don't care if you give me ten bad reports. I will complain that you have been sitting down, reading magazines, and leaving me to do the work of four nurses." She was shocked. How could a student nurse be so rude to her greatness? She turned her back and took off to the nurse's station as fast as fat legs would take her. I gained the reputation of being insubordinate and rude as well.

I had two more unpleasant experiences in my student years. I was working in the day surgery ward. That ward was run like an army barracks by a nurse whose father was a high-ranking army officer. She carried herself around and talked as if she were an army major, and she was referred to as such by students. She was careless and lax in her duties.

It was an extremely busy shift, and I was seven months from graduating. One day she handed me a syringe with premedication in it, which she hadn't checked with me. She handed me the dish and said, "Give it to Mrs. X, bed number N."

I hesitated for a moment, wanting to say, "I haven't checked it with you, and you need to come with me." That was the rule.

She imperiously said, "Go on. I've checked it. We are too busy." There was no arguing with her; she had made it clear in the past that she didn't like me and that I was disobedient. Those days, student nurses did as they were told. We had just started being taught to say no to bad practices and to not walk behind the doctor, but the old-school, battle-axe nurses weren't ready to give up their authority and follow protocol. The old, grandiose doctors weren't ready to be taken off the pedestal. Against my will, I went and gave the premedication to Mrs. X in the bed number given. When I came back, she signed it, but I should have signed it, and she should've co-signed it.

Forty-five minutes later, she gave me another premedication and said, "Give this to Mrs. X," and it was the same name and same bed number.

I looked her and said, "You told me to give Mrs. X's premedication nearly an hour ago. Does she get double?"

She looked shaken momentarily but quickly recovered and said, "Give this to Mrs. Y, then." She handed me the tray with the filled syringe. I waited for her to say, "We'll fill in the incident report later," but she didn't. I looked at her long and hard, she got the message. She knew that she was negligent in her duty in more ways than one. She also knew that I knew, and she didn't like that.

The time came for me to finish my placement in that ward and get my report. It was unfair and untruthful. I don't remember all the comments in it except one, and that stuck in my mind as far off the truth. It said, "She is not coping well. She does not perform well under stress." I smiled, and she noticed. She was watching my reaction as I read.

Without looking up at her, I took the pen out of my pocket and started writing in the section for the nurse's comments. She read as I wrote. "I have been most unhappy working in ward four. I have been treated as if I were incompetent, ignorant, and stupid. I felt unsupported and was treated unfairly. My medical questions were ignored."

She became uncomfortable, shifting from foot to foot. "Aren't you happy with the report?" she asked in an angry manner. "Do you want me to change it?"

"No, it is fine," I said calmly. "It is as much of a reflection on me as it is on you. Thank you." I finished writing and handed it back to her. She grabbed it and took off in a hurry.

I was not worried. Back at the nurses' station, she looked at me with hatred. "When did I treat you as if you were ignorant and stupid?" she asked.

"Every time I asked you a question, you'd look at the three bars on my cap as if to say, 'You should know this, stupid.' And you never answered my questions." She was ropeable but said nothing. Whenever we met in the hospital corridors, she ignored me. She left the hospital soon after giving me my report.

Yvette was one of the nurse educators at the hospital. We became friends and kept in touch over the years. I mentioned the incident to her thirty years later. "I remember that report very well. You weren't the only one to complain about the working conditions in that ward, but we smiled at the way you wrote your comments."

The third unhappy experience was in the paediatric ward. I didn't fit in no matter how hard I tried. I couldn't gain recognition or approval. I was an outsider. I loved the children, and the children trusted me.

At the school of nursing, we had a student meeting. Both the director and her deputy were present. The director started the meeting without too much ado. After the preliminaries, she asked, "How do you like working in the kids' ward?" There was a general silence.

I groaned and almost with pain said, "I wake up in the morning and say to myself, 'No, not in that ward again!' And I am tempted to stay home." There was a general consensus, which surprised me. I thought I was the only one that was treated like dirt. I suspect the young nurses acted on their feelings and stayed home, prompting the powers that be to investigate the high sick leave of students in that ward. Not long after that, the charge nurse left the hospital.

Another nurse took over. She was a middle-aged lady who was friendly and fair. She didn't have much to say to me, but I noticed she observed me closely. One day during handover, children playing around us, my favourite little boy, Matthew, was walking towards me wanting to sit on my knee. A little girl saw him and ran to overtake him. They both arrived by my side at the same time. Without thinking, I turned them around and sat them back to back, one on each knee. The new charge nurse noticed and smiled but didn't comment. From then on, I had no problems in that ward, and neither did the other students.

My relationship with Edward didn't improve. I was happier away from him. In my mind, my marriage was over. I didn't know how to tell him or whether I had the right to a divorce. Biblically and according to the Church, we couldn't divorce because neither of us had committed adultery. The stress I was under was immense, and the strain showed in the way I treated the children. This made me feel guilty, realising they were made the scapegoats because of my unhappiness with Edward. I felt guilty and depressed. I found no happiness in anything in life. I felt devoid of any emotion, positive or negative. I felt hollow, like an empty shell. I was dead inside, useless to anybody, and a burden to those around me. I distinctly remember my neighbour's reaction when I told her, "I don't care about anything or anybody any more. All I want to do is finish my nursing and get out of here." Only people who experience this emptiness know what it feels like. In all the years of my psychiatric nursing, I heard of only two other people describe depression in those terms. I understood them perfectly and feared for their safety. The only thing that stopped me from killing myself was my purpose in finishing nursing. I was so depressed I didn't even think of my children.

Chapter 59

My Marriage on the Rocks

My relationship with Edward was in tatters. I hated him touching me, and I cringed when we were intimate, but I felt he still had conjugal rights and that I had a duty as a wife. It was a duty performed under duress. The thought disgusted me—and worse still, filled me with guilt and self-condemnation. Why, oh why did I feel this way? Why couldn't I love this man who was kind to me, never ill-treated me physically, and was gentle and generous? I shed buckets of tears trying to find a reason for our drifting apart, my withdrawal from him, and my loathing of being close to him, but I could find none other than that we'd grown apart. As we grew older, we became two different people with different views on practically every aspect of life, including religion and its philosophy, which we'd previously had in common for seventeen years. It was becoming clear to me that the situation was untenable. I could not live the rest of my life like this. I contemplated divorce. The one and only comforting thing was that by the time the divorce would come through, the children would be independent.

I finished nursing in February 1978 and worked at the local hospital. In good faith, I applied to do midwifery in a hospital in Sydney before I'd even had my exam results. It was not because I was confident I would pass, but I hoped that I would. The examination paper that year was extraordinarily hard, and we students came out of the exam room looking glum. When the paper was dissected at the school of nursing, all the educators agreed it was one of the hardest exams they had come across. This was a good reason to feel pessimistic, but I needed to have a year's separation from Edward before I could apply for a divorce, according to the law of the land.

I was praying for a pass, even a low one. The exam was in February. Late in March, I rang the Nurse's Examination Board and asked if the results were out. A man answered the phone and said yes but wouldn't give results over the phone; we had to go and get them personally. Given my bad sense of direction, my worry and excitement, and the complicated road system in Canberra, I didn't feel confident driving myself. I rang Sandra, another mature student, and told her the results were out, but I couldn't drive myself. I asked her if she wanted to come with me by taxi. She said, "No, I'll drive, and I'll pick you up on the way." She was at my place within twenty minutes. In my worry and excitement, I didn't even think to change my gardening clothes!

At the Nurse's Board, I couldn't wait to get the results quickly enough. "We came to get the results," I blurted out, Sandra next to me.

"What's your name?"

"Koutsadam," I said. Before he even looked at the list, he tried to pronounce my given name. My knees went like jelly. How would he remember my name unless I was one of the few who'd failed? He went as far as pronouncing my legal name, "Mala …" He had difficulty pronouncing the rest, I helped him.

"Did I pass?" I asked anxiously.

Slowly, softly, and deliberately, he said, "High distinction."

In my state of mind, it didn't sink in. All I wanted to hear was a yes or a no. I asked again louder, "Did I pass?"

He seemed to be enjoying the torment he was putting me through, and he again said, "High distinction." He kept looking at me, saying no more and relishing my torment.

Sandra saw my distress, she leaned over and whispered in my ear, "Yes, it is a good pass," stressing *yes* to make sure I understood. It was a relief I've felt only a few times.

Then Sandra got her results. "High distinction," he said to her. I was so excited that I wanted to run away, but Sandra calmly asked if everybody had passed. "No, three failed," he said, but he wouldn't give their names. Not a bad result considering there were nearly 140 nurses who'd sat a very hard exam. There were three high distinctions, all in my class, and one failure. The students who sat the exam were from Young, Orange, Goldburn and elsewhere. Word went around like a wild bush fire that the results were out. The next thing we heard was that Margie, the class clown, went to get her results and grabbed the list out the clerk's hands to check the results for herself. Not only did she check her own results. She grabbed the paper form the clerk's hand, checked her results and everybody else's as well. I dare say he tried the same trick on her as he tried on me, and she wasn't going to stand for it. She then rang the school of nursing and gave them the details. "Estella, 247. Sandra, 246. Stephanie, 245. Julie failed." The marks were out of 250, if I remember correctly. Whatever it was we were just three to five marks short of 100 per cent

Later Yvette rang to congratulate me. "Why are you so bloody humble? Why didn't you tell me you got an HD?" I told her all I wanted was a pass; a higher mark did not necessarily make a better nurse. She agreed.

I rang the hospital in Sydney and told them I'd passed. They arranged an interview for the following week. Edward drove me and the kids to Sydney. By now the children knew we were separating. Rose never commented on the situation, but Timotheos was upset. He said to one of his friends, "It's the worst thing that can happen to you." I was sad and upset.

Two weeks after the interview, I received a letter saying I was accepted to do midwifery starting in two weeks, in mid-April 1978. Everything went to plan. I would do midwifery. I'd get free accommodation, cheap meals, and a basic wage while studying and filling in the year of separation needed before my divorce. I was now sure in my own mind that I was doing the right thing, even if the Church disapproved. I figured out I was miserable in myself and made everybody else around me miserable. I put my children in my position and decided I would not like to see them spend their lives in misery. "If you being evil want to give your children good things, how much more your Father in Heaven wants to give you good things," said Jesus (Matthew 7:11). I figured that God didn't want to see me in a miserable relationship anymore than I wanted to see my children miserable.

Right or wrong, I was comfortable with my decision, resting assured that God would not condemn me even if the Church did. Edward drove me to Sydney to start my midwifery course, and I took notice of every turn and every sign on the road, knowing that the next time I'd have to drive to Sydney myself. (There was no GPSs then.) He returned to Canberra, taking the kids with him. Timotheos did year ten and Rose was in year twelve. They were old enough and were used to looking after themselves. Edward was at home with them. I waved to them with a smile but pain in my heart. Sadness, guilt, relief— I was all mixed up and on the verge of tears.

On my next days off, Edward came and picked me up. I was glad to be home with the kids I'd missed them. My days off were spent cleaning, washing, and cooking. Things weren't good at home. I felt the kids were neglected, and Rose had a lot of responsibility with little help.

On my next extended four days off, I took the kids with me to Sydney, where Timotheos bought a new motorbike. I didn't look forward to going home on days off. Edward expected us to have a normal physical relationship. In no uncertain terms, I told him it was over. He wouldn't accept it. I told him to stay away from me. He said I was cruel.

He realised our marriage was over, and now he was hell-bent in saving it. He bought me chocolates and flowers. The gesture had the opposite of the desired effect. I ran out of the lounge crying and shouting, "It's too late, it's too late! Why couldn't you do this earlier?" The kids looked on, wide-eyed, the chocolates and the flowers, lying on the couch. He involved Pastor Goodwin to mediate. Pastor Goodwin visited on my next days off and tried to tell me that all marriages go thought a rough patch, including his. I listened without commenting.

Camp time for the south New South Wales area came. Edward booked a tent for him and the kids. I went to camp on my two days off, but I refused to stay in the tent with Edward, who ended up staying with Pastor Goodwin. I stayed with the kids.

The next time I was in Canberra, Pastor Goodwin visited again. Edward wasn't there. He said, "Edward is a good man and wants to start again. Give him another chance. He deserves that much." I told him how desperately I'd tried to save that marriage, and how long and hard I'd prayed for over three years. I'd shed buckets of tears and I refused to take no for an answer, but Edward would not accept there was a problem.

The next time Pastor Goodwin visited, Edward was home. He again tried to mediate. I told him that I'd tried to salvage our marriage till the last time he came down from Papua New Guinea on holidays. I told him how, after my bath, I knelt by the bed which Edward was in and awake. I prayed and said, "Dear Lord, I have been praying for a long time to save this marriage and for Edward to see sense. I am praying again, and for the last time, I will ask if he loves me. If he acknowledges me in any way at all—even if he as much as looks at me—I will persevere." I told him how I got into bed put my arm on his chest and asked him if he loved me. I got no reaction at all as if I didn't exist, as if he were dead. Then he wanted sex. "Do you have any idea how that felt?" I asked.

Edward had his head down and said, "I was stupid."

On another occasion, I took Pastor Goodwin upstairs and showed him Edward's room, with dirty clothes mixed with clean ones strewn all over the floor. Pastor Goodwin was astounded and disgusted. "He says he loves me. I had eighteen years of this. I am tired." Pastor Goodwin said nothing.

"Is there anything else I can do to help?" he asked before leaving.

"If you can make me respect and love him again, start now," I said.

"Hmm. It might be a bit late now," he agreed. He didn't visit for a couple of months.

On my next days off, Edward said, "Graham is in Sydney on a work assignment. He rang to ask for your phone number. He doesn't know anybody there, and he wondered if he could see you sometime. I told him I'd let you know when you got home later today."

My heart missed a beat. This was not what I wanted just now. I wanted to forget Graham. I thought I was over him. I wanted to finish my studies, work and travel around Australia, and start my life over again.

I took the phone number and casually said, "I'll ring him when I get back."

Chapter 60

A Blossoming Romance

Graham and I had a nice meal at a restaurant and enjoyed a glass of wine. He was a novice in wine drinking. He asked the waitress for a suggestion, and she suggested a Moselle. It was too sweet for me, but he enjoyed it. "The church has put it over me, there is nothing wrong taking a glass of wine with one's meal," and there isn't. We talked for a long time about the church, our families, and our present lives. During the week, he came down from country New South Wales, where the conference was. We sat and talked again. He told me that Valerie was living and working away from home. He lived in Latrobe Valley, where he worked. I told him that my marriage was on the rocks, and that was why I was in Sydney. He didn't comment one way or another. Eventually, he caught the train and returned to his hotel.

He rang during the week and asked if we could go out for a meal. I had the afternoon off and was working a late shift the next day, so I said OK. He drove this time and had booked a restaurant not far from the hospital. While he was driving to the restaurant, I impulsively and without thinking put my hand on his knee in the same manner I used to do when Edward was driving. I was shocked at my action and withdrew my hand immediately. He looked at me and calmly asked, "Who's kidding who?" In my shocked state of mind, I didn't understand what he meant, and so I ignored the question. We had another meal together, and by this time he made his feelings for me clear. He said the reason he didn't visit us in Port Moresby on his return from Japan was that he was afraid of his feelings for me.

He suggested we spent a couple days together somewhere. I said OK. He decided to go by the beach. I didn't know Sydney and so agreed. We walked and talked and returned to the motel. He was nervous and awkward while we were having a cup of tea, which he made. In an almost aggressive, business-like manner, he said, "Listen. I have a wife and kids." He looked at me for a reaction.

"I know," I said calmly. "I don't want your wife or your kids. I just want you." He said nothing. His kids were adults. His eldest daughter was married with two children, the second was twenty-three, and the youngest was nineteen. Valerie was living away from home. His marriage was broken down. His kids were aware of the situation. I had no qualms about getting into a relationship with him. I longed to matter to someone, to be told I was important, to be acknowledged as a person, to be loved and made to feel worthy, even if it didn't last forever. That latent fire sparked and became a raging inferno physically and emotionally.

We spent two days and one night at the motel. We had a good time walking by the beach, holding hands, and talking like two teenagers. He was forty-seven and I was thirty-nine. As he drove me to work the next day, he played "Spanish Eyes" all the way.

Pastor Goodwin visited again. I told him I had a lover, and Edward was free to do as he wished. I knew he was interested in Leonie, and so did Pastor Goodwin. I said, "I wish them all the very best."

"But he can't marry her," he said.

"Yes, he can, and he will. You might even officiate at the wedding," I told him. "Go tell the brethren I have committed adultery."

His jaw dropped "Do you really want me to tell them that?"

"Yes," I said emphatically. "It's the last favour I can do him."

Pastor Goodwin visited me once again, for the last time. We discussed the state of affairs and how I felt. He was concerned. "This fellow might walk out of your life and leave you hurt."

I told him, "Right now, I need his support and his love. I need to know that I matter to someone. If he later leaves me, I might be stronger, less vulnerable, and better able to cope with whatever happens."

"Will I tell the brethren what you have just told me?"

"Yes. I told you before, Edward's free to marry. I have a lover."

He seemed disappointed and unwilling to do so, but he had no choice. My name was struck off the church roll in Canberra.

Graham and I saw each other frequently. Either he came to Sydney or I went to the Valley. I'd drive to Canberra, stay there overnight, and go to the Valley the next day. Our meetings were filled with pleasure, not just physical but in every way. We'd talk for hours of past events, religious points we had in common, church matters, the different personalities of various ministers, and the effect they had in either building or tearing down the church. Sometimes we'd sit silently, each lost in our own thoughts.

One day Graham asked, "How do you justify before God what you and I are doing?"

I said, "To start with, my marriage to Edward was over before you came along. As a parent, I looked at my children and asked, Would I want them to stay in a wretched relationship just because they chose the wrong companion, or because they grew apart from each other? Must they be miserable because the Church says so? Certainly not. I would like to see them happy with someone else. Did I break the vow I took before God and man to love and to care, for better or worse, till death do us part? Edward plainly told me he did not love me any more. He broke his vow before God well before I broke mine. No, I don't think I am committing adultery, and I can stand before God and say so. I have not deceived or cockled Edward. I told him, 'Don't touch me. I have another man.'"

Graham looked at me pensively. I don't know what he thought, and it didn't matter to me. My passion for him was rekindled and there was no holding it back. I was with a man who, to my mind, was perfect. He was my Absalom (more fitting than I realised then). "There was no fault in him from the hair on his head to the sole of his feet" (2 Samuel 14:25). I saw him as mature, intelligent, well-adjusted, and you can add any other positive quality to the list you can think of. I'd say, "Amen, amen," to all of them. He was perfect. I was blind to any and all weaknesses or foibles in his personality, and I refused to accept it even when his own daughters told me clearly or indirectly.

I now accept that we only believe what we want to believe and see only what we want to see, regardless of facts or what others say. Love is not blind, but infatuation or Eros is. We see our beloved as they really are only when all the arrows in the quiver of Eros have been spent. It is then that the reality sets in, and it is only then that we accept facts. There is no point in trying to make a blind man see because he just can't.

Edward refused to accept that our marriage was over and that I had a lover. He kept asking me who the other man was and what he did for living. I refused to tell him. One day, just to get him of my back, I said he was a chook farmer and a second-hand dealer; it was the first thing that came to my head. He didn't believe me. He didn't stop asking, refusing to accept the facts. Somehow I had to make him understand that it was over, that our marriage was dead and impossible to resurrect. He'd had his opportunity and thrown it away.

Too much water had gone under the bridge. I had accumulated much anger and resentment. Even had I decided to stay with him, it would have taken me a long time to get over my anger and respect him again. His life would have been miserable, and he didn't deserve that. I told him all I wanted to do was to finish midwifery, get my divorce, and start my life again. He refused to accept it. My mind was preoccupied with how to convince him that I was telling him the truth, that I had a lover, without revealing his identity.

One day I got an evil idea. "Why not get Graham to put a love bite somewhere nobody could see? Then I could show Edward the next time he refused to accept facts." It was a terrible way to shock someone into reality, but it worked. The next time he said, "You are only telling me you have a lover. I know you don't," I calmly pulled my dressing gown collar open and pointed to the love bite just beneath my collar bone. His reaction surprised me. He was dumbfounded, turned around, and went away in silence. I felt very sorry for him, particularly for the way

I went about convincing him of the truth. It worked, and that saved us both heartache and angst.

My divorce came through in April 1979, eighteen years after we were married. Edward suggested I move out of the house. Like a fool, I did so and lived in the nurse's quarters for four months. I decided to move back with my kids. He was angry. "What did you come back for?" I told him this was still my home and my kids were still here. I knew he was seeing Leonie, and I was happy that he too was happy.

I'd visit Graham and stay at his house. Valerie would be away. Graham's kids knew, and Jane was happy that her father had found some happiness at last. I did not tell my kids where I was, thinking they didn't care about me. I felt that I was a bad mother (which I was) and that I didn't deserve their affection. I couldn't get rid of my guilt, then or now.

The house in Canberra went up for sale. I got that one, and Edward got the house in Canberra North. At this stage, I was still depressed and torn between my duty to the children and my wish to move away from Canberra and be with Graham. Edward and I lived in the house while we waited for it to sell.

One afternoon, I was sitting on the front steps. Timotheos' little dog, Topsy, a part Pomeranian, sat by my side. I stroked him as he looked up at me lovingly. We were communicating silently as humans and animals do. Edward arrived home and watched in silence. Then he said, "You show more affection to the dog than me."

"Yes," I said. "And for the last few years, you treated me worse than a dog. Why are you complaining now?" He said nothing. We spoke little and only when necessary.

The house sold quickly, and we got the price we wanted. After settlement, I hired a small truck. Edward helped me load the furniture. John, next door, gave us a hand with the piano. We laughed while packing so that we wouldn't cry. When the truck was nearly packed, Edward stopped, looked at me long and hard, hesitated for a moment, and asked, "Do you want to reconsider?"

I thought he was joking. "Now? Now?" I asked, surprised and angry. "The truck is almost packed. It's too late now. Would it be worth our living together, trying to get rid of the resentment and pain that has accumulated over the years and bridge the rift? I don't think so. I'm happy with my new-found love. I wish you luck." I left Canberra mid-morning that day. The children and Edward moved into the house at Canberra North.

It took me nineteen hours to get to Melbourne. The twin tub washing machine in the cabin sat precariously on the front seat and wobbled all the way to Melbourne. The small truck was overloaded and slow. I held the traffic up for miles from Canberra to Melbourne on the old, one lane highway. To top it all up, halfway to Melbourne when I stopped to get petrol, I took the wrong turn back to Canberra. It was miles before I realised I was heading the wrong direction. When close to Melbourne, my brother-in-law, Tinny, met me somewhere in Campbefield. I followed him home from there and stayed with them for a few weeks while buying a house.

I drove the truck back to Canberra and went to see the kids. Jan and her husband were there, and as always I was glad to see them. Edward made it plain I wasn't welcome there. "What are you doing here?" he asked angrily.

I told him, "I came to see my kids, not you." It was a feeling I cannot put down in words. Devastated would probably fit. My children were in limbo while waiting to start their careers. Rose was seventeen and would be starting nursing in Sydney. Timotheos was fifteen and would be starting his apprenticeship with the armed services in New South Wales in a few weeks. This would be a heart-rending experience for any parent under the best of circumstances, let alone coupled with a recent divorce.

I wanted Timotheos to come to Melbourne, finish year twelve, and do engineering, which he wanted to do. However, his childhood experience of a city school spoiled his view of Melbourne. He refused to come. I was happy for Rose to do nursing in Sydney. I comforted myself with the thought that at least they would both have accommodation and meals, but it hurt me to part with them under these circumstances.

I drove my car back to Melbourne with the two little dogs, Timotheos's Pomeranian and Rose's little Maltese cross, keeping me company.

I started working at a repatriation hospital close to where I'd bought a house. It was comforting to come home after a late shift and find something alive and intelligent that was glad to see me. This was my family now. It was a very poor substitute for parting with my children, but if it wasn't for those little dogs, I would have gone mad. They kept me sane. I went back to Canberra to see Timotheos before he left to join the armed services, but I couldn't locate him.

At this stage, Edward had moved in with Leonie, and I didn't know their phone number or their address. I rang the new minister, Pastor Braham, a young man, to ask for Edward's phone number. He told me I was a bad woman for leaving my husband. I said to him, "I'd like to see you and discuss things face-to-face, instead of you abusing me over the phone." He said he wouldn't waste his time talking to a woman like me and hung up. I found Edward and Leonie by ringing some other church member.

Edward didn't come out to talk to me. He left a message in his own handwriting on a small box with some of my belongings and Timotheos' address, saying, "No more contact here." I respected that and never contacted him again.

I found Timotheos, who was sharing a house with his girlfriend, Marie, and a friend from church. Later, Timotheos told me he had asked his father if he could leave his motorbike in his garage for three days. Edward refused. That upset me, but I knew whose decision that was. My kids suffered the effects of divorce. Thankfully, it was only for a short while. When I hear of families breaking up, I feel sorry for both parents and children. They don't realise how much they will suffer in the long run. Here, I must qualify my statement. Violence and cruelty of any kind should not to be tolerated. Children are better off with one parent and living in peace than two parents and living in fear.

Another incident that upset and angered me was when Rose and her girlfriend, Ariane, went to Canberra for a few days. Rose asked her father if they could stay with them for the weekend, but he refused to give them shelter. Edward had been a good father to them. He did other things uncharacteristic of him. Later, I realised he was controlled by a very possessive and cruel woman.

I worked at the repatriation hospital for over a year. It had a psychiatric ward, but it didn't offer a psychiatric training course. I wanted to know more about psychiatry, and so I started my psychiatric nursing at the local psychiatric hospital near Bundoora. The extra qualification would come handy.

Halfway through my psychiatric nursing, Graham moved in with me. He'd had a confrontation with Valerie, packed up his personal belongings, and left. Jane rang to warn me he was on his way and that he was very upset. She was crying and asked me to take care of him. When he arrived at my place, he was in a terrible emotional state. He took a few days to calm down and function properly. He never told me what had happened, and I didn't ask. We started our life together in March 1980.

When Timotheos got his first holiday from the the Air Force, he came to Melbourne. At seventeen, he looked grown-up and good in his uniform. He looked happy. I was proud of him and still am. He stayed with us for a few days and then returned to Wagga Wagga to continue his apprenticeship. When Rose got her first holidays, she too came down. She too had grown up in the year I hadn't seen her. They had both changed so much. I was glad to see them and happy they were doing well, but for some reason I had a very uneasy feeling which I could not fully define. Was it guilt, sadness, or shame? I felt I'd abandoned them, that I had been an irresponsible mother, and no matter how I saw it, I saw some truth in it. It saddened me.

Part 3

Chapter 61

My Life with Graham

Graham was the man of my teenage dreams. He had the looks, the brains, and the personality, everything a girl wanted in a man. What's more, in that small church group he was the best. He had a good job with a big company, and he was influential. I perceived him to be mature, cool, calm, and collected. I considered myself privileged to be seen by his side. I would do anything for him. He liked to entertain, and that was a plus considering Edward preferred a quiet life. I did the cooking, mostly Greek. My house was too small for the scale of entertaining he had in mind. At times there would be ten people in a small dining room. He wasn't happy, and it was difficult for me in a small kitchen.

One day after dinner, he said, "I have no stakes in this house; it's all yours. I have no rights and have not contributed anything."

I was starry-eyed and blinded by infatuation. I wanted him to be happy with me. "We can sell this house and buy another one," I said. He agreed. The house was nearly paid off. I had money for deposit to invest in another house. At that stage, I had already made my will and left everything to him if I died. The solicitor was surprised and said something like, "What about your children?" I was ignorant of the law and presumed that after his death, it would go to my children. Anyway, that was far into the future. Just now, he was my all in all. I didn't think to say, "Graham, pay me half the value of the house, and half can be yours," but infatuation blinds.

We looked around and bought a house closer to the city, near completion. We sold my house in $55,000, and I put it all on the new house which cost $65,000. Graham put in the rest. The house was bought in both names with an equal share. If I died or if the relationship broke down, half was his, which I didn't know. But I didn't care. As far as I was concerned, I was going to be with him for the rest of my days.

We moved into the new house. I had enough time to make curtains before we left for a four-week holiday in Greece. I had no desire to go, but he said he hadn't been there and wanted to go. To please him, I'd go to the ends of the earth. He suggested I get an international driving licence, which I did, but I told him that I was not driving in Greece. He said he would.

We landed in Athens and got a taxi to the hotel. On our first day touring, we stood on the footpath in front of the hotel. We looked around at the traffic. I asked if he was going to hire a car and drive. "No," he said. We used either public transport or taxis.

My time in Greece was not enjoyable. I hated the place. My paternal cousins thought I went there to take my father's property from them. It hadn't entered my mind. We stayed with my maternal cousin Kostas and his wife, Marina. Kostas drove me crazy with his political talk, and I was sick and tired of translating. Obviously, Kostas hadn't changed even though communism was dead. However, they couldn't do enough for us.

We spent about a week with them and looked around the place. I told Graham I'd had enough of translating all day. I was exhausted and wanted to leave. We went to Thessaloniki, spent a few days there, and continued on to Turkey, where we spent two weeks. Our time in Turkey was pleasant. I looked across from Saint Sophia's Temple in Istanbul, where my father had grown up and where my beloved grandmother's home had been, and for some strange reason I felt as if this was where I belonged. I haven't felt like this anywhere on earth before or since.

I stood in silence, looking across the water, wondering where her house had been, and where her spirit was wandering. Was it hovering over the holy ground where this temple stood? It was then that I understood why she hated Greece so much. Here in Turkey, she'd had everything she'd wanted. My grandfather had been a seaman and brought home delicacies and luxuries from all over the place. In Greece, they were thrown inland and were expected to cultivate the earth. They hadn't seen a plough before, let alone use one. No wonder they were all miserable.

It was while in Turkey that I accepted the fact that Graham was tight-fisted. Both Jane and Rhonda had told me so, but I dismissed them. My Graham was perfect. There was no fault in him. One day he was with me at the supermarket, doing the weekly shopping. When we went through the checkout, he was surprised at the bill, which was $120. "Gee, that cost a lot," he said.

I looked up at him, and lovingly said, "Did you think the forty dollars would cover it, darling?" The next week, he gave me sixty dollars.

We stayed in Turkey for two weeks, looked around the markets, and bought all sorts of things (as tourists do) which I neither needed nor used. While in Turkey, whenever it was time to pay a bill, he was always elsewhere, looking at something. Whenever he had to pay, he did it reluctantly, throwing the money on the counter rather than handing it to the salesperson. (his eldest daughter had told me this) It was very embarrassing.

I paid for everything—accommodation, bus fares, and food—while travelling in Greece, and even the small gifts I bought for his daughters and his sisters. He didn't offer to reimburse me, pay for anything, or buy them anything. I was more disillusioned than annoyed, and as much as I hated it, I said to him, "Graham, I will pay for the holiday, but you will pay for the carpet when we go home."

He looked at me, shrugged, and said, "OK." I think he feared that the carpet might cost more than the holiday. It didn't. In all fairness to him, he paid for my air fare, which wasn't the costliest part of the holiday.

I took my first disappointment and disillusionment with a prayer on my lips. "Lord, I too have faults and shortcomings. Please help me love him as he is."

Chapter 62

My Sin of Omission

We bought our bus tickets for Athens, but we were going to get off in north-east Greece so that Graham could see where my mother's family and siblings lived. We boarded the bus. On the seat across the aisle from us sat a young, good-looking Spanish tourist. His face has been etched in my memory, and the encounter caused me much pain, shame, and regret. I spent many sleepless nights castigating and hating myself. How could I treat another human being like this? How could I be so heartless? Where did my Christianity go? And where did my sense of helping another human in need go? Oh, how I wish I could make amends, meet that young man again, throw myself at his feet, and ask forgiveness. How I wish I could forget those big, serene, beautiful blue eyes looking up at me silently but unmistakably asking for help. I ignored him. Tears of shame run down my face when I remember the incident, which I will take to the grave with me. I often wondered if the universe would be kind to bring him my way again when I walk the Camino in Spain. Small chance, but not impossible. I wanted to believe in my grandmother's saying: "Only mountain and mountain don't meet, humans might."

It happened like this. We boarded the bus in Turkey and sat on our seats. Just before the bus left, a man with a uniform got on the bus and asked for our tickets. I thought it was strange, but we all gave them to him, thinking he was going to check them. The Spanish young man gave his to the "inspector" too. A little way down the road, with the bus coughing and spluttering, the young man looked at us and in good English said, "They won't take us to Athens. They will take us to the border and leave us there. They have done it before." I didn't believe him. Surely bus companies would not be so corrupt! If this young man knew what he was talking about, why did he give his ticket? Why didn't he warn everybody? I didn't give it another thought and tried to enjoy the rough ride.

We arrived at the Greek border at dark. The driver ordered us to get out. We protested that we'd bought tickets to Athens. He asked for our tickets. The guys at the terminal laughed. "Give us your tickets?" one asked. We told them that the Turkish inspector had taken them from us. They roared with laughter and were greatly amused. I was furious at being duped, and I was furious at the young man who'd known what was going to happen but stupidly gave away his ticket. I was furious at being laughed at and made the butt of a joke. I became even more furious at him when he said in a self-righteous tone, "I told you so." I could have clobbered him there and then. I could have twisted his neck around a couple of times. I was blind with rage.

"What do we do now?" I asked the guys at the bus terminal.

"You can buy another ticket," they said, roaring with laughter again. I felt frustrated, angry, and helpless. I translated this to Graham and to the young man, who at this stage was sitting on the curb. "But I don't have any more money," he said. I could have throttled him! Momentarily I felt sorry for him. I was going to buy him a ticket, but I was immediately overcome by all the other emotions, and my compassion and reason fled.

I did not help that man, and Graham made no effort to either. The young man did not ask for money; he was too dignified. Instead, he took some bracelets and necklaces made out of beads and asked if we wanted to buy some. "No," I said in anger as I turned away.

I don't know where he slept, what he ate, or how he returned to Athens. At that moment, I did not want to know. But I've had thirty-five years to wonder, to think about him, to regret my heartlessness, to put my son in his position, to cry with bitter tears, and to ask God to forgive me. I don't know if any good ever came out of that incident for that young man. It did two things for me.

It caused me a lot of pain and shame. I hope I will never, ever act in that manner again. It made me more ashamed than stealing money from my beloved grandmother as a sixteen-year-old. It was due to this experience that I decided to try to be a blessing to someone each day, even if it was giving them a smile. It made me decide to help my fellow man with my means and to help as many people as I could, because I have been blessed over and above many. May God help me in this.

Oh, how I wish I could make amends. But this is not possible now. I wish I could forget it. In life, we fall, get up, and go again. Hopefully we learn from our mistakes. They make us more understanding and forgiving of other people's mistakes. Then I thought, *If I forgot all the horrible things I have done, what would I be like as a person?* I hate to think of it. I can pile a lot of epithets on me, but will summarise it. Arrogant, not understanding, self-righteous, and friendless. Unfit to live on this earth and unworthy of heaven.

This has been a horrible experience for me. It took me much courage to put it down on paper. I hope those who read this find it in their hearts to forgive me, because I am truly sorry.

That incident taught me a very important lesson: the sins of omission are much harder to bear and deal with than the sins of commission. It is much easier to go to the person wronged and say, "I owe you an apology. Please forgive me for saying such and such. How can I make amends?" than to say, "I should have helped you when you needed me," because by the time of the apology, the person may not need help.

****

Back home, I made the rest of the curtains and planted the small garden around the house. The house and garden was finished. On my weekends off, we'd go for drives and picnics most of the time, or we'd stay home and enjoy each other's company. This was a happy time for me.

One weekend during a drive down a country road near Wallan Wallan, I spotted a "for sale" sign on the road side. I asked Graham to drive in and have a look. He did so reluctantly. My breath was taken away by the views from that place. I told him, "I want this block of land, and this is where I want to build the house." He didn't react. I took the name and phone number of the agent, rang the next business day, and made an appointment with the agent, who took us for a look. He said the owner wanted $41,000. I told him I wanted the land, I made an offer, which he took to the owner. I didn't even try to knock the price down because I thought it was a fair price for fifty-one acres. I told Graham again, in front of the agent, that I wanted it, and this was where I wanted the house built. I was eager and enthusiastic about it. The agent saw it and took advantage of it. He came back and said, "The owner changed his mind. He won't sell it under $43,000." I couldn't be bothered arguing for two thousand dollars. Graham was wary, not wanting to commit himself. I told him, "I'll buy it anyway," and I did.

I paid nine thousand for the deposit. It was all the money I had left, having paid for the holiday and curtain material. The sale went ahead, and the title was in my name because we weren't married yet. I was thrilled. There would be lots of space for a garden, it was only one hour for Graham to travel to work, and it was fifty minutes for my job.

Soon after that, Graham suggested we get married, and I accepted. I loved him and had promised God a long time ago that if He ever brought Graham my way, I would love him and spend the rest of my days with him. We planned on a very small affair at the registration office with two witnesses and a dinner afterwards. I accepted his stinginess as part of his negative traits; it wasn't an issue because I was financially independent.

I rang Rose and Timotheos to tell them. They were very happy. Rose rang back, saying that she was able to change her roster and was coming, and so was Timotheos. I didn't have the heart to tell them our plans, so we changed them. Graham's sisters, his children, and their families and my sisters and their families were there to share our happiness.

On the day of the wedding, I felt excited but uneasy. Just as I finished getting dressed, Graham came in. I said to him, "I am not going to say, 'Till death do us part.' It is going to be, 'For as long as you love me and want to be with me. If you find someone you are happier with—someone younger, better looking, or better endowed physically—that day I want you to come to me and tell me it is over."

"OK," he said.

"But this is going to apply to me too," I said. He looked surprised. I was not going to live with someone who didn't love me. The feeling of being unloved was still vivid in my mind and raw in my heart. We were married at the registration office and celebrated in our new home.

The wedding over, a year after we bought our new house, we went around looking for a builder to build us a house on the land in the country. By this time, Graham was happy to go along and move out to the country. We found one. As soon as the building started, we put our house up for sale, hoping that the building and the selling would coincide. It didn't. The house sold early, and the new owners wanted an early settlement, a few weeks before our house was finished. We hired a caravan, put it under the big machinery shed, and lived there, much to the chagrin of the builder, who said we had no right to be there legally because the land was his till we paid him off completely. Tough! We were there and were staying put. We lived in the caravan with our three dogs: Lisa, a Labrador; Butch, a border collie cross; and Rose's little dog, Tootsy.

It was winter and very cold in the caravan. Graham had to go to Wallan to collect his mail and do some shopping at the only shop in town. He looked around for his binny but couldn't find it. "Here, this will do. It will keep your head warm," I said, taking the cosy off the teapot and throwing it to him. He put it on, the spout opening at the back of his head. It was a bit small, but it kept his bald patch warm. Off he went.

He returned irate. "What's the problem?" I asked.

"These two women in the shop looked at me and burst out laughing," he said indignantly. I took a critical look at him and laughed too. There was the teapot cosy, sitting smugly just over his prominent ears, the pompoms dangling on his head. The bright orange and aqua blue stripes clashed with his long grey hair. He looked like an oversized gnome and was a sight to behold.

Soon after we moved into the caravan, our neighbour, Patrick, and his family came and introduced themselves. His wife was Anja, and their three children were Matias, ten; Delores, eight; and Bernie, four. They were lovely, helpful people. A little farther down lived Julie and Alfonso. We became good friends and kept in touch for many years. Julie was one of those people God put on this earth to brighten the lives of many. I admired her philanthropy, maturity, kindness, and cheerfulness. Every Tuesday we'd get together for lunch. She brought the champagne, and I provided chicken and salad. I'd have some with her, making sure it was a little or else I'd fall asleep. She remembered our Tuesdays together and used to say how much she enjoyed the good old days. She died in 2012, two weeks short of her eighty-seventh birthday. I missed her very much.

Graham, Patrick, and Frederick (who lived across the road) became friends and worked well together. Once again, I was flat out making curtains at night and setting up a big garden during the day, which I enjoyed more than any other activity in my day. We concreted and paved a large area. Graham bought a tractor and built retaining walls, and we planted about one thousand carob trees. Timotheos and Marie helped dig holes. Timotheos was posted to Sale when he finished his apprenticeship.

I loved living in the country. The views were absolutely beautiful. From the balcony, we could see across the valley, and the mountains far in the distance. From the back of the house, a bit higher, we had a 360-degree view, miles away of the township, and the hill where *Picnic at Hanging Rock* was filmed. The sunsets were stunningly beautiful, and the double rainbows were glorious, full circle and bright. At night, the stars shone brighter than I have seen them anywhere on earth, except in my dream. There were no artificial lights to dim their brightness. God's handiwork surpasses the most beautiful artwork ever made by human hands.

But as with everything else, we get used to beauty or desolation around us, and we don't notice it any more. Two years after we were there, I said to Graham, "We'll stay here ten years, and we will re-evaluate." He was non-committal. He loved living in the country more than I realised. He chopped wood during the weekends and cleared the land. We grassed the bare slopes and took measures to stop erosion. He made a platform for his tractor and carted dead wood for winter fuel. Graham bought an attachment for his tractor to grade the road, which became corrugated after heavy rains. We enjoyed living there.

Chapter 63

Disillusioned

One day, Patrick asked Graham to grade his road and asked how much it'd cost. Graham said he'd do it as a favour, which Patrick accepted gracefully. Graham waited for Frederick to help him with some work on the tractor, and they talked while working. Graham mentioned that he was going to grade Patrick's road. Frederick said, "You could get a lot of money grading that long driveway." At the sound of money, Graham's ears picked up. He changed his mind and asked Frederick to tell Patrick that he wanted to get paid for the job. When Graham went to grade the driveway, Patrick had already left for work. Frederick was working there, and he told Graham what Patrick had said.

Graham came home upset and told me why. I told him, "I'd do exactly the same. You offered to do him a favour, but at the sound of money, your ears flapped and you wanted payment. This is not how friends work. You got what you deserved." I was disillusioned and disappointed. They say love is blind. No, love is not blind. Infatuation is, and she is blind, deaf, stupid, irrational, and unable to see reason. We are under the power of the magic mushroom. I am well qualified to say so; I've been there and done it, and in my type of work, I've verified it in others.

Graham had another dreadful habit, one Jane had warned me about, but I was still under the influence of the magic mushroom. I dismissed her. He'd creep up on me, scaring me half to death. It delighted him, and he'd laugh raucously. It was very childish behaviour that I'd actively discouraged in my own children. The first time he tried it, we were still living in town. I was hanging the washing out. I had put the linen on the front lines, away from the fence, and was hanging the small things on the back lines against the fence. I was absorbed in my thoughts, miles away in the past, back in the village, thinking of the gypsies singing and the bears dancing. I didn't hear him come home. Graham crept up on me amongst the flapping linen and bent down to kiss me, his long hair falling on my face. I wet myself. I thought it was a bear attacking me. I did the only thing I could: I bit him on the lips as hard as I could! He yelped in pain. I hoped he wouldn't try this childish trick again, but he tried it many times. I protested, telling him it was immature and childish. It made no difference. I hated it.

One morning, during winter and still dark, before driving to work I noticed the right front tyre was flat. I went upstairs and told him. He put on his dressing gown, went downstairs, and was absorbed in changing the tyre. He didn't hear me come. I thought, *Here is my chance to teach this old bastard a lesson.* I crept close behind him, bent over him, spread my arms out, and roared like a lion with all my might. He was terrified and screamed in fear like a trapped animal, so much so that his knees gave way and the spanner fell from his hand. He didn't even have the strength to swear at me. He was undone! I knew I'd have to soak his pyjamas well before washing them, but the effort and extra work was well worth the satisfaction I got at seeing him scared half to death.

I burst out laughing just as he used to do. In between fits of laughter, I managed to tell him, "Now you know what it feels like. I'll scare you every chance I get if you do it to me again." Did that cure him? Well, nearly. He still kept creeping up on me.

Another trait that annoyed me was his inquisitiveness. If he wanted to get some information, he'd rephrase the question, interrogating till he got the information he wanted. I used to tell him he missed his vocation—he should have been a detective. and I didn't mean it in a flattering way either. But he was good to me. Our relationship was satisfying emotionally, psychologically, and physically for over ten years.

Chapter 64

Sophia

I was still working at the oncology unit part-time. I found it depressing to see young people die of cancer. I remember a lot of them and the stories behind them. A few stand out in my mind. The thirty-six-year-old woman dying of lung cancer, leaving three young children behind, the oldest twelve years old. We had to take her outside in a wheelchair for a smoke till she took her last breath. My heart broke for those kids.

I was angry at the tobacco companies, who presented smoking as glamorous and sophisticated, showing beautiful actresses and actors enjoying a smoke. The beautiful, single mother of a nine-year-old boy who found a lump in her breast went to her doctor only to be told, "Don't worry. You are too young to have cancer." Later, it was too late. There was the forty-year-old mother of a twelve-year-old daughter and many, many others. The one that upset me most was a middle-aged woman who suffered for a long time, taking days to die. I'd go off duty, hoping she would die on my days off. The first thing I'd ask before starting the shift would be, "Is she still alive?" My heart would sink when heads nodded. The poor woman. Every day, we expected her to die. It was a month before she passed.

Then there was Maree, a middle-aged little lady who met her fate with much courage. She was an inspiration to all. She never complained, and she never tired of the endless visits from her family and friends. She was bedridden and in pain, but she never complained. She was a perfect little lady who liked her make-up. No matter how busy we were, I'd find a few minutes to put it on for her after her bath. She died peacefully while I was on duty. I have never seen a dead person with such a peaceful expression on her face. A young Vietnamese nurse and I laid her out. For the last time, I opened her drawer, pulled out her make-up bag, and respectfully and reverently put it on her. The young nurse who was helping me was surprised. "You are not going to put make-up on her, are you?" I nodded. She watched me, not knowing what to make out of it. At the end, she looked at me and said, "She looks so peaceful."

"And so beautiful," I said. It was her inner beauty that shone out even in death. It was that day that I accepted that there is some beauty in death. I'd ridiculed the hospital chaplain saying it. I also saw the futility of fighting death, like the hospital chief radiologist who refused to accept it and didn't find peace till the last two weeks of his life.

It was in that ward that I met Sophia, a forty-year-old single mother of a five-year-old son, Damien. She had acute myeloid leukaemia. At the time of the diagnosis, she was given six months to live. She defied all odds and was still alive three years later. She had a relapse and was hospitalised for over six weeks, but she was not improving. We became friends. Her friends brought Damien in to see her. He was an intelligent child, took note of everything around him, but said little. He occupied himself with toys or drawing. He was a good little artist and was no trouble in the ward.

September holidays were approaching. I asked Graham if we could take Damien for the three days I had off. He agreed, and Damien stayed with us. He enjoyed his stay on what he called the farm. We took him to the horse riding school nearby, whose owner we knew. He got lots of attention and had a great time. When we went to visit his mother again, he said, "It's a funny farm, Mum. They only have three dogs and lots of kangaroos. But I liked it. Can I go again?"

Sophia's social circumstances were sad. She had no relatives in Australia and her mother who lived overseas was unable to look after the child alone. She said she would look after him part-time, but he'd have to stay with relatives some of the time. Sophia wanted a stable home for her child. Her friends and Damien's godmother offered to take him, but they couldn't manage him because there was conflict between their children and Damien. It lasted between two and five months. A friend of hers would take him but wanted ninety dollars a week, which was a lot of money. Sophia said, "If she wants money, she'll look after him as a job, not as a labour of love."

The child protection system found some families who wanted him. When Sophia went to check them out, she didn't like what she saw and heard. One family, in a posh suburb with two children of their own and a fostered son, were very keen to take Damien. When she casually asked the fostered child what he got for Christmas, the child said, "My foster brother's old bike." They were well off in a beautiful house with a swimming pool and all the mod cons, but they were not kind enough to give a disadvantaged child a new gift for Christmas. Their children had new gifts. "My child is not going there. I don't know what to do, I can only pray," Sophia said.

For weeks, I'd drive home crying. I talked to Graham about Sophia and her plight. He was sympathetic.

School holidays were about to start. Sophia wasn't ready for discharge yet. I suggested to Graham, who had retired, that we take Damien for the two weeks of the September school break. It was OK with him and with Sophia. I worked three days a week. Damien was glad to come back to the "farm" for two weeks in September. I'd take him to see his mother on my days off. One day he was horsing around on her bed like any five-year-old. He lost his balance, fell, and hit his head at the bed's end. He got down from the bed and came to me for comfort instead of going to his mother, who was closer to him distance wise. She noticed and looked pleased but said nothing.

Sophia improved a little and went home for Christmas, but a week later she was readmitted. She was wondering what to do with Damien again. We agreed to take him for the rest of the Christmas holidays. Two weeks later, Damien asked Mark, Sophia's ex-partner, to bring his bed and toys to our place. She allowed him to do so. Their relationship had broken down, but they remained friends. Mark supported her and was fond of Damien, but he was working full-time and was unable to care for the child. Damien was happy staying with us, and she could see it in his behaviour. She said, "Estella, I haven't seen him as happy as this in a long time. It makes me happy too."

Poor darling. It must have been hell for her, knowing she could well die and there would be nobody to look after her child. She didn't want to contact his father even though she knew where he was. She had a relationship with Damien's father some years after the death of her older son, who'd drowned at a swimming pool aged 11. She wanted another child. Her partner, whose name she never mentioned, was a "a con man." She was seven months pregnant when she found out that he was having a relationship with a forty-year-old woman—as well as with her eighteen-year-old daughter. She confronted him and asked him what he wanted to do in regards to the child. She gave him the option of giving the child his name and paying child support, or disappearing and having nothing to do with it. He chose the latter. She never saw him again.

When Damien was born, she wanted to call him David Anthony. She filled in the birth registration form and gave it to the nurse, asking her to check it for any mistakes. The nurse looked at it and said, "I thought you called him David."

"Yes, I did," she said.

"But this doesn't say David. It says Damien."

She later told me, "I thought for a minute and said to the nurse, 'Bugger it. Damien is a nice name too. Leave it as it is.'"

About this time, I was asked if I wanted to work in the psychiatric unit of hospital. I was glad for the change because the oncology ward was depressing me. At times we had four deaths a week, and most of them were young people. I was transferred to the psychiatric unit, and I'd visit Sophia every day I was on duty.

The Christmas school holidays were nearly over, but she was not getting any better. She wondered what to do with the child, who was happy with us. She didn't want to unsettle him again. I talked about it with Graham, and we suggested to her that Damien could start school at Kilmore. When she got out of hospital, she could either take him and go to her own home, or if she wanted, she could move to Wallan or

Kilmore, and we could help her if she needed us. Sophia liked the plan. Damien was settled in, played well with the kids next door, and was spoiled by Julie, who was naturally kind but had no children of her own.

He started school in a church primary school at Kilmore, where the neighbour's children went. He'd have friends, and he'd go to school on the bus with them. In between treatments, she came to our place a couple of times, and all she talked about was her eleven-year-old son Damir, who'd drowned, and for whom she was still grieving about. Her description of a parent losing a child was an apt one. She said: losing a child was a bit like losing an arm or leg: you never get over it you just learn to get on without it. "Damir was loving, considerate, and affectionate. Damien is different," she'd say.

She went on to tell me how, when Damien was three years old, she took him to church. She gave him some money to put in the offering plate. When it came around, he stood up on the seat, looked in the plate, put the money in his pocket, and sat down again. When she asked him why he didn't put the money in the plate, he said, "They have plenty. We need it more." She was flabbergasted and so was I, but even aged three, he could reason.

Chapter 65

Sophia's Dreams

Time went by, Sophia's health deteriorated. She wasn't responding to treatment and was told the truth about the state of her health. She was asked if she wanted to continue her treatment. Her insensitive social worker, Monica, said to her, "What's the point? You are only suffering."

Sophia was upset and said, "The point is I have a young child, and every minute I have with him counts." Monica advised her to set her affairs in order and make permanent arrangements for the child. I can't imagine how she must have felt. She didn't do anything straight away.

One day Monica came to the psychiatric unit and said, "Sophia is very upset and wants to see you urgently." I went to see her after work. She was visibly upset and worried.

Without preamble, she said, "I'm going to die soon. I need to make arrangements for Damien."

I tried to calm her down and asked her why she suddenly felt like this. She hadn't felt this way when she'd been given the bad news a few weeks earlier. She said she used to have a recurrent dream which meant that someone was going to die. I interrupted her, saying, "Perhaps it is because so many people have died here in the last two weeks, and it was unusually high."

"No, no," she said. "That dream never fails." In the dream, she saw a carriage drawn by two white horses. In it was her father and herself dressed as a bride. She said emphatically. "I was the bride in that carriage. I will die." Her father, whom she was close to, had died a few years earlier. I felt very sorry for her and tried to change the subject, but she came back to the point and the question she wanted to ask. "Will you look after Damien for me?

My heart broke. How would you feel leaving your child to almost a stranger? I had only known her for eight months. I told her I would talk to Graham and let her know tomorrow. I had no doubt that Graham would agree; we were half expecting it because the boy was settled with us and at school. I cried all the way home that day too.

I told Graham about her request, and he said, "How can you say no?" We were agreed. The next day when I saw her, I told her we would look after Damien for her, and we would try our best to love him and care for him. She was pleased, thanked me, and said she'd start proceedings to give us legal guardianship of the child.

Her heart must have been breaking, but she was too tough, realistic, and busy arranging for his welfare to shed tears. The next time I went to see her, I took Damien with me. She was beaming with joy. I was taken aback. I had expected to see her upset, throw her arms around Damien, and cry. Instead, she was joyful. After the preliminaries and a short play with Damien, she said, "I'm very happy. I know he is going to be OK."

"How is that?" I asked.

"Last night, I dreamed that my father came and said, 'Sophia, don't worry about Damien. He is going to be well looked after, even better than you could do yourself.'"

I was shocked and said, "I don't understand How could a child be better off with anybody other than his own parents?"

"I don't know, but I believe in what my father told me in my dream." I promised her to do the best we could.

How good is the Lord! He never leaves us to bear our pain alone, and He never allows us to suffer more than we can bear. She was a believer in God, and she had a simple faith. In a simple way, God reassured her that her much-loved son would be OK. I was glad that she would die knowing that her precious little boy would be provided for.

We did the best we could for him. I can stand before God and honestly say, "Lord I have made mistakes, but I did the best I knew how."

The legalities were rushed through. She gave me sole guardianship and made provision for everything. She allowed for his school expenses and other costs, which we didn't touch till he went to high school as a boarder. She died six weeks to the day after her dream. I was off duty when she died. Even though I had asked the nursing staff to let me know any time of day or night, they didn't till morning. Sophia died quickly and peacefully, and the peace showed on her face when we went to see her body that day. Damien was too young to comprehend what was happening, and he was well prepared for the event by someone wise and well qualified, though I don't know who. Also, children under the age of nine don't grieve in the same way adults do. She died on May 24 just forty-one years old. Damien was seven on May 4.

On the day of the funeral, Damien was given a lot of attention. By this time, he had been with us for eight months and was well settled. Fate would have it that I ended up with a ready-made son called Damien. Little did Sophia realise that when she was putting her child's name on his birth certificate, an unseen being was guiding her hand. Every time I called his name, I thought of my little brother. I loved Damien not because of his name but because he was now mine. Many times, I dreamed that Damien was a baby, my own baby, and that I was feeding him.

Damien had difficulty showing warmth, and he was uncomfortable with close physical contact. It took him months to show any emotion. I was thrilled when one day while driving the camper van, he sat between Graham and me, looked at me, smiled, and put his arms around me. I hugged him as tightly as I could, the safety belts restricting our movement. He chose to call us Mum and Dad, and we were pleased with that. He didn't seem to be missing his mother. I never saw him cry. I put her photo on the fridge door and talked to him about her

He shed tears twice while I was telling him about how sad I was when'd I lost my good friend. My heart went out to him, and I tried to be as loving and caring as I could. I might not have been the perfect parent, but I did a much better job with him than with my own children. Graham was very good to him. We had the wisdom of being older parents. Damien was headstrong, but he tried to please us and was a good kid. As he grew older, he tested limits like kids do, and he went all the way.

By the time he was eleven, he was a handful like any other kid. Given he wasn't our natural child, we thought twice before discipline him. I always wondered how his own mother would have disciplined him for the same offence. Many times I felt guilty. He was a quick thinker and a smart kid. At times I was frustrated and angry, and it did neither of us any good. The idea of sending him as a boarder was becoming more and more attractive as time passed. I spoke to Graham about it. He wasn't happy with the idea but didn't say much at the time. Damien was getting harder and harder to get on with and was constantly testing limits.

I decided to speak to the school principal, who suggested we consult a child psychologist. They weren't happy with his performance at school either; he never paid attention and didn't concentrate. They suggested I give him a more nutritious lunch.

"I wish I could," I said. "The only thing he will ask for is bread and jam. He brings the fruit back and throws it in the bushes." He refuses anything else. I made sure he had a good breakfast, camouflaged the egg in pancakes or drinks, and made sure he ate or drank it.

The psychologist's report astounded me! After she wrote her observations and his behaviour in the classroom (e.g., "played with his pencils, lined them up, fidgeted), she concluded with, "His behaviour at home is not unusual for an adopted/fostered child. His foster mother works. Damien is left at home to do as he wishes, and when she is home, he refuses to do as she asks him to. His obstinacy is a common trait of fostered children." What a lot of rubbish! To start with, by that time I was only working three days per fortnight. Graham had retired and was home all the time. On the rare occasion he needed to be looked after, either Julie or Anja would pick him up from the bus stop, andbothe women spoiled. The psychologist never bothered to investigate the situation at home, never rang to ask me what was happening, and never offered any "good advice" if she thought I was doing the wrong thing by the child. Their presumptions were wrong and their inaction was negligent. What if that child was being neglected, as they had intimated in their report? I was disgusted and too angry to bother contacting them.

By the time he was in year six, he was impossible. He didn't do his homework. He spent his time watching TV. Halfway through year six, I made up my mind that he was going to the local college as a border. That way, we could keep a better relationship. I didn't tell him till the last few weeks of the year. "I don't want to be a boarder," he said emphatically.

I did not argue the point with him then other than to say, "You don't have a choice." He was warned and would be prepared for the event when time came.

When it did, he kicked like a mule. When he realised that crying wasn't going to work, he promised he was going to be good, but that didn't move me. Many times in the past, we'd sat down together and drew up a contract, but he never stuck to his side of the deal. Nothing worked—he wanted it all his way. He had no option now. He was going to college as a border

On enrolment day, he cried, tears rolling his face. The brother tried to comfort him and reassure him he'd like it. There was lots of fun, other boarders, sports, and more. However, Damien cried all the more. I suggested we break him in gently, a few nights at home and a couple nights at the college. The brother said, "This is not a usual practice, but we'll make an exception." For the first six weeks, this was how it was, reducing the time at home and increasing the time at college till he was comfortable to be there full-time.

At the end of school term, I went to pick him up. A kid from Western Australia called out to him, "Bye, Damien, I'll look after the TV for you." Obviously, he was the TV manager.

At college, he played up. He refused to hand in his assignments, was disruptive in class, and was rude to his teachers. I was forever being called to the college to discuss his attitude towards his homework and his teachers. His religious instruction teacher, a young girl, was at her wits' end. I said, "I have no suggestions. Deal with him as you see fit.

Kick him out of class, if you like." She wasn't impressed. The same thing happened a couple more times, and I wondered how to handle his behaviour.

The next time I was called up, it was by his maths teacher, a young man in his mid-thirties. Damien was present at that meeting. The teacher had the same complaints and went on to say how Damien wouldn't be able to get a good job if he didn't change his attitude to his studies. I glanced at Damien. He was sitting there with a smug look on his face. I realised then that he was manipulating the lot of us by misbehaving. He achieved his purpose admirably.

I was not going to play his game any more. I let the teacher finish and thanked him for being so caring and trying to make Damien see the importance of studying. "But in the end, we can't force him to do anything he doesn't want to do. After all, he's fifteen now. He can decide for himself what he wants to do with his life."

"But the way he is going, he is not going to pass," the teacher interrupted.

"That's OK by me," I said. "Will you still get paid whether he passes his exams or not?"

The teacher was surprised, and Damien looked uncomfortable. When the teacher recovered from the shock, he nodded and quietly said, "Yes, I will still get paid."

"That's all that matters. I'm not worried about Damien. There will be plenty of unskilled labour jobs for him to do. That's if he wants to work at all. Please don't call me again to complain. It wastes my time as well as yours. He can do as he pleases." I got up to go, turned around, looked at Damien, and asked, "Is this fair enough?" He looked at me defiantly, saying nothing.

The responsibility was thrown on him, and his manipulative tool was taken away. He didn't like it. I wasn't called back again to discuss his progress. Time went by. I don't know whether or not his attitude changed. There was nothing I could do and no point in worrying about it. He was now near the end of year nine.

One day I received a distressed call from him, crying on the phone. I couldn't understand what he was talking about. "He bashed me, he threw me against the wall," was all I could make out in between sobs, but he couldn't or wouldn't tell me why. I understood it was one of the brothers at the college, but I didn't know the reason for the ill treatment.

I made an appointment to meet with the school principal and the teacher concerned. I won't forget the atmosphere in the room; it was thick and heavy. The principal opened the door for me and greeted me with a sombre look on his face. The teacher was sitting with his head bowed, his hands clasped on the table. I felt terrible for him and wished I could put my arms around him and comfort him. Nobody spoke for a few moments. I took a deep breath, trying to relax and said the first thing that came into my head. "I sympathise with anyone wanting to kill Damien. He has a way of bringing the worst out in people. The reason he's here as a boarder is because I couldn't cope with him at home. Now, let's see what we can do to help him."

I heard the sound of relief in both men. I saw it on their faces and felt it myself. They both looked up at me with a faint smile and nodded. The teacher spoke first. "He is certainly a difficult child to deal with, headstrong and unreasonable at times."

I couldn't disagree with that. "What happened, anyway?" I asked.

Damien left his bag in the middle of a walkway. The teacher asked him to move it, and Damien defiantly said, "You move it." With that, the teacher got him by the scruff of the neck and pushed him. He went flying ending against the nearby wall. I told the teacher I knew exactly how he felt. I told him that the punishment didn't fit the crime; he needed something that would make him think twice before he was rude to his teachers again. I could not tolerate rude kids myself, and Damien could be insolent if he chose, just like most teenagers.

I had no suggestions as how to deal with him, I told them. The principal said something like, "It's not the punishment but rather the way it was served that you object to, then?" When I analysed my feelings, that was just how I felt.

Later, Damien rang me complaining for not defending him. I told him in no uncertain terms that he deserved what he got, and he should get more. "Being rude to anyone is bad enough. It's much, much worse when it is your teachers. If this happens again, don't come to me for sympathy—you won't get any." This is the story I was told by his teacher. I hadn't heard the other half of the story, either from the teacher or from Damien, till many years later. What Damien told me upset and angered me. Talking to him about it just recently, I was angry at the treatment and more so about being told only half the story, leading me to believe a lie all these years. The teacher had really bashed Damien. His screams and noise of chairs being thrown around brought in another teacher, who put an end to the vicious attack on the child. The teacher was transferred to another school at the end of the term, which wasn't long after that incident. I am sure Damien told me the truth. I have no reason to believe otherwise.

Year ten started, and I was still preoccupied with Damien's welfare. I wanted to make sure he'd have some money saved when he finished school. We decided to pull him out of the boarding school, bring him home, and enrol him at the local college—a very good one for day students. It offered lots of subjects such as music and languages, including Croatian. I hoped he would be interested in it because it was his mother tongue. By now we were living in Altona. We approached him with the idea, and he was thrilled. He couldn't leave the boarding school quickly enough, which surprised me because the college was a good school and he had a lot of friends. When I went to pick him up, he was waiting for me. A few of his friends were with him. He had tears in his eyes while waving goodbye.

Back home, he behaved for a few weeks. Then he started refusing to get up for school, and when he did, I wasn't sure that he went. I started following him because the college was a short distance from home. Then started the rudeness, the teenage "I don't care, whatever!" kind of thing. "I will do what I want." At this stage, he was still in the first term of year ten, and I wondered whether he intended finishing the year. His attitude to his studies was appalling. He'd spend the odd weekend with Eva, who liked having him, and he got on well with my nephew Alexi.

One long weekend, we decided to go to New South Wales to see Timotheos and his family. We told Damien, who didn't commit himself one way or another. The day before the trip, I asked him to put a few things in his suitcase to be ready for the trip tomorrow. He said, "No, I'm not coming," but he wouldn't give a reason.

"OK," I said. "Get ready. You will stay with aunty Eva. I'll go ring her now to make sure it's OK with her." I rang her, and she was glad to have him. Damien refused to go to Eva's or come with us. He was determined to stay home on his own, and I was determined he would not. We locked horns, the ram against the bull.

He locked himself in the toilet and refused to come out. Graham said, "I can put the hose through the louvers and flush him out." Instead, he rang the police and explained the situation.

Two policemen arrived reasonably quickly. Damien got out of the toilet. Being articulate, he spun a good sob story, a "poor me" kind of a thing. When the policeman wouldn't buy into his story, he became rude and told them how I didn't give him any money but instead gave it to the Salvos. Damien became ruder and more insolent. The interviewing policeman pulled him up and told him in no uncertain terms that he wasn't going to take his rudeness. "Watch it, mate." I was so glad the officers were firm. Damien stayed with Eva. After that, he became harder to cope with. We tried to do the best we could for him, but he was too young to understand. I rang his boarding school and asked them if they would take him back. They said they would.

When he came home from school, I told him he was going back to the boarding school. He was not pleased and tried to persuade me he would behave. As far as I was concerned, he'd had his chance. I bundled him up and took him to the college the next Sunday. I'd tried to save him a few thousand dollars in school fees, but it wasn't worth the pain for either of us. He finished his education at the boarding school, coming home for school holidays. Although he had the ability to excel, he didn't apply himself to his studies. He had a mathematical brain, was articulate, was good at drama, had some leading roles at school plays, and did it well. I was so proud of him, and during the play I kept thinking of his mother; I felt her pride.

By the time Damien finished year twelve, we were living in Melbourne's West. He moved back home, and I expected he would start looking for a job or further studies. He did neither despite us being on his back to do something about it. He wasn't anxious to get a job. He had plenty of money left to him by his mother. An eighteen-year-old boy thinks a good sum of money is inexhaustible. He refused to work. He listened to loud, banging music, always coming up with smart answers. He was rude and angry. We argued a lot, and he always had the last word.

One day after a heated argument about him not making plans for further study or work, I went close to his face, shaking my fist and with teeth clenched, I said to him, "I feel like killing you." Then I left the house, fuming, and went next door to Alana's. She made us a cup of tea, and when I cooled down, I told her what the problem was.

Just as we finished our drink, Damien came and said, "Phone call for you from the police."

My knees went to jelly. Trembling and fearful, I picked up the phone and asked, "What's wrong? Who is it? Who is hurt?"

The policewoman answered calmly and said, "Nothing is wrong. Damien just rang to say you have bashed him." I breathed with relief! "Where is he? I'll get him. He can repeat this to my face," I said in anger.

"Oh, no, that won't be necessary. I just wanted to verify that this wasn't true. I didn't think it would be so." She told him he could move out of home because he was now eighteen. Then she hung up.

Soon after that, he moved out, rented with his friends, got a part-time job, and entered a private college to do filming and photography. He did well, but he abandoned it halfway, saying it wasn't what he wanted to do for the rest of his days. He worked and supported himself. I was so happy and proud of him. He bought a car and he was happy.

By the time he was twenty, he'd matured, and our relationship improved tremendously. He would visit and spend holidays with us. He worked, studied economics and statistics, and got his degree. He got a job with the public service and was quickly promoted. He studied for his master's degree. I am very proud of him and told him so. He became a mature and loving adult. Our relationship is wonderful now.

He is my much-loved son, and I am as proud of him as of Rose and Timotheos. I can stand before God and say, "Lord, I have done the best I could for him, the best I knew how." Barring his mother's death, Damien had a better childhood than Rose and Timotheos and many other children I know.

Chapter 66

Graham's Business Adventure

Graham retired at fifty-five, he was strong and healthy. He got his superannuation, a respectable sum, and we went together to see his accountant, Chris. They discussed this and that investment, as well as the pros and con of each, about which I had no clue. At a lull in the conversation, I suggested he buy a couple of houses in Melbourne's West, close to the city; real estate was still affordable. Graham looked at me condescendingly, as if to say, "Shut up. It's my money." Chris noticed and shifted uncomfortably in his chair. In a quiet manner, Chris added "We had real estate, and we got out of it."

I said no more. Later, I reminded him that when he moved in with me, I had a house nearly paid off and had a good deposit to buy another one. "Now I have nothing. All I want from you is a house in my name." He reluctantly agreed. We bought a three-bedroom house in Altona in my name, which we let.

He wanted to do some building to occupy himself. He did a builder / owner course and was ready to start. Having invested all his money, he needed to borrow to build. He put our house as a guarantee. All up, he borrowed $300,000, and at 18 per cent interest! I shuddered, but he was happy. He said, "It's OK. I am getting good interest on my investments." I said nothing. I owned a house in Newcomb Geelong, on a large block of land. He built a unit on it. He bought three blocks of land west of Melbourne and built a house on one of them. Graham was a good mechanic, not a businessman. He was disorganised and impractical. He took every Tuesday off to play golf while paying over four thousand dollars a month in interest.

Working with him was frustrating. We were tiling in Geelong. He cut the tiles, and I put them down. The cutter was under the carport at the front of the house, which was OK. He was cutting one tile at the time, going around, while I waited for tiles. He could have brought the cutter to the side door, or walked through the front door five steps away. He refused to do either. He looked at me as if to say, "No, I'll do it my way, just to get under your skin." He carried on in a passive-aggressive way. At times I'd be sitting down, frustrated and angry, my gut churning and in pain. It was times like this that I wanted to run away and leave him to his own devices. But I had promised God a long time ago that if He ever brought Graham my way, I would stand by him, love him, and be true to him. I would not break the oath I took before God. At times like this, I would be praying earnestly and saying, "Lord, I too have faults. Please help me love him as he is." As time went by, my prayer became, "Lord, please help me. I can't do it on my own. I can't live like this for the rest of my days. Please give me strength to cope.

In the end, we couldn't keep up with the repayments. The stock exchange crashed, the building industry came to a halt. We sold at a loss everything we owned except the house in Altona, paid the bank, and got out of it with a bit of cash in hand. That was the end of Graham's business adventure and his big dreams of building multi-storey units. Everything went down the gurgler.

We were now financially ruined. He was upset and inconsolable. He'd lost all his money and had made no provision to get part of his superannuation in pension. We had no income other than mine, and I was working part-time. One day we were sitting down and discussing our financial state and the options we had, which were none. How were we going to survive? He felt lost, hopeless, and depressed. He looked at me and in all seriousness said, "I can't cope with all this. I am going to blow my brains out."

I was surprised. He was feeling very low, and knowing how much money meant to him, I feared he might do something stupid. I had to think fast to bring him back to reality. "OK," I said, "but not before I give you a couple of hypothetical scenarios." He looked at me, puzzled.

Scenario One

Imagine your investments flourished and your business made you millions. You are the envy of your friends and the bane of your enemies. You drive an expensive car, you wear designer clothes, and you eat caviar. You say to your soul, "Graham, eat, drink, and be merry, for you have goods for many years to come."

One night, there is a knock on the door. You answer it. Two policemen are standing there. "Hello, is this Mr. Dawson?"

"Yes," you say.

"Can we come in?" they ask, you let them in. "Can we sit down?"

By now you are scared shitless, and you can't wait to hear what they have to say. "What's the matter? What's happened? Who is hurt?"

To cut it short, they say "Sorry, Mr. Dawson, but there has been a terrible accident. Your daughter Jane and her family have all been killed. We are terribly sorry." They stay for a few minutes, ask if there is anything they can do, and leave.

****

I paused a few moments to let reality sink in. He looked stunned.

I emphasised every word. "Now, what would you rather have? Your daughter, or your money?"

He looked at me and slowly said, "My daughter."

"OK," I said. "Here's one more scenario."

Scenario Two

"Imagine that your investments and your business flourished as before. You are sitting pretty and in great luxury. One morning, I wake up and find you still in bed, unable to talk. The right side of your face is drooping, and you are unable to move. I call the ambulance. Yes, just as I thought, you had a terrible stroke. After three months in hospital and rehabilitation, you come home. The best you can do is walk supported on a four-prong stick. I buy you a state-of-the-art wheelchair and a suitable flash vehicle to accommodate it. I put you and your chair in the car and take you to the shops. You point with your good hand at all the things your soul desires. You indicate with a grunt that you want this, that, and the other. I buy them. We go home. I spread all the goodies around for you to look at and enjoy."

I paused again for him to ponder on this situation. "Now, what would you rather have? Your money, or your health?"

"My health," he said decidedly.

"Good," I said. "Now, you can go and blow the brains out, but do it somewhere I won't find you, because I don't like the mess it makes." Thirty-four years later, I am still waiting for him to blow his brains out.

After the settlement of the house in Upper Plenty, we moved to Altona. The house needed work done to it. We replaced the shabby kitchen with a good second-hand one, added a bathroom, and painted it. It looked good. It was an easy house to live in. Graham went on the age pension, which he took badly. "On the scrap heap," he would say in a defeated and self-pitying manner. He felt humiliated and ashamed to say he was relying on government handouts to survive. Here was a man who had been on the top 10 per cent of wage earners and had been proud of his job. He'd lost everything. "How the mighty have fallen," he would wail (2 Samuel 1:25; King David's lamenting King Soul and Jonathan dying in battle).

When Rose got married, she bought an old house in a busy street west of Melbourne. After Louise was born and before Rose was ready to go back to work, we sold the Altona house and bought an old one closer to her for less, which gave us the money we needed to renovate. Rose was the interior decorator, advisor, and helper. I was the tiler, painter, wallpaper hanger, and lackey around the place. Graham did the structural work, plumbing, and plastering. We added a bathroom and a family room. When the place was finished, it looked good. We paved a large area at the back and built a double garage. We had all we needed. By now I was working at a psychiatric hospital doing night shift five nights a fortnight, and looking after Louise.

She was an easy baby to look after, and because I couldn't go to sleep until lunchtime, I'd take her to bed with me, and we'd both sleep. When she gave up her midday sleep, Graham would look after her until I got up. I'd prepare dinner and go to work. I managed well for three years, but night duty caught up with me. I felt constantly tired, irritable, and unable to sleep day or night. I ate because I had to, but I felt no pleasure in life. I had to stop and think. I decided I was not doing myself a favour. I told Graham I had had enough and I was going to resign. I couldn't cope any more. He wasn't happy about it, but he had no choice. I took a long time to get back to sleeping and eating normally and be myself again. Now we had to budget to the last cent, but that wasn't new to me. I simply took over where I had left off years earlier.

When our house was finished, Graham renovated Rose's house with our help. Three years later, she sold her newly renovated house and bought another one in the same suburb, but on a quiet street. This house needed a lot of work too.

Because Graham was retired, he undertook to renovate this house too. He took a long time to finish it. To him it was a hobby, with no urgency to finish the job. Anybody who went by and wanted a chat was welcome to do so. I was looking after Louise and couldn't work with him all the time.

Little by little, my frustration and unvented anger eroded my remaining respect for him, and my relationship with him suffered. I found myself praying for strength to cope with him.

When the structural work was finished, Rose did the wallpaper and interior painting. My late sister-in-law, my neighbour, and I painted the outside. It looked very good when it was all finished.

Chapter 67

Dog Business

Alana, next door, wanted a puppy. Together we went looking for one all over Melbourne. We answered an advertisement in Werribee. It was a Maltese male pup that was snow white and adorable; she called him Charly. The more I got to know Charly, the more I wanted one myself. All three of our dogs had died of old age within three months. I was not working now, and I had a bit more time to myself—a bad thing for me. I decided to get a puppy. I talked it over with Graham, and he had no objection to us having another dog. I rang Charly's breeder, and he said he had a litter of two females and two males; they would be ready in two weeks. I asked him to put down my name for a female. I couldn't wait to pick it up.

Alana and I went to pick the pup up, and as it is with most people, I couldn't decide which one to take. The breeder must have been busy, sick and tired of waiting, or wanting to sell both, he said, "I'll tell you what. I'll make you a good deal if you want to take them both." The temptation was too much. I took them both and went home, delighted. Graham didn't object because he too was a dog lover. We called one Peggy and the other one Pixie. Peggy was the smarter one, with a lovely nature and personality. We loved them both. I wanted to breed them once before sterilising them. They say they settle better after they have a litter, but that's not true. Anyway, by selling a litter, I'd get my money back.

Looking after Louise, house-training two pups, and keeping the house clean was a full-time job. The year went by quickly, and they came in season one after the other. They had seven beautiful, healthy pups between them, and all in two weeks. There was great excitement when Peggy was whelping. Alana and I stayed with her till the fourth pup was born. She was treated like Queen Lizzy. The same applied to Pixie. I was flat out with two mothers and seven pups. It was a constant round of mopping, feeding, and cleaning.

One day while looking at the paper, I noticed an ad about a breeder closing down, with Maltese females for sale. I went to have a look. What I saw shocked me. The poor animals were kept in a cold, dark, and damp shed; some of them were running around filthy, and one in particular ran away to hide. I felt sorry for them. I never do things in half measures, so I took all four of them, including the scared one, which the breeder chased, cornered, and caught.

I brought them home. The first question Graham asked was, "What are you going to do with all these scungy dogs?"

"First of all, give them a bath, feed them, and hopefully find decent homes for them," I said.

I started with the scared one. Her ears were full of brown gunk from untreated infections. As I was cleaning her, she whined. Amazingly, she made no effort to pull away. She looked at me as if to say, "Please carry on. Clean me up." I was nearly in tears. This was the animal that ran away from people. I was angry at their inhumane treatment. They were kept for the sole purpose of making money. their welfare was the last thing in the minds of those heartless breeders.

Now we had a few problems I hadn't foreseen. The animals needed treatment for ear infections, worms, and general checking. That meant big money, which we couldn't really afford.

They barked. If the neighbours complained, we'd be in trouble with the council for keeping all those dogs (and two pups) without a permit. In town, I was allowed to keep two dogs, but now I had eight! The biggest problem was, where would they live?

First problem first: to the store for eardrops and worming tablets. Then to the vet for a check-up. When I told the staff their story, they thought I was mad. Fortunately, they were healthy enough—nothing a good feed and a bit of care wouldn't fix.

Then we made beds, using clean, warm boxes in the garage. The car was parked outside, and Graham organised to put up a shed for them in the backyard. He put a bench, a trough, and hot and cold water in it for bathing them. He insulated the roof and even put a shade cloth for them to sit under on a hot day. Compared to what they'd had, this was luxury. That shed became my refuge, my prayer and meditation place, when things were too hard to bear.

Now the biggest problem: what would I do about the barking, which wasn't too bad because I was with them practically all day. When I was inside, they'd sit at the back door, waiting for me.

I had to approach the council and ask for a permit sooner or later. I prayed and prayed about it. I drafted a letter and asked the neighbours to sign it if they didn't object to me keeping my eight dogs in the yard. They all signed the petition! The block to the right of us was vacant, and behind was Leander Street. Armed with the signatures, I was ready to go to the council for the permit, fully aware that I'd exceeded the number of animals allowed in suburbia. As much as I feared going, I had no choice.

With my heart thumping and a prayer on my lips, I opened the council door and rang the bell. A young man in his early thirties came to the desk with a welcoming smile. Trembling, I told him the story of how I went to get one dog, felt sorry for them, and rescued them. Now I would like to keep them, and the neighbours didn't mind; here were their signatures and my application to keep them.

The young man looked me up and down. The desk hid most of me. He couldn't see or hear my knees knocking, and I tried to keep calm. He looked at the signatures I handed him. "It's terrible how some people treat helpless animals. They shouldn't be allowed to keep them." I agreed wholeheartedly. He handed me a form to fill, which I did. I paid the fee and expected a letter from the council refusing me the permit, but I didn't hear anything from them.

The following year, when I went to the council to pay the registration fees, a female clerk came to the desk and asked sweetly, "who gave you the permit to keep eight dogs?"

"A man," I said. She wanted to know his name. "I don't know," I replied. She said no more. So I'd had a permit, and I didn't know it!

I was flat out with the endless round of keeping the pups and dog house clean, as well as the animals fed. As any breeder will tell you, you don't make money from breeding just a few dogs, if you want to do the right thing by them. Feeding and vetting costs are high and the work is endless, but still they paid for their keep, and there was a little bit leftover. The advantage was they kept me occupied and sane.

I'd always wanted a pug dog, and so did Rose since she was a little girl. I talked about it with Graham, he shrugged and said, "OK." I kept a lookout for one. There was one available in the country a few miles from our place. Graham drove us there, and we picked her up. She was a beautiful, healthy pup with a wrinkled face. We called her Soufra, or "Wrinkles" in Greek. We loved her, and the extra bit of work didn't matter.

We became registered breeders. I enjoyed learning how to train dogs for showing, and I liked the socialising aspect of the shows. It took me out of the house, mostly to the country, and I talked to people with the same interests. Before long, I realised that our backyard was too small, and the neighbours were too close. I told Graham that I'd like to go somewhere with a bigger backyard. His first reaction was, "We have just finished renovating. We've been here only two years, and you want to move? No, I like it here". "But there is no harm in looking. If something more suitable comes up, we'll look at it. If not, we stay put." I took it as licence to go looking.

I contacted an agent and told him what I was looking for. He said, "We have one just listed in Maidstone. It needs a lot of work, but it has a big block of land." I couldn't wait to see it. I took the address and without telling Graham went on my own to have look. I loved it. It was a corner property with a huge block, no houses opposite, a wrecking business across the road, only two neighbours to worry about, and a dead-end street.

I thought it would suit us well. I told Graham about it. He reluctantly agreed to look at it. He was not enthusiastic. He looked around silently and with a long face. We drove home in silence. For the next two days, I prayed constantly. I talked hard and fast and pointed out all the advantages of the place, in order to get him interested enough to take another look. He agreed. The second time, we went with the agent. He inspected it carefully, and when he said he'd like to look up in the roof, I knew half the battle was won. They refused the offer we made, the auction was only a week away. We bought it at auction at a better price than our original offer. We paid the deposit, and I was over the moon. I rang Timotheos and asked him if he was still interested in buying our house. He said yes. We again had enough money to pay for the house and renovate, with a bit left over.

We moved in, and the first thing we did was to sort out accommodation for the dogs. The garage and the shed were converted to kennels. We put the air conditioner we'd taken out of the house in the shed. The majority of the yard was divided for the dogs, and behind the shed we allowed a patch for vegetables. It was more comfortable in the dog shed than in the house. I spent most of my day there again.

The renovating started with Rose being the interior decorator again. It looked pretty good when it was finished. The back veranda was converted into a whelping room with hot and cold water, a bench, a sink, and even a bed for me to sleep in when expectant mothers were close to term. By this time, we had four Maltese and four pugs.

Maltese mothers are good. Pugs are stupid. They also have a high incidence of caesarean sections. When their pups are born, the mothers don't have the sense to move the pups out of the way before sitting. They turn around and around, sitting on them and suffocating them. I lost count of how many times in a night I'd get up to rescue a pup from under its mother. Breeders lost whole litters because of it. Also, in a large litter, the bigger pups feed first, and the smaller ones die quickly if they miss a couple of feeds. They either need to be helped or bottle-fed. Very often I had to bottle-feed, keeping the small pups warm in my bosom. One day while looking in an op-shop, I found an electric slipper, which I bought to keep the small, weak pups in. I didn't lose one. Later, we found that there were electrically heated beds for breeders, and we got some of them too. Those dogs lived in luxury. I'd spend three weeks with each pug mother, one week before whelping and two weeks till the pups were big enough to move out of her way. It was tiring.

It was much easier looking after pugs than Maltese (less grooming), eventually I got out of breeding Maltese and sterilised Peggy and Pixie; they were our house dogs, and we had pugs only for breeding. I loved going to shows. I wasn't a show person because I couldn't walk with the grace others walked, and I couldn't show my dog with the flare others did. The breeds were shown alphabetically. We usually stayed behind to watch the other breeds shown. Again I fell in love with another breed, this time a Scottish terrier. The beauty and grace of that breed is only surpassed by its energy and capacity to defend itself, but I didn't know it. I was hell-bent on getting one. We got one from South Australia, and later we got two pups from New Zealand. I loved them. I had professional grooming lessons with my usual enthusiasm. It was all good till I had to strip them a few times. My old shoulder injury, sustained at work a few years earlier, flared up. I was in constant pain. I gave away the stripping and started shaving them. Even that was too much. I had to give up my favourite breed and find homes for them.

After a while, Graham lost his enthusiasm for shows. He didn't say so. Instead, he refused to load the trailer with the tent and cages, the night before. He'd get up late, and consequently there was rushing and hard-to-find parking, creating stress and tension between us. I preferred to get ready the night before, and in the morning I'd put the last few things in and take a leisurely trip. When I asked Graham to pack up the day before, he told me he didn't enjoy the shows any more. We stopped going altogether. That was my only social interaction other than going to church weekly and the soup kitchen every three weeks.

Chapter 68

Providence

Graham became restless and harder to live with. He wouldn't talk, and he was distant and often grumpy, even more so after visiting his daughters, whom I liked. One day he asked me to tell my kids not to come. I became furious and balked. I told him, "You can tell yours not to come, but I would die before I said this to mine. They are most important to me and are welcome here any time.

One day he returned from visiting his daughters. I went to open the door to greet him and give him a hug as usual. Before he came in, he said coldly, "I want my name in the equity of the house."

I was surprised. "But Graham, this is my house, what I bought with the money I got when I split with Edward. You, at my suggestion, gave everything you had to Valerie: two houses, a block of land, your car, your life insurance, and your sailing boat. You came to me with your clothes and your father's antique plumbing tools."

"Well," he said in a business-like manner, "I did work on this house, and I am entitled to it by law." He was right.

"OK," I said. "If this is what you want, you will take it—but you will go." He agreed. My first reaction was, *Quick, before he changes his mind.*

We were unhappy together. My prayer when we got together was, "Dear Lord, please take days from my life and give them to him." As time went by, it became, "Dear Lord I too have faults. Please help me love him as he is." But for the last few years, it was, "Lord, how am I going to put up with this for the rest of my life? Please help me. I can't do it alone."

The first thing I did was get a sworn valuation. The house was valued at $180,000. Graham took the little bit of cash we had, Rose borrowed the rest, and he left. He bought himself a house in the Latrobe Valley, which he renovated.

I packed linen, crockery, glassware, and cutlery. He took his tools and any gifts I gave him, and he walked out. That was a relief. He walked out of my life, and I didn't have to break the vow I had consciously and knowingly taken before God more than twenty-five years ago. He released me of that vow, and I was grateful. On the day we said our last goodbyes, I felt an undefined sadness. Here was a man I had known for forty-one years as a friend, and twenty-two of them as a husband. On his way out, for the last time I looked him in the eye and asked, "Is this what you really wanted?"

He looked at me and with sadness said, "Don't ask." We parted on good terms without bitterness.

Two months after we parted, he visited and he suggested we go to marriage counselling. He said he had a good one he saw himself, and she would like to see us together. He also generously offered to pay for the consultation. I had to try very hard to be civil while talking to him. I thanked him for the offer but refused. I was happy with the way things were. My divorce came through within three months.

We continued to be on friendly terms, and he visited again many times. On one of those visits, Rose was at my place. Graham was sitting in his usual chair, I on mine, and Rose next to me. We talked, and at one stage I said to Rose, "Last night, I had a strange dream."

He interjected. "I too had a very strange dream last night," and he proceeded to tell us his dream. "I dreamed that I was renovating my house. I pulled the mantelpiece off the wall, looked behind it, and saw Estella's name written on it."

I was stunned and looked at Rose, who was surprised. Then I looked at him long and hard. He put his head down. No words were needed.

Later, I told my sister his dream. She said, "The hearth, the fireplace, is the heart of the house. It is the whole house" I didn't need any more explanations.

A little while later, he visited again. While we were having a cup of tea together, he said, "And if you like, I will come and live with you and help you look after the dogs."

This was as much as I could take. I lost my cool and bluntly said, "Like hell you will. You will go as far away as you can and a little farther. I don't need you, and now I don't want you. Do you get the difference?"

He looked at me and said angrily, "Of course I do. You made it bloody plain." In the past, he'd refused to accept that there was a difference between the "I want you" and "I need you" statement, no matter which way I tried to explain it. He insisted there was no difference. He left and didn't visit for a couple of years.

Here are some precious lessons I learned while living with Graham.

I've learned to appreciate people for what they are, not for their appearance.

Love is born out of respect. It is impossible to love without respect.

I learned the difference between confidence and arrogance. They're easily confused when one is young or infatuated.

I've learned the difference between wisdom and knowledge. Wisdom is inherent. Knowledge is acquired.

Maturity is inherent, and it does not come with years. Years only bring experience.

Yes, it takes two to tango, but it takes only one to spoil the dance.

I learned to appreciate qualities such as generosity, honesty, humility, and altruism. I saw negative traits such as selfishness, stinginess, and greed in their true and soul-destroying effect, the source of all evil and suffering in the world.

Part 4

Chapter 69

Trying Times

I will lift up my eyes to the hills … My help comes from the Lord, which made heaven and earth. (Psalm 121:1–2)

Now I was alone with eight dogs and six pups. I was on the single pension, and I had not a cent in the bank to fall back on. I wondered where would the money come from to pay the next bill, but I did not despair. I left my case with God once again. The last time I was utterly and completely helpless and alone was after my mother's death. He didn't forget me then, and I knew He wouldn't this time either. I had to trust Him to rescue me in His own time and in His own way. He might test me and try me again, but it wouldn't be beyond my endurance—of that I was sure.

I struggled financially for a few months, and I can only say I lived by faith alone because I couldn't see beyond the present moment. For about four months, I lived from hand to mouth, budgeting to the last cent, and I was always short of money.

Sometime in December 2003, my friend Yvette paid me one of her rare visits. We were talking about each other's kids and our lives. She talked about her job at the arts centre and how unhappy she was. She didn't get enough work while the younger ones got in first. She casually said, "I'd be better off doing a couple night shifts either in a hospital or in a nursing home." That statement hit me like a thunderbolt. I don't remember what else we talked about that day. That statement kept resonating in my mind. While Yvette was talking, I kept saying to myself, "I can do that too. I can do it!" I was sure that Yvette came to me that day with a message from God, and neither she nor I knew it. He sure works in weird and mysterious ways.

As soon as Yvette left, I rang Rose at work and told her what Yvette had said. I wanted to go back to nursing. I needed to know where I could do a refresher course. After I'd resigned from nursing at the psychiatric hospital and when we were short of money, I let my registration lapse, and I needed to do a refresher course before I could re-register.

Rose said, "Mum, if you are going to do that, you need to do it immediately because the government is planning to cut funding to this course soon." She gave me the names of some of the hospitals that still offered it. The Austin was one of them. I got off the phone from Rose and called the Austin hospital. My heart sank when the person at the other end of the line said, "There are no positions in this intake, the next one is in May, would you like to enrol for that intake?"

"Yes, please," I said eagerly. "I was hoping to do it sooner, but I'll just have to wait."

"OK, I'll put your name down for the May intake, and if there is a cancelation in February's class, I'll let you know." I hoped and prayed there would be a cancelation—a slim chance, but possible. I kept praying and hoping.

On January 7, the Austin hospital rang to say, "There is a cancelation in February's re-entry class. Did you want it?" It was heaven-sent. The interview was arranged for January 23, 2004. I wrote in that day's diary,

> The Good Lord takes care of everything … Yvette put it into my head to work, the position came up just on time, and I won't have to worry about Louise. Tory and she would be going to the same school and home together. What a blessing! Praised be His name. He has faithfully led me, sometimes through narrow and dark paths, but He has never left me stranded. I am grateful.

I just wonder if this is going to be the beginning of my dream's materialisation. I hope so, though I have no idea how. One thing I am sure of: that with Him holding my hand, I can turn the world upside down.

The refresher course went well. I did my presentation on spinal cord injuries on April 14 and passed with flying colours. I couldn't wait to show my grandkids my results, hoping it would inspire them. If their grandmother could get 100 per cent, then so could they. The course finished on April 19, 2004. I was now registered again and started looking for a job. I posted my CV and an application for a job at the rehabilitation centre on April 26, and I applied for a casual position with a nursing agency. It signed me up, and they asked me when I wanted to start. I said the week starting May 10.

Chapter 70

Better Things

I started work on May 15 and never looked back. I worked days and nights, frequently seven days straight, and very often double shifts. Before long I didn't need to be on the pension anymore.

What a blessing! What freedom, what dignity, what pride and independence does work bring to a person! To me, no matter what type of work a person does, from the prime minister of a country to cleaning streets, if that work is done well, that person is dignified and well respected by anybody who understands the dignity and value of work. It gave me much pride to say, "I am working." Nursing was easier than breeding animals, and the money was infinitely better. The only problem I had was getting used to the new equipment and taking blood with vaquets. I managed the technique, but I still prefer the old-fashioned syringe; it's much easier on the veins, with no bruising.

I had a problem getting from hospital to hospital on public transport, which meant I had to get up very early for an early shift or get home at midnight after a late shift. As I was running with a knapsack on my back to catch the train, I would say, "Lord, I knew it was going to be hard, but not as hard as this." Fortunately, I got a lot of shifts at the Sunshine Hospital. I liked working there because it was close to where I lived, but above all the staff were really good. They were friendly and helpful until I orientated myself in the ward. I decided to apply for a job at the hospital's psychiatric unit, and I kept praying for a permanent position there or somewhere nearby. As always, God answered.

On November 25, 2004, at 6:00 a.m. I received a phone call and presumed it was a call for an early shift somewhere. I answered it, and at the other end was Maria, one of my favourite nurses from the psychiatric unit of the local hospital. Without much ado, she said, "There is a permanent nursing position coming up. Do you want to apply for it?"

I was half asleep and thought I was dreaming. "Do I want what?" I asked. Maria repeated herself. When it sunk in, I couldn't believe my ears. "Do I want to? I have been praying for it! I already have an application in, together with my resume," I told her.

On December 2004, the unit manager, Shelley, and Adrian interviewed me. The interview went well, but the last question took me by surprise. "And how will you manage making friends and all that?" asked Shelley.

I looked at her, surprised, and said, "The good old book says if you want to have friends, you must be friendly yourself—Proverbs 18:24. I don't know of another way."

She looked at me, pursed her lips, and shrugged as if to say, "Fair enough." I started working as a permanent nurse on February 4, 2005, and true to my way of doing things back to front, I entered the work force full-time at age sixty-four, when everybody else was exiting. I hoped to be able to work for three years before I'd be asked to retire. Nearly thirteen years later, I am still working, and I hope to be working till I drop dead, preferably in my garden with my dirty boots on. I wouldn't want to do it in the ward—it would create too much paperwork for my colleagues, and I don't want to subject them to that.

On December 31, 2004, I closed the year by writing, "Watched the New Year ushered in, and I'm glad to say the old one is over. I hope I never ever have another one like it, being involved with the suicide of Bradley, a young man I was looking after in another hospital. A heavy burden to carry … I achieved my aim for the year in saving $15,000 before the year is out, and it's a good feeling. I now hope to save another $30,000 before 2005 is out."

I closed 2005 by writing,

I turned my diary on January 1 and read my aim for the year, which was to save $30,000. Not only did I reach my aim, but I exceeded it by far. This year has been a tumultuous one for me. It has been full of fear, full of hope, full of prayer and of necessity, full of faith … full of doubt … I doubted … my ability to achieve my aim … but also my sanity … I had to rely on my faith in God, as I had to do many times in the past. I still doubt myself, and when I think of the enormity of my plan, I tremble and shake, my spiritual knees knock and buckle under me, and I raise my soul to God for help. There is so much to consider … it boggles my mind, but my dream comes back to me, and those stars popping up and out of the Great Bear Constellation like popcorn in a frying pan, filling the sky as far as my eye could see. It spurs me on, and I say to God, "Dear Lord, You gave me the dream, and I made it my own. Now You have to take the lead and bring it to fruition. On my own I can do nothing, but with You holding my hand, I can turn the world upside down. So please, God, hold me up lest I fall. Thank You for the myriad blessings, keep me humble and in your love."

Chapter 71

Building the Units

Sometime soon after Graham and I divorced, there was a knock on the door. There were two men, one middle-aged and the other in his mid to late twenties. They introduced themselves as father and son builders. They wanted to talk to me about developing my land. I let them in. The long and the short of it was they wanted to build three to four townhouses on my land, and they would give me one townhouse. I rejected the offer, saying, "It's not good enough."

Without hesitation the son said, "OK, what about a townhouse and $50,000 cash." I told them I'd think about it and let them know. That got me thinking. If those fellows were happy to give me a townhouse and $50,000 cash, there must be money to be made here, and it might as well be me who makes it, not them. I thought about it for a week, and when they came for my answer, I told them I didn't want to proceed with the project. They left, saying they were disappointed.

The more I thought about it, the more obsessed I became with the idea of building. I was convinced I could do it and should do it. I decided four units would be too crowded. Three would be better, and there'd be a bit of land around each for a small garden and a bit of privacy. The only problem was that I had no money for such a venture. However, I rang the council to inquire what was needed before I can start the process of building, before I engaged a draftsman or an architect. I was told by the clerk, "All we need at this stage is the size of the land, the number and size of the units you want to put on it, the distance between them, and the buildings behind, to the left, to the right, and opposite."

Here I was once again, nearly three years after Graham left, excited but with not enough money. I sat down, put pen to paper, and started working out the plans for three two-storey units, how and where I wanted them placed, and more.

Here are entries from my diary chronicling the process.

31/3/2005

> Fooled around for a while drawing and redrawing the plans for the upstairs units ... I worked on them for thirty hours, and when I thought I had them perfect, I went to the council and presented them with great pride. So easy, I thought, but it wasn't. The clerk I spoke to on the phone ... wasn't there. Another clerk attended the desk, took one look at the plans, and got on her high horse.

4/7/05

> They want to see how the building is going to impact in the area. They want the height, orientation, and what's opposite, behind, and on either side of the buildings. I told her that I had already seen someone only two weeks ago, and was told ... all that was needed at this stage ... She interjected, "But it must be shown on the plan." I was annoyed and frustrated. I asked for an appointment with the town planner before I engaged a draftsman. All I want to know for now is whether I can put three or four units on the land and take it from there. Easy, I thought, but no, it can't be done. She had more questions, such as where was the access for the corner unit. I told her from Ashley Street, and then she came up with all the difficulties I'd have with

Vic Roads ... how the neighbours might object, and a few other problems including the weather (not really). I thought I could hear Graham talk. I told her we will cross those bridges when we get to them, took my precious plans, and went.

7/5/05

Home by 10:30 p.m. Fed the animals again and hit the sack at about 11:30 p.m. I couldn't resist the temptation of opening my plans and giving them another admiring look. I now had to go back to square one, buy a battery for the camera, take some photos of buildings I like, and take them to a draftsman to get the ball rolling. I know what I want. I have to be able to pass the vision on to the experts.

21/7/05

In the morning, I rang two draftsmen and talked to them about my plans to build. They were more helpful than the one I saw last week, who looked at me as if to say, "The poor old soul is demented." He said he wasn't interested. Just the same, the enormity of my project was being reinforced ... my fears and doubts ... magnified. I am doubting my sanity. I need all the encouragement I can get ... but since I haven't spoken to anyone for fear of ridicule or discouragement, I am keeping this ... dream too, hidden in my heart, and I seek comfort from the stars even though I do not believe in their predictions.

30/6/05

In the Herald Sun, I read, "Jupiter's opposition to Mars has left you feeling like the owner of a brand-new car. You want to go places, make journeys, see and do things and generally explore your new possibilities.

Unfortunately, all the roads seem to be blocked. Or, if there are no traffic jams, you have commitments that prevent you from travelling anywhere for a while. That may be frustrating, but it's hardly a terrible state of affairs. Psych yourself up for a wait and be glad, at least that you have something worth waiting for." That was a timely message of great encouragement after the knockdown by the draftsman last week. As far as the waiting bit goes, it was a great thing in that I was able to save a bit more money, which meant that I didn't have to borrow so much from the bank.

13/4/05

At work … in HDU [High Dependency Unit] again … One of the patients was given a book by his aunt written by Susan Hayward, titled *Begin It Now*, to replace the one "the police took when they raided the house." I read the preface and did just what it suggested. "Open … at random and there will be your answer." The answer was interesting, to say the least. It helped disperse my fears and doubts, and it encouraged me to keep trying and with the help of God materialize my dream. I often think I must have misinterpreted that dream. I must be mad thinking it would be possible to achieve it and madder still to be … taking the first step to materialise it. Then faith kicks in, and I say, "Dear Lord, on my own I can do nothing …" I have repeated those same words hundreds of times since 1997, and they are still on my lips now. I am fully aware of the magnitude of my dream and my own insignificance.

19/7/05

In the *Herald Sun*, I read my stars. "Your determination is admirable. It is also appropriate. There are times when we find ourselves getting all fired up for doubtful reasons. Something or someone provokes a strong reaction in us and before we know it we have made some big commitment that we then have to see through. You though, are now acting on a feeling that has been slowly growing within you over quite some while. You have given the matter a lot of thought. You have reached a valid conclusion." There were many more encouraging predictions which I kept but later threw out; too bulky in a diary.

My preoccupation with reading the stars bothered me. First of all, I didn't believe in them; I laughed at them. Second, I was led to believe that it was of evil origin, and my religious background emphasised that nobody can see the future but God, which is true. But I was hooked on them just the same, and I tried to analyse my obsession with them and justify my behaviour. First of all, I was scared of entering the building project. The memory of borrowing from banks was still fresh in my mind; I perceived them to be ruthless when it came to collecting their due. It reminded me of drug lords not hesitating to kill rather than lose their ill-gotten gains. The banks will not literally kill you, but they will destroy you financially. Second, would I be able to sell on time to pay the bank before they started charging me exorbitant interest rates? I wasn't sure.

27/7/05

I still feel very nervous about my building project, especially with my long-term dream. I am discouraged and doubt my sanity … the messages in my stars give me some encouragement to keep on going, even though I feel blindfolded. "By faith alone," and I hang on the words. I'd go to work, my mind would fleetingly go to my building project, and I'd be trying to work out how long I'd have to work to save enough to at least pay for one unit and borrow to build the others.

11/8/05

We had a good shift. At home, I felt lazy, sat at my little desk, made an entry in my diary, and daydreamed. I worked out there are 143 days left this year and 365 next year. All up, I'd have to work at least 508 days before I have enough money to start building. Then I thought of the suggestion of Anders, the draftsman: that the builder could foot the bill and get one unit. That idea didn't appeal to me. Then a brilliant idea occurred to me ... that I could borrow the money and pay the bank when the units go up in lottery. That's if Mr. Tatts Lotto agrees to cooperate! Ha, ha, ha ...

12/8/05

I do my calculations on newspaper while watching the patients. I don't dare tell anybody what they are about for fear of ridicule; they may suppose they are Mal's calculations. He is always working out how many millions he has in the bank, and he sends telepathic messages to George Bush to deposit forty million in his bank account and to John Howard to organise two hundred kilograms of dope to be delivered to his home address. I often wonder and fear that I too am deluded and grandiose, as Mal is. I doubt my sanity, even my motives, and I ask ... God to hold my hand and lead me on because on my own I can do nothing; all my dreams and good intents will remain just that. I will not give up until I have exhausted all avenues humanly possible, and only then I will admit defeat, saying, "Lord, You know I have tried. I accept Your verdict." I am loath to think of that. I know God hears prayer and believe He will ... bless my plans. I bring them to him in faith.

"Commit to the Lord whatever you do and your plans will succeed" (Proverbs 16:3). I hang on that promise.

16/9/05

The building venture has been going through my mind, and I'm scared out of my wits. The only thing I can do is pray … I take God at His word, "for He who promised is faithful (Hebrews 10:23_. Surely the arm of the Lord is not too short to save, nor his ear too dull to hear (Isaiah 59:1) … He challenges us to test Him, saying, "Test me in this … and see if I will not throw open the floodgates of heaven and pour out so much blessing that you will not have room enough for it" (Malachi 3:10).

I reminded God again that He sent me the dream in the first place; I'm only the vessel through which He will fulfil it, and I'm willing to do His bidding, but He will have to carry me all the way. I cannot do it on my own; I am too ignorant, too small, too insignificant for such a mammoth undertaking. I thought how God works in weird and wonderful ways to carry out His plans, and I took courage for a moment. I thought of how Graham removed himself out of the way … and left me free to do my own thing. I prayed for humility and strength to resist pride and to give all credit to God. I am worthless on my own, and if whole "nations are regarded as dust on the scales" (Isaiah 40:15), what am I? But with God holding my hand, I can turn the world upside down.

Chapter 72

Finding an Architect

I kept praying, looking, and asking around for a good draftsman to draw the plans for the three units. I asked the council if they could recommend anybody, but they were not allowed to do so. I had no choice but to do my own research. I looked at newspapers and other places and came across the name of Anders K. I had a good gut feeling. I rang him, hoping he'd be the one meant to draw the plans. On the phone, he sounded interested. He asked a few questions, took the address, and came to take a look at the possibilities. He said he would be happy to take on the job. I explained what I had in mind and gave him my precious plans. He had a quick look at them. I noticed a faint smile on his face. He wanted the first instalment for his work and gave me his bank account.

10/10/05

> To the bank to sort out some banking and pay the first instalment to the draftsman for the plans. With the first payment down, the project of building became a reality, and this posed a change to my original plans of doing all those weird and wonderful things. It gave me a new direction and new ideas as to what I could do, which was more realistic and achievable.

13/11/05

My mind is preoccupied with my dream and the building project ... but above all borrowing ... It frightens me to death, but by the grace of God, I will cross that bridge when I come to it. I can only jump one obstacle at the time. I went to bed thinking about the building and the risks involved. Would I lose my house? And if I did, would I ever be able to buy another one? I knew I'd find it impossible to get a loan from the banks, and the thought of being homeless terrified me. If I have nothing else on this earth, I must have a home, even if it is a little shack, a one-room place, as long as I can call it mine. My childhood obsession of owning my home is still with me and will always be. With these thoughts going through my mind, I fell asleep. I had a dream.

28/11/05

I have four types of dreams. (1) The same type as every other human has: I dream, and by morning I forget it. (2) A dream in colour, in which the picture is sharp and distinct, and in which mostly I do something in it. I am the actor ... and I remember it forever. (3) A vision? A revelation? A prophetic dream? I don't know ... (4) The dreaded recurrent dream, in black and white. It is in a huge, framed picture, but the subjects in it are animated. I see it when someone is very ill, is very worried, or will die. Last night's dream was no exception. I went to bed thinking again of the enormity of my plan, and I prayed again and wondered if I could ever accomplish it ... The dream gave me the answer, and I want to believe it. I said to God, "Dear God, You gave me the dream. I didn't go looking for it, and I can't do it on my own. It will only come true by Your power and Your might."

The dream was as follows. It was dusk. I was riding a tree trunk that was roughly cut, the bark still on it. I was flying over a dark forest, high above the trees, and only just below the very tallest ones ... The thickness of the trunk would be equivalent to a horse's girth. I was sitting astride flying at high speed, and I had no way of guiding it through the tall trees (I had no reins), but the tree trunk dodged all trees and branches amazingly well. I hung on as best as I could, and I realised I had some control over the trunk by moving my body, much as a motorcyclist does when he takes a turn. By moving my legs as a horse rider does, I could control the speed. I felt more relaxed.

The flying log took me out of the forest. By now it was getting darker. I looked down. I was flying over a very wide, muddy river, and the flying log was taking me straight to it and lowering me in it. Before I knew it, I was in the water, still riding it. From the water level, the river looked like a lake. I couldn't see the riverbanks and said to myself, "I will never get across. The under current is very strong and turbulent; I will be swept away. As I thought this, the log already started to get carried away by the current, and no matter how hard I tried to guide it, I could not control it. I sat on it, resigned to the fact that there was nothing I could do to get to the other side. The next thing I knew, I was very close to the bank and off the log without any effort on my part. I was neither wet, nor muddied. I don't know who got me out or how. I was standing on the bank, an d looking at the great river, the likes of which I hadn't seen before. I looked for the log, but it was nowhere to be seen.

I woke up scared. I did not want to think of the meaning, or even that there was one ... The muddy water in Greek culture is a bad omen. I was so distressed that I didn't have the presence of mind to analyse the dream logically. Looking back now ... the meaning is very clear. Yes, I was confused and lost, had no one to turn to, and had no control over the situation. But there was an unseen hand guiding me safely through my confusion; I was not swamped by my fears.

Chapter 73

My Fear of Pride

Amongst my many fears during building, there was another underlying one: that of pride. I always disliked pride, and in my later years I came to hate and fear it. I saw it as one of the biggest negative characteristics in a person, next to arrogance. In my philosophy, pride and arrogance go hand in hand, just as selfishness and stinginess go together. You cannot have one without the other, just as you cannot have kindness without generosity. You can say they are conjoined twins.

15/12/05

My fear has always been, "What if my plans succeed? What if there is enough money to feed millions, and then pride sets in?" I dread the outcome of this because I firmly believe that "when pride comes, then comes disgrace" (Proverbs 11:2). My prayer has always been, "Lord, teach me humility and help me be like Jesus," who, being the prince of heaven, took it upon Himself to become a human, a condescension in itself. But He humbled Himself even more and became the lowest of the low. He humbled Himself enough to wash the feet of his fellow man, a job assigned to servants or little children in his day. I remember my mother saying that as a little girl and the youngest in the family, she was assigned the duty of foot washing when they had visitors. Can I withstand the temptation of feeling smug, important, or benevolent? I doubt my ability to do it on my own; I must rely on God's strength to protect me from this evil.

The architect Anders K and I worked well together. He had his ideas, and I had mine. At times we clashed and frustrated each other, but on the whole, we could see each other's good points and came to a compromise.

Fighting with the council was a different story. The experienced town planner we were working with, and who had originally approved the temporary plans, resigned, and another took over. His assistant, a young and enthusiastic woman, thought that everybody should comply with their ideas, building houses the size and design she wanted. They rejected the final plans of the third unit and wanted the balconies on all three town houses deleted. They disregarded a lot of what the previous town planner had already approved and had a whole lot of new ideas and demands.

We'd made changes just to appease the council, but this was too much. I told Anders the plans are staying as they are, and we are taking the matter to court. He was reluctant. He thought it was likely that we would lose the case, and then what? But I was determined. He shrugged and reluctantly said, "OK."

In the meantime, I sat down and wrote an angry letter to the council, pointing out that what we were proposing to build on the land was within the residential code, that they had previously agreed to the plans, and the council had no power to dictate to the residents what size and style houses to build, especially on Radio Street, which was not a heritage assigned area. I told them that we did not agree to the changes and that the matter was going to court and be resolved there. This was a risky step to take because at that time, the court was deciding in favour of the councils, but that didn't stop me. I couldn't see the reason for refusing the final plans especially deleting the balconies!

I received a letter from the council on September 8, 2006 outlining the reasons for the refusal of the permit; all the issues outlined had been dealt with before.

Anders, guided by experts, suggested I engage an experienced town planner who would prepare the case to present to the court at a cost of five thousand dollars, and for them to be present at the court at eight hundred dollars per day. If I wanted a solicitor to represent me, it would cost twelve thousand dollars for the first day and at two thousand dollars for every day after that. I nearly fainted. After the shock was over, anger overwhelmed me. To start with, I didn't have that amount of money to spend on "experts." Earlier, I engaged an engineer at Anders' suggestion, he did nothing and cost a lot. I felt we weren't building anything different than what was already there, and the plans had been approved before by the same council, which was giving us the run-around now. All this has taking too long already. I'd had enough.

Bugger them all, I thought. *I will do my own footwork. I will gather all the relevant information and evidence and represent myself at court.* Anders agreed to come for support and to verify technical points. Armed with a seven-metre measuring tape, camera, pen, and paper, I went around photographed and measured the set back of every house on the street. Thankfully the street was a short one—no buildings opposite, because the golf course was there.

With photographs taken and developed, I went to the local butcher and asked for two lengths of paper, on which I stuck the photos with the measurements of the setbacks of each house under its photograph. Anders looked at them, half-smiling. I also typed a petition and asked the neighbours to sign if they didn't object to my developing the land. Everybody who was home signed it. The neighbours close to me even wrote their comments. Frank, next door, wrote, "I am of the opinion that the units are not bulky nor massive, as described by the council ... The proposed development is better looking and more pleasing to the eye than some of the recent developments in the street." Others wrote similar comments.

I was armed with my four-page letter to the mediator outlining all the reasons why I thought the council should approve my application.

The photos were beautifully arranged on butcher's paper with the positive comments of my immediate neighbours. Two neighbours came as witnesses, and I had twenty-two signatures, which was nearly all the residents of the short street. I took myself and the witnesses to court in Melbourne, where I was to meet Anders without a clue as to what to expect.

Chapter 74

At Court

31 /01/07

> I slept reasonably well last night, woke up at about 6:00 a.m., and stayed in bed relaxing, wondering what the day would bring. I was out of bed at 7:00, got ready, and rang Frank to make sure he was awake. "Yes," he said. "I'll be there about 9:00 a.m."

Then I rang John. His brother said he was on his way. He was knocking on the door as I hung up the phone. Suddenly I felt the need to run to the bathroom, feeling nervous and harassed. I had ordered the taxi the night before for 9:00 a.m., but it hadn't arrived. I rang the company, they said as always, "It's on the way." It arrived late. The driver said, "We might make it on time if the traffic isn't too bad." Not very comforting.

We were at King Street at 9:40 a.m., and the clerk directed us to the right place. I looked for Anders, couldn't see him, and rang him on his mobile, he answered saying, "I'm here." I turned around as he was coming around the hallway. He looked a bit nervous.

At the court, we were ready for the hearing. Anders asked the mediator for a few moments' leave, which was granted. We went and saw Legal Aid. They suggested mediation first, and so we went back to the courtroom. Anders said, "We would go for mediation," she made a call, and we started.

The mediator addressed us first, directing the questions to Anders as if I weren't there. She glanced at me a couple of times dubiously, wondering what the hell was I doing there. She questioned Anders, who would then consult me. At one stage, I noticed his lips quivering, but he soon re-gained his composure and carried on admirably. She then asked the council representative, who was the town planner, if the council was prepared to compromise. The town planner became anxious and uncertain and timidly said, "Yes, I suppose so." The mediator then looked at the plans and wanted the council to present their objections first.

The town planner went as far as the second objection when the mediator cut in and in a tone of surprise said, "What? why do you want all the balconies deleted? They look good, they add style, and they make the buildings look finished. Aren't you being a bit too severe? They face the golf course, they will be used, and there are no neighbours across from them." Anders and I exchanged glances.

Then the issue of the setbacks, fences, cladding, and windows came up. The mediator asked if cladding was very important to the council and why. The town planner said, "Appearance."

I couldn't hold back and said, "Matter of taste."

She then asked Anders if we'd compromise. I nodded to him, and he went on to draw on the plan a few changes. By now she had already looked at the photos of the street and asked if the units at 25 and 27 were built in the 1920s. "They were built around 2005," I said.

She looked at the town planner. "And you gave permits for them, didn't you?"

By now the young town planner looked decidedly uncomfortable, shifted on her seat, and said, "It wasn't me."

The mediator looked at 35 and 37 Radio Street and commented on their bulk, and their setbacks. The town planner said, "We want the units to fall in line with the property next door."

I couldn't hold back again and pointed out that the setbacks varied greatly, ranging from just over 9.2 metres next door to 3.2 metres down the road, and the neighbour didn't mind. I said, "The neighbour is here—please ask him." I turned around and asked him myself.

"No," he said in his heavy English accent, "I don't mind at all."

The mediator then said to the town planner, "The neighbour might want to put some units there too sometime. Are you concerned that you might be setting a precedent of increasing or reducing setbacks?" The town planner didn't answer. The mediator then looked at the photo of exhibit two and wanted to know at which end the street was closed. Anders had explained it before.

Half an hour into the negotiations, she asked to see the town planner alone outside. John wanted to know why. Anders said, "To tear strips off her, most likely!"

They returned after about ten minutes The town planner looked humbled, and the mediator was worked up. "All right," she said. "Let's see how far we can compromise. The balconies are over the front door, aren't they? They provide protection from the weather. How much will you compromise?"

Anders looked at the plan and without consulting me said, "Seven hundred millimetres." The town planner nodded—it was too late for me to object.

She then asked the town planner to consult her boss about a roof change, which she did. The council argued that unit three would overshadow the property behind. Anders argued it was within residential code rules. "OK," said the mediator. "I order the council to issue a permit provided all the changes are met and provided unit three does not overshadow 156," which was the property next door around the corner of Ashley Street. The town planner made another call.

Anders said he was short of time and was catching a plane to Brisbane. There was paperwork to sign, which I had to sign. As Anders was getting up to go, the mediator asked him while looking at me in a condescending manner, "Is she savvy?" I stared at her through narrowed eyes. I was angry, but she'd fought valiantly on our behalf. I swallowed my pride and anger, saying nothing.

Anders answered, "Hmm. Very," and left.

The changes were made and written in point form. The town planner faxed the appropriate forms quickly because the mediator wanted to wrap up the case today because she had other engagements. We were ready to start signing. The mediator asked me if I understood what I was signing. "Yes, I understand," I said.

She then said, "You understand you have two years to start and two years to finish?"

"Two years to start and four years to finish," I corrected her coldly. She looked at the town planner for verification.

"That's correct," said the town planner.

"There you are then," she said with some acknowledgement. I was even more annoyed. We finished at nearly 1:30 p.m., took a photocopy, and left. I was on cloud nine. I was tired but couldn't relax. With my dinner, I had a glass of wine that would normally put me to sleep for ten hours, but even that didn't work. After nearly two years of dealing and fighting with the council, drawing and redrawing plans all at a cost, finally the plans were approved on January 31, 2007!

I took a long walk down the corner street, reflecting on the events of the day. I remembered my prayer in the morning, and sure enough, the Lord once again was with me, leading me. My prayer before I left was, "Dear Lord, this is another step closer to materialising my dream—the dream You gave me. I made it my own. Please go before me, soften the hearts of the panel to look favourably on our application, and give me the appropriate words to speak." I thanked God once again.

I waited three months for the plans to arrive. Anders was getting worried. I went to the council to investigate, and the clerk told me I should have received them within a week of approval, which neither Anders nor I knew. I asked, "Why the delay?

I was told matter-of-factly, "They must have forgotten them." They gave no apologies. Was this their revenge for taking them to court?

Chapter 75

Finding a Builder

Anybody who has done any building will tell you that it's harder finding a good builder than a good husband. But here again, God answered my prayer. I looked at newspapers and asked friends and acquaintances for recommendations of a good builder. I stopped at every building site, got the phone number from their advertising board, and rang the lot.

One day while going to work, I drove past a building site on Furlong Road and noticed the nearly finished string of two-storey townhouses. The front door of one was open. Two men were there working. I went in and I asked if I could have the name of the builder. One of them came forward and said, "I am the builder." He introduced himself as David, and the other man was William, the painter. I told him my plans. He asked the usual questions. "Have your plans been approved? Do you have finance? What do you want to build?" I answered all questions correctly and confidently. David said, "We are nearly finished here. If you like, I can come and have a look at your plans, give you a rough estimate of cost and time of commencement." It suited me fine. We organised to meet at my place in two weeks, the day and time organised during my days off to suit me; we met in the evening to suit him.

4/7/2007

> The day of the appointment, I cleaned the place, especially the table, ready to spread the plans. There were a few bits and pieces of paper and an old magazine, *The Record*, a Seventh-day Adventist news magazine which I'd intended to put away too, but I was caught up doing other things and completely forgot about it. David and Tim, his business partner, came on time. I offered them a hot drink of tea or coffee, and they declined and opted for water. When I came back with the water, I noticed Tim was looking at the magazine in great interest. "You get this magazine too?" he asked in his heavy Slavic accent.

I put two and two together and answered him with a question, "Are you Seventh-day Adventists?"

"Yes, we are," they answered simultaneously. My heart missed a beat. How lucky can one be? I call it providence, an answer to prayer, because I was nervous about getting just any builder. I instinctively knew I was in good hands and silently thanked God. They looked at the plans; Tim's English was poor, and so David spoke to him in Croatian. They took the plans to work out the cost and give me an accurate quote.

A few days later, David and Tim came with their quote. They couldn't match the price of the last quote I'd had, and I didn't expect them to; the other builders were a big company and David wasn't. David wanted $330,000 to build the two units. I offered $325,000, and we settled for $327,000. We were all happy. We agreed for him to pick up the first payment tomorrow, paying a little more than the required 5 per cent. I was happy to do so, trusted him explicitly.

On July 25, we signed the contracts, and David hoped to have the concrete slab laid before August 16. He would start as soon as he could after his holidays. He picked up the down payment for the project on July 26, 2007. During the building, I rented in St. Albans.

4/8/2007

The demolisher rang at 7:15 a.m. to say ... they started demolishing the house yesterday. I needed to be there to take any plants if I wanted any. My sister had taken most of them already.

5/8/07

I went past the building site on the way to visit Eva and stopped to see what was happening ... The bulldozer was hard at work. I watched the old but recently renovated house come down by the expertly manoeuvred bulldozer operator. Sadness, fear, gratitude, and hope were all mixed up within me, and once again I thanked God for all my blessings ... My faith is almost sight now, and in my mind's eye, I can see the buildings go up. A thrill and a fear seized me ... How, who, and when should I approach someone and explain to them my long-term dream and what I want to do? Will they laugh at me? Will they see it as impossible, too hard, too silly? Again I prayed that God touch and prepare the hearts of the experts and put everything together. From now on, I am sailing in unchartered waters, not in regards as to the building or financing it, but as to how to go about using what God has given me, and which I dedicated to Him ... for His glory, and for the benefit of my fellow man.

13/8/07

I met the concreters and their young apprentice. All were down to earth with nothing artificial or superficial. I love these kinds of people. I thanked God because so far everything was on course and going according to plan. As always, I felt this to be the easy step, the part I had some control over, and that gave me some confidence ... But when I think of the next step, I shudder, I tremble ... I have to rely on faith alone, and I call on God ... to hold me up ... Again, I wondered whom, when, and how I'd go about finding out what to do in order to materialise the next part of my vision. I know nothing about finances and money. I can hardly count a cupful of coins twice and get the same sum ... But I have no choice other than to call upon my God to prepare the way ... I believe He will. My pact with God for a long time now has been, "Lord, I'll do my best; You do the rest." This has saved me a lot of anxiety over time.

5/9/07

Home via the old house. Joy of joys! They had the foundations almost done; concrete will be poured on Friday ... After work, I'll be there to thank God and to celebrate with a glass of champagne.

7/9/07

Slept till 12:30 p.m. ... At Ashley Street, the concrete was poured this morning ... by the time I got there, it was hard enough for me to walk on. I stood there and thanked God for bringing into being the first part of my dream. As I thought of the second part of my dream, I again ... felt fearful ... I know God is bigger than all my fears and that He is faithful in all his promises to us. With a heart full of gratitude, I walked away ... went home, and headed back to bed for a rest before work tonight.

The carpenters started today, and all the wall positions have been marked ... I met David at 12:30 p.m. and sorted out the changes we made to the plans ... took them to the Council no issues there. Right through the building process, working with David was a pleasure.

Nothing was too hard for him; "There's always a solution to every problem" was his philosophy. If the walls hadn't been put up, he didn't charge me for the changes. If extra material was needed, I paid for it.

Chapter 76

More Fearful by the Day

12/10/07

I went back to bed to study Spanish, but I spent most of my time agonising about taking the next step. I had set the time to contact one of the TV channels to say what I was doing, hoping that they would direct me to the right people for guidance. That time would be when the brickwork was up. Now that it isn't too far away, I am growing more fearful by the minute. For a good while, I've been wondering as to which channel would be the best to approach, and the question bugged me for a couple of years now … It wasn't urgent then, but it is now and scares me. I thought of casting lots, and that seemed reasonable up to now, but now even that scares me. "What if I pick the wrong channel? What if they laugh at me? What if, if, if?"

I prayed again … and acknowledged my weakness and my dependence on God's strength and wisdom. I thought of Gideon, who was called to lead the Israelites and free them from the Midianites. How he too feared and doubted, and how he asked for reassurance, some sign that God was leading. God patiently gave him the reassurance he wanted and more. I heard this story as a child and read it many times, but while reading it today, I wept.

I empathised with Gideon's fears and doubts. I understood how insignificant he felt. Judges 6:12–39. The angel of Lord appeared to Gideon and said, "The Lord is with you mighty warrior." Gideon argued with God … "But Lord, how can I save Israel? My clan is the weakest in Manasseh, and I the least in my family." He was given more signs than he asked for. "Fire flared from the rock, consuming the meat and the bread." Not only that, the Lord reassured him even more. (Judges 7:10). "If you are afraid to attack, go down to the camp … and listen to what they are saying … You will be encouraged" (Judges 7:11-13) Gideon heard a man telling his friend his dream. "I had a dream … A round loaf of barley bread came tumbling into the Midianite camp. It struck the tent with such force that the tent overturned and collapsed." His friend responded, "This can be nothing other than the sword of Gideon son of Joash, the Israelite. God has given the Midianites and the whole camp into his hands." Obviously, God does not see us as we see ourselves. Gideon was scared out of his wits, but God saw him as, and called him a "mighty warrior." God disregards our strengths and overlooks our weakness and ignorance. He sees only our willingness to let ourselves be used by Him. We are merely the instruments by which God brings about His will. "We are workers together with God," said the Apostle Paul. A thousand times, I said; "Lord I'll do my best; you do the rest."

13/10/07

I went back to bed … One thought led to another and ended up with Gideon again, where he heard one soldier telling another the above dream. What an odd way for God to encourage Gideon! There must have been a hundred ways God could reassure him. A dream, a vision, an actual scene of the future battle, a sound or light from heaven. Or send an angel as he did to Abraham, even take him to heaven as he did with Paul and showed him "things that are not lawful for men to speak about." But no, God gave Gideon a message through a most unlikely channel. He used the mouths of the Midianites, "infidels and gentiles," to give Gideon the message bearing the reassurance he so desperately needed. How odd! …

Chewed over it and wondered why. I burst out laughing. Laughed as heartily as I wept bitterly yesterday. What a similarity! When I felt most frightened, most anxious and discouraged, where did I get some comfort and encouragement? From the stars! The message was so fitting and so timely, I could not help but cut and paste it in my diary as a reminder that God knows, hears, and answers. I laughed some more.

Well, Hugh, my dear colleague, your favourite saying was "God works in weird and mysterious ways His wonders to perform." Thank You, Dear God, for more often than not, you condescend to come down to our level because it's impossible for us to rise to Yours.

13/10/07

I found this passage in the *Herald Sun* today.

Greased lightning? You surpassed that slow speed some time ago. To suggest that things are moving fast for you now, is to make a glorious understatement. You are-or soon will be-hurdling towards a date with a new element of your destiny. Is there anything you need fear or guard against? Absolutely not. Whether events are unfolding as a direct result of some conscious strategy or whether you feel as if you are being dragged towards this destination by a series of powerful forces beyond your control you are heading in the right direction.

I want to believe I am.

25/11/07

The frame is up in the second unit too. David said by the end of this week, the roof should go on. My deal with God was, "As soon as the brick work is done, I'll take photos and start from there." I also said to myself I will need to pray for three days and hopefully fast as long. Then I'd let God decide which channel I should go with. But ... I am terribly fearful about it. The old fears of how I will be received ... occupy my mind. But I also see the hand of God leading in all this; last Sunday's Spanish sermon came to my mind, and it comforted me. *"El a movio montes ante esta hora"* (He has moved mountains before now). I believe He can and will do it again. He has moved the biggest ... mountain, Graham, out of my way, and I didn't have to say a word, to lift a finger ... But like all humans, I too have feet of clay, and at times of fear I notice them more—the devil always makes sure of that.

I finished my diary of 2007 writing,

Another year has gone; my dream and the building of the units are behind schedule, but on course. As time approaches for me to take the last step, a great leap into the unknown, I am becoming more and more nervous ... A great fear seizes me, which paralyses me ... Will they laugh at me as others did before? Their derisive laughter still echoes in my ears ... "Oh, dear God, please help me," I pray over and over again.

Chapter 77

My Literal Dream

On 16/3/15, I was reading several of my old diaries and was amazed at how God works to answer our prayers. The house Frank showed us was just what I was praying for, and we ended up buying it. On its land, three units are now standing. My dream about the stars filling up the dark sky and making it look brilliant remains a mystery. At times I'd get angry with God and would say, "Lord, You, gave me that dream for a reason. Why do You take so long to fulfil it?" But I realised that God's clock and my clock are not synchronised. My time is finite, His is infinite. I'll just have to wait for God to work in His own time and in His own way. I am convinced that what I saw was a vision rather than an ordinary dream; it has a special meaning and a purpose, but what? One thing I know, and this is that even after twenty-one years as I am typing this: that dream is vivid in my mind, and I still have a burning desire to do something for my fellow man who is less fortunate than I am.

I have thought long and hard before I plucked up courage to open the secrets of my heart—my thoughts, my hopes, and my aspirations. I find it difficult to let you into my innermost self because I myself doubt my sanity.

Many times I made plans, went to see bank and credit union managers, and asked how to start a financial institution of some sort.

I'd say to myself, *Estella, you are crazy. You are stark-raving mad.* I feared I had schizophrenia with grandiosity features, and at times I still do. I contacted the Salvation Army. I even engaged two financial advisors, and one told me, "Enjoy what you have while you are alive. Then make your will to whatever charity you want to help after your death." The other one told me that what I wanted to do was nigh impossible and very risky. I saw Tatts and explained what I wanted to do. They looked at me kindly as if to say, "Poor soul. She is going crazy." They politely said, "At this stage, we are unable to help."

I wasn't offended. I myself doubted my sanity. I made phone calls and during one of them while explaining to the person at the other end what I wanted to do, I heard giggling in the background, but they sent me the information I needed to start my "Financial Institution." I even had a name for it. It was going to be The People's Bank or The Battlers Bank. I wrote to TV channels, and only Channel 7 answered, saying, "Organise all the legalities, and we will be happy to take over from there," or words to that effect. It was signed by "Nicole."

24/6/2005

> Visited my niece. Went by public transport and had plenty of time to think … Usually when I feel tired, my imagination becomes vivid and wild … My dream came back to me with much clarity. I felt insignificant, impotent, ignorant, and stupid for even contemplating such a dream, which at that moment … felt impossible. My faith faltered, and doubts rose up like mountains … I prayed, "Dear Lord, take my hand and lead. On my own I can do nothing, but with You holding my hand, I can turn the world upside down. Please hold me up lest I fall." I have prayed this prayer a thousand times over the years.

> I know God hears prayer, and I knew He heard me again. I know He does not get sick and tired of my asking, and I felt a bit better, though still tired and still

busy planning how to make money to feed the poor, dress the naked, educate the underprivileged, and give sight to the blind. Thoughts raced into my mind. All of them were plausible, and all of them needed expertise and lots of money, of which I had neither. One of them was to start a chain of supermarkets, with all profits going to feed and clothe the poor. One was to start a chain of restaurants. Now, that was a good one; it kept me busy organising the equipment, the menu, the price, the crockery, and the cutlery. I decided disposable plates would be cheaper. Working out the menu was a bit trickier. I decided to have a set menu of sausages, fish, chicken, and beef, with chips, a salad, and bread rolls. Say the first helping for eight dollars and a second helping four dollars. But I couldn't work the price out. I couldn't work how to run the restaurants. I got muddled up, and in the end I decided I could go and see how Hungry Jacks and McDonald's do it and take it from there.

Then I felt stupid. Not only did I doubt the plausibility of my plans, but I also doubted my sanity. This is too big a vision for an old, little lady like me, who is completely ignorant of commerce and business. What's more, I don't like cooking; I'm not interested in that kind of business. I wondered if my mind was a bit shaky, as my grandmother used to say. I wondered if I'm stupid altogether, deluded, grandiose, simpleton, stark-raving mad, or what?

Thankfully, the tram came to the end of the line. I got off and had to gather my wits about me to find my way to my niece's place … That ended my torment for the time being.

My obsession did not deter me then, and even eighteen years after that phone call, I still hope and pray that my dream will materialise somehow. I know I cannot do it on my own, and it will be done only by divine intervention, in God's own time and in God's own way. There are people out there who will extend their hands to guide and help me materialise my dream. Now, what I would like to do is to put up in a lottery all I have, set up a trust fund to support my favourite charities (Fred Hollows is one of them), and allocate funds for educating underprivileged children. I always wanted an education, which I couldn't have as a child. But then again, He didn't forget me. He knew the desire of my soul, and without me even asking, He sent me a schoolteacher, private and exclusive, 24/7! How good is that?

24/8/03

I wrote. I thought again of my dream and had to admit it's all but dead. All the money I had has been spent, and what little was left has gone to Graham ... Now it's humanly impossible to do anything about it. I often wonder whether I misinterpreted my dream or whether it is still that period of darkness and inactivity. Whatever it is ... unless the Lord takes over, I can do nothing. I have no money and no knowledge ... "but all things are possible with God."

24/3/1997

The Lord has realised all my dreams, so why shouldn't He bring this one to fruition also? I'm sure He will, or He has something better in mind for me. For I've learned to say, "Your will be done in my life Lord, on this earth as it is in heaven. Supply according to Your knowledge, Your love and wisdom." I have asked for things in the past urgently and persistently. I received them, but I had plenty of time to repent ... and to wonder if that was what I really needed.

Chapter 78

My Literal Dream of the Stars

24/2/1998

Last night I had a very strange dream. It was a very dark night. I was standing at front of the house at 158 Ashley Street, looking up in the dark, starless sky to the north. I noticed the constellation of the Great Bear. It was the brightest I have ever seen it. My attention was drawn to it. As if magnetically, my eyes rested on the tail and in particular on the middle star, Orion. I observed it for a few moments. From the middle star, a bright arrow of light appeared, like a comet makes when it falls. The arrow moved around, forming a bow. At the end of the bow of light and attached to it formed a flower. I looked at it, it was a large, four-leafed clover of light. The arrow of light made a short semicircle from Orion and rested in the inner side of the pan of the Great Bear, as if someone was waiting, ready to shoot it.

As I watched the light of arrow move, thinking it was a falling star, I prayed, "Dear Lord, make my wish come true," just as we used to say when, as kids, we'd watch comets fall. As I was wishing, I looked at the pan of the

Great Bear and saw a lone bright star light up. After a pause, another one lit up; a pause, and another one lit up. After the fourth pause, the stars were filling the pan fast, without a pause, till the pan of the Great Bear was full of bright stars. When the pan was filled, the stars started spilling out of the pan of the Great Bear in great speed, like popcorn out of a frying pan, filling the whole sky as far as my eye could see and making it look brilliant, the brightest I have ever seen it.

I woke up feeling that God was trying to tell me something, I wanted to believe it. I wanted to believe that my wish to start something to help my fellow man will materialise, and that we somehow will get a place with a bigger yard. I didn't care where, even if it is in Shitsville where nobody else wants to live. I wanted to believe that my wish to start The People's Bank or somehow be able to help my fellow man will materialise, and that somehow … we would get a place with a bigger yard. I didn't really care where. That part of my wish has been fulfilled" the house Frank showed us suited us well. and it wasn't in Shitsville. I am still waiting for the first part of my wish to be fulfilled.

Ever since I was a very young child, I got a lot of pleasure helping others in some way, or by doing the right thing. After I was baptised in the Seventh-day Adventist church in Thessaloniki, my prayer was, "Lord, here am I. Use me in Your service."

In one of my sleepless nights in 1997, as I was reflecting on the events in my life and recounting each one of them, I realised that each event helped strengthen my faith and made me who I am. Even though Graham was on the pension at that time, with strict budgeting we lacked nothing. There was always enough food on the table, we managed to pay the bills, we had clothes to wear (bought from the Op Shop and remodelled). I compared myself to the millions of people who came to this world and went out of it without ever knowing what it is like to go to bed with a full stomach, or those who were half-naked, had nowhere to sleep, and had no one to turn to, because everybody else around them was in the same situation. And yes, I went hungry, went to bed in freezing nights, with the temperatures plummeting to minus twenty degrees Celsius, taking hours to warm up. But all that is over now.

At times, I still smile sadly when I think of bribing my sister Eva, with a trinket, a blue stoned ring, to let me put my cold feet next to hers till I warmed up. She looked at the ring, put it on her finger, cocked her head sideways, and reluctantly said, "OK. I warm you up anyway." She was just twelve years old. Whenever she complained of my cold feet, I'd remind her of the deal with the ring, and she'd stop complaining. She always stuck to the deal not because of integrity but out of pity for me. Even late in her dementia, she'd remind me of the incident. She'd laugh heartily, dimples still on her cheeks and her face lighting up. I would cry inwardly. I thanked God for that stint of hardship; it gave me an insight to what millions of people have gone through all their lives—and are still suffering, even in Australia, which I call God's own land, a land flowing with milk and honey.

I realise I am blessed in many ways. First of all, my children have enough to eat. I have a loving foster son who has given me much pride and joy. They have houses to live in. My grandchildren have good educations; they are all healthy and well adjusted. What a great blessing! I thanked God countless times, for that blessing alone.

Second we all have comfortable houses, warm beds, and hot showers. You may not believe this, but after fifty-seven years in this land, I still thank God every time I get in my warm bed or get under a warm shower. The warm, relaxing water trickling over me is a luxury I don't take for granted. I don't know what all this thanking and praising does for God, but I know what it does for me. It helps me wake up every morning with gladness in my heart and a song of gratitude on my lips.

On March 7, 1998, I took my now deceased friend Eva and went to the local plant nursery for a look around. I told her my dream but not my plans. She had a different interpretation than my sister's. She said,

"It's a good dream. The dark sky means you have a concern or a worry, but the fact that the sky was filled with millions of stars and the bow and arrow lit up means that your worries will disappear, and your wish will be granted." I wanted to believe she was right.

Sixty years after my prayer, "Here am I, Lord. Use me in Your service." Twenty years since my dream of the stars and nearly ten years after the completion of the three townhouses, dedicating them to God for His glory and to benefit my fellow man, I am still waiting. Compared to how much others can give and have given, mine is a bit like the widow's mite. But then again, it was the widow's mite that Jesus noticed and commented on, for she gave all she had willingly, and so do I. It was a little boy's lunch, given willingly to Jesus, which fed five thousand people. God does a lot with the little we give.

I am still waiting for God to send someone who will take my hand and fulfil the dream He gave me, which I nurtured in my mind and heart and towards which I directed all my energies and my earnings. I did everything possible in my power to materialise it, but my knowledge ends here. My expertise is non-existent. The advice I received from the experts does not satisfy me. I don't want to be hanging onto the equivalent of two houses' worth of money till I die. My deal with God on May 22, 2006, was, "That of all You have given me, or might give me yet, 90 per cent is Yours and 10 per cent is mine." I know how He loves to give His children good gifts, and that He returns a full measure and well pressed down. I know I will never go hungry or naked.

Are you the one or ones whom God has chosen to be the instrument in His hands, the arrow of light that will show me the way? Are we going to work together to give sight to the blind, feed and clothe the naked, and educate little minds, enabling them to do great things not just for themselves but also for humanity? And who knows? We might raise another Fred Hollows, another Booth, another Pappaphy (the Greek philanthropist who built an orphanage in Thessaloniki where hundreds of children had food, shelter, and an education).

If we can't fix the whole world, why not take Mother Teresa's advice? She said, "If you can't feed the whole world, feed one person." I would like to say, "If we can't help the whole world, let's help as many as we can." My prayer has always been, "Lord, I want to be a blessing to as many people as I have been blessed over and above, and they are millions."

Please take my hand, and together while hanging on to the hand of God, we can materialise the dream He gave me. Make it your dream too. By holding on to His hand, we can turn the world upside down. "Madness, Madness!" some might shout, and madness it could well be. But my interpretation of madness is "any thought or action outside the square is madness." If what I have been striving for so long to achieve is considered to be madness by few or by many, then so be it.

I would like to close my life story up to today with Proverbs 14:31. "He who oppresses the poor shows contempt for their maker, but whosoever is kind to the needy honours God." I want to honour my God. Please join me in this.

I hope this is not going to be the end of my story, I hope I will be able to say, "It is done. My dream has been fulfilled! Thank You, God, Thank you, all."

My Prayer of Gratitude

Thank You, Lord, for hearing me when I pray.
Thank You, for taking my fears and troubles away.
Thank You for "peace that passes all understanding."
Thank You for holding me up when my knees give way.

Thank You, Lord, for reassuring me when I am afraid.
Thank You for not forsaking me when I miserably fail.
Thank You for rushing to my help and softly to me say,
"Child, hush. Your cries I hear; I'm never too far away."

Thank You, Lord, for in Your Word You plainly say,
"Come, let us reason together. I Am always the same",
Loving, your needs I know. I'm willing and able to save.
If you remember My promises, you'll never suffer pain."

Lord I know: Your arm is not too weak all of us to save.
In many places in Your Word, You plainly to us say,
"Surely the arm of the Lord is not too short to save.
Just come to Me, your troubles before My feet to lay."

Estella

My Philosophy in Life

Life is like a river which we all have to cross. The river
is full of obstacles. Dead tree trunks, huge rocks, deep
pools, and horrible little creatures like leeches. Some of
us use those obstacles as stepping stones to get across to
the other side to do bigger and better things. Others use
them as obstacles to stay back, do nothing other than
blame others, and talk about their bad luck. I don't want
to be one of them. I want to see myself as a victor over
life's battles, not as a victim.

Estella

Printed in the United States
By Bookmasters